GLOBAL SPIN

GLOBAL SPIN

*The Corporate Assault
on Environmentalism*

Sharon Beder

GREEN BOOKS
&
CHELSEA GREEN PUBLISHING COMPANY

First published in the UK in October 1997
by Green Books Ltd
Foxhole, Dartington
Totnes, Devon TQ9 6EB

First published in the USA in February 1998
by Chelsea Green Publishing Company
Post Office Box 428
White River Junction, Vermont 05001

Typeset in Adobe Garamond
at Green Books

Cover design by Rick Lawrence

Printed on acid-free paper
by J.W. Arrowsmith Ltd, Bristol, UK

A catalogue record for this book is
available from The British Library

Library of Congress Cataloguing-in-Publication data
is available on request

ISBN 1 870098 67 6 (UK)
ISBN 1 890132 12 8 (USA)

Contents

Contents *(continued)*

Acknowledgements

I would like to thank Richard Gosden who advised me, encouraged me and commented on an earlier draft of the book. The research for this book was also aided by a Small Australian Research Council Grant awarded through the University of Wollongong.

Foreword

Before I began reading and writing about politics, I used to while away the hours writing science fiction stories. In one of them, my hero became convinced that he and everyone else had somehow been placed in a virtual reality machine that was able to reproduce the world just about perfectly. He was sure that that everything he saw, everyone he knew and everything that happened to him was a computer-generated illusion, that he was imprisoned in some kind of electronic tomb. Naturally, his friends feared for his sanity and assured him that he was suffering from advanced paranoia. In the end he determined to put his theory to the test: he leapt in front of a bus. Sure enough, instead of being crushed beneath the wheels, he opened his eyes to find the canopy of a virtual reality machine lifting away from his body. He had been right. Around him, armed guards and a sinister commissar were waiting to escort him to a kind of prison commune reserved for people who had exceeded the capacity of the programme to maintain the illusion. The twist to the story, of course, was that my hero was still inside the machine: his apparent partial escape to the commune was simply another layer of deception. There was no escape.

Imagine my surprise some years later when I discovered that our condition in modern 'democratic' society is not all that dissimilar from that faced by my fictional hero. While there is of course no evil conspiracy, no perfect virtual reality machine, and certainly our situation is far less hopeless, we too are living in a world in which everything we see, think and believe is influenced by powerful interests determined to shape our version of what is real and true to suit their requirements. We, too, are living in a world where we are convinced we are free for the very reason that the forces by which we are constrained are so adept at controlling us that it never occurs to us to question the true extent of our liberty. And, as in my story, escape or progress in the real world is often merely a transition to a new kind of deception: consider, after all, the Earth Summit, green consumerism, sustainable growth, 'New' Labour, and so on.

The book you are holding is the first I have come across to deal with the real environmental crisis—the one that consists not of decaying eco-systems, ozone depletion and global warming, but of the corporate domination of what we are able to hear, see, know and think; the crisis that lies in the fact that the modern mass media system is not a medium for the 'free' discussion of ideas and viewpoints, but is deeply embedded in, and dependent on, the wider corporate status quo, and on the related capacity of corporate communications and economic power to boost facts, ideas and political choices that are conducive to profit maximization, and to stifle those that are not.

In this situation, specific environmental issues can hardly be considered the central—let alone the sole—problem for environmentalists, given that corporate

domination makes the raising of public awareness and concern for these issues all
but impossible. After all, it hardly matters whether a person is bleeding to death,
poisoned, or dying from hypothermia, if some kind of obstacle is preventing all
medical aid from reaching the patient. The real problem, for now, is the obstacle
that prevents the public from coming to the aid of the environment.

Consider for example the issue of press freedom, in the context of the following excerpt from a letter sent by the Chrysler Corporation to over a hundred
magazines:

> In an effort to avoid potential conflicts, it is required that Chrysler Corporation be
> alerted in advance of any and all editorial content that encompasses sexual, politi-
> cal, social issues or any editorial content that could be construed as provocative or
> offensive.[1]

If a class of teenagers were asked whether the above quotation in any way
compromised the notion that we are proud inheritors of an advertising-depen-
dent but 'free' press, they would surely laugh. Try, however, convincing any mainstream journalist, or editor, that there is any kind of problem here. Try, indeed
(and I have, for one), convincing the leaders of our mainstream green movements. And yet Chrysler's stance is the rule for all corporate advertisers, who are
all equally sensitive to "potential conflicts". Moreover, the mainstream media are
themselves all owned by large, parent corporations, all tied into the stock market,
all owned by wealthy people with fingers in any number of other corporate and
political pies.

Meanwhile, the only problem exercising the minds of our senior journalists,
it would seem, is whether it is always right to be completely neutral and objective
in accordance with the grand traditions of the 'free press'. Thus the former BBC
journalist Martin Bell caused quite a ruckus by declaring:

> I do not believe we should stand neutrally between good and evil, right and wrong,
> aggressor and victim.[2]

The subsequent argument raged between journalists and editors defending
"our obligation to be impartial"[3] and the idea that "As well as straight reporting
there is room—and sometimes a need—for a more engaged form of writing."[4]
Even as this foreword was being written, veteran BBC foreign editor John
Simpson made his feelings known in no uncertain terms: "Martin Bell is talking
nonsense and he knows it. He was one of the most objective journalists."
Simpson added, apparently with a straight face, "You don't watch the BBC for
polemic."[5]

The question, then, is not whether our corporate media system is objective
and neutral—that is taken as read—but whether it should sometimes allow itself
to indulge in the luxury of a little subjectivity. As so often in the mainstream, the
truth is hidden by and beyond these two opposing arguments. The absurdity of
both becomes immediately clear when we recognize that it is actually impossible
for any journalist, even a corporate one, to be objective and neutral. Historian
Howard Zinn made the point well in his essay 'Objections to Objectivity':

The chief problem in historical [and journalistic] honesty is not outright lying. It is omission or de-emphasis of important data. The definition of 'important', of course, depends on one's values.[6]

The point about 'the facts' being, as Zinn suggests, that they are always value-dependent: data reported, emphasized, stressed, headlined, or neglected, are selected—or not—on the basis of what the historian or journalist deems important. There is no way around this: a journalist must have values, priorities (conscious or otherwise), must filter facts, must report subjectively. Bias and subjective opinions are inherent to the profession of journalism, indeed human existence itself, not 'bad form' to be avoided wherever possible.

The notion that a journalist can be impartial and neutral, can produce 'straight reporting', then, is a logical absurdity. Like so many other logical absurdities, however, it is useful to the interests of the powerful, and one that the 'free press' is only too happy to present as 'indisputably true'. The reality and the determined denial of reality surrounding the issue of media freedom verges on the surreal and is easily as bizarre as any primitive religious dogma, belief in a flat earth, or faith in a kindly Fuehrer plotting global conquest.

* * *

In another of his essays, 'History & Warfare', Howard Zinn made a striking point about war—that great, damning, perennial blight of human affairs:

It seems to me it only takes a little bit of thought to realize that if wars came out of human nature, out of a spontaneous urge to kill, then why is it that governments have to go to such tremendous lengths to mobilize populations to go to war? It seems too obvious doesn't it? They really have to work at it. They have to dredge up an enormous number of reasons.[7]

Zinn notes that governments are also always required to appeal to our moral sentiments—we will not simply go out and kill for greed, or for the fun of it. Zinn concludes that the sheer extent of government propaganda is therefore hugely flattering to human nature and the moral potential inherent in it.

As Sharon Beder points out, the same is true for environmentalism and the corporate assault against it that she has documented with such marvellous clarity in this book: it is only because so many people do care about the environment and that they really are capable of changing the world, that corporations are near-hysterical in their determination to "put the environmental lobby out of business", to render it "superfluous, an anachronism", as one consultant to the oil and gas industry put it.

Indeed, if the corporate media were to be believed, everything would appear to be hopeless, with people utterly passive and indifferent now that "history has ended". It is an interesting paradox, then, that the common conviction that the situation is hopeless has actually been brought about by a no-holds-barred campaign by the big corporations, which in turn has resulted from their crystal-clear awareness that this is not, in fact, the case!

To be an environmentalist today must mean understanding and exposing the nature and logic of this attempt to stifle environmentalism. As Sharon Beder says:

> A new wave of environmentalism is now called for: one that will engage in the task of exposing corporate myths and methods of manipulation.

In this book she helps us to do just this, showing the way for environmentalists to move from a position of political naivety and relative impotence to a new radical depth of understanding how corporate propaganda can be effectively countered.

If you think that caring is pointless, that effort leads nowhere, that radical change is unnecessary or impossible, I recommend that you read this book. By revealing how these beliefs, far from being 'cold facts of life', are actually vital components of the corporate assault on environmentalism, this book easily qualifies as the most important contribution to the environmental debate I have ever read.

David Edwards
Bournemouth, England
August 1997

References:
1. Quoted by Wayne Grytting in *Z Magazine*, June 1997.
2. *The Guardian*, 23 November 1996.
3. Richard Sambrook, Head of BBC News Gathering, quoted in *The Guardian*, 23 November 1996.
4. Alan Rusbridger, editor of *The Guardian*, in *The Guardian*, 23 November 1996.
5. *The Guardian*, 5 August 1997.
6. Howard Zinn, *Failure to Quit*, Common Courage Press, 1993, p.30.
7. Howard Zinn, *Power, History and Warfare*, Open Magazine Pamphlet Series, 1991, p.4.

Chapter 1

Introduction

This book examines the way that corporations have used their financial resources and power to counter gains made by environmentalists, to reshape public opinion and to persuade politicians against increased environmental regulation. Corporate activism, ignited in the 1970s and rejuvenated in the 1990s, has enabled a corporate agenda to dominate most debates about the state of the environment and what should be done about it. This situation poses grave dangers to the ability of democratic societies to respond to environmental threats.

Between 1965 and 1970 environmental groups proliferated; environmental protection, especially pollution control, rose dramatically as a public priority in many countries. *Time* magazine labelled it a "national obsession" in America. A "sense of urgency—even crisis—suddenly pervaded public discussion of environmental issues. The press was filled with stories of environmental trauma. . ."[1]

As environmental concern grew, so did distrust of business institutions, which were seen to be the primary cause of environmental problems such as air and water pollution. Public respect for business fell to an all-time low and "for the first time since the Great Depression, the legitimacy of big business was being called into question by large sectors of the public."[2] Surveys showed increasing percentages of people nominated "factories and plants" as the major source of air pollution. The distrust of business and support for environmentalism was highest amongst the young and the college or university educated.[3]

Governments worldwide responded with new forms of comprehensive environmental legislation, such as Clean Air Acts and Clean Water Acts and the establishment of environmental regulatory agencies. These new environmental laws were part of a general trend in legislation aimed at regulating corporate activities and constraining unwanted business activities. In the UK, new environmental legislation included a Clean Air Act in 1968, a Water Act in 1973 and the Control of Pollution Act in 1974. In the US, there was even more legislation:

> From 1969 through 1972, virtually the entire American business community experienced a series of political setbacks without parallel in the post-war period. In the space of only four years, Congress enacted a significant tax-reform bill, four major environmental laws, an occupational safety and health act, and a series of additional consumer-protection statutes. The government also created a number of important new regulatory agencies, including the Environmental Protection Administration (EPA), the Occupational Safety and Health Administration (OSHA), and the Consumer Product Safety Commission (CPSC), investing them with broad powers over a wide range of business decisions.[4]

Businesses found that their past ways of dealing with government no longer sufficed. The scope of political conflict widened. "For the first time since the 1930s, business found its political influence seriously challenged by a new set of interest groups."[5] Grefe and Linsky describe the traditional business approach in their book *The New Corporate Activism*:

> Back then, it was standard for organizations to conduct their government relations in accordance with a "fix-it" mentality. They had a problem. They hired a lobbyist. They said, "Fix-it!" What they meant was "Kill it or make it go away". . . It was 'influence peddling', quite simply—that is, finding the person who knew the legislator or regulator and getting him (it was always a 'him' in those days of the old-boy network) to bury the problem.[6]

The First Wave of Corporate Activism in the US

In various business meetings, corporate executives lamented their decline in influence. "The truth is that we've been clobbered", the Chief Executive Officer of General Motors told chiefs from other corporations. The Chairman of the Board of General Foods asked "How come we can't get together and make our voices heard?"[7]—which is of course what they did. Throughout the 1970s, US corporations became politically active, getting together to support a conservative anti-regulatory agenda and financing a vast public relations effort aimed at regaining public trust in corporate responsibility and freedom from government regulation.

According to David Vogel in his book *Fluctuating Fortunes: The Political Power of Business in America*, "It took business about seven years to rediscover how to win in Washington." Once they realized how the political scene had changed, corporations began to adopt the strategies that public-interest activists had used so effectively against them—grassroots organising and coalition building, telephone and letter-writing campaigns, using the media, research reports and testifying at hearings, "to maximize political influence".[8] To these strategies, corporations added huge financial resources and professional advice. "A new breed of public affairs professionals began emerging" who could service corporations in their new activism.[9]

> For business, the turbulence of change was a nightmare of new regulations and increasingly vocal interest groups that needed pandering to. The rules of the game had changed, and new ways had to be found to at once get what one needed from government, shout down the opposition, and harness the power of interest groups for one's own benefit through persuasion.[10]

They established 'public affairs' departments, increased the funding and staffing of those departments, and allocated responsibility for public affairs to a senior company executive, such as a Vice-President. The offices of these public affairs units were increasingly sited in Washington. Chief Executive Officers also devoted increasing amounts of their time to government relations. A survey of four hundred public affairs units in large and medium-sized firms in 1981 found that most received more than half a million dollars each year in funding, and more than half had been set up after 1970.[11]

The number of business lobbyists in Washington increased rapidly through the 1970s. By 1982, 2,445 firms "had some form of political representation in Washington" compared with 175 in 1971. Trade associations also moved to Washington, often being restructured and given increased budgets.[12]

> All told, as of 1980 there were in Washington 12,000 lawyers representing business before federal regulatory agencies and the federal courts, 9,000 business lobbyists, 50,000 trade-association personnel, 8,000 public relations specialists, 1,300 public-affairs consultants, and 12,000 specialized journalists reporting to particular industries on government developments affecting them. The number of individuals employed by the 'private sector industry' exceeded the number of federal employers in the Washington metropolitan area for the first time since before the New Deal.[13]

In response to government regulations brought on by the activities of environmentalists and public interest groups, businesses began to cooperate in a way that was unprecedented, building coalitions and alliances and putting aside competitive rivalries. This was facilitated by the introduction of legislation such as the Clean Air Act that affected large numbers of industries as opposed to one industry at a time. "They learned to find people who were similarly situated and form ad hoc committees with these people and have a concerted, organized effort across the board of a number of industries who were similarly situated to fight the thing together."[14]

Broad coalitions of business people sought to affect "a reorientation of American politics". The Chamber of Commerce and the National Association of Manufacturers were resurrected and rejuvenated, and new organizations such as the Business Roundtable (for large corporations) and the Small Business Legislative Council (for small businesses) were formed to lobby government. The Business Roundtable, established in 1972, consisted of the chief executive officers of almost 200 corporations. It "cranked out smooth public-relations messages" warning of the costs of environmentalism. One of the Roundtable's early successes was its opposition to the Consumer Protection Agency in which it used strategically designed polling techniques and employed a public relations firm to distribute editorials and cartoons to thousands of papers and magazines.[15]

This trend towards corporate activism could be observed in other countries too. In Australia, corporations "substantially increased their level of resources and commitment to monitoring and influencing the political environment"; ensured their senior executives were effective political operatives in their dealings with politicians and bureaucrats; hired consulting firms to help with government submissions; and established government relations units within their companies with direct access to the Chief Executive Officer. Also, as in the US, "concerted efforts were made to improve and centralize business representation at the national level" so as to mobilize and increase their power.[16]

The Confederation of Australian Industry (CAI) was established in 1970 and the National Farmers Federation in 1977. The Australian Business Roundtable, modelled on the US Business Roundtable and made up of chief executives of twenty of Australia's largest companies, was founded in 1980. The Business Council of Australia was formed in 1983 by the chief executives of sixty-six large corporations, following what they perceived as a weak showing by business at the Economic Summit organized by the newly elected Labor Government. The Business Council now represents big business in Australia.[17]

Rejuvenation of the activism of business in the US happened at a time that political power in Congress was becoming more decentralized and fragmented, and party loyalty was weakening. Individual politicians were increasingly susceptible to pressure from interest groups. Whereas previously business leaders could effectively lobby key people in Congress, they now had to adopt a new lobbying strategy that focused on a wide number of individual members of Congress. This required organising support in a number of electorates so that "by 1978, corporations and trade associations were spending between $850 million and $900 million a year on mobilizing their supporters throughout the United States."[18] Trade associations did this by organising the owners of large numbers of small businesses to lobby their Congress Representative while large corporations mobilized shareholders, suppliers, customers and employees.

The War of Ideas

Far more important than the money invested in political campaigns, however, was the money invested in other forms of political influence, particularly in influencing the political agenda through the dissemination and selling of ideas:

> Right-wing businessmen like Richard Mellon Scaife and Joseph Coors, and conservative treasuries like the Mobil and Olin foundations, poured money into ad campaigns, lawsuits, elections, and books and articles protesting 'Big Government' and 'strangulation by regulation', blaming environmentalists for all the nation's ills from the energy crisis to the sexual revolution.[19]

Corporations put large amounts of money into advertising and sponsorships aimed at improving the corporate image and putting forward corporate views. Much of this advertising was on environmental issues. One 1974 survey of 114 large companies "found that thirty to thirty-five per cent of corporate advertising addressed environmentalism, energy-related issues, or the capitalist system". During the mid-1970s over $100 million was being spent each year on this sort of advocacy advertising, particularly by oil companies, electrical utility companies and the chemical industry.[20]

The Advertising Council also became active: using funds from the US Department of Commerce, it attempted to educate the public about the benefits of free enterprise, distributing millions of booklets to schools, workplaces and communities. It blamed inflation on government regulation. The idea for this campaign came from the Chairman of the Board of Procter and Gamble, the largest advertiser in the US, in a speech in which he called for American people to be better educated about the free enterprise system, so that business people need not be defensive about their work.[21]

In Australia, after the election of a 'progressive' Labor government in 1972, the Australian Chamber of Commerce reacted with a nationwide 'economic education campaign' to promote free enterprise; and in 1975 Enterprise Australia was established by the Free Enterprise Association (funded by multinational companies such as Esso, Kodak, IBM and Ford Motors) to take part in the "propaganda warfare for capitalism". In 1977, the president of the Institute of Directors in Australia told his fellow directors that the Institute should, in conjunction with Enterprise Australia, "publicise and sell the benefits of the system it espouses".[22]

Another area of corporate investment in the US, Britain and Australia was to support scholars whose views were compatible with the corporate view by funding them in universities or non-university research institutes, otherwise known as think-tanks. This was seen as a way of countering some of the anti-business research that was being produced in universities, particularly in the social sciences. Irving Kristol, one of those widely credited with persuading the US business community of the merits of this strategy, argued: "You can only beat an idea with another idea, and the war of ideas and ideologies will be won or lost within the 'new class', not against it."[23] The 'new class' comprised people—such as government bureaucrats, academics and journalists—who dealt in ideas rather than products.

Another person who persuasively made these arguments was William Simon, head of the Olin Foundation. He argued that rather than fight each piece of legislation as it came up, or spend money getting particular candidates elected, business people should foster a 'counterintelligentsia' "in the foundations, universities, and the media that would regain ideological dominance for business". Three of the wealthiest US foundations funded the establishment of the Institute for Educational Affairs (IEA), which was conceived by Kristol and Simon to coordinate the flow of money from corporations into the production of conservative ideas. Millions of corporate dollars was distributed each year in this way.[24]

Corporations continued to fund the sciences and engineering, but became much more political in other university funding, endowing forty chairs of "free enterprise" between 1974 and 1978, to promote business values to undergraduate students at colleges perceived to be liberal. They also spent millions "to influence the teaching of business and economics in the nation's high schools". They sponsored or funded educational films promoting free-market economics and screened on public television, such as Milton Friedman's series *Free to Choose* and five films on American Enterprise supported by Phillips Petroleum Company. The Business Roundtable also sponsored economics courses in primary and secondary schools.[25]

In Australia, the Australian Chamber of Commerce and Enterprise Australia used surveys of school leavers to find the 'deficiencies' in their attitudes to the free enterprise system and then circulated corrective material through schools. They also produced fifteen videos and films with titles such as *Profits, Advertising and The Market Economy*. Their material was made available to school resource centres with the approval of the departments of education in each state.[26]

Enterprise Australia produced a series of television programmes called

Making it Together, distributed a text book by one of its directors entitled *The World of Business*, presented awards to Young Achievers and broadcast commercials promoting the benefits of free enterprise on over one hundred radio stations. Business groups such as chambers of commerce, the Australian Bankers Association and the Australian Mining Industry Council ran conferences and made presentations to teachers, business people and school students.[27]

Part of the aim of all this 'education' was to get people used to the idea that "it is an appropriate part of business's role in democracy to judge what beliefs we must hold in order to be 'economically educated'." They juxtaposed personal, political and economic freedom, arguing that constraints on economic freedom were tantamount to reducing personal and political freedom and that those who sought to "intervene excessively in the play of market forces", however well-intentioned they might be, posed a major threat to those freedoms. Criticism of the economic system amounted to subversion of the political system.[28]

Think-tanks also took a leading part in the war of ideas in various countries. In the US in particular, conservative foundations and large corporations established and/or funded a new set of think-tanks which were ideologically compatible with right-wing causes and corporate interests, promoting the free market and attacking government regulation.

> Funded by eccentric billionaires, conservative foundations, and politically motivated multinational corporations, right-wing policy entrepreneurs founded think-tanks, university centers, and political journals, and developed the social and political networks necessary to tie this nascent empire together. The end product was a tidal wave of money, ideas, and self-promotion that carried the Reaganites to power.[29]

This influx of money meant not only that conservative think-tanks proliferated but that other think-tanks moved towards the right. As Jerome Himmelstein points out in his book *To the Right*: "The political mobilization of big business in the mid-1970s gave conservatives greater access to money and channels of political influence. These helped turn conservative personnel into political leaders and advisers, and conservative ideas, especially economic ones, into public policy."[30]

In the mid-1970s the corporate-owned media announced that a conservative mood had set in. Although there was indeed a 'backlash' from conservative groups, the media exaggerated what was happening by portraying it as a widespread change in public mood. This in turn helped shape public opinion into a conservative mould. Michael Parenti, in his book on the politics of the mass media, says:

> In discovering a 'conservative mood', the news media had to overlook a great deal about the 1970s and 1980s including the various polls conducted during that period—which showed a shift in a *progressive* direction (even among many who labelled themselves conservative) on issues such as military spending, environmental protection, care for the elderly, tax reform, and race relations. . . By crediting conservative policies with a popular support they did not have, the press did its part in shifting the political agenda in a rightward direction.[31]

Robert Entman, in his book *Democracy Without Citizens*, agrees that the public's policy preferences had not changed much but "the media-fed perception that they had swung right influenced politics", legitimizing the conservatism of Reagan's administration, and allowing him to implement a policy agenda that lacked majority support.[32] During the late 1970s and early 1980s, protest activities by environmental and other public interest groups were mostly either unreported or dismissively reported as being a hangover from the past.

Vogel argues that by 1978 US business had "clearly regained the political initiative" and defeated many of the regulatory measures hard won by public interest activists. They achieved the abolition of the Consumer Protection Agency, the reduction of automobile emissions standards, the deregulation of energy prices and the lowering of corporate taxes.[33] In the late 1970s US business was spending a billion dollars each year on propaganda of various sorts "aimed at persuading the American public that their interests were the same as business's interests". The result of all this expenditure showed in the polls when the percentage of people who thought that there was too much regulation soared from twenty-two per cent in 1975 to sixty per cent in 1980.[34]

Ronald Reagan, who was elected President in 1980, owed his success partly to conservative corporate interests, which he served faithfully once in power through a combination of deregulation and political appointments and by directing funding away from agencies such as the Environmental Protection Agency (EPA). During the 1980s, under Reagan's administration, the numbers of trade and professional associations, corporations and interest groups with offices in Washington continued to grow. By 1985 an estimated 80,000 employees of these associations were being serviced by accountants, lobbyists, lawyers, trade paper journalists, public relations advisers, direct mail consultants, economists and think-tanks.[35] It was a huge information industry, and all this information was shaped and presented to promote the interests of the associations and corporations generating it.

The New Corporate Activism

Corporations managed to achieve a virtual moratorium on new environmental legislation in many countries throughout the late 1970s and most of the 1980s. However, towards the end of the 1980s public concern about the environment rose again, reinforced by scientific discoveries regarding phenomena such as ozone depletion and weather patterns that seemed to indicate that global warming had already begun. Local pollution events, such as medical waste washing up on New York beaches and sewage pollution on Sydney beaches, also contributed to the public perception of an environment in decline.

A 1989 *New York Times*/CBS poll found that eighty per cent of people surveyed agreed that "protecting the environment is so important that standards cannot be too high and continuing environmental improvements must be made regardless of cost." Green parties in Europe attracted fifteen per cent of the vote. Sixteen per cent of Canadians surveyed said the environment was the most important problem in Canada—more important even than unemployment—and most people felt that solving environmental problems required government action. An Australian survey found that fifty-nine per cent of people believed that protecting the environment was more important than other issues including the economy, and eighty-one per cent said they were prepared to pay for environmental protection.[36]

A Saulwick Poll in 1990 also found that sixty-seven per cent of people thought Australia should "concentrate on protecting the environment even if it means some reduction in economic growth".[37] Similarly, a 1991 Gallup Poll found that seventy-five per cent said environmental protection should be given priority, "even at the risk of curbing economic growth". In this poll, eighty per cent of those surveyed called themselves environmentalists.[38]

Amidst all this public concern, regulatory agencies in various countries got tougher and new laws were enacted. In the US, the highest-ever number of environmental convictions were recorded by the EPA in 1989, and half of those convicted got jail sentences. Environmental indictments by the Justice Department increased by thirty per cent in 1990 over the previous year.[39] In New South Wales, Australia, an Environmental Offences and Penalties Act was introduced in 1989, which provided for jail terms and million dollar fines for senior executives of polluting companies.

This heightening of public anxiety in response to scientific confirmation of environmental deterioration induced a new wave of corporate political activity. This time the corporate backlash was able to utilize the techniques and organizations that had been established in the 1970s for the same purpose. With their activist machinery already in place, corporations were able to take advantage of the new PR techniques and information technologies available for raising money, building coalitions, manipulating public opinion and lobbying politicians. And this time, rather than focusing on defending the free enterprise system and opposing labour unions, the attack was primarily targeted at environmentalists.

For example in 1991 Bob Williams, a consultant to the oil and gas industry, wrote in his book *US Petroleum Strategies in the Decade of the Environment* that the industry needed "to put the environmental lobby out of business. . . There is no greater imperative. . . If the petroleum industry is to survive, it must render the environmental lobby superfluous, an anachronism."[40] Similarly Ron Arnold, another industry consultant, told a meeting of the Ontario Forest Industries Association: "You must turn the public against environmentalists or you will lose your environmental battle as surely as the US timber industry has lost theirs."[41]

Frank Mankiewicz, a senior executive at transnational PR firm Hill and Knowlton, observed:

> The big corporations, our clients, are scared shitless of the environmental movement. . . They sense that there's a majority out there and that the emotions are all on the other side—if they can be heard. They think the politicians are going to yield up to the emotions. I think the corporations are wrong about that. I think the companies will have to give in only at insignificant levels. Because the companies are too strong, they're the establishment. The environmentalists are going to have to be like the mob in the square in Romania before they prevail.[42]

Having observed the rise in environmental consciousness and the defensiveness of US industry, C.J. Silas, Chief Executive Officer for Phillips Petroleum Company, wrote in *Public Affairs Journal* at the beginning of 1990: "There's no reason we can't make the environmental issue *our* issue. If we wait to be told what to do—if we offer no initiatives of our own and react defensively—we're playing not to lose, and that's not good enough." (his emphasis)[43]

It has been during the 1990s that the application of public relations to environmental concerns has really come into its own. Environmentalism was labelled "the life and death PR battle of the 1990s" and "the issue of the decade" by public relations personnel. Activist Brian Tokar suggests the rise in environmental PR was because, with the collapse of communism in many parts of the world, "the growth of ecological awareness in the industrialized countries may be one of the last internal obstacles to the complete hegemony of transnational corporate capitalism."[44]

The coalition building which began in the 1970s continues to grow. A survey of thirty of the largest firms in the US found that each firm was involved in an average of 5.7 coalitions, such as The Business Roundtable; most of them "formed for legislative and regulatory purposes and focused primarily on national issues" such as the environment. More than a third of the corporations surveyed spend over a million dollars each year on "coalition activity".[45]

Some corporations have gone beyond their corporate allies in their organising efforts, hiring specialized public relations firms to set up front groups that promote the corporate agenda but pose as public interest groups (see Chapter Two). Public relations firms also have become adept at creating the impression of grassroots support for corporate causes so as to convince politicians to oppose environmental reforms. A 1992 survey by the US Public Affairs Council found that seventy-three per cent of the 163 large companies surveyed had a senior executive responsible for grassroots organising, a newly acquired responsibility growing at a rate second only to environmental affairs.[46] There are now also several firms in the US which specialize in creating grassroots support for industry causes.

Industry interests have been able to turn the disaffection of rural and resource industry workers, farmers and small business people into anti-environmental sentiment. Nowhere has this been more spectacularly achieved than in the US with its Wise Use Movement (see Chapter Three). The Wise Use Movement has attained grassroots support through enrolling thousands of people in the US who are worried about their future and feel individually powerless to do anything about it. A similar coalition has been formed in Canada, called the Share movement, and elements of this type of movement are spreading to Australia.

Those who oppose undesirable developments and unfettered resource extraction are now finding that they are not only subject to the abuse of industry funded anti-environmental groups but they are also vulnerable to a new wave of law suits filed against them for exercising their democratic rights to circulate petitions, write to public officials, attend public meetings, organize boycotts and engage in peaceful demonstrations. Every year thousands of environmentalists and ordinary citizens are sued for speaking out against governments and corporations (see Chapter Four).

Corporate political donations have also increased. Organizations involved in influencing environmental legislation in the US since 1989 have included the American Farm Bureau Federation, which has contributed almost a million dollars to congressional candidates between 1989 and 1994 in its efforts to get the Clean Water Act controls on factory farms removed: the Republicans have introduced a bill that does just that. Oil corporation and land developer Chevron Corporation, which is a member of the Alliance for Reasonable Regulation, has spent over a million dollars on congressional candidates during the same period, and managed to introduce the concept of "plausible risk" into the same bill so that acceptable toxicity levels would be reduced, According to the EPA's Toxics Release Inventory, Chevron releases millions of pounds of toxic material into the environment each year.[47]

Exxon, with a similar annual discharge of toxic material, has also been a member of the Alliance for Reasonable Regulation, and also spent over a million dollars in that same period on lobbying congressional candidates in its efforts to prevent the Clean Air Act being strengthened. Dow Chemical and its affiliates have also given over a million dollars and opposed the strengthening of the Clean Air Act, as well as pushing for cost-benefit analysis to be incorporated into the Clean Water Act. Chevron, Exxon and Dow Chemical all give financial support to a range of front groups including Allliance to Keep Americans Working, American Council on Science and Health and the National Wetlands Coalition.[48]

In Europe, lobbyists and corporate consultants are flocking to Brussels to influence policy making by the European Parliament:

> Leading the most recent wave of arrivals are large US law firms with strong Washington, DC, lobbying experience. They join an international armada of advocates already active in Brussels, including. . . public relations groups, confederations of European trade associations, representatives of US states, German lander and British municipalities, small 'boutique' consultancies, in-house representatives of individual US, European, and Japanese companies, European trade unions, agricultural groups, and a growing number of public-interest associations.[49]

Conservative think-tanks, having been instrumental in bringing Ronald Reagan to power in the US and Margaret Thatcher to power in the UK, have turned their attention to environmental issues and the defeat of environmental regulations. They have sought to cast doubt on the very features of the environmental crisis that had heightened public concerns at the end of the 1980s, including ozone depletion, greenhouse warming and industrial pollution (see Chapters Five and Six).

Think-tanks have opposed environmental legislation in a variety of ways. In the US they have attempted to hamstring the regulatory process by advocating legislation which would ensure that regulatory efforts become too expensive and difficult to implement, by insisting on cost benefit analyses and risk assessments of proposed legislation and compensation to state governments and property owners for the costs of complying with the legislation. Throughout the Western world, these think-tanks have promoted free-market techniques such as tradeable property and pollution rights, pricing mechanisms, tax incentives, and voluntary agreements for dealing with environmental degradation. These have been taken seriously by governments and in some cases accepted by environmentalists as a valid alternative to tougher legislation (see Chapter Six).

Corporations have also turned their attention to the next generation, through the development and distribution of 'educational' material to schools. The potential to shape environmental perceptions and improve corporate images at the same time has attracted many customers to the firms designing educational materials for corporations. These materials inevitably give a corporate view of environmental problems, and avoid solutions that would involve reduced consumption, increased regulation or reduced corporate profits (see Chapter Ten).

The combination of activist techniques and corporate money is a powerful weapon in the battle of ideas. In the US, opinion polling indicates corporate funded anti-environmental efforts produced a major shift in public opinion within the space of a single year. In 1992, fifty-one per cent of those surveyed agreed that environmentalists had "gone too far", compared with seventeen per cent the year before.[50]

Andrew Rowell, in his book *Green Backlash*, dates the arrival of the anti-environmentalist backlash in Britain as Spring 1995, when the media took up the "anti-green tune" and a number of books were published that attacked environmentalism. These included a book by Richard North, whose research, according to Rowell, was funded by British chemical company ICI, and another published by the conservative UK think-tank, the Institute of Economic Affairs.[51]

The corporate muscle of multinational (also known as transnational) corporations is formidable. In 1995 the UN Conference on Trade and Development (UNCTAD) reported that these corporations—40,000 of them—controlled two-thirds of the world's trade in goods and services.[52] According to *New Internationalist* magazine in 1993:

> The combined sales of the world's largest 350 multinationals total nearly one third of the combined gross national products of all industrialized countries and exceed the individual gross national products of all Third World countries.[53]

Many of the largest multinational corporations are headquartered in the US and it is not surprising that the strategies they have pioneered there to combat environmental regulations are now being used in other countries. This book examines this second wave of corporate activism that has emerged in the US, Canada, UK and Australia and elsewhere.

Chapter 2

Fronting for Industry

When a corporation wants to oppose environmental regulations, or support an environmentally damaging development, it may do so openly and in its own name. But it is far more effective to have a group of citizens or experts—and preferably a coalition of such groups—which can publicly promote the outcomes desired by the corporation whilst claiming to represent the public interest. When such groups do not already exist, the modern corporation can pay a public relations firm to create them.

The use of such 'front groups' enables corporations to take part in public debates and government hearings behind a cover of community concern. These front groups lobby governments to legislate in the corporate interest; to oppose environmental regulations and to introduce policies that enhance corporate profitability. Front groups also campaign to change public opinion, so that the markets for corporate goods are not threatened and the efforts of environmental groups are defused. Merrill Rose, Executive Vice-President of the public relations firm Porter/Novelli, advises companies:

> Put your words in someone else's mouth. . . There will be times when the position you advocate, no matter how well framed and supported, will not be accepted by the public simply because you are who you are. Any institution with a vested commercial interest in the outcome of an issue has a natural credibility barrier to overcome with the public, and often with the media.[1]

The names of corporate front groups are carefully chosen to mask the real interests behind them but they can usually be identified by their funding sources, membership and who controls them. Some front groups are quite blatant, working out of the offices of public relations firms and having staff of those firms on their boards of directors. For example, the Council for Solid Waste Solutions shares office space with the Society of the Plastic Industry, Inc and the Oregon Lands Coalition works out of the offices of the Association of Oregon Industries.[2]

Corporate front groups have flourished in the United States, with several large companies donating money to more than one front group. In 1991 Dow Chemical was contributing to ten front groups, including the Alliance to Keep Americans Working, the Alliance for Responsible CFC Policy, the American Council on Science and Health, Citizens for a Sound Economy and the Council for Solid Waste Solutions. According to Mark Megalli and Andy Friedman in their report on corporate front groups in America, oil companies Chevron and Exxon were each contributing to nine such groups. Other companies which donate to multiple groups include Mobil, DuPont, Amoco, Ford, Philip Morris,

Pfizer, Monsanto and Proctor and Gamble.[3] These large corporations "stand to profit handsomely by linking their goals with what they hope to define as a grass-roots populist movement".[4]

The use of front groups to represent industry interests in the name of concerned citizens is a relatively recent phenomenon. In the past, businesses lobbied governments directly and put out press releases in their own names or those of their trade associations. The rise of citizen and public interest groups, including environmental groups, has reflected a growing scepticism amongst the public about statements made by businesses:

> Thus, if Burger King were to report that a Whopper is nutritious, informed consumers would probably shrug in disbelief. . . And if the Nutrasweet Company were to insist that the artificial sweetener aspartame has no side effects, consumers might not be inclined to believe them, either. . . But if the 'American Council on Science and Health' and its panel of 200 'expert' scientists reported that Whoppers were not so bad, consumers might actually listen. . . And if the 'Calorie Control Council' reported that aspartame is not really dangerous, weight-conscious consumers might continue dumping the artificial sweetener in their coffee every morning without concern.[5]

The American Council on Science and Health has received funds from food processing and beverage corporations including Burger King, Coca-Cola, PepsiCo, NutraSweet and Nestlé USA, as well as chemical, oil and pharmaceutical companies such as Monsanto, Dow USA, Exxon, Union Carbide and others. Its Executive Director, portrayed in the mass media as an independent scientist, defends petrochemical companies, the nutritional values of fast foods, and the safety of saccharin, pesticides and growth hormones for dairy cows. She claims that the US government spends far too much on investigating unproven health risks such as dioxin and pesticides because of the public's "unfounded fears of man-made chemicals and their perception of these chemicals as carcinogens".[6]

The American Council on Science and Health is one of many corporate front groups which allow industry-funded experts to pose as independent scientists to promote corporate causes. Chemical and nuclear industry front groups with scientific sounding names publish pamphlets that are 'peer reviewed' by industry scientists rather than papers in established academic journals.[7] Megalli and Friedman point out: "Contrary to their names, these groups often disregard compelling scientific evidence to further their viewpoints, arguing that pesticides are not harmful, saccharin is not carcinogenic, or that global warming is a myth. By sounding scientific, they seek to manipulate the public's trust."[8]

The Corporate Strategies of Front Groups

Corporate front groups use various strategies to promote the corporate agenda in environmental affairs. In the case of pseudo-scientific groups, the aim is to cast doubt on the severity of the problems associated with environmental deterioration, and create confusion by magnifying uncertainties and showing that some scientists dispute the claims of the scientific community. Some groups such as the Information Council on the Environment, which is a coal industry front group, publish propaganda which argues that global warming will not happen. Other groups emphasize the uncertainty associated with global warming predictions or argue that the United States could be better off in a warmer world.

The Global Climate Coalition, a coalition of fifty US trade associations and private companies representing oil, gas, coal, automobile and chemical interests, uses these sorts of arguments to fight restrictions on greenhouse gas emissions. Its tactics have included distributing to hundreds of journalists a video which claims that increased levels of carbon dioxide will increase crop production and help to feed the hungry people of the world. In the lead-up to the Rio Summit the Coalition successfully lobbied the US government to avoid mandatory emissions controls; and in 1994 it called for the Clinton government to resist international agreements to reduce greenhouse emissions because they "would damage the US economy and the competitiveness of American business in the global market-place". The chair of the Coalition at the time was also president of the National Association of Manufacturers.[9]

Some corporate front groups acknowledge environmental problems but argue that the solutions being promoted are too expensive, cost jobs, and would have detrimental economic consequences. For example the Alliance for Responsible CFC Policy, representing chemical companies, argued that the substitution of hydrochlorofluorocarbons (HCFCs) for chlorofluorocarbons (CFCs) would not be in the public interest because of the costs.[10] They were thinking of course, of the costs to the chemical companies.

Such front groups tend to portray themselves as moderate and representing the middle ground; they therefore often use words like 'reasonable', 'sensible' and 'sound'. The use of these words is a way of implicitly saying that environmentalists are extremists—whilst hiding their own extreme positions. They downplay the dangers posed by environmental problems whilst emphasising the costs of solving them. Examples include the Coalition for Sensible Regulation, which is a coalition of developers and corporate farmers in the West, and the Alliance for Sensible Environmental Reform, which represents polluting industries. The Citizens for Sensible Control of Acid Rain operated between 1983 and 1991 to oppose amendments to the Clean Air Act which threatened stricter standards on electricity generating emissions. It did not have a membership of individual citizens yet spent more money lobbying in Washington in 1986 (thanks to funds from coal and electric-utility companies) than any other lobby group.[11]

Another strategy used by corporate front groups is to recognize environmental problems that are caused by corporations, but to promote superficial solutions that prevent and pre-empt the sorts of changes that are really necessary to solve the problems. Sometimes they shift the blame from corporations to the individual citizen. The Keep America Beautiful Campaign focuses on anti-litter campaigns but ignores the potential of recycling legislation and changes to packaging. It seeks to attribute litter and waste disposal problems to the irresponsible actions of individuals and admits no corporate responsibility for such problems. In the

1970s Keep America Beautiful opposed bottle deposit legislation, and more recently it has sought to discredit recycling with television advertisements, reports and brochures which emphasize the cost and limits of recycling.[12]

The Keep America Beautiful Campaign receives approximately $2 million per year from "some 200 companies that manufacture and distribute the aluminium cans, paper products, glass bottles and plastics that account for about a third of the material in US landfills", including Coca-Cola, McDonald's, 3M and Scott Paper. It is also funded by waste companies that landfill and incinerate hazardous wastes and prefer waste disposal to be focused on the tidy disposal of litter. The Campaign's directors include representatives of Philip Morris, Mobil Chemical, Procter and Gamble, and PR giant Burson-Marsteller. In the past it has been coordinated by the Public Relations Director of Union Carbide.[13]

Perhaps the most common strategy of corporate front groups is to portray themselves as environmentalists, and the views they are promoting as those of environmentalists. In this way, corporate interests appear to have environmental support. The names of groups are chosen because they sound as if they are grassroots community and environmental groups, such as the Environmental Conservation Organisation, founded by the Land Improvement Contractors of America; the Sea Lion Defense Fund, a legal arm of the Alaska fishing industry fighting limits on fishing; and the Coalition for a Reasonable Environment (CARE) which consists mainly of developers, builders, lawyers and investors.[14]

The National Wetlands Coalition, which has a logo that shows a duck flying over a wetland, is not, despite its name, campaigning to protect wetlands. The group was formed in response to a policy statement made in 1989 by President George Bush that his government's aim was to have no net loss of wetlands. The Coalition, which is largely made up of oil and gas companies including Exxon, Shell and Mobil, was formed to protect the right of its members to build and drill in wetlands without impediment.[15]

Consumer Alert, another group which has been supported by corporations like Exxon, Eli-Lilly, Chevron, Estée Lauder and Philip Morris, campaigns against safety regulations for consumer products. It has fought against such measures as mandatory air bags in cars, safety seats for babies in aeroplanes and acid rain regulations, as well as filing a law suit against protesters at a Californian nuclear reactor.[16]

Pacific Lumber/Maxxam have hired a PR firm to put together a coalition to obstruct environmentalists wanting to save the 60,000-acre Headwaters Forest in Humboldt County, California. A coalition called the "Headwaters Consensus Council" was put together by the Sacramento PR firm. It says it too wants to save the old growth redwoods of the Headwaters, but is campaigning to preserve only "the 3,000-acre headwaters grove of virgin old growth redwoods"; and it wants to do this by getting the Californian government to acquire the 3,000 acres from Pacific Lumber/Maxxam for about $500,000 "or a swap of like value".[17] This would be an ideal solution for the corporations which could go ahead and log most of the forest whilst being paid handsomely for that small portion that they almost certainly wouldn't be permitted to log anyway.

Some groups are formed purely to oppose a particular piece of legislation, such as the Clean Air Working Group which was formed by coal companies— who invested millions of dollars in the campaign—to fight the Clean Air Act of 1990. The group Nevadans for Fair Fuel Economy Standards was formed in 1990 by car manufacturers who wanted to put pressure on a Nevadan Senator to oppose a Federal fuel-economy bill. It employed consultants to get members by writing to "Nevadans who owned taxis, recreational vehicles, pickup trucks, and other gas guzzlers", telling them the new bill would make running their vehicles very expensive. The letters did not mention that the group was a car industry front group; some people who had acted on the letters felt deceived when they later found out.[18]

Similarly, the Coalition for Vehicle Choice was established in 1991 by the Motor Vehicle Manufacturers of America, with a $500,000 grant and the help of public relations firm E. Bruce Harrison, to fight standards for fuel consumption in new cars. Its members include a variety of automobile manufacturers' associations, motorists' associations and business groups. Behind the facade of the front group, these organizations argue that fuel efficiency means smaller, less safe cars—a claim that is hotly denied by non-industry groups such as the Center for Auto Safety.[19]

Corporate front groups are less well documented outside the United States, although it is reasonable to assume that wherever the multinational corporations who support them operate, they do also. Bob Burton, who has been investigating front groups in Australia, believes that the Forest Protection Society is one such group. It was established in 1987 with the support of the Forest Industry Campaign Association, whose Executive Officer claimed the funds were just to get it started but that it would be an independent community group. Some years later about eighty per cent of the Society's funding was still coming from the Association.[20]

The Forest Protection Society shares the same postal address as the National Association of Forest Industries, uses an industry spokesperson as a contact for job advertisements and uses the services of Burson-Marsteller. Yet the Forest Protection Society is listed as an 'Environmental Protection Organisation' in the 1994 Directory of Australian Associations. Its fact sheets promote logging in rain-forests as "one of the best ways to ensure that the rain-forests are not destroyed". Burton claims to have uncovered minutes of a Forest Protection Society meeting where ways to take over meetings of local environment groups and distract them from their campaigning were discussed.[21]

Mothers Opposing Pollution (MOP) is another Australian front group which has been exposed. Its prime purpose seems to have been to champion cardboard milk cartons against plastic milk bottles. A report in the *Courier Mail* informed readers that MOP's sole spokeswoman not only owned her own public relations company but also co-directed another company with a consultant to the Association of Liquid Paperboard Carton Manufacturers.[22]

Manufacturing Grass Roots

Front groups are not the only way in which corporate interests can be portrayed as coinciding with a greater public interest. Public relations firms are becoming proficient at helping their corporate clients convince key politicians that there is broad support for their environmentally damaging activities or their demands for looser environmental regulations. Using specially tailored mailing lists, field officers, telephone banks and the latest in information technology, these firms are able to generate hundreds of telephone calls and/or thousands of pieces of mail to key politicians, creating the impression of wide public support for their client's position.

This sort of operation was almost unheard of ten years ago, yet in the US today, where "technology makes building volunteer organizations as simple as writing a check", it has become "one of the hottest trends in politics" and an $800 million industry. It is now a part of normal business for corporations and trade associations to employ one of the dozens of companies that specialize in these strategies to run grassroots campaigns for them. Firms and associations utilising such services include Philip Morris, Georgia Pacific, the Chemical Manufacturers Association, General Electric, American Forest & Paper Association, Chevron, Union Carbide, Procter & Gamble, American Chemical Society, American Plastics Association, Motor Vehicle Manufacturers Association, WMX Technologies, Browning Ferris Industries and the Nuclear Energy Institute.[23]

When a group of US electric utility companies wanted to influence the Endangered Species Act, which was being re-authorized to ensure that economic factors were considered when species were listed as endangered, their lawyers advised them to form a broad-based coalition with a grassroots orientation: "Incorporate as a non-profit, develop easy-to-read information packets for Congress and the news media and woo members from virtually all walks of life. Members should include Native American entities, county and local governments, universities, school boards. . ." As a result of this advice the National Endangered Species Act Reform Coalition was formed, one of a "growing roster of industry groups that have discovered grassroots lobbying as a way to influence environmental debates".[24]

Artificially created grassroots coalitions are referred to in the industry as 'astroturf' (after a synthetic grass product). Astroturf is a "grassroots program that involves the instant manufacturing of public support for a point of view in which either uninformed activists are recruited or means of deception are used to recruit them."[25] According to *Consumer Reports* magazine, those engaging in this sort of work can earn up to $500 "for every citizen they mobilize for a corporate client's cause".[26]

Mario Cooper, senior vice president of PR firm Porter/Novelli, says that the challenge for a grassroots specialists is to create the impression that millions of people support their client's view of a particular issue, so that a politician can't ignore it; this means targeting potential supporters and targeting 'persuadable' politicians. He advises: "Database management companies can provide you with incredibly detailed mailing lists segmented by almost any factor you can imagine."[27] Once identified, potential supporters have to be persuaded to agree to endorse the corporate view being promoted.

Specialists in this form of organising use opinion research data to "identify the kinds of themes most likely to arouse key constituent groups, then gear their tele-marketing pitches around those themes."[28] Telephone polls, in particular, enable rapid feedback so that the pitch can be refined: "With phones you're on the phones today, you analyze your results, you can change your script and try a new thing tomorrow. In a three-day program you can make four or five different changes, find out what's really working, what messages really motivate people, and improve your response rates."[29] Focus groups also help with targeting messages.

Demographic information, election results, polling results and lifestyle clusters can all be combined to identify potential supporters by giving information about people's age, income, marital status, gender, ethnic background, the type of car they drive and the type of music they like. These techniques, which were originally developed for marketing products to selected audiences, are now used to identify likely political attitudes and opinions. In this way the coalition builders don't have to waste their time on people who are unlikely to be persuaded, and at the same time can use different arguments for different types of people.

Jack Bonner of Bonner & Associates is one of the leading specialists providing grassroots support for his clients, who include the Association of International Auto Manufacturers, Chrysler, Dow Chemical, Edison Electric Institute, Ford, General Motors, Exxon, McDonnell Douglas, Monsanto, Pharmaceutical Manufacturers Association, Philip Morris, US Tobacco Co. and Westinghouse.[30] When the amendments to the Clean Air Act were being debated in 1990, Bonner managed to get some large citizen groups, who had no financial interest in the matter, to lobby against amendments which would have required car manufacturers to make their cars more fuel efficient.

Bonner's firm, working on behalf of the automobile industry, persuaded these citizen groups that the legislation would have meant that large vehicles would not be manufactured. "Bonner's fee, which he coyly described as somewhere between $500,000 and $1 million, was for scouring six states for potential grassroots voices, coaching them on the 'facts' of the issue, paying for the phone calls and plane fares to Washington and hiring the hall for a joint press conference."[31]

The Society for the Plastics Industry hired Bonner after a law was passed in 1987 in Suffolk County, New York, banning some plastic products which were filling up landfills. The law was expected to be the first of many in other parts of the US. The Society also challenged the law in the courts. Subsequently the law, which had been approved with a twelve to six vote, was suspended with a twelve to six vote by the same body.[32]

Bonner's Washington DC office has three hundred phone lines and a sophisticated computer system. His staff phone people all over the country, looking for citizens who will support corporate agendas. He targets members of Congress who are unsure of how to vote or who need a justification for voting with industry against measures that will protect the environment.

Imagine Bonner's technique multiplied and elaborated in different ways across hundreds of public issues and you may begin to envision the girth of this industry. Some firms produce artfully designed opinion polls, more or less guaranteed to yield results that suggest public support for the industry's position. Some firms specialize in coalition building—assembling dozens of hundreds of civic organisations and interest groups in behalf of lobbying goals. . .This is democracy and it costs a fortune.[33]

Another expert in creating grassroots support for corporations is John Davies, who features a picture of an old lady carrying a sign "Not in my backyard" in his advertisements. The picture is captioned:

Don't leave your future in her hands.
Traditional lobbying is no longer enough. Today numbers count. To win in the hearing room, you must reach out to create grassroots support. To outnumber your opponents, call the leading grassroots public affairs communications specialists.[34]

In his promotion, Davies explains that he will use mailing lists and computer databases to identify potential supporters and telemarketers to persuade them to agree to have letters written on their behalf. In this way he is able to create the impression of a "spontaneous explosion of community support for needy corporations".[35]

The practical objective of letter-writing campaigns is not actually to get a majority of the people behind a position and to express themselves on it—for it would be virtually impossible to whip up that much enthusiasm—but to get such a heavy, sudden outpouring of sentiment that lawmakers feel they are being besieged by a majority. The true situation may be quite the contrary.[36]

Other less specialist firms also create such coalitions for their clients. Edelman PR Worldwide has created such a coalition for Monsanto to oppose the labelling of genetically engineered food. Burson-Marsteller, one of the world's largest public relations firms, also organizes grassroots coalitions and corporate front groups for many of its clients. Since 1985 it has had a team of people in its Washington, DC office specialising in designing coalitions to build allies and neutralize opponents. In 1992 Burson-Marsteller created an independent grassroots lobbying unit, Advocacy Communications Team, to counter activists that threaten corporations by organising "rallies, boycotts and demonstrations outside your plant".[37]

Burson-Marsteller used their grassroots lobbying unit to create the National Smokers Alliance in 1993 on behalf of Philip Morris. The millions supplied by Philip Morris and the advice supplied by Burson-Marsteller's Advocacy Communications Team allowed this 'grassroots' alliance to use full-page advertisements, direct telemarketing and other high-tech campaign techniques to build its membership to a claimed three million by 1995, and to disseminate its pro-smoking message. The Alliance's president is the Vice-President of Burson-Marsteller, and other Burson-Marsteller executives are actively involved in the Alliance.[38]

Burson-Marsteller is heavily involved in similar activities on behalf of clients who have been threatened by the rise of environmentalism. It helped create the Coalition for Clean and Renewable Energy, organized to support its client Hydro Quebec, which was embroiled in controversy with environmentalists over its dams, both existing and proposed.

> The masquerade is part of the game. B-M and companies like it have become masters of manipulation. If a pro-utility group calls itself by a nice, green-sounding name, if speakers at public forums are not identified as being on the Hydro Quebec payroll, and if supposed activists are really moles for the opposition, image triumphs and truth becomes a casualty.[39]

A new coalition, The Foundation for Clean Air Progress, is currently operating out of Burson-Marsteller's offices. According to CLEAR, an organization which monitors anti-environmental activities in the US, the Foundation is "in reality a front for transportation, energy, manufacturing and agricultural groups". It is attempting to influence the re-authorization of the Clean Air Act due in 1997 by setting up chapters in various cities and 'educating' the public about the progress made in air quality over the past twenty-five years. Its focus is on individual responsibility for pollution, as opposed to the regulation of industry to achieve further improvements.[40]

Influence on Politicians

According to the people who staff congressional offices, grassroots campaigns are far more effective than traditional lobbying—or even monetary contributions—in persuading politicians to vote in a particular way. One survey, by a doctoral student at the University of North Carolina Business School, found that 'grassroots activism' was ranked as the most effective strategy by fifty-seven per cent of respondents, compared with twenty-eight per cent who said 'lobbying by company executives' and five per cent who said 'political donations'.[41] The rationale for this is that politicians have to worry about being re-elected, so they care what voters think.

Environmental and public interest groups pioneered the use of printed postcards as an effective means of grassroots campaigning, but as this method was adopted by corporations, and as competition between various interest groups increased, politicians become more cynical of these grassroots lobbying techniques. They realized that "10,000 pre-printed postcards arriving within five days of one another may not be a unilateral groundswell of democracy."[42] Postcards were soon replaced by form letters and then telegrams, faxes and phone calls.

> As a result of advances in technology, the realization on the part of elected officials that form letters were merely a product of a relentless coordinated campaign (it only took Washington half-a-decade to figure this out), and because the public is demanding a more responsive government, the art of grassroots campaigning has advanced to a science.[43]

The more personalized the communications, the harder it is for the targeted politician to tell if it is a genuine, spontaneous expression of voter sentiment or an organized push by a corporation. And public relations people have become expert at faking the real thing. Davies, speaking at a conference in Chicago on *Shaping Public Opinion: If You Don't Do It, Somebody Else Will*, explained how his firm creates 'personal' letters for his clients, after gaining agreement from the person on the telephone:

> If they're close by we hand-deliver it. We hand-write it out on 'little kitty cat stationery' if it's a little old lady. If it's a business we take it over to be photocopied on someone's letterhead. [We] use different stamps, different envelopes. . . Getting a pile of personalized letters that have a different look to them is what you want to strive for.[44]

Telephone calls also tend to be more personal and, according to public relations people, the staff in politicians' offices often keep a tally of calls in favour of and opposed to particular bills. "Some even get callers' names and addresses and add them to their database."[45] Companies such as Optima Direct have sophisticated telephone communication equipment that enables them to redirect calls directly to politicians. Employees of Optima Direct contact potential supporters by telephone, talk to them, and suggest they talk to their representative. If they agree, they are connected straight through before they change their mind. In this way politicians can be flooded with calls from their local constituents on an issue and get the impressions that these calls are manifestations of a vast groundswell of opinion out there on that issue. Such calls can be spaced out through the day and each week to further increase the apparent realism of the groundswell.[46]

This telephone connection technique (called 'patch-through') has also been used in conjunction with talk-back radio shows to give the impression of mass opposition to government reforms. For example, a conservative radio host such as Rush Limbaugh, whose show is broadcast to twenty million people via 650 stations across the USA, will argue against health reforms and work people up about them; then a commercial during the next break, paid for by the health insurance industry, will give listeners a free phone number to call for more information. These calls will be put through to a telemarketer who will talk to the callers and put them through to their representative in Congress.[47] Similar techniques have been used against environmental reforms and regulations: a "massive phone patch campaign was credited with defeating the corporate average fuel economy standards provision of the energy bill in the Senate in 1992".[48]

Television advertisements have been used in a similar way. A free call number, given in the ad, can generate thousands of callers who are then recruited to lobby their local politicians. The advertisements are carefully targeted to reach those most likely to do this, being shown on news and public affairs programmes on particular cable channels and CNN, rather than in prime time on entertainment channels.[49]

Randy Haynie, whose firm represents corporations such as Philip Morris and WMI (formerly known as Waste Management Inc), explains how they categorize politicians according to their past votes and other factors into those likely to support a bill, those likely to oppose it and those who could go either way. It is this last category that is targeted by grassroots campaigns. Corporate lobbying now commonly includes a grassroots component.[50]

The letters and telephone calls resulting from these PR efforts tend to have an exaggerated effect on politicians, because most operate under the traditional assumption that a letter writer or caller is extremely committed and motivated; and that for every letter that the politician receives, there are hundreds or thousands of citizens who feel the same way but who lacked the time, resources, skills or motivation to write a similar letter. Someone who goes to the trouble of writing a letter is likely to feel strongly enough to actually monitor how the politician votes on the issue and decide their own vote accordingly when he comes up for re-election. With grassroots organising, however, these assumptions about letter writers and callers are totally invalid because of the way the lobbying is engineered by the PR companies.

According to Edward Grefe and Marty Linsky in their book *The New Corporate Activism*, letters, particularly to state, county and city legislators, are especially influential because people at these levels seldom get more than one or two letters on any subject.[51] Even at the national level letters are important. A 1992 Gallup Poll found that over seventy per cent of members of Congress said that they paid "a great deal of attention to (a) personally written letters from constituents, (b) meetings with heads of groups, (c) CEO visits representing companies with a job presence in the district, (d) personally written letters from heads of groups in the district or from company officials with a job presence in the district, and (e) phone calls from constituents."[52]

Another study of congressional staff found that seventy-nine per cent said that individually written letters were most effective form of grassroots campaigning; sixty-four per cent said phone calls were most effective; and letters and phone calls were more effective than public demonstrations and petitions, which in turn were more effective than mass mail responses. When their estimates were averaged, respondents said that it would take 2,035 mass mail responses to get a legislator to place a high priority on an issue, compared with 156 individually written letters and 188 phone calls. In order to change their position on an issue, staff suggested it would take almost 20,000 mass mail responses compared to about 700 letters and 1,500 phone calls.[53]

Front groups and PR-generated grassroots responses also help politicians who want to vote for or against a piece of legislation because of corporate inducements, but also want to be seen to be responsive to voters. According to Michael Pertschuk, co-director of the Advocacy Institute: "Fronts are useful for politicians who essentially want to do industry's bidding but are reluctant to be seen as tools of industry."[54]

These methods are not confined to the US: they are also available in Canada. In his speech to the 1993 Wise Use Conference entitled *How to use communications technology to compete with radical environmentalists*, Ross Irvine, President of the Canadian firm Public Relations Management Ltd, explained to the audience the value of computer-generated letters as a powerful way of influencing

Canadian politicians. "Politicians feel compelled to respond to letters, and for each letter they receive politicians believe there are 10, 100, 1,000 or 10,000 voters who feel the same way as the letter writer."[55]

> How about if you make a few copies of the computerized list of law makers and prepare form letters which can be merged with your list of names. . . Then you give copies of these computer disks to all your members, to all your friends, to all your neighbours,—to everyone you know—and ask them to send letters to the law makers.[56]

James Gardner, author of *Effective Lobbying in the European Community*, has described "the soaring growth in transnational lobbying by giant global corporations" and contended that in future grassroots lobbying is likely to be used widely in many countries. He notes, for example, that there is provision for citizens to petition the European Parliament and that this "furnishes a framework for a grassroots lobbying campaign aimed at the Parliament and indirectly at the Commission and the Council".[57]

Grassroots firms also specialize in generating attendance at town hall meetings and public hearings, as well as signatures on petitions and attendance at rallies. National Grassroots and Communications sets up local organizations to support their clients, using selected individuals from the local community who are paid and supervised by their own staff.[58] The business of collecting signatures for petitions has also become a professional activity that corporations can pay for.

In California, where bills can be initiated through petitions, the use of professional petitioners seems to be the way to ensure success. Two companies have been responsible for seventy-five per cent of the 65 initiatives that qualified for the California ballot in the decade from 1982 to 1992. These companies also operate in Oregon, Nevada, Washington, Michigan, Ohio, Oklahoma and Colorado. The people who collect the signatures get paid 25 to 35 cents per name. Often they have several petitions going at a time, which makes the operation more efficient. Increasingly it is only the well-financed who can afford to get such an initiative qualified.[59]

Grassroots: Mobilising Family, Friends and Neighbours

Consultant John Brady concentrates on what is known in the business as 'treetops' lobbying, which involves activating smaller numbers of more influential citizens to contact their local government representative. He has over a hundred 'field operatives' working for him throughout the country. These are people with contacts and political savvy who can identify twenty to sixty business people or respected citizens able to clearly present the client's viewpoint on an issue. These people are then asked to contact the targeted politician, preferably with a visit or phone call.[60]

Some firms run their own version of this sort of programme, known in the business as a 'key contact approach': "Each member of management is assigned one or more legislators or administrators—members of Congress, state legislators, governors or regulators—with whom they are expected to develop a relationship."[61] This personal relationship gives the firm access to government and sometimes influence in times of need.

Large corporations are increasingly turning to their own business networks for grassroots support. Such organizations have access to many potential allies through their own employees, shareholders, customers, suppliers and vendors. One of Burson-Marsteller's directors told a gathering of British chemical industry leaders:

> Don't forget that the chemical industry has many friends and allies that can be mobilized. . . employees, shareholders, and retirees. . . The industry needs an army of spokespeople speaking on its behalf. . .Give them the songsheets and let them help industry carry the tune.[62]

Edward Grefe and Marty Linsky, in their handbook on 'Harnessing the Power of Grassroots Tactics for Your Organization', point out that any corporation will have three potential constituencies for its grassroots efforts: 'family', 'friends' and 'strangers'. 'Family' are employees and shareholders, and perhaps their close families, "whose livelihoods depend on the organization's success"; as a result they have a strong economic interest in—and emotional commitment to—the company. 'Friends' are people who have less direct connections to the company but still have some sort of economic tie or common interest. These people would include customers, suppliers and trade associations.[63]

'Strangers' are those who have no connection to the company, are not aware of the issue being debated, and yet can be influential in its outcome. They include the media, politicians, the business community, opinion leaders, scientists and academics; the key is to find those who "may have an intellectual or philosophical perspective that puts them into alignment with your organization". Grefe and Linsky recommend that family should be mobilized first: "Once involved, family are the best ambassadors, not only for reaching out to the friends but more importantly for reaching out to strangers as well."[64]

Grefe and Linsky argue that getting employees on side is not enough. They have to be activated—involved in political activity on the company's behalf: "People on the assembly line are always more credible spokespersons than people in sterile corporate offices." The model they refer to is that of the Nationwide Insurance Company, which has set up a Civic Action Program (CAP) for employees and agents. Volunteers are offered "speaker training, drills on how to make a call to a legislator or write him or her a letter, and information on the importance of being present at hearings at which issues are being debated. . . Trips to Washington or a state capital are planned."[65]

> CAP volunteers are also asked to fill out cards that indicate who they know among the political leadership and how well they know that person, what community-based associations they are members of, whether they have ever held office or are active in a political party, and other information that would prove helpful in the development of coalition grassroots activities. . .[66]

Grefe and Linsky don't question the infringement of privacy this may involve, nor how voluntary such activities can be for people dependent on their employers for a livelihood, promotion prospects and references. However, in *Toxic Sludge is Good For You!*, their book on the PR industry, Stauber and Rampton argue that this sort of employee mobilization "is in fact a top-down command system, under which employees are expected to vote and agitate not for what they as free citizens consider politically good or desirable but for the political interests of the company that employs them."[67]

Public affairs consultant Gerry Keim points out that companies that direct their employees to write letters and lobby on their behalf are far less successful than those that give their employees a "deeper education. . . it is easy to induce employees to take political action with education".[68] Persuasion is better than coercion, and that persuasion is much easier in a situation where the persuader is able to offer substantial rewards to those who will be persuaded. Grefe and Linksy note that a major key to the success of Nationwide's programme—forty-six per cent of its 5,000 agents and fifty per cent of its 15,000 employees are actively involved in the CAP—is the 'reinforcement' that 'volunteers' get.

Keim notes that with the increasing use of grassroots campaigns, and the growing cynicism about them on the part of politicians, the use of employees is particularly effective in ensuring that grassroots efforts have a genuine appearance. In fact, knowing that the employees are part of a grassroots programme can have even more impact on a politician, because he or she knows that these voters will be kept informed of how the issue is progressing and reminded of how the politician voted when it comes to re-election time. One company sends politicians copies of the newsletters it distributes to employees to show that "educated and politically informed constituents are working for it".[69]

Nationwide pass on names of employees and agents willing to work on campaigns to local legislators: "a particularly powerful message when the candidate is an incumbent legislator seeking re-election. It's a reminder that among the legislator's constituents are many who also happen to be Nationwide employees or agents."[70] Such tactics are particularly effective in influencing politicians. As one politician said:

> You can give me $1,000. That helps. But stimulate a number of your employees to volunteer for my campaign and, following my election, I'll remember those who stuffed envelopes or walked precincts in my behalf long after I've filed the report on the contribution from your PAC.[71]

Some companies also encourage their employees to attend 'town hall' and other meetings organized by politicians and to join local civic organizations that have influence in the community, and they subsidize their membership of them. This enables the company to give presentations and discuss issues informally with other influential members of the community and thereby foster the support of 'strangers'.[72]

Grefe and Linsky surveyed 119 companies, finding that thirteen per cent had a key contact programme, thirty-one per cent put together grassroots coalitions "*only* on an ad hoc or as-needed basis" and thirty-six per cent had an ongoing grassroots coalition with "activities in which their employees or members were involved in specific public affairs efforts". Only twenty per cent did no grassroots coalition work at all. Some corporations, such as Glaxo Pharmaceutical, have even utilized their sales forces in a political "outreach effort".[73]

By getting together in trade associations and federations, smaller businesses can help each other in the same way. The US Chamber of Commerce has 220,000 member businesses, trade associations, and local and state chambers of commerce; in 1993 it established its "Grassroots Action Information Network (GAIN) with state-of-the-art technology and networking capabilities".[74] The National Federation of Independent Businesses has 617,000 members, and from these members it is able to construct a database of members classified into categories which include political backgrounds, position on particular issues and the extent to which they have been 'activated' in the past by direct mail approaches. The computer database is connected to laser printers and broadcast faxes. When an issue comes up, the Federation can instantly contact and activate thousands of specially selected members, or alternatively space out the contacts over a number of weeks to give the impression of a spontaneously growing public reaction.[75]

Workers who can be persuaded that their jobs are at risk from some government action such as environmental regulation are an obvious source of grassroots support for corporations, and indeed for whole industry sectors. In a speech to the American Mining Congress, Tamara Johnson of the Citizens United for a Realistic Environment, a mining workers group, said:

> An inferno is advancing toward us at an alarming rate. It is primarily in the form of the preservationist movement and the political ramifications it brings with it. . . Why have mining companies been losing the battle against this blaze? Because historically you have counted only on slick lobbyists in three-piece suits and upper-echelon management to get the message delivered. . . We have discovered that by forming grassroots groups such as ours and then linking up with other groups which have similar goals and forming multi-sector coalitions, we indeed can become a force to be reckoned with.[76]

One of the most successful grassroots campaigns utilising these multi-sector coalitions mobilized farmers, coal-miners, aluminium manufacturers, the natural gas industry and others to oppose President Clinton's proposed energy tax.[77]

Successful grassroots campaigns go beyond employees and 'family' to activate potential allies. Bruce Harrison, who specializes in environmental public relations, recommends to companies who have been attacked by an activist group that they encourage their allies to speak to the press and the activist group on their behalf. For this to be effective, these allies—who might be business associates, friendly politicians or academics—need to be armed with the right information. "Put them on a mailing list and service them aggressively."

> The critical point is to immediately reduce or remove the 'us vs. them' element, the polarity of the one-on-one relationship. You'll lose if it's like this, because press and politicians will not get into the act unless they see others take your side.[78]

It is important to enrol strangers because their views will have more weight with the general community since they are not seen as self-interested—as employees and others may be—and so they can "offer to the uncommitted community an endorsement that is seen as pure", a third party endorsement.[79] Phil Lesly, author of a handbook on public relations and communications, advises organizations facing opposition to identify those whose viewpoints are different from those of their opposition—both those who share the views of the organization and those who don't agree with the opposition for other reasons. "Both can become your allies," he says.[80] The aim in fostering allies is to give an impression that there is strong support for both sides of a controversy.

Chris Crowley, of the Seattle-based Crowley/Ballentine public affairs consulting firm, wrote in *Oil & Gas Journal* that grassroots organising "may just prove to be industry's best weapon" for countering environmentalists who oppose resource developments. He describes the success of Citizens for Full Evaluation, formed as a front group to support Trans Mountain Pipe Line Company's plans to construct an oil tanker terminal and underground pipeline in Washington state. Polls commissioned by the company had found that sixty-five per cent of local people were concerned about an oil spill in Puget Sound, but also that some people supported the development. Trans Mountain sought to activate these unknown allies.

> Citizens for Full Evaluation (CFE) was built primarily through the mail. More than 200,000 issue-oriented brochures and letters were mailed to registered voters along the proposed route, sounding themes developed from the poll. Supporters were quickly and cost-effectively identified where no organized support had existed before. . . CFE's mailing list grew to more than 5,000 in six largely rural counties. Entered into a computer database, the list could be broken down geographically, by level of support or by what members were willing to do.[81]

Using this mailing list, supporters could be mustered for public meetings and meet in advance to be briefed. Letters to newspapers by opponents could be answered by CFE members with more credibility than the company. A county commissioner was targeted, as was a congressman with "more than 1,000 post cards to his office. He got the message and remained neutral on the project. . ." In the end the project did not go ahead for "economic reasons" but Crowley argues that CFE managed to redefine the debate: "The group was critically important in helping to shift the focus of the debate from 'David vs. Goliath' or, 'people vs. big oil' to opponents vs. supporters of the project."[82]

A variation on this theme is for PR firms to set up 'Community Advisory Panels' for their clients. These panels have about a dozen people from the community and the corporation, especially those who are respected or opinion leaders. The aim is to improve the image and credibility of a corporation in the region and foster community support by creating a forum for "carefully modulated" dialogue that engenders trust and avoids embarrassing issues. One PR professional explained: "People in a community are usually more concerned about such issues as trust, credibility, competence, fairness, caring and compassion than about mortality statistics and the details of quantitative risk assessment".[83]

Community Advisory Panels were first established by chemical companies, which formed hundreds of such panels around the US; waste management, car manufacturing and oil companies have followed suit. Members of these panels are generally chosen by the companies or their consultants and environmental activists are often excluded. The panels tend to be dependent on the company for technical information and expertise; or academic experts who are dependent on the company for research funding are included. The resulting panel begins with little knowledge of the environmental problems and the politics of the issues surrounding those problems. They learn only what the company tells them in closed meetings or gives them to read (which they are not supposed to show to others). This information is explained and interpreted by company officers or those sympathetic to the company. It is not surprising that the panels often become great supporters and advocates for the company. [84]

Examples of such compliant panels are given in the Chemical Manufacturers Association's Handbook. They include the Citizen's Advisory Council, set up by Rohm and Haas when it wanted to build a hazardous waste incinerator in Kentucky. Members of this Council got company paid trips to Germany and New York to learn more about incinerators. The advisory panel set up by Syntex Chemicals in Colorado helped the company put its views on a local zoning issue. Another set up by Kerr-McGee Chemical "had become staunch supporters" within two years.[85]

In 1990 the embattled Sydney Water Board decided to form a number of community advisory panels, which it called community consultation forums. Those wishing to be on these panels had to apply or be nominated by groups such as local councils, and the Board hired consultants to screen the applicants and nominees and choose suitable people. It soon became evident however that environmentalists who had been active in the issue of sewage pollution had been screened out of these forums. Richard Gosden of Stop the Ocean Pollution (STOP), one of the Board's main adversaries,[86] had been nominated by Randwick Council but had been left out of the local forum (no reason given) whereas an executive of ICI, the multinational chemical company and major user of the Board's sewers for disposal of trade waste, was put on one of the panels as a local resident. When environmental groups, including Friends of the Earth, STOP and Greenpeace, complained about the exclusion of environmentalists, the Board offered to have a consultation forum of environmentalists, but this was rejected as a way of separating the environmentalists from the community groups so that environmentalists would not be able to influence the community representatives.

Community advisory panels can also serve another purpose. Susan Schaefer Vandervoort advises companies wanting to engage in green marketing campaigns to assemble an environmental team then invite "opposition representatives, such as community action groups, environmental activists, political or regulatory officials, and academics" to join the team to help the firm "broaden their strategy and hone their tactics".[87]

Manufacturing a Mass Movement

Ron Arnold is another of the new breed of public opinion entrepreneurs who have advised industry about the need for front groups and the manufacture of grass-roots coalitions to successfully counter environmentalism. Throughout the 1980s he was advising the timber industry that its arguments would always be seen to be self-interested unless it could get citizen action groups to give the same arguments:

> The public is completely convinced that when you speak as an industry, you are speaking out of nothing but self-interest. The pro-industry citizen activist group is the answer to these problems. It can be an effective and convincing advocate for your industry. It can utilize powerful archetypes such as the sanctity of the family, the virtue of the close-knit community, the natural wisdom of the rural dweller. . . And it can turn the public against your enemies. . . I think you'll find it one of your wisest investments over time.[88]

> Long experience has shown that it is the plain, unvarnished truth spoken by plain, unvarnished citizens, not statements by full-time lobbyists or public communicators, that is most persuasive in shaping public opinion.[89]

In 1989 he recommended to Canadian timber executives that they organize grassroots organizations that could be "an effective and convincing advocate for your industry".[90] But Arnold has gone far beyond the front groups and grassroots alliances of ordinary public relations firms. With the help of Alan Gottlieb, a direct mail fund-raising specialist and founder of the Center for the Defense of Free Enterprise, Arnold has managed to engineer a whole movement of hundreds of groups in the US with an anti-environmental, pro-development, right-wing agenda.

During the late 1970s and 1980s Ron Arnold, acting as a consultant to industry, was helping to publicize a number of these pro-industry citizen groups. He realized that each group was being treated in the media as an isolated phenomenon, and that for these groups to have any influence they needed to be linked together in some way so that each group would seem to be part of something larger. He became convinced that if industry was to successfully counter the environmental movement it needed its own activist movement.[91] To do this he needed a label that would connect these groups and imply that they were part of a trend—a movement.

> We called it the pro-industry movement for a long time. . .The major response we got from that was, well that's just old gut rock to protect his ill gotten gains. So that sunk. . . And I wanted to use conservation, because that's really my favorite label. But it had already been coopted by the preservationists that mean preservation, no use. And so it had been corrupted beyond thinking. We couldn't use it. And one day it hit me. . .[92]

On that day Arnold noticed a saying on a calendar which said: "Conservation is the wise use of resources." The saying came from Gifford Pinchot, an early twentieth century conservationist and head of the US Forest Service. Gifford argued for the 'wise use' of natural resources and promoted principles of multiple use, scientific management and sustained yield. For him natural resources, like time and money, were limited and therefore should be used wisely. This was in contrast to his friend the preservationist John Muir, who founded the Sierra Club. Muir didn't view nature as something to be used, rather held nature as sacred, having inherent value outside of its commercial potential. The two men parted ways over plans to flood the scenic Hetch-Hetchy Valley to supply water and electricity to San Francisco. For Pinchot the scheme was a wise use, for Muir it was sacrilege.[93]

Arnold liked 'Wise Use' as a name because it was short and would fit neatly into newspaper headlines, and because it was ambiguous: "It was symbolic, it has no exact definition, anymore than environmentalism or the environment. . . It can mean anything."[94]

In 1988 Arnold and Gottlieb organized a conference of over 200 groups for the purpose of starting a movement that would oppose the environmental movement. Groups attending the conference included the American Mining Congress, the National Rifle Association, the American Motorcyclists Association and the National Cattlemen's Association, as well as corporations such as Exxon, DuPont, Macmillan Bloedel, Louisiana-Pacific, Georgia Pacific and Weyerhauser. At the time Congress was about to consider renewal of the Endangered Species Act, renewal of the Clean Waters Act, and repeal of the 1872 Mining Law which enables mining companies to buy public land very cheaply; the organisers felt it was time to flex their collective muscle. The possibility of environmental reforms galvanized all those who believed they would be worse off into a liaison against environmentalism, and marked the beginning of the Wise Use Movement and its Canadian equivalent, the Share Movement.[95]

Chapter 3

The Wise Use Movement

The Wise Use Movement (WUM) today is a broad-ranging, loose-knit coalition of hundreds of groups in the United States which promote a conservative agenda. Many groups within the movement receive substantial industry funding and support, but the movement prefers to portray itself as a mainstream citizens' movement. Indeed, its extended membership includes farmers, miners, loggers, hunters and land-owners as well as corporate front groups. Local versions of the Wise Use Movement have emerged in countries such as Canada and Australia, but they have yet to have the same impact as the movement has had in the US.

The Wise Use Movement began in 1988 when two hundred and twenty-four groups and individuals from the US and Canada met at a conference in Reno, Nevada. The conference was co-sponsored by groups such as the National Association of Manufacturers, the United 4-Wheel Drive Association, the Independent Petroleum Association of America, the National Forest Products Association, the American Sheep Industry, Exxon USA and the American Pulpwood Association. Canadian groups attending included the Council of Forest Industries, MacMillan Bloedel, Carriboo Lumber Manufacturers Association, and the Mining Association of British Colombia.[1]

Today the WUM is able to claim millions of members through the association of large organizations within its domain, such as the American Farm Bureau which represents four million farmers and the Blue Ribbon Coalition, backed by Yamaha and Kawasaki, which represents 500,000 off-road vehicle enthusiasts. However whether all these indirect members endorse the Wise Use Movement's agenda is questionable. David Helvarg, who has written a book about the movement, suggests that there are probably fewer than 100,000 active members, whilst law professor Charles Wilkinson from the University of Colorado estimates a few hundred thousand active supporters: less than one hundred people attended the 1994 Wise Use conference. Nevertheless, the WUM is an influential political force in the American landscape. Its ability to turn out a couple of hundred vocal protesters for key meetings and hearings has a significant impact on decision-makers.[2]

The Wise Use Movement is stage-managed by Ron Arnold and Alan Gottlieb from their base at the Center for the Defense of Free Enterprise, a non-profit 'educational' foundation "devoted to protecting the freedom of Americans to enter the marketplace of commerce and the marketplace of ideas without undue government restriction". There is no formal structure for the coalition; cohesion comes from shared enemies (environmentalists) and a few key leaders. Says Arnold, "We provide the Jello mold. . . The rest of the movement fills it." He sees himself as the Wise Use Movement's thinker and philosopher.[3]

Those attending the inaugural 1988 conference approved the movement's manifesto, *The Wise Use Agenda*. It has been described as "a wish list for the resource extraction industries": many of its twenty-five goals are about guaranteeing access for mining and forestry on public lands. They include "immediate wise development of the petroleum resources of the Arctic National Wildlife Refuge (ANWR) in Alaska" and the opening of "all public lands including wilderness and national parks" for mineral and energy production.[4]

Some of the Wise Use goals are aimed at changing definitions and common understandings in order to weaken environmental legislation and allow further development, timber cutting and resource extraction. They call for a Global Warming Prevention Act that would replace old growth forests with plantations or, in their words, "convert all decaying and oxygen-using forest growth on the National Forests into young stands of oxygen-producing carbon dioxide-absorbing trees to help ameliorate the rate of global warming and prevent the greenhouse effect. . ." They also propose that the Endangered Species Act be amended so that some endangered species are reclassified as "relict species in decline before the appearance of man, including non-adaptive species such as the California Condor" and others be classified as "endemic species lacking the biological vigor to spread in range".[5]

Other goals are aimed at preventing or deterring environmentalists from taking legal action that might lead to restrictions on resource extraction and other activities. These and other goals in *The Wise Use Agenda* are aimed at protecting property rights, opening up wilderness areas to commercial development and motorized recreational use, and highlighting the economic costs of regulatory activity.

Wise Use Philosophical Underpinnings

There is great diversity within the Wise Use Movement but members share a dislike of environmental regulations, which affect parts of the movement in various ways: by constraining what they can do on private property and how they can use public land and water. Rural dwellers in the US often identify with an individualist and pioneering spirit of self-determination that upholds free enterprise and property rights as sacrosanct and opposes government intervention, even if that intervention is in the public interest:

> They proclaim values associated with John Locke, values that impelled the founding fathers. In this tradition, that government is best which governs least. The right to life, liberty, and the pursuit of happiness includes the individual's right to appropriate wealth from nature. If no one has claimed it, it's yours. In this view, government's role is to help convert natural resources into private property, and then to protect that property.[6]

In their campaigns against environmental regulation, Wise Use leaders highlight anecdotes of individuals treated unfairly by the government, such as small landowners unable to develop their land because of regulations designed to protect wetlands or endangered species. Such individuals testify at Wise Use conferences and become legendary in the movement. Their stories are told and retold for the media and congressional committees, are spread from group to group, published in their newsletters and told again at conferences to promote outrage.

There seems to be no shortage of such stories in an inequitable system which allows large corporations to evade the laws and comes down hard on the small business or property owner, "creating a vocal constituency for deregulatory measures that ultimately benefit those already in power". Anyone who has had problems with government bureaucracy becomes a potential recruit to the anti-governmental rhetoric of the Wise Use Movement: "Widespread distrust of government bureaucracy shared by people across the political spectrum can be manipulated to benefit élite interests, especially in the absence of visible anti-corporate movements."[7]

However not all the stories disseminated by the WUM can be taken at face value: often they are cut and tailored to suit the anti-regulatory agenda. For example, the story of the man who was fined $4,000 for shooting a grizzly bear that was trying to kill him gained widespread currency. Yet Helvarg relates a different version of the story:

> That man, Montana sheep rancher John Schuler, shot the bear after it repeatedly raided his sheep corral. The Montana Department of Fish and Game had offered to finance the installation of an electric fence. . . In court Schuler claimed he shot the bear in self defence, an argument the judge didn't buy. Two environmental groups have since paid to have an electric fence installed around Schuler's corral.[8]

Ralph Maughan and Douglas Nilson, academics from Idaho State University, suggest that the Wise Use agenda stems from an ideology that combines laissez-faire capitalism with "cultural characteristics of an imagined Old West". The resulting beliefs include the following:[9]

1. Human worth should be measured in terms of productivity and wealth. Status and power are a reward for hard work.

2. Nature is there for the use of humans.

3. Real wealth derives from extracting and adding value to primary material resources.

4. "Productive lands and waters should be owned (or at least controlled) and tamed by producers. Regulations should be kept to an absolute minimum."

5. Free markets benefit both producers and consumers and constraints on these free markets should be eliminated.

6. Depletion of energy and mineral resources is not the problem that environmentalists make it out to be.

7. Government's role is to protect property and property rights.

8. The quintessential Western person is self-reliant, male, and tough.

These beliefs blend well with libertarian philosophies and those of other free market proponents, including corporate executives. Yet the truth is that much economic activity in the West is heavily subsidized by government, and doesn't fit the laissez-faire ideal at all. Nevertheless, the articulation of these beliefs helps groups which are fighting for self-interested reasons to appeal to a wider constituency. For example, the Blue Ribbon Coalition represents those who want to be free to enjoy the recreational use of off-road vehicles—four-wheel-drive vehicles, motorbikes etc—in national parks. It campaigns against the Endangered Species Act, which has been used to limit their access to these areas. Its rhetoric draws heavily on the above laissez-faire/Old West ideology:

> The Endangered Species Act has failed in large part because it has engendered a regulatory regime that has:
> • violated the rights of individuals, particularly property rights;
> • destroyed jobs, devalued property, and depressed human enterprise on private and public lands;
> • hidden the full cost of conserving endangered species by foisting those costs on private individuals; and
> • imposed significant burdens on State, county and local governments.[10]

Common Enemy: The Environment Movement

Wise use leaders have easily translated this opposition to environmental regulations into an opposition to environmentalists who promote the regulations. In their book, *Trashing the Economy: How Runaway Environmentalism is Wrecking America*, Ron Arnold and Alan Gottlieb argue: "Behind each one of these laws stands an environmental group that lobbied it into existence and made sure the costs were pushed onto private budgets. . ." And in the Preface to *The Wise Use Agenda*, Gottlieb argues that environmentalists have promoted environmental legislation which he says is pervaded with the attitude that "man has no right to be here" and "people are no damn good".[11]

> We have more than twenty years worth of 'command and control', 'do it this way or else' legislation enshrined in court test case decisions that uphold these stupidities. The result is a gigantic morass of regulations that virtually stifle human intellectual and economic progress while doing little to solve actual environmental problems.[12]

Opposition to environmentalists is the glue that holds the Wise Use Movement together. Before the WUM was established, Gottlieb said: "Right now the environmental movement is a perfect bogeyman for us. In order to get people to join and donate money we need opposition." Arnold has been reported as saying that "fear, hate and revenge are the oldest tricks in the direct mail book."[13]

The designation and ridicule of environmentalists as the enemy unites people who might not have much else in common. In this way, fishing people can identify with loggers or with mining workers or with free-market ideologues, because they all feel environmentalism is threatening their goals. "For people in desperate circumstances whose needs are not being met by the system, Wise Use has provided an identifiable enemy, 'the preservationist', on which to focus their anger and vent their rage."[14]

The theme that environmentalists put nature ahead of people is an oft-repeated one. Charles Cushman, one of the Wise Use Leaders, is reported to have said that "the preservationists are like a new pagan religion, worshipping trees and animals and sacrificing people"; and from Arnold and Gottlieb: "We see that every place where people want to make a living is suddenly recognized as the habitat of The Last Big Old Tree or The Last Cute Little Animal or even The Last Ugly Bug. . ."[15]

Wise Use Leaders feed the distrust of environmentalists by highlighting and exaggerating the most radical and extreme elements of the environment movement, and focusing on the elements to which rural people will be most hostile: animal rights, anti-hunting and gun control campaigns. In a speech in 1992, Ron Arnold stated his intention to destroy the environment movement: "There is no compromising with the environmental movement, there is no redemption for it. It cannot be reformed. It must be dismantled entirely and replaced. . . "[16]

Some Wise Use groups actively sabotage environmentalists. One group in Southern California, the Sahara Club, its name a parody of the Sierra Club, says it is "dedicated to fighting eco-freaks and keeping public lands free". In its newsletter, it boasts about how it has managed to disrupt public meetings organized by environmentalists by its members showing up, dispersing themselves through the audience and shouting. Another tactic the group claims is to write inflammatory letters to the local papers pretending they are from environmentalists so that people will "get really pissed off at the eco-freaks". "We do not condone or encourage any illegal activities of any sort," their newsletter says. "However, we get a real kick out of legitimate irritation of the ecofreak community."[17]

Wise Use leaders encourage their members to see environmentalists as 'freaks'. Whilst anti-environmental groups in some other countries such as Australia tend to characterize environmentalists as welfare dependent no-hopers, in the US they characterize environmentalists as élitist, 'overwhelmingly white', 'overeducated' urban people.[18] They label them as 'preservationists' and 'pointy-headed' or 'communists'. Another favourite is to compare an environmentalist to a watermelon: green on the outside and red on the inside.

The Wise Use Movement likes to portray itself as a poorly financed, grass-roots movement representing the average American, the 'little guy', and the environmental movement as a series of well-funded, professional lobby groups representing sectional and élite interests. Arnold and Gottlieb describe the environment movement as "the most powerful superlobby on Capitol Hill". They depict environmentalists as affluent city dwellers who want "to preserve western public lands as their summer playgrounds".[19] In his 1992 speech Arnold claimed;

When you're talking about environmentalists, you have people who, in my experience, are divided into two classes, the upper class and the upper class. One of the upper class is academics. There are an awful lot of people in either academia, or from academia and nice posts such as mathematicians in large aerospace companies who have tenure and therefore the ability to say or think anything they want, are comfortably off, but not particularly wealthy. And then there's the coupon-clippers that are living on daddy's money. I've had any number of those on the hiking trails. But there's a predominance of those people in the environmental movement, and that second bunch is the ones who tend to show up in the actual power structures. The academics tend to show up in the volunteer structures.[20]

Arnold uses such rhetoric to tap into the anti-intellectual tradition of the West of America where 'common sense' is considered to be far superior to book learning, and where farmers and landowners believe they know better than any outside professional how best to manage their land.[21] The Wise Use Movement argues that the true environmentalists are those who work in the environment rather than those environmentalists whom they characterize as living in the cities, divorced from nature's realities. Such rhetoric also finds a place in Australia, where a spokesperson for an emerging local version of the Wise Use Movement argued that his members were the real Greens: "the people who actually use the bush rather than just talk about it."

In the Preface to *The Wise Use Agenda*, Gottlieb states that "Wise Use will be the environmentalism of the 21st Century."[22] Gottlieb and Arnold describe the Wise Use Movement:

> They are the true guardians of the environment, the farmers and ranchers who have been stewards of the land for generations, the miners and loggers and oil drillers who have built our civilisation by working in the environment every day, the property owners, workers and technicians and professionals who provide all the material basis of our existence.[23]

Nevertheless, the Wise Use Movement's claims to be the true environmentalists are belied by their crass attempts to deny environmental problems exist. They deny problems from acid rain to ozone depletion, whilst they exaggerate and distort the arguments of environmentalists. In *Trashing the Planet*, Arnold and Gottlieb claim:

> We are beginning to notice that the big mainstream environmental organisations have lost their way, no longer just identifying crises, but fabricating them, so there will be something to do with all their huge fund-raising infrastructure. . .We are told that man-made chemicals are depleting the ozone in the upper atmosphere, creating an ozone hole which will let in more ultraviolet radiation and kill all life on earth except for a few resistant creatures such as cockroaches and spiders. Do scientists who disagree get quoted in the daily newspapers or network television news programs? No. Because they would point out that the ozone hole over Antarctica has always been there, and that we only became able to detect it in the recent past. . .The ozone hole is a manufactured doom.[24]

Enrolling the Alienated and Dispossessed

The Wise Use Movement has sought grassroots support by enrolling thousands of disaffected people in the US, particularly from rural areas in the West of the US, who are worried about their future, who feel individually powerless to do anything about it, and who are ready to blame environmentalism for their woes.

Wise Use groups have successfully attracted rural workers by arguing that environmental protection costs jobs and threatens their land, and that environmentalists care more about animals and plants than people: "When jobs are lost to protect some tadpole, environmentalists have gone too far."[25]

The movement draws membership from people who are pro-development, anti-big government, opposed to environmentalists, or just plain worried about their future economic prospects. Many people in rural USA are suffering the effects of economic recession and are only too willing to blame environmental protection measures. It provides them with a focus for their fears.

> The Wise Use Movement regards wilderness, wetlands and endangered species as the unholy trinity responsible for most of its gut worries—from the loss of timber jobs in the Pacific Northwest to the locking up of public and private lands to protect plant and animal species.[26]

The leaders of the WUM and their corporate allies have exploited the fears and suffering of workers and rural citizens. Arnold and Gottlieb generate opposition to environmentalists by blaming them for economic problems in the US: "Increasing out-of-pocket cost of regulation to the average American is not the only way environmentalists trash the economy. Preventing economic growth— lost opportunity costs—is another way to bring about industrial collapse," they claim. "Every time an environmental group draws a line around a new place on a map and convinces Congress to 'protect' it, thousands of people are pushed out of productive employment."[27]

The anti-environmental, deregulatory, property rights rhetoric of the WUM is "designed to transform the real anger and anxiety over the changing economic conditions of the West into a forceful political movement" that can be utilized by conservative interests. It is powerful because many rank and file Wise Use members are angrier and more motivated than the supporters of environmental groups, since they are fighting for their self-interest and their economic well-being.[28]

And whilst some environmentalists are willing to admit that the US environmental movement has tended to neglect workers' issues,[29] the Wise Use leadership don't seem to have any genuine concern for workers' issues either. Gottlieb reflects on his 1984 decision to team up with Arnold and build a movement:

> It worked out far better than I would have predicted. I've never seen anything pay out as quickly as this whole Wise Use thing has done. What's really good about it is it touches the same kind of anger as the gun stuff, and not only generates a higher rate of return but also a higher average dollar donation. My gun stuff runs about $18. The Wise Use stuff breaks $40.[30]

The irony is that most of the major corporate financiers of the movement are not supporting it so as to protect workers' jobs and have themselves been a major cause of job losses. Thousands of jobs have already been lost from the timber industry in the US and Canada through automation, economic rationalisation and export of raw logs.[31] Yet none of these groups blame the corporations for the job losses because they have been provided with a convenient scapegoat—

environmental protection and environmentalism: "A decade of low timber demand, of low prices, of lay-offs and closures could now be fairly and squarely blamed on environmentalists."[32] William Street, the Director of Research for Woodworkers of America explains:

> Once you have folks that are scared, then you have folks that are receptive or vulnerable to any kind of solution. At that point, the wise-use groups speak to the woodworkers' fears better than most of the locally based and certainly better than the nationally based environmental groups.[33]

The corporate supporters of the movement have nothing to boast of when it comes to labour policies. But they do have an interest in driving a wedge between environmentalists and workers. When reporting about Wise Use groups in Canada, a Canadian Government Report said that:

> The forest companies have provided these 'local citizens coalitions' with much of the organizational impetus and financial backing. Their apparent objective has been to put labor against environmentalists and environmentally oriented persons. Their effect has been to divide communities and create animosity in the very places where honest communication and consensus should be encouraged.[34]

Strategies and Tactics

Maughan and Nilson sums up the strategy used by the Wise Use Movement:

(1) bill itself as the "true" environment movement
(2) try to marginalize environmental groups by highlighting the views and actions of the radical fringe of environmentalism, and in other ways promote the perception that environmentalists are atypical of the public
(3) downplay threats to the environment
(4) try to form coalitions with interests who perceive they have been harmed or are threatened with harm from environmental policies
(5) form coalitions with groups that share part of the Old West ideology
(6) stress the economic costs of environmental policy
(7) create the perception that the real goal of environmentalists is attainment of authoritarian power[35]

The last tactic is necessary because the question arises: Why do environmentalists bother if there is not really a problem? It also counters the observation that most environmentalists have nothing personal to gain from environmental regulations and can therefore legitimately argue that they are concerned with the common good. Few Wise Use Movement members or supporters can make the same claim.

The Center for the Defense of Free Enterprise provides ready access to the media for the Wise Use Movement through various media outlets owned by the Center which include a radio station in Oregon, a network of eighty-five affiliated radio stations, a talk show, and interests in half a dozen television stations.

Both Arnold and Gottlieb appear as columnists and guests in the media and distribute opinion columns, media releases and "public service announcements" widely to print and electronic media outlets.[36]

The Center has an Investigative Task Force which "probes the personnel, programs and funding sources of those who systematically oppose free enterprise and are aligned with big government". This information is then published. It also helps free enterprise oriented groups to network with each other, and trains activists from these groups to "stage non-violent protest demonstrations" and other activities to achieve their aims.[37]

The Center's Free Enterprise Legal Defense Fund files 'Friend of the Court' briefs on behalf of small businesses, home owners and individuals who are harassed by big government as well as analysing government rules and regulations for possible legal challenges.[38] The Center also owns a publishing house, Free Enterprise Press, which publishes Wise Use Movement books.

As environmental groups feel the pinch of shrinking budgets, Wise Use groups seem to be expanding at an accelerating pace. The WUM uses the strategies and tools of environmental groups; petition drives, fax and letter campaigns, protest meetings, rallies and demonstrations, lobbying etc. Arnold is well versed in the tactics and strategies of the environment movement. He once worked for the Sierra Club before (as he describes it) the Club "evolved out of being a conservation group into being an environmental group".[39]

Arnold has equipped his Wise Use Movement to use those very tactics against environmentalists on industry's behalf. Journalist Richard Stapleton says that Arnold "has torn whole chapters from the text-book of grassroots activism and used them to rewrite industry's rules of engagement".[40] However the Movement has been able to go further than environmental groups by using public relations techniques and corporate resources, mainly supplied by the timber, mining, agriculture, real estate, chemical, oil and gas and vehicle manufacturing industries. It claims it is able to "inundate legislators with thousands of letters against pending environmental legislation in just hours via a nationwide fax network".[41]

Chuck Cushman, another of the Wise Use leaders, is another ex-Sierra Club member who now uses environmentalist grassroots strategies against environmentalists. He founded the National Inholders Association in 1978 to fight the regulation of private property which falls within the boundaries of national parks and federal preserves. Since becoming part of the Wise Use Movement he has successfully defeated or slowed down many preservation initiatives. Cushman tells his audiences "I've always said wilderness is like aspirin. Two are good for you; one hundred will put you in the hospital."[42] His political strategy is one of coalition building:

> What are the three most important words in political action?. . . Lists, lists, lists. If you don't have a list you're not in the game. We have a list on computer of every miner in the country, every rancher who has a grazing permit, every timber purchaser on federal land. Every special use permittee in a national forest. This is not rocket science to realize we have to stay competitive with the other side. The next most important words are network, network, network."[43]

Cushman runs a "sophisticated, high-tech fundraising and lobbying operation that would make many an environmental activist feel like a Luddite", including nine fax machines that can send out 4,000 faxes overnight. He charges up to $20,000 for his services.[44] According to T.H. Watkins from the Wilderness Society:

> These organizations now have money and power and they know how to use both—
> to buy television, radio and print ads; pack hearings halls and meeting rooms; hire
> the best legal firms in Washington, D.C., to represent them; manipulate the press
> with 'spontaneous demonstrations' and broadcast outrageous charges so repeatedly
> that they begin to be accepted as unvarnished fact.[45]

Support from Conservative and Corporate Quarters

Wise Use groups are keen to point out that they work with corporations, not for them: not all the Wise Use groups get industry funding. In fact a few are anti-big business, although the rhetoric of most groups indicates strong free enterprise and libertarian ideals. Similarly, many businesses don't tend to openly endorse the Wise Use Movement for fear of alienating potential customers. Helvarg argues that the movement pushes "a more radical core agenda of 'free-market environmentalism', 'privatization', and the deregulation of industry" than most corporations are willing to own up to.[46]

But the Wise Use agenda is very much a corporate agenda, and this is why corporations and industry associations provide significant funds, support and services to individual Wise Use groups. What is more, corporations are pleased to see Wise Use groups on the offensive against environmentalists; something they are unable to do directly themselves for public relations reasons. The founder of the Alliance for America, one of the larger Wise Use coalitions, points out: "We do have one important thing in common with business: We're all being crushed by regulations that simply don't make sense."[47]

Industry support for grassroots lobbying ensures not only that such efforts are well-funded and well-organized, with in-kind support such as media consulting and advertising, but also that events are well-attended. Workers are given paid leave to attend rallies and sometimes transported there. They are encouraged to wear work clothes, including boots and hard hats, to emphasize their grassroots credentials. One journalist noted of a rally in Washington DC that "the working-class getup proved to be far more effective than the pin stripes of most industry lobbyists."[48] The Wise Use Movement has organized seminars where public relations experts teach loggers how to speak effectively to the media.[49]

Whilst many of the Wise Use groups get industry funding directly, money is also raised by Gottlieb, who runs a direct-mail operation with a claimed five million addresses of possible donors, which he says has raised $5 million for Wise Use groups. Gottlieb is also a fund-raiser for Republican candidates and conservative causes including the National Rifle Association.[50]

The Wise Use Movement is fairly influential in the Republican Party. Gottlieb's involvement in fund-raising for Republican candidates has included

Ronald Reagan's re-election campaign in 1984 and parts of Bob Dole's 1988 presidential campaign. *The Wise Use Agenda* features George Bush on its back cover shaking hands with Allan Gottlieb; in 1992 Bush denounced "environmental extremists" for locking up natural resources. A number of congressmen from Western States have also endorsed the Wise Use agenda. In 1992, Audubon magazine reported that the advisory board of the Center for Defense of Free Enterprise included seven US senators and nine members of the House, including the Secretary of Defense.[51]

There have also been allegations of connections between a Wise Use Movement association and right wing militias, and also with Reverend Sun Myung Moon's Unification Church. According to the New York based *Village Voice* and the environmental journal *Sierra*, Ron Arnold was on the council of a Wise Use group called the National Federal Lands Conference (NFLC) which "enthusiastically endorsed the creation of militias in its October 1994 newsletter". However, since the Oklahoma City bombing in April 1995 the Wise Use Movement has done its best to distance itself from the militias; Arnold says that the NFLC is the only Wise Use group that he knows which supports militias. Nevertheless environmentalists claim that anti-environmental, property rights literature is distributed at various militia meetings and that the militia groups use Wise Use groups as an organising base.[52]

Another group that has been bringing disrepute to the Wise Use Movement is the American Freedom Coalition (AFC). AFC is reported to have been founded by one of Moon's 'lieutenants' and funded to the tune of $5 million by 'business interests' of the Unification Church to campaign for far-right political causes. According to some writers, AFC is a key group in the Wise Use Movement. In 1989 Ron Arnold was president of their Washington State Board and a registered agent of the AFC; Gottlieb was a director of the Washington State Board and owned the building in which the AFC had its office. Another movement organiser was also paid by the AFC. It has sponsored several Wise Use conferences, including the first in 1988. However, Wise Use activists strongly deny any connection with Moon or his Unification Church.[53]

Because of these alleged connections, which have had a fair bit of publicity, some Wise Use groups have tried to distance themselves from Ron Arnold and the Center for the Defense of Free Enterprise and even from the term Wise Use by using terms like 'multiple use' and 'prudent use' and portraying themselves as more moderate.[54]

People For the West!

People for the West! (PFW!) is one group that likes to distance itself from Ron Arnold and his connections. PFW! uses the term multiple use rather than wise use and describes itself as "a non profit, grassroots organization dedicated to preserving the traditional multiple use of Western and Midwestern public lands". It is one of the largest, best financed and most powerful of the Wise Use groups, with a claimed grassroots membership of 18,000 including "farmers, ranchers, oilmen, miners, timber workers, recreationists, elected officials and people from all walks of life".[55]

PFW! is funded by mining and petroleum companies who want cheap and easy access to resources. In 1991 its funding came from almost two hundred companies, including $1.6 million from the mining industry. Its thirteen-member board of directors included twelve mining company executives.[56] PFW! organizers tend to downplay their industry connections and portray themselves as a genuine grassroots organization concerned about local issues.

PFW! was formed by John Wilson, head of the Western States Public Lands Coalition and Chief Executive Officer of the mining corporation Pegasus Gold. Its original aim was to fight a proposal to repeal an old law (the 1872 Mining Law) which enables mining companies that have found mineral deposits to buy up public land for between $2.50 and $5.00 an acre. The law was established at a time when mining exploration was generally the work of pick-axe prospectors. It was intended to encourage them by giving them cheap rights to mine on federal lands.

Nowadays the Mining Law prevents taxpayers from recouping some of the benefits of the minerals found on public land by large mining companies and enables those companies to make huge profits from selling off the land, when they have finished with it, at market rates. Nor are there any provisions in the law for cleaning up land polluted with mining wastes before it is sold off. In 1991 an industry-financed poll found that eighty-two per cent of those surveyed believed that mining companies should have to pay royalties on what they extract and rehabilitate the sites of their activity. As a result of this finding "the polsters cautioned the industry not to debate the mining law in public forums." PFW! enables the industry to put its views in the name of the concerned citizens.[57]

PFW! doesn't baulk at using the tactics of the environment movement. It has copied the exclamation mark of Earth First!, and its logo bears striking similarities to the logo of Citizen's Clearing House for Hazardous Waste. It also uses the environmentalist strategy of grassroots organising, collecting signatures on petitions in rural minority communities by knocking on doors, and organising letter-writing events and large numbers of telephone calls at short notice. Its members visit and lobby mayors and county commissioners, as well as lobbying government by picketing government buildings and testifying at public hearings.[58]

Its grassroots organising is aided by industry funding and support. PFW! managed to have a big grassroots showing at the congressional hearing on mining law reform in Santa Fe, New Mexico, by arranging for at least one company to bus employees there from around the state and for school children to wave placards. PFW! argued that repeal of the 1872 law would destroy families and communities. Reform of the Mining Law was successfully stopped in September 1994.[59]

Its aim is now broader than just mining. PFW! organizes grassroots groups in grazing, logging and mining communities and is responsible for dozens of local groups in various states. Like other Wise Use groups, it gains members by appealing to their fears. "They seek out the aggrieved and disenfranchised. Whenever there is a mill closing, for whatever reason, PFW is there directing people's anxieties and fears toward the convenient scapegoat of the environment movement."[60] One foreboding PFW! pamphlet warns that if mining, grazing or logging are restricted, "people will lose jobs, rural communities will become ghost towns, education for our children will suffer and state and local governments will forfeit critical income for police, fire protection, roads and services."[61]

PFW! has been involved in the fight to oppose an environmental protection plan for the Greater Yellowstone Area, which covers three state jurisdictions. PFW! became part of the Yellowstone Regional Citizens Coalition, a coalition of forty "commodity, multiple-use, recreation, and local government groups" including the Montana Mining Association, the Idaho Farm Bureau, the Petroleum Association of Wyoming, the Multiple-Use Land Alliance and Montana Wood Products Association.[62]

This coalition of industry and interest groups produced letters, leaflets and press releases, and organized a grassroots campaign against the proposed plan. Environmentalists claim they whipped up emotions at rallies and grossly overstated the proposed changes in their literature in an attempt to frighten people into opposing them. This they did successfully, and the government bureaucrats mostly backed down from their original commitments, "leaving environmentalists to battle industry and other opponents of the Vision document while the agencies sat in judgement". The final document was so watered down that the word 'vision' had been left out of its title.[63]

Property Rights Groups

The term 'wise use' is now being used by two main types of groups:

(i) those who advocate opening up of public lands for logging, mining and cattle as well as off-road vehicles and motorcycles, and

(ii) those who lobby against any restriction of use of private lands—property rights advocates.[64]

Wise Use groups in the west of the USA are dominated by "western ranchers, corporate farmers, and business people whose margin of profit is directly threatened by any fee increases on grazing, water reclamation, and other uses of public lands". One of their heroes, Wayne Hage, has published a book called *Storm Over Rangelands*, which argues for private property rights on federal grazing allotments. Environmentalists counter that grazing rights on public lands, for example, affect only one in fifty livestock operators, most of whom are big businesses.[65]

Meanwhile Wise Use groups in the eastern USA have also taken up the theme of private property rights and their protection. They argue that environmental regulations impede their ability to develop their land in the way they want. By taking up this issue the Wise Use Movement has been able to expand into the Eastern states. In *Trashing the Economy*, Arnold and Gottlieb argue that private property rights are sacred. They claim that the environment movement is "actively destroying private property rights on a massive scale" by preventing people from using their land. Their Center for the Defense of Free Enterprise argues that "the right to liberty is dependent upon the right to own property—

together they form the most basic civil rights."[66]

Whilst the anecdotes of suffering at the hands of the government always involve the 'little' people, those who have most to gain from any further protection of private rights are the large landowners such as the banks, developers, agribusiness and the timber industry. Companies such as the US Sugar company have invested millions of dollars to this end.[67] And whilst "the key players in the property rights movement are upscale conservatives, more likely to own a second home than a second mortgage, they try to portray their interests as compatible with those of rural, low-income property owners."[68]

Property rights advocates cite the Fifth Amendment of the US Constitution to support their case. This amendment includes a clause that says that private property taken for public use should not be taken by the government without just compensation. Property rights advocates infer from this that government regulations that restrict their use of their property are 'takings'. Rather than seeing regulation as an attempt to balance conflicting rights, property rights activists see property rights as absolute and any restriction put in place to protect the public interest as an unjust imposition: "In effect, government is making private property owners provide a public good—the protection of wetlands—at private expense without compensation."[69] It has however been recognized by the US Supreme Court that property rights are limited by the requirement that the property owner not use their property in a way that harms the rights of others.[70]

Wise Use groups are fighting to have legal definitions of "government takings" expanded to cover regulations which inhibit all sorts of development from mining to filling in wetlands on private land; by the end of 1992 they managed to get such legislation introduced in twenty-seven states. The purpose of this expanded definition is to force the government to compensate a developer for profits they might have made had they been able to develop the land in the way they wanted. The effect of this would be to make the implementation of environmental regulations ridiculously expensive. "A single lost takings case could bankrupt most state regulatory agencies. The takings movement would, if successful, effectively end environmental protection in the United States."[71]

One such piece of legislation has already been established: the Private Property Protection Act passed in Arizona in 1992 requires state agencies to "identify government actions that have any impact on private property. The attorney general can prohibit that action if it has such impacts. State agencies may not take action based upon potential threats, such as suspected carcinogens, but only upon proven threats." Even undue delays in decision making, for example those caused by public hearings, may be considered a taking under the legislation. This has had the effect of deterring government agencies from implementing health, safety and environmental regulations and the government from introducing new ones. Similar legislation has been introduced in Utah and Delaware and has been proposed in many other states.[72]

The passing of such legislation is not necessary for individual or corporate developers to sue government agencies for takings. As far back as 1922 a company was able to win a takings case against the government (corporations are considered as 'persons' by the US Supreme Court and so are protected by the Constitution and can claim compensation for takings). In *Pennsylvania Coal v. Mahon* the US Supreme Court decided that a local rule prohibiting mining below ground under surface structures restricted the use of the company's property so significantly that it could be considered equivalent to taking the property from them.[73]

However the takings argument was not widely used until the publication of *Takings, Private Property and the Power of Eminent Domain* by law professor Richard Epstein in 1985. After this book had been published, the Reagan administration issued an executive order which required federal health, safety and environmental regulations to be examined for their impact on private property. The executive order recommended that regulatory authorities avoid possible compensation claims from property owners by not enforcing regulations too aggressively.[74]

It seems that the agenda behind the push for takings legislation is to achieve deregulation by making it too expensive to regulate. According to a former US Solicitor General who served in the Reagan Administration:

> Attorney General Meese and his young advisors—many drawn from the ranks of the then fledgling Federalist Society and often devotees of the extreme libertarian views of Chicago Law Professor Richard Epstein—had a specific, aggressive, and, it seemed to me, quite radical project in mind: to use the takings clause of the Fifth Amendment as a severe brake upon federal and state regulation of business and property. The grand plan was to make government pay compensation as for a taking of property every time its regulation impinged too severely on a property right. . . If the government labored under so severe an obligation there would be, to say the least, much less regulation.[75]

Using the 'takings' argument, opponents of environmental regulations can claim the moral high ground by arguing that they are not opposed to environmental protection but they are just ensuring that regulation is fairly paid for by the taxpayer rather than the poor, overburdened property owner.

The Wise Use Movement is attempting to get takings legislation into state legislatures because judges frequently consider that in some situations governments have the right to regulate private property. In a 1992 case, *Lucas v. South Carolina Coastal Council*, the US Supreme court ruled that a beach protection act constituted a taking from one of the local property owners, but the presiding judge left the way open for certain types of government regulations that "diminish private property value substantially". Lucas, a developer, had bought some land for building two houses. He sued for the loss in real estate value of his property when the Coastal Commission changed their management plan so as "to prevent development on sensitive coastal land". [76]

It is claimed that "almost all of the 'takings' bills that have been proposed in state legislatures around the county are written by a little right-wing think-tank, the American Legislative Exchange Council, funded by the usual long-lived cast of conservative businesses and foundations."[77] The Council is aiming to introduce stronger takings laws in various states with its model takings legislation, which gives property owners automatic compensation if the value of their land is diminished by fifty per cent or more by government regulations or plans. In 1995 thirteen states passed takings bills, and the Private Property Protection Act, part of the Republicans' Contract with America, was passed in the House. If this Act is also passed in the Senate, the cost is estimated at $28 billion. An even more extreme and expensive takings bill was proposed by Republican Senator Bob Dole.[78]

It is not only in the area of 'takings' legislation that the Wise Use Movement has been successful. The movement has been credited with getting the Interior Secretary "to reconvene a special endangered species committee to reconsider the protection of the spotted owl", and the Vice-President's Council on Competitiveness was seen as having the power to achieve many Wise Use goals in blocking Federal regulations. Other achievements include rewriting the Endangered Species Act to give more weight to economic considerations and an extended moratorium on new federal environmental laws. Arnold has claimed that Bush didn't sign the Biodiversity treaty at the Earth Summit in Rio because of pressure from the Wise Use Movement (although others have attributed this to pressure from the biotechnology industry). More recently, the Republican-dominated congress has set in train anti-environmental legislation that is in line with the agenda of Wise Use groups.[79]

The combination of corporate financial resources and public relations techniques for mobilising grassroots support has made the Wise Use Movement in the US into a formidable conservative force that seeks to thwart environmental reforms. Its success will no doubt encourage corporate interests to try to achieve similar results in other countries.

Chapter 4

Lawsuits against Public Participation

In 1986 a woman in Texas was sued by a company, Hill Sand Co., for $5 million for using the term 'dump' for a landfill; her husband, who had not been involved in the protest, was also sued because he "failed to control his wife". After nearly three years of court appearances and thousands of dollars in legal fees, during which time many people withdrew from the campaign in fear, the law suit was dropped. Hill Sand closed down and a couple of years later the landfill was investigated by the Environmental Protection Agency as a hazardous waste site that needed to be cleaned up.[1]

Every year, thousands of Americans are sued for speaking out against governments and corporations. Multi-million dollar law suits are being filed against individual citizens and groups for circulating petitions, writing to public officials, speaking at, or even just attending, public meetings, organising a boycott and engaging in peaceful demonstrations.[2] Such activities are supposed to be protected by the First Amendment to the US Constitution, but this has not stopped powerful organizations who want to silence their opponents.

This trend is now spreading to other countries. In Canada the transnationals MacMillan Bloedel Ltd and Fletcher Challenge have between them sued over a hundred individuals and four community and environmental organizations who opposed the logging of an ancient rainforest on Vancouver Island.[3] And in a highly publicized case in Britain, McDonald's, one of the largest companies in the world, sued two unemployed activists for distributing pamphlets critical of the company.

In Australia, business people attending the Third Annual Pollution Law Conference were presented with a paper entitled *Legal Rights of Industry Against Conservationists*, which advised them about legal action that could be taken against environmental activists. Conference attendees were told about developments in the US which were relevant to Australia, including the widespread use of lawsuits to intimidate environmentalists.[4]

Wise Use groups in the US use this tactic against environmentalists. The Oregon Lands Coalition sponsors seminars for Wise Use activists on using injunctions and 'intent to sue' letters against environmental groups and government agencies. *The Wise Use Agenda* calls for "industry advocates" to be given standing "to sue on behalf of industries threatened or harmed by environmentalists".[5]

However developers, corporations and small businesses don't need such advocates to launch lawsuits against citizens who oppose their plans. In Missouri a high school teacher, in a letter to the editor of a local paper, urged her local community to attend hearings being held by the state environmental agency on a

medical waste incinerator and to testify against approval being granted. The
Canadian incinerator company sued her for $500,000 for libel.[6]

Betty Jane Blake opposed a developer, Terra Homes Inc, that wanted to cut
down some trees in her street. She put up signs saying "This neighbourhood will
not be Terraized" and tied red ribbons around the tree trunks. She was hit with a
$6.6 million dollar law suit for defamation, interference in business and trespass-
ing. The company also sued all the residents who attended a meeting at the Town
Hall to discuss the development. The company eventually dropped the suit, but
not before residents had one by one signed affidavits swearing that they had not
taken part in putting up signs and ribbons, and dropped out of the campaign
from fear.[7]

These cases are indicative of a trend which began in the 1970s as a response
to the increasing number of citizens who were speaking up about environmental
and other social issues. The law suits have been labelled "Strategic Lawsuits
Against Public Participation", or SLAPPs, by University of Denver academics
Penelope Canan and George Pring, who have been studying such suits for more
than a decade with the help of funding from the US National Science
Foundation. They began their research after they noticed an increasing number
of environmentalists were being named as defendants in large civil damage cases.[8]

Canan and Pring define a SLAPP as a civil court action which alleges that
injury has been caused by the efforts of non-government individuals or organizations to influence government action on an issue of public interest or concern.
They found that "SLAPPs are filed by one side of a public, political dispute to
punish or prevent opposing points of view." Of course people using SLAPPs in
this way cannot directly sue people for exercising their democratic right to participate in the political process, so they have to find technical legal grounds on
which to bring their cases. Such grounds include defamation, conspiracy, nui-
sance, invasion of privacy or interference with business or economic expectancy.[9]

Such cases seldom win in the courts. The charges often seem extremely flimsy
and the damage claims outrageously large. Most are dismissed by the courts, and
77% of those that are heard by the courts are won by the people being sued. Less
than ten per cent of such cases in the USA result in a court victory for the filer of
the action.[10] In their article in the *Journal of Law & Politics* on the misuse of libel
law for political purposes, Edmond Costantini and Mary Paul Nash observe that
"One would be hard-pressed to find another area of the law in which so overwhelming a proportion of defendants brought into court are eventually vindicated."[11] But companies and organizations taking this legal action are not doing
so in order to win compensation: their aim is to harass, intimidate and distract
their opponents. They 'win' the court cases when their victims "are no longer able
to find the financial, emotional, or mental wherewithal to sustain their defense."[12]
They win the political battle, even when they lose the court case, if their victims
and those associated with them stop speaking out against them.

One trial judge pointed out:

> The conceptual thread that binds [SLAPPs] is that they are suits without substantial
> merit that are brought by private interests to 'stop citizens from exercising their polit-

ical rights or to punish them for having done so'. . .The longer the litigation can be stretched out, the more litigation that can be churned, the greater the expense that is inflicted and the closer the SLAPP filer moves to success. The purpose of such gamesmanship ranges from simple retribution for past activism to discouraging future activism.[13]

The cost to a developer is part of the cost of doing business, but a court case could well bankrupt an individual or environmental group. In this way the legal system best serves those who have large financial resources at their disposal, particularly corporations. In 1983 the US Supreme Court stated in one such SLAPP case that a lawsuit may be used "as a powerful instrument of coercion or retaliation" and no matter how flimsy the case the defendant "will most likely have to retain counsel and incur substantial legal expenses to defend against it. . ."[14]

Such a case takes an average of three years to be settled, and even if the person being sued wins, can cost tens of thousands of dollars in legal fees. Emotional stress, disillusionment, diversion of time and energy, and even divisions within families, communities and groups can also result. George Campbell organized his neighbours to protest against the expansion of an airport near their homes in Worcester, Massachusetts. After he was threatened with a lawsuit from the city council for $1.3 million he thought he was going to lose everything and ended up in hospital as a result of the stress. The council dropped the suit a few weeks later.[15]

The Chill Effect

Not only does a SLAPP deter those involved from continuing to freely participate in political debate, but it also deters others from speaking freely and confidently about local public issues. In Putnam County, New York, residents opposing a zoning decision were sued for conspiracy and "interference with contractual relations" by the developer which would benefit from the zoning decision. The residents agreed to cease opposition in return for the developer's dropping the lawsuit.[16]

Dixie Sefchek says that when she and three other leaders of Supporters To Oppose Pollution (STOP) were SLAPPed it was "like a death threat to your organization. People, organizations, and churches stopped giving money. Individuals resigned their memberships." The suit was later dropped and the landfill they opposed ordered to be closed a few years later because of contamination of the groundwater.[17]

Research by Canan and Pring in fact shows that people who know about SLAPPs are more cautious about speaking out publicly than those who have never heard of them.[18] Judges in one US court decried a SLAPP for this very reason:

[W]e shudder to think of the chill. . . were we to allow this lawsuit to proceed. The cost to society in terms of the threat to our liberty and freedom is beyond calculation. . . To prohibit robust debate on these questions would deprive society of the benefit of its collective thinking and. . . destroy the free exchange of ideas which is the adhesive of our democracy.[19]

One tactic sometimes used by developers is to include John Does and Jane Does and "unnamed persons" as defendants to "spread the chill".[20] This is a way of claiming that there are additional 'offending' citizens who could not be identified before the suit was filed and leaves the way open to sue other citizens later. It puts would-be activists on notice that they too could be added to the list of defendants.

SLAPPs often do not go to trial because the objective—to scare off potential opponents—can be achieved merely by the threat of the court case. Kim Goldberg points out that "company lawyers will usually go to great pains to warn activists of impending defamation suits. After all, why waste time and money filing legal papers to initiate a lawsuit if the mere threat of a suit will silence your critics?"[21]

Another effect of the SLAPP is to distract the key antagonists from the main controversy and use up their money, time and energy in the courtroom, where the real issues are not discussed. Activists use the political arena to expand the debate, enrol other citizens on their side and spread the conflict. The firms and developers that utilize SLAPPs are trying to subvert and circumvent that political process "by enlisting judicial power against their opponents". SLAPPs "are an attempt to 'privatize' public debate—a unilateral effort by one side to transform a public, political dispute into a private, legal adjudication, shifting both forum and issues to the disadvantage of the other side."[22]

SLAPPs can also shift the balance of power, giving the firm filing the SLAPP suit the upper hand when they are losing in the political arena. Action tends to be taken against citizens who are successfully opposing them because those taking the action are afraid that they will not win in the public, political forum. In the courts, the wealth of the disputants and their ability to hire the best lawyers can influence the outcome. "Whereas in the political realm the filer is typically on the defensive, in the legal realm the filer can go on the offensive, putting the target's actions under scrutiny."[23] Prolonged litigation can even achieve community compliance through delay and loss of sustained interest among the broader public.

In the US, SLAPPs are used in controversies over development and zoning issues (twenty-five per cent), environmental protection and animal rights (twenty per cent), when public officials are criticized (twenty per cent), as well as various neighbourhood problems, human and civil rights cases and consumer protection issues.[24] Canan and Pring found that those filing the suits assumed that economic rights were superior to public interests. "The idea is that because a business has money at stake, business should receive priority over civic, communal opposition."[25] The introduction of 'food disparagement' laws in several states has opened up new avenues for SLAPPs to operate. These laws, which prohibit people from publicly criticising corporate food products, were promoted by agriculture, chemical and biotechnology industry lobbyists.[26]

The targets of these law suits are generally not radical environmentalists, nor professional activists: they are ordinary middle-class citizens who are concerned about their local environment and have no history of political activity. This concentration on middle-class citizens is no accident. They often have most to lose, and don't have the support and ideological commitment that a professional environmentalist in a large environmental organization usually has. However Al Meyerhoff, a senior attorney with the Natural Resources Defense Council, claimed in 1992 that "what started as a tactic against small targets is now expanding to national groups. . . It is part and parcel of an overall counterattack by the polluter industry against the environmental community."[27]

Identity of First Party in 100 SLAPPs

	Targets	Filers
Individual Participants		
Family Member	7	1
Citizen	38	4
Voluntary Organization Member	3	2
Economic Role (e.g. Owner)	8	20
Occupational Role	8	25
Group Participants		
Industry Group	1	39
Labor Organization	1	1
Public Interest Group	14	2
Civic/Social Organization	13	1
Political Organization	2	0
Membership Organization	5	2
Total	100	100

Source: Canon & Pring 1988, p. 511

Law suits are clearly aimed at intimidating middle-class citizens who have assets that could be seized, and are less threatening to young activists who have little to lose. Kelpie Wilson, who was one of six activists SLAPPed in Oregon by the logging company Huffman & Wright Logging, argues that:

> Non-violent civil disobedience, historically a political tool of great importance to this country, is no longer a viable option for many activists. . . in future activists will probably have to divide into two camps. Those who do direct action will have to stay lean, mean and low on the food chain. They can't keep suing us when they don't get anything out of it.[28]

Wilson and her colleagues had chained themselves to a yarder and hung a banner from it saying "From Heritage to Sawdust, Earth First!" They were arrested for interfering with the property of another and sent to jail. They thought it was all over when they got out of jail, but then they were SLAPPed and Huffman & Wright won an award of $25,000 in punitive damages and $5,717 in actual damages. Wilson observed:

> It seems so unfair that they can sue us for our little actions that barely even slow them down, but we can't sue them for destroying our ecosystems, stealing our trees, bribing politicians, calling us 'eco-terrorists', beating us up, creating an atmosphere of hate and violence and otherwise being selfish, ignorant jerks.[29]

SLAPPs Outside the USA

The burger company McDonald's seems to have made a mistake in suing two unemployed activists, Dave Morris and Helen Steel who, unlike others McDonald's have threatened, were willing to fight the case. It seems to be the first time that McDonald's has actually gone to court in the UK after making such threats. It has forced apologies from a number of media outlets, including the BBC and Channel 4, major newspapers such as the *Guardian* and the *Nightline* programme in New Zealand. McDonald's has also sent solicitors' letters to the Vegetarian Society of the UK about their publication *Greenscene*, to the publishers of a Polish primary school handbook, and to publishers of a UK *Home Ecology* handbook, all of which linked McDonald's to rainforest destruction and in other ways criticized the company.[30] Morris argues that a climate of fear had been created and the word had gone out that if you said anything against McDonald's you would get a writ.

Morris and Steel are members of London Greenpeace (an anarchist group not affiliated to Greenpeace International), and were distributing pamphlets entitled 'What's Wrong With McDonald's'. The pamphlets claimed that McDonald's sold food that was unhealthy, exploited its workers, promoted rainforest destruction through cattle ranching, added to the litter problem and targeted advertisements at children. They were sued for libel; in Britain legal aid is not available for libel cases, so they represented themselves against McDonalds' top lawyers. Even before the case went to trial in 1994, there had been several years of pre-trial hearings. It became the longest trial in UK history.[31]

McDonald's claims that it took legal action to establish the truth. Prior to the case, McDonald's infiltrated the meetings of London Greenpeace to gather evidence against them; the private investigators who did this later gave evidence at the trial. McDonald's was also successful in petitioning the judge not to have a jury for this case, arguing that the issues were too complex for a jury to understand.[32]

British libel laws clearly favour those who bring a case to court. To win their case, Morris and Steel had to prove that every statement in the pamphlet was true, rather than McDonald's having to prove that it was untrue (as would be the case in the US). Nor does a corporation such as McDonald's have to prove that its reputation was damaged or sales were harmed as a result of the libel. Keir Starmer, a lawyer who has given free advice to Morris and Steel, argues:

> The problem with the law as it is now is for libel is that its not a battle for the truth in court, it's a battle of the purse. If you have the money you can hire a good legal team. If you have no money you can't hire a legal team and you run huge risks because if you lose you could pay the costs of the person that's suing you. Now that is a huge incentive [for] those that can afford to pay lawyers to suppress information and opinions of those they know can't.[33]

Morris and Steel were supported by an international 'McLibel Support Campaign' which raised money to help with costs. They called over 100 witnesses to give evidence against McDonalds' practices and products. They also sued

McDonald's in what is termed a SLAPP-back (also sometimes used by US targets of SLAPP suits), for distributing leaflets calling them liars.[34]

When the trial ended in February 1997 after two and a half years, it had cost about £10 million and generated 40,000 pages of documents and 20,000 pages of transcripts of testimony. The trial judge found that some of the claims were true, such as the poor dietary value of their hamburgers, the exploitation of children through their advertising, cruel animal practices in producing the meat for the hamburgers and the low wages of McDonalds' employees. However he found that other claims were untrue and therefore the pamphlet had harmed the reputation of McDonald's and was libellous. He ordered that the defendants pay McDonald's £60,000. However Morris and Steel felt they had won a moral victory because McDonalds' practices had been put on trial and they had defeated the company's efforts to silence its critics. The pamphlet has been distributed to an estimated two million people since the trial began, and an internet site has been established which is accessed by people from all over the world.[35]

SLAPPs are far less frequent outside the US. As regards Canada, Chris Tollefson suggests this is because SLAPPs are a response to the drive for and exercise of citizen participation rights and that "Canadians enjoy few of these rights." In the US "the enactment of statutory regimes contemplating or requiring public input" and liberalisation of the rules as to who can take court action on environmental matters mean that citizens have "unprecedented access to government and the courts with respect to decisions affecting the environment". Tollefson sees SLAPPs as a tactical response by business interests to the increasingly effective use that environmental and citizen groups make of these opportunities.[36]

Nevertheless, the number of SLAPP cases outside of the US is increasing and taking its toll, especially because legal assistance is not readily available in cases such as libel. Mirabelle, one of the Canadian protesters being sued by Fletcher Challenge, points out that most of the defendants in her case are representing themselves because they can't afford lawyers and were unable to get legal aid. Six of them have already lost the case before trial for not following "proper procedure" because they didn't understand the legal process. This means that their assets can be seized and part of their wages forfeited for the next twenty years to pay the company. And because of a legal concept of 'joint and several liability', if anyone can't pay then the others must make up the difference. Mirabelle says that this is one of the reasons why "SLAPPs are potentially a very divisive tactic."[37]

A similar situation has arisen in Britain, where the Department of Transport (DOT) is using SLAPP tactics on demonstrators opposing a motorway at Twyford Down. When seven demonstrators were jailed for twenty-eight days for breaking a court injunction banning them from protesting on the construction site of the motorway, they received favourable publicity and praise from the judge who stated that civil disobedience was an "honourable tradition". However the high court injunction is being used by the DOT to sue the protesters for damages and legal costs of two million pounds.

Under the terms of the injunction, those breaching it are held "jointly and severally liable" for the legal costs and for damages. Because others may not be able to pay, according to the defence counsel Liz Loughran this means that "a single individual, who may have been on the site only once. . . could be held entirely responsible for the £2,000,000 the DOT is claiming." The threat has already had its casualties. One well-respected campaigner who had been fighting the motorway for over twenty years was able to settle out of court to relieve the anxiety caused to his family by the injunction, "on the condition that he refrains from further protest". A similar injunction on Friends of the Earth has caused it to withdraw from the Twyford Down campaign.[38]

Another tactic that has a similar effect to injunctions is used in both the UK and Australia. Protesters are arrested *en masse* and bail conditions are set that require protesters not to return to the site of protest. "In most people's opinion it is the most effective tactic at stopping a protest. For months and months you are banned from protesting, and then when it finally gets to court, the police do not even bother to turn up." In Britain this has been aided by the 1994 Criminal Justice and Public Order Act which makes various protest actions, such as trespass for the purposes of blocking development work, criminal offences.[39]

In Australia, Bill Ringland, chair of the Clean Seas Coalition, was sued by his local council for putting out a press release that the council claimed was defamatory. The press release, which was quoted in the local paper, *The Northern Star*, said that sewage "will continue to be pumped out surreptitiously at night" from the local ocean outfall.[40] Ringland was referring to Ballina Shire Council's practice of discharging sewage effluent from its treatment ponds at night, and the fact that most local residents were unaware of this practice. The Council chose to interpret the use of the word 'sewage' in Ringland's press release as raw sewage rather than treated sewage, and the word 'surreptitiously' as secretly and unlawfully, and therefore claimed that the press release was falsely accusing the Council of breaching its licence requirements.

The Council, via its solicitors, demanded an apology from Ringland, who declined. *The Northern Star*, however, printed a full apology on its own behalf, saying that it accepted "the view of the Ballina Shire Council that there is no sewage being put into the sea by the council".[41] The newspaper also suggested that the Clean Seas Coalition was unjustifiably trying to discredit the council.

The Court of Appeal of the Supreme Court of New South Wales found, in a two to one decision, that a Council could not sue for defamation (although individual councillors could). In his judgement, Judge Gleeson stated that

> The idea of a democracy is that people are encouraged to express their criticisms, even their wrong-headed criticisms, of elected governmental institutions, in the expectation that this process will improve the quality of the government. The fact that the institutions are democratically elected is supposed to mean that, through a process of political debate and decision, the citizens in a community govern themselves. To treat government institutions as having a 'governing reputation' which the common law will protect against criticism on the part of citizens is, to my mind, incongruous.[42]

Australian Jenny Donohoe, her husband and her neighbour Tim Tapsell were all sued by a developer in 1993 for campaigning against a housing development that they believed would be environmentally damaging. According to the writ against them, they had forwarded letters to the council promoting re-zoning; printed and arranged for about 1,085 people to sign copies of letters promoting the re-zoning which they delivered to council; and written articles in favour of the re-zoning which were subsequently published. The developers argued that the effect of this re-zoning (for environmental protection) would be to prevent them from developing their land and that "the defendants were aware of that effect and sought to achieve that effect".[43] They therefore sought to obtain damages from the defendants to cover those losses.

The writ has already cost the defendants thousands of dollars, even though the case has yet to come to court and the developers are unlikely to win if it does. It has also taken its toll in stress and sickness within the families involved. For Jenny Donohoe there is no doubt that SLAPPs do work to intimidate community-minded citizens and to victimize key individuals so that their voice is not heard. She points out that, for a relatively small amount of money, "anyone can put up a statement of claims against you", whether or not they have any evidence to support their case. What is more, it doesn't take much for a public statement to be defamatory but the defences which are available to a defendant—for example that the statement is fair comment and made in good faith—have to be established in court. This means that it is unlikely that a writ can be summarily dismissed by the courts in Australia without a full hearing.[44]

While legal aid to low-income litigants is being cut back in Australia, companies receive a massive subsidy for their legal expenses through being able to claim them as tax deductions, no matter whether a case has any merit whatsoever nor how much they spend on lawyers. Recently the Australian multinational BHP, which was being sued by Papua New Guinea citizens for environmental damage caused by its mining activities, managed to persuade the PNG government "to pass legislation guaranteeing the right to claim against tax all of what it paid the lawyers to defend and settle the case in Papua New Guinea and Australia—about [A]$7.6 million".[45]

Other legal mechanisms have also been used against protesters involved in civil disobedience in Australia. In one case, five protesters superglued and bolted themselves onto logging machinery in Badja State Forest in NSW. They were charged with 'intimidating' the logger, who was 600 metres away at the time. Such protesters have often been charged with trespass, but charges are usually dismissed by the courts. However the criminal charge of 'intimidation', which has been on the statute books for almost a hundred years, carries with it the possibility of jail sentences. It was only recently discovered by local police, who say they will use it more often in future. In 1993 the protesters were found guilty and fined A$4,000 in the first conviction of this kind. The Australian Council of Civil Liberties backed an appeal against the convictions saying that they were an "outrageous" interference with the "basic right to protest".[46]

In other cases the Trade Practices Act has been used against environmental activists. The Act contains 'secondary boycott provisions' that were originally introduced to stop trade union actions, including strikes. It made it illegal for a group of people to interfere with the provision of services or products that one party has contracted to provide to another party.[47]

This act was used against Greenpeace Australia in March 1991. The ship *Western Odyssey* was undertaking seismic testing in Victorian waters so that BHP Petroleum could investigate the feasibility of drilling for oil. Greenpeace was concerned about the impact that the sonic booms would have on the Southern Right Whale, for whom the area was a breeding and calving ground (the area is now a whale sanctuary). It was also concerned about the environmental impact of off-shore drilling. BHP had said that it wouldn't drill whilst the whales were calving, but Greenpeace campaigners felt they couldn't trust BHP to stop a multi-million dollar operation for six months of the year.[48]

Greenpeace Australia, using the *Rainbow Warrior*, interfered with the seismic testing by continually moving a buoy that the testing boat was dragging behind it to receive back the resonations from the sonic booms, thus interfering with their measurements. In response, BHP used section 45D of the Trade Practices Act to gain a court injunction to stop Greenpeace from coming near the testing boat. The injunction was taken out against Greenpeace, as well as the captain of the Rainbow Warrior, Joel Stewart, and the campaign coordinator, Molly Olson.[49]

The application to the court also "sought declarations against Greenpeace for conspiracy and trespass and an order for damages". Damages, including the costs such as the hire of the boat and lost oil production, could potentially have amounted to millions of dollars. But BHP withdrew the charges before the case reached court. This case has been cited by lawyers as an excellent example of legal action being used against environmentalists "as it highlights the combination of a number of different types of actions (breach of Section 45D, interference with agreements, conspiracy and trespass) with a range of remedies (injunctions and damages)."[50]

The Trade Practices Act, whilst not used much in the courts, is often used as a way of intimidating protesters. The Forest Products Association threatened to use it against the North East Forest Alliance activists who were trying to prevent logging in the Chaelundi wilderness area. A separate court case, which declared logging in this area illegal, saved the activists at the last minute. It was also used by Australian Paper and Pulp Manufacturers (APPM) in 1993 to threaten the Wilderness Society in Tasmania, which was campaigning against the export of woodchips, and by the Federal Airport Corporation against fishing people who were interfering with the dredging of Botany Bay to construct a third runway for Sydney's Mascot airport. The fishing people were concerned that the dredging would adversely affect the Bay and therefore reduce their fish catches by up to seventy-five per cent. The Australian Consumers Association (ACA) and the Australian Federation of Consumers Organisations (AFCO) have had legal advice that consumer boycotts against environmentally damaging products might also be illegal under the same Act.[51]

Secondary boycott provisions have also been used against Canadians. In 1996 the Japanese multinational Daishowa Paper Manufacturing Co. won a case in an Ontario court against the Toronto-based Friends of the Lubicon (FoL), which

was promoting an international consumer boycott of Daishowa's packaging products. The court decision prevents FoL from picketing or threatening to picket
Daishowa customers, and Daishowa is suing FoL for more than $5 million in
damages.[52]

Responses to SLAPPs

Several US states have responded to the epidemic of SLAPP cases with legislation
aimed at making it more difficult for developers to sue. Californian Senator Bill
Lockyer, a supporter of such legislation, argued that "Our courts are being used
by wealthy and special interests to prevent citizens from speaking out on legitimate public controversies."[53] California, New York, Washington, Nevada,
Florida, Texas and several others have all introduced SLAPP-deterring legislation.
In New York, for example, people filing lawsuits have to show that the person
being sued acted in malice and with "reckless disregard for the truth".[54] In a
Californian Supreme Court case in 1995, the court upheld a ruling that citizens
can make comment and give criticism during formal reviews authorized by law,
without fear of libel suits, no matter what their motivation.[55]

In countries where the constitution does not guarantee the right of citizens
to petition government, it is more difficult for state or provincial governments to
enact legislation to discourage SLAPP suits.[56] However Stephen Keim, Barrister-
at-Law, argues that there is in the Commonwealth Constitution an implied protection of free speech that could be used to make it more difficult for SLAPP
writs to operate in Australia. He cites a 1992 case (Nationwide News Pty. Ltd vs.
Wills) in which the judge said that the doctrine of representative government
which the Constitution incorporates "presupposes an ability of represented and
representatives to communicate information, needs, views, explanations and
advice. It also presupposes an ability of the people of the Commonwealth as a
whole to communicate, among themselves, information and opinions about
matters relevant to the exercise and discharge of governmental powers and functions on their behalf."[57] Keim believes that there is scope for test cases to explore
the potential of this doctrine of representative government as a way of summarily dismissing suits that offend against the rights of citizens to communicate
among themselves on matters of public importance.

Another option is for people who are targeted for SLAPPs to SLAPP-back (to
sue the developers in return). Grounds for such cases in the US can include abuse
of legal process, malicious prosecution and "interference with the exercise of con-
stitutional rights of free expression".[58] Some people in the US have won large
amounts of money in this way. In Australia, the torts of abuse of process and
malicious prosecution are available for this purpose, but such responses depend
on the willingness and financial ability of those involved to use them. It really
requires special legislation to deal with the phenomenon of SLAPPs in a more
integrated and comprehensive way.

The development of a climate of fear that dissuades citizens from speaking
out on matters of public interest and discourages activists from continuing the

'honourable tradition' of civil disobedience is a threat to democracy and healthy political debate. Lawsuits are not the only way to dissuade healthy debate on issues of importance, but litigation is increasingly used to intimidate people who cannot be influenced in other ways, for example through pressure from employers or professional associations.[59]

Chapter 5

Conservative Think-Tanks

In the conservative revolution which has swept the world in the last fifteen years, think-tanks have played a vital role.

John O'Sullivan, National Review [1]

Conservative think-tanks have played a central yet largely unexamined role in the corporate battle against environmental policies and reforms. Think-tanks are generally private, tax-exempt, research institutes which are sometimes referred to as 'universities without students'. Their tax-free status depends on their ability to maintain a superficial appearance of political independence, so they present themselves as providing impartial, disinterested expertise. However they are generally partisan, politically or ideologically motivated and practise the art of 'directed conclusions'.[2]

Think-tanks generally tailor their studies to suit their clients or donors. Writing in the *National Catholic Reporter*, Thomas Blackburn describes think-tanks as "home to non-teaching professors and shadow cabinet ministers hired to spread a patina of academese and expertise over the views of their sponsors."[3] In recent times, an increasing number of think-tanks are openly ideological, fitting their research into an conservative philosophical framework such as libertarianism or economic liberalism, and producing ideas and research that has appeal to their donors.

These conservative think-tanks aim to influence government and set the agenda in a variety of policy arenas, including that of the environment. To be effective, they insinuate themselves into the networks of people who are influential in particular areas of policy by organising conferences, seminars and workshops and by publishing books, briefing papers, journals and media releases for policy-makers, journalists and people able to sway those policy-makers. They liaise with bureaucrats, consultants, interest groups, lobbyists and others, and seek to provide advice directly to the government officials in policy networks and to government agencies and committees, through consultancies or through giving testimony at hearings. Ultimately, think-tank employees become policy-makers themselves, having established their credentials as a vital part of the relevant issue network.

In their efforts to influence and become part of the policy-making process, think-tanks, sometimes referred to as 'advocacy think-tanks', have more in common with interest groups or pressure groups than academic institutions. Nevertheless, employees of think-tanks are treated by the media as independent

experts and are often preferred to experts from universities or interest groups as a
source of expert opinion. When they appear as experts on television shows or are
quoted in the newspapers they have more credibility than a company expert or a
representative of a business association, even though they may be pushing the
same line.[4] They are trained to perfect the TV sound bite and give quotable
quotes for newspapers. Many write their own newspaper columns.

News Shapers on US Network Television News 1987/88

Think-tanks	72
Experts, Analysts, Consultants	57
Former Politicians and Officials	50
Academics	37
Journalists	26
Economists	9
Others	9
Total	260

Source: Gellner 1995, p. 506

Think-tanks often employ former government officials and politicians, as
this gives them influence in government and credibility in the media, besides providing their funders with access to and influence in the policy-making process.
Some US politicians have found that setting up their own think-tanks is a useful
way to capitalize on their own access as they can thereby avoid limits on political
donations and taxation of those donations.

House speaker Newt Gingrich has a very close relationship to the Progress &
Freedom Foundation, which was set up in 1993. As a result the Foundation has
received millions of dollars from 'access-hungry' corporations. Communications
and pharmaceutical companies have been large contributors, each donating far
more to the think-tank than they could legally donate to a political action committee. The Foundation is putting together proposals for deregulating the activities that these companies are involved in.[5]

Corporate Funding

Think-tanks are found all over the world, although the highest density is in the
US where they have a long tradition and ready access to funds. There are currently over a thousand think-tanks in the US, with a diversity of agendas and with
varying degrees of success and influence. More than one hundred are situated in
Washington, DC; most are funded by foundations and corporations, and many
were originally established as part of the conservative backlash against the
counter-culture movements of the 1960s and 70s.

In response to the proliferation of conservative think-tanks in the 1970s, liberals set up their own 'progressive' think-tanks in the early 1980s.[6] However these
were never as well-funded or focussed as the conservative think-tanks, which
provide a powerful vehicle for business interests to change the political agenda
and have been influential because of the corporate financial power behind them.

The tactic by which such changes in the political agenda are secured is for corporations to search out articulate conservative economists and amenable academics, gather them together in lavishly funded tax-deductible think-tanks and pay them handsomely to inundate relevant debate with an endless stream of books and research reports.[7]

Like corporate front groups, think-tanks are more useful to corporations when they are not obviously associated with business interests. The commitment of conservative think-tanks to free-market ideals means that "their views are often indistinguishable from those of the business leaders and associations that support them financially", but because they are funded by multiple donors they can claim independence from 'particular' vested interests.[8]

Whilst conservative think-tanks may not represent the interests of individual companies, the ideas they promote serve the interests of corporations in general, which is why they are able to get so many donors. These ideas include industry deregulation and 'supply-side economics', which advocates reduced taxes. (Lower taxes, they claim, will provide a greater incentive for the wealthy to invest in productive activities that will boost economic growth and provide more employment.)[9] Conservative think-tanks also tend to oppose environmental reforms that threaten industry—this will be discussed further in the next chapter.

For many corporations, the investments they make in think-tanks, which produce and market ideas that benefit corporate interests, are small change when compared with the hundreds of millions of dollars that they spend on advertising their products. Such investments are also considered to be more cost-effective than funding university researchers, who tend to be more concerned about peer review and academic quality and don't seem to have, what John Hood, a 'scholar' with the Heritage Foundation, one of the leading US think-tanks, refers to as "a clear understanding of who their customers are".[10]

Academic research can be full of jargon, and often goes no further than academic journals with a very small readership. Politicians seldom read academic research and therefore "a lot of useful knowledge remains politically inert". In contrast, think-tanks "are geared toward political activism and propaganda, rather than towards scholarship".[11]

Conservative think-tanks don't usually carry out original research, but adapt and apply existing research; although their ideas are not new, they are promoted vigorously. David Ricci, in his book on the rise of think-tanks in Washington, observes that "Conservatives enlarged the think-tank business while openly assuming that such institutes were not places where people developed new ideas but where they advanced a truth known already." Many think-tank employees have been able to bypass the academic route to expert status, avoid the peer-reviewed journals, and write and speak in a way that would be unacceptable in academic circles.[12] The first priority of researchers in think-tanks is to make their papers as accessible as possible.

Think-tanks put a great deal of effort and expense into ensuring the work of their 'scholars' is marketed and disseminated effectively. In the US there is fierce competition between them to attract corporate funding and to get ideas heard. Developing effective marketing techniques has become a major concern for many think-tanks, who have adopted strategies used by interest groups to "promote their causes in the political arena".[13]

Some Conservative US Think-Tanks

The Heritage Foundation has often been credited with changing the face of think-tanks with its aggressive marketing strategies; others are now following suit. The Foundation spends only forty per cent on actual research: more than half goes on marketing and fund-raising, including thirty-five to forty per cent on public relations.[14] Foundation president Ed Feulner says: "We view production—that is, conducting research, analyzing the data, and publishing the findings—as only part of the total process. The other key part is marketing—the way in which we package our findings, our distribution network, and the various activities aimed at building support for our ideas."[15]

All this marketing enables the Foundation to successfully attract mass media coverage for its publications and policy proposals. The Foundation claims that it usually gets 200 or more stories nationwide from each of the position papers it publishes. In the first six months of 1992 the Heritage Foundation was covered in forty-three stories in the *New York Times* and *Washington Post*, according to a survey in the *National Journal.* It also has its own syndicated newspaper features service.[16]

The Foundation produces hundreds of publications every year, including books and a quarterly journal, *Policy Review.* Its speciality is its 'backgrounders' or 'bulletins' which are short essays (between two and twenty pages) on current issues—"brief enough to read in a limousine ride from National Airport to Capitol Hill". These are provided without charge to government officials, employees and journalists, and are usually personally delivered. The Heritage Foundation, like other think-tanks, conducts public opinion polls as a means of—as a Foundation employee put it—"influencing public opinion, not just reflecting it". This is done by selecting questions that will influence the results and then getting wide media attention for the supposedly objective poll findings.[17]

The Heritage Foundation promotes deregulation of industry, an unrestrained free market and privatization, including the sell-off of public lands. The *Economist's Good Think-Tank Guide* described the foundation's ideology as "red-blooded, celebratory capitalism". In line with this ideology it advocates free-market solutions to environmental problems or 'free-market environmentalism' (discussed further in the next chapter). Policies promoted by the Heritage Foundation include replacing fuel economy standards for corporate cars with pollution fees, supporting 'takings' legislation and opposing mandatory recycling and packaging reduction legislation.[18]

The Foundation was formed in 1973 by a group of "conservative legislative aides" with a budget of more than $250,000. Early support came from beer magnate Joseph Coors and petroleum tycoon Edward Noble. The Foundation also developed a very successful direct mail programme for fund-raising. By 1983 it was spending $10 million a year, and had bought its own building in Washington

DC. It had become one of the dominant conservative think-tanks in the US.[19]

The Heritage Foundation is now the wealthiest Washington-based think-tank, with a budget of over $25 million per year of which almost ninety per cent comes from more than 6,000 private donors. These include corporations such as automobile manufacturers, coal, oil, chemical, tobacco companies, foundations (about twenty-five per cent of the foundation's total income), as well as individuals contacted via their direct mail programme. The Heritage Foundation has 165 employees, including fifty 'resident scholars'.[20]

The Foundation aims its publications at government and the media:

> Its most avid consumers are members of the conservative congressional staffs who must brief their bosses and supply them with legislative arguments, pro or con; the conservative appointee in an executive agency who is leery of relying on the expertise of civil service employees and may want to consult with an ideologically compatible expert; and the journalist who wants to balance an article with insights drawn from an authoritative conservative source.[21]

It is illegal for non-profit groups such as the Heritage Foundation (which has a tax exempt status) to lobby government, but it gets around this by having a disclaimer on its publications saying that they should not be "construed as necessarily reflecting the views of the Heritage Foundation or as an attempt to aid or hinder the passage of any bill before Congress". However this does not stop the Foundation from putting out press releases headed, for example, "Fifteen reasons why the Clinton tax package is bad for America's Future".[22] The Foundation has also been one of the forces behind the Republicans' 'Contract with America', which incorporates a range of measures aimed at reducing environmental regulation (see next chapter).

The Cato Institute, established in 1977, is another major Washington-based think-tank that opposes environmental regulation and promotes free-market environmentalism. It is a medium-sized think-tank whose research reflects its ideological stance—libertarian and therefore anti-government. It tends to publish longer, more philosophical papers than the Heritage Foundation's 'backgrounders', but it does detailed policy work as well and testifies with increasing frequency before government committees. It also sponsors policy conferences, provides radio commentators and even has its own daily radio programme.[23]

Like other libertarian think-tanks that have followed it, the Cato Institute calls for many government functions to be turned over to the private sector. James Smith, author of *The Idea Brokers*, says "its blend of fiscal conservatism, social tolerance, and a principled selfishness grounded in writers from Adam Smith to Ayn Rand" make it "the think-tank for yuppies".[24] However, according to *The Economist*:

> Cato's vision, taken to its logical extreme (and people at the institute are keen on taking things to their logical extremes), would be an America in which a family does whatever it likes at home; pays virtually no taxes and expects no state provision or support; has its own tank and machine gun for defence; and ignores other countries. In short, an updated version of the Wild West.[25]

The Cato Institute has an annual budget of $6 million, of which almost ninety per cent comes from private grants and gifts from foundations, individuals and corporations, including such organizations as the American Farm Bureau Federation, the American Petroleum Institute, Coca-Cola, Exxon, the Ford Motor Company, Monsanto, Philip Morris and the Procter & Gamble Fund.[26] It has a full-time staff of thirty-five, including sixteen resident scholars and over sixty adjunct scholars who do work on contract for the Institute. It campaigns for reduced government and deregulation of the economy, and so opposes environmentalists who seek to introduce environmental regulations that will constrain the free market. The Institute argues that environmental regulations impose excessive costs on industry and that government bureaucracies such as the Department of Energy with its "fanatical promotion of energy conservation" are a waste of taxpayers' money and should be abolished.[27]

Conservative Think-Tanks In Other Countries

In Britain, conservative think-tanks have also been influential, although there are only a few of them and they are much smaller than the major US think-tanks. Similar groups have been established elsewhere in Europe, such as the Frankfurt Institute and the Institute for Political Science in Germany, and the Institut de L'Entreprise and the Tocqueville Foundation in France. In France, as in Japan, there are also government equivalents of think-tanks, such as the French Commissariat du Plan.[28]

One of the oldest think-tanks in Britain is the Institute of Economic Affairs (IEA), which has promoted *laissez-faire* libertarian views[29] or 'economic liberalism' for decades, keeping it "alive when academic opinion had pronounced it brain-dead".[30] The IEA, inspired by the work of economist Friedrich von Hayek, seeks to apply free-market solutions to all aspects of society, including environmental problems, and to reduce the role of government and regulation. For example, one of its publications states:

> There is a strong case for letting market forces work in energy, partly because of government failure but also because rivalrous (not 'perfect') competition will lead to a beneficial discovery process. . . A policy for energy is not only unnecessary but undesirable. It hampers market adjustment and induces producers to spend time influencing government rather than improving efficiency.[31]

From its inception in the 1950s, the IEA set out to gain wide acceptance for the "philosophy of the market economy" through education directed at opinion leaders such as intellectuals, politicians, business people and journalists. It started as a one-person operation; at its height in the 1980s it had fifteen full-time employees, with a half-million pound budget provided mainly by about 250 companies, including large multinational companies.[32]

During the 1970s the IEA managed to get several academics and influential journalists to promote economic liberalism, as well as some prominent MPs, most notably Margaret Thatcher. In its early years the IEA also had some influence in the universities, and produced undergraduate and secondary school texts. It trained young economists at the IEA early in their careers, which helped provide personnel for the free-market think-tanks established in the 1970s and 80s.[33]

The Centre for Policy Studies (CPS) was to some extent an outgrowth of the IEA, having been founded in 1974 by Sir Keith Joseph, an active member of the IEA, and Margaret Thatcher, who had also been associated with the IEA. Whilst the IEA pledged itself to be "independent of any political party" and therefore did not publish policy recommendations, the CPS was set up to convert the Tory party to economic liberalism and formulate policies for the Party that were in line with this philosophy. It seldom exceeded seven full-time employees and an annual budget of £150,000.[34]

The IEA, CPS and other think-tanks, including the Adam Smith Institute and the Institute of Directors (also small compared to the average US think-tank), were nonetheless effective in the British environment because of the "extreme centralisation of British political and public life". This gave easy access to key people within government, the media and the financial sphere, and they needed only to concentrate their persuasion on "a strategic policy-making élite" to be effective.[35]

> These 'second-hand dealers in ideas'—to use the IEA's own description of its role—were typically not intellectual originators but served to collect, distil and preserve certain strands of ideas and to diffuse them more widely, not least as detailed interventions in current policy debates.[36]

The CPS in particular has been accused of being an "intellectual jackdaw, gleaning most of its ideas from overseas experiments— and in particular from the US. These were then reworked to fit Britain, packaged in pamphlet form and fired across the media's bows."[37]

These two organizations, the IEA and the CPS, "provided the ideas which gave intellectual shape to the instincts and energy of Thatcherism" in Britain. They helped to convert the Tory leaders to economic liberalism whilst they were in opposition, and gave the Thatcher government "a style of politics whose cutting edge was its ideological crusade".[38] When elected as Prime Minister in 1979, Thatcher nominated Ralph Harris, head of the IEA, for a seat in the House of Lords. She wrote to thank him and two of his colleagues: "It was primarily your foundation work which enabled us to rebuild the philosophy upon which our Party succeeded in the past. The debt we owe you is immense and I am very grateful."[39]

In Australasia, the largest think-tank is the Sydney-based Centre for Independent Studies (CIS), established on a very small basis in 1976. Although it claims to be independent, the Centre is funded by businesses and its work is shaped by its libertarian/*laissez-faire* philosophy. It is committed to "an economy based on free and competitive markets" and "individual liberty and choice" including "the right to property".[40]

The Centre deals with "practical public policy issues" as well as "more intellectual issues focussing on the way societies work and the importance of liberty in securing prosperity both economically and socially."[41] It publishes the work of various conservatives, including media baron Rupert Murdoch; economists such as Hayek (whom the Centre brought out to Australia in the 1970s) and Milton Friedman; conservative law professor and 'takings' expert Richard Epstein; Nick Greiner, a former premier of New South Wales; Gary Sturgess (former Director-General of the NSW Cabinet Office under Greiner); and various think-tank scholars from the US and the UK. It also distributes in Australia material from US and UK libertarian think-tanks, including IEA free-market literature.[42]

Another prominent (and the oldest) Australian conservative think-tank is the Institute of Public Affairs (IPA). The IPA describes itself as "a political organisation in the sense that it influences the political agenda" but claims that it "avoids political-party partisanship". It stands for, among other things, "less regulation and smaller government generally" and "rational economic policies".[43]

Almost one third of IPA's $1.5 million annual budget comes from mining and manufacturing companies. It has 700 corporate members and 3,000 individual members, some of whom are subscribers to its various publications. Its council has included Murdoch as well as other conservative business leaders. Like many of the conservative US think-tanks, the IPA has good connections in the media by means of right-wing commentators with regular columns in major newspapers. It also has good political connections: two of its three units are headed by former senior public officials from the Australian Treasury, and the former Secretary of the Treasury, John Stone, is an IPA consultant. The third unit is headed by Dame Leonie Kramer, Chancellor of the University of Sydney.[44]

The Centre for Independent Studies and the IPA both publish material attacking environmentalists and promoting 'free-market' environmentalism. The Centre has published a book which it claims "checks predictions of environmental doom against current scientific knowledge, and finds them to be at best unproven and at worst plain false."[45]

A number of Australian think-tanks are modelled on those in the US and have close ties with some of them, including the Heritage Foundation, the Cato Institute and the American Enterprise Institute. The Institute of Public Policy, now amalgamated with the IPA, modelled itself on the Heritage Foundation as well as the British IEA. The Committee for Economic Development in Australia (CEDA) was originally modelled on the US Committee for Economic Development, and in 1984 it made a conscious decision to move towards an American Enterprise Institute (AEI) model. It promotes conservative ideologies and policies, publishes reports, articles and pamphlets which are widely distributed, organizes conferences and seminars, and holds "regular private briefings with key financial journalists, and regular luncheons with editors of newspapers and executives of TV and radio stations".[46]

The growth of conservative business-financed think-tanks in the 1970s contributed to the "new prominence of neo-conservative ideas in economic debate in Australia" which was labelled the 'New Right'. Millions of dollars are being channelled into these organizations each year for the promotion of conservative, market-oriented ideas.[47] The sociologist Michael Pusey says:

No one can doubt the tremendous success that the 'New Right' American and British policy organisations and think-tanks have had in cloning themselves in Australia, and then in reorganising the public policy agenda along Anglo-American 'free' market lines—continental European social democratic experience is excluded almost to the point of invisibility.[48]

Fostering Think-Tanks

One reason why there are so many think-tanks in the US and why some are so large is the ready availability of funds: "A lot of rich foundations are ready to pay good money to people to sit and think." In contrast, there are few wealthy foundations willing to fund UK or Australian think-tanks. The large foundations which fund US think-tanks are themselves financed by wealthy families and corporate profits from family businesses. They include the Smith Richardson Foundation, run by the son of the founder of the Vicks Chemical Company, the Coors Foundation, whose fortune comes from beer, the Lilly Endowment from Eli Lilly pharmaceuticals, and the Olin Foundation, founded by Olin Chemical. Also there are the Lynde and Harry Bradley Foundation, whose fortune is from electronics, and the Scaife Foundation, whose fortune is from Gulf Oil, each with assets of well over $100 million. As few as fifteen such foundations, together with various corporations "are able to finance hundreds of ultra-right and conservative organizations, thus creating the illusion that the far right is a diverse and growing group of Americans. . ."[49]

A second explanation for the proliferation of US think-tanks is in terms of the American system of government: "Think-tanks and foundations perform the research and advocacy functions that in many other industrial nations would be undertaken by the organized political parties."[50] American political parties do not play much role in policy development and do not have policy research units. It has been suggested that American political parties are not only unable to come up with ideas, but that they lack any ideological coherence: "Think-tanks have played a crucial role in building and supporting policy consensus and thereby replaced American parties which tend to work rather as electoral coalitions than as places of ideological discussion and policy planning."[51]

In the US, the political party has much less power over how its members vote than in countries like Britain and Australia, where members of parliament can be punished and even expelled from the Cabinet for not maintaining solidarity in voting. In the US there is much more scope for influencing the votes of individual politicians. The policies favoured by the party executive may not be favoured by Congress, who are likely to be willing to listen to criticisms of those policies and to alternative policies put forward by think-tanks.[52]

A third explanation sees think-tanks as a functional response to information overload. Ricci, in his book *The Transformation of American Politics*, argues that politicians, government officials and policy-makers looked to experts who could summarize and interpret the screeds of information coming their way. As a consequence of the undermining of the prevailing consensus of traditional values by the counter-culture of the 1960s and 70s, and the crisis of confidence in the US brought on by the Vietnam War, policy-makers often lack the vision, philosophy or coherent set of values that would enable them to deal with the information: to distinguish between the "good and bad, significant and insignificant, relevant and irrelevant". Politicians and government officials therefore looked to experts in the think-tanks to interpret and make sense of the massive amounts of information that they were receiving. This gave rise to a set of policy entrepreneurs based in think-tanks who often had the coherent vision that politicians lacked, particularly in the conservative think-tanks which promoted the market place as an alternative to big government.[53]

An additional function that think-tanks provide in the US, which is often carried out by political parties in other countries, is the facilitation of 'élite transfer'. In Britain and Australia, cabinet ministers are chosen from the elected members of government, whereas in the United States this is not necessarily the case. The American system also allows each new administration to appoint its own senior bureaucrats including the staff of government departments, heads of departments and advisory councils. These are not necessarily selected from the public service, as is the case in other countries.[54]

This means that when a new US government is elected, top-level personnel in the administrative arm of government are changed for people whose ideology is more suited to the incoming government. Think-tanks provide a ready source of such personnel, and Presidents from Carter through to Clinton have made great use of them to fill high level government positions. Think-tanks provide a fast track to a political career and a public profile in the policy arena. They also provide a place for discarded government officials to go when there is a change of government, where they can be employed until 'their' government is re-elected, whilst still having some influence over public policy in the meantime.[55]

> The revolving door between government and think-tanks is well-established. . . When Ronald Reagan took office, no fewer than twenty of the research fellows at the neo-conservative American Enterprise Institute (AEI) joined his administration. Now that Mr Reagan has left power, many of his appointees, such as Jeane Kirkpatrick and Richard Perle, are working at AEI. Every American think-tank director has a dream and a nightmare. The dream is to house the next administration; the nightmare is to house the last one. AEI seems to have managed both in the course of a decade.[56]

The circulation of personnel suits the think-tanks well. Employing ex-government officials gives a think-tank access to politicians and others in government and attracts the funds of corporations who want access. When think-tank employees are taken up by a new administration, the think-tank has its best chance to have its ideas and agenda accepted by the government and to influence policy. Those employees are then able to recommend others in the think-tank for government positions.

With an eye to the revolving door between think-tanks and government positions, the Heritage Foundation and the Cato Institute have sought to nurture a new generation of conservative leaders within their ranks by sponsoring college students and promising junior bureaucrats, and providing them with a place to meet and socialize. The Heritage Foundation also promotes a 'talent bank' of potential candidates for official positions in government administrations on the premise that its policies will be more influential if its people are in positions of influence. It was able to place thirty-nine of its staff in government jobs whilst Reagan was president.[57]

> In the past two decades, the most important function served by the network of conservative think-tanks has not been the germination of new ideas, but the creation of a 'new cadre' of professionals. . . Not only have the dozens of conservative think-tanks created a framework for disseminating ideas that exists largely outside the established infrastructure of academic journals, university presses, and commercial publishing. . . they have also designed career vehicles for conservative activists and thinkers.[58]

There is far less scope for political appointments in the UK government administration because of a permanent and powerful civil service that acts as a stabilising agent when governments change. However, this latter has also been used as an argument for the influence of think-tanks during the Thatcher years:

> The civil service is constitutionally incapable of generating the policy innovation which the prime minister craves. The typical civil servant enters Whitehall in his or her early 20s. . . and settles down for a lifetime career: there is little infiltration from the outside of new people with new ideas and new methods. A reforming prime minister has little choice but to go round them and listen to the think-tanks.[59]

In Britain and the US the think-tanks provided a platform and training ground for conservative thinkers who later came to power. In Australia, opportunities for 'élite transfer' have become available with the creation of the Senior Executive Service during the 1980s. For example, in the state of New South Wales, the senior executive service consists of hundreds of public officials employed on contracts. Continuing appointment depends on "yearly appraisals made by a private firm of consultants. . ."[60]

In a study of the Australian Senior Executive Service, Pusey found that they were predominantly conservative in their political views, tending to emphasize individualism, small government and free-market economics or what he called 'economic rationalism'. In the powerful departments of Treasury, Finance, and Prime Minister and Cabinet, he found that seventy per cent were economic rationalists. He argued that they "tend to see the world in terms that neutralize and then reduce the norms of public policy to those of private enterprise".[61]

However in Australia think-tanks don't play a significant role in training future public servants; the conservatism of the senior executive service results from a selection process that favours people with private school backgrounds and training in university economics departments, where the philosophy of market economics prevails. The economists that dominate the Senior Executive Service have their economic rationalism reinforced by fellow economists in key university departments, "in peak business groups, the private sector economists in the finance sector, and with the staff of the economic 'think-tanks'."[62]

Political Influence

Conservative think-tanks have played a leading role in the conservative resurgence in English speaking countries. One White House official told *The Atlantic* that the AEI played a large part in getting Ronald Reagan elected by making conservatism 'intellectually respectable'. During the Reagan years, the Heritage Foundation provided information to members of Congress and their staffs, and was extremely influential. Most of its policy recommendations were adopted by the Reagan administration, including a proposal to allow strip mining in designated wilderness areas.[63] Edwin Feulner, President of the Foundation, received a Presidential Citizen's Medal from Ronald Reagan for being "a leader of the conservative movement. . .who has helped shape the policy of our Government".

Like the Heritage Foundation, the Cato Institute was influential during the Reagan years. William Niskanen was acting chair of Reagan's Council of Economic Advisers in 1985 when he left to become chair of the Cato Institute. He was previously a Director of Economics at the Ford Motor Company, a founder of the National Tax Limitation Committee, a defence analyst at the Pentagon and author of the book *Reagonomics: An Insider's account of the Policies and the People.*[64]

One survey published in 1982 found that most officials "in the Department of State, the Central Intelligence Agency, the National Security Council, and the Department of Defense" were more influenced in the long-term by think-tanks than by public opinion or special interest groups, and many were more influenced by think-tanks than by the media or by interaction with members of Congress.[65]

In Britain, a few conservative think-tanks were extremely influential in Thatcher's government. According to *The Economist,* "Politicians looked to the think-tanks for instant policies, journalists for instant opinions, and people on the make used them for instant connections."[66] Academic Simon James says:

> The tiny handful of think-tanks operating in Britain have a very mixed track record. The larger and less ideological amongst them have exercised a moderate influence on certain specific public policy issues. As to the smaller and more ideologically zealous think-tanks, most have made no impression worth writing about. But one or two have exercised an influence greatly disproportionate to their size, and played a key role in making Britain in the 1980s to a surprising extent a testing ground for the ideas of the radical right.[67]

These think-tanks, particularly the CPS, played a major role in setting the policy agenda of the Thatcher government, providing it with most of its policy initiatives including trade union 'reforms', privatization of public authorities such as water and electricity, and welfare cuts. Thatcher's chief of staff, economic adviser and all four heads of the No. 10 Policy Unit were former contributors to the CPS. The Policy Unit served as a conduit for ideas from CPS and other conservative think-tanks.[68]

Whilst the British think-tanks have had less influence since the demise of Thatcher, with the Republican domination of the US Congress the conservative think-tanks in the US are again experiencing a resurgence of importance and influence. According to *The Economist*, the influence of the Cato Institute is again on the rise "because its fundamentalism offers Republicans a reminder of the true faith". Similarly, a *Wall Street Journal* journalist wrote that the "less government, more freedom" approach of the newly elected Republicans "echo the libertarian Cato Institute".[69]

However, according to another *Wall Street Journal* journalist, "No policy shop has more clout than the conservative Heritage Foundation." House Speaker Newt Gingrich has said that "Heritage is without question the most far-reaching conservative organization in the country in the war of ideas" and he is reported to be "a regular visitor to the foundation's plush building near Capitol Hill". Edwin Feulner, the Foundation's President, was appointed by Gingrich and Republican Senate Majority Leader Bob Dole as Vice Chairman of the National Commission on Economic Growth and Tax Reform.[70]

Traditionally, newly elected members of congress have attended Harvard's Kennedy School of Government for their orientation programme, but now Republican congresspeople are flocking instead to a programme set up by the Heritage Foundation and Empower America to hear speeches from the likes of Charles Murray (of *The Bell Curve* fame) and Rush Limbaugh (right-wing radio talk-back host).[71]

Heritage employees claim that much of the Contract with America was shaped by them. Indeed some members of Congress admit that Foundation researchers were 'key architects' of some proposed legislation, including the plan to overhaul welfare. "When GOP congressional staffers met in June with conservative leaders to help map current legislative efforts to cut federal funding for left-leaning advocacy groups, the closed-door meeting took place at Heritage headquarters."[72]

According to the Foundation's policy analyst John Shanahan, a former labour-management specialist in the Bush administration, "Our influence comes from ideas. When we put out something and say this is what conservative thought should be, Congress listens. . . The 'Contract with America' wouldn't be there without groups like Heritage."[73] They listen largely because the new Republican congresspeople share ideological outlooks with the Foundation.

Michael Warder, Executive Vice-President of the Rockford Institute, describes the influence that the conservative think-tanks have on policy making in Washington today. He asks: "When congressional hearings are held, who or what is generating the body of data and the categories of that data upon which the law will be based? Chances are the vocabulary, the categories for the data, and the data derive from someone at a think-tank."[74]

Long-Term Influence

More important, however, than their ability to shape individual policies, has been in the ability of the conservative think-tanks to move the whole policy agenda to the right. Heritage Foundation's Edwin Feulner explained to an international conference in 1978 that the ability of free-market think-tanks to dominate public debate had been effective "in keeping. . . debate within its proper perspective".[75] The debate has been moved to the conservative end of the spectrum:

> First, they help to set the agenda of the political debate. They inject arguments (neatly packaged for a copy-hungry media) into the public arena before they are raised by politicians. This both softens up public opinion and pushes the consensus farther to the right.[76]

Even after Margaret Thatcher's departure, the ideas of the conservative think-tanks continued to influence Prime Minister John Major. Richard Cockett, who in his book *Thinking the Unthinkable* has charted the rise of conservative think-tanks in Britain, notes that a new consensus, which included keeping government control of industry to a minimum, has been achieved by those think-tanks. The free-market ideas of think-tanks such as the IEA have become the new conventional wisdom, so that even the Labour Party in Britain "employs the language of economic efficiency and choice, albeit reluctantly."[77]

> Furthermore, most of the economic liberal agenda that the Conservative Party espoused during the 1980s was duly adopted by the Labour party in the wake of their 1987 election defeat. . . Indeed, by the 1992 election it became very hard to tell the two main political parties apart on economic policy.[78]

R. Desai, writing in *New Left Review*, agrees: "The Labour Party, by the late 1980s, resigned itself to operating within the political parameters laid down by Thatcherism." However he adds that the think-tanks have been disappointed that more of their agenda has not been taken up and that "political and electoral convenience" continued to remain the overriding consideration of the Thatcher government. He also notes that the wider public was never really converted to 'economic liberalism'.[79]

Noel Malcolm, writing in *The Spectator*, says of these think-tanks:

> Their most valuable effect on policy has been long-term and indirect: over nearly thirty-five years, the IEA has changed the way people think by putting a whole range of ideas into more general currency among academics, politicians and economic journalists.[80]

Similarly, more moderate liberal think-tanks in the US have been influenced by the conservative ideas promoted by the conservative think-tanks. The Brookings Institution, one of the larger and more respectable think-tanks, is sometimes referred to as a 'liberal' or 'left of center' think-tank. It had become a base for so called 'liberal thinkers' who became part of various Democrat administrations from Kennedy through to Clinton. Brookings is far less dependent on corporate donations that most conservative think-tanks, since it has a $90 million endowment and gets almost one third of its income from sales of its publications (compared with five per cent in the case of the Heritage Foundation). Nevertheless it has been moving to a more conservative stance for some years. According to Brookings' spokesperson Stan Wellborn: "Our economics department is just full of antigovernment free-marketeers."[81]

In Australia, economic rationalism has been reinforced by conservative think-tanks which have "captured the policy agenda" of the Liberal Party which is now in power, as well as that of the opposition Labor Party which, whilst in power, copied a number of Liberal Party policies, including privatization and the deregulation of financial markets.[82]

> For nearly a decade economic rationalism has been the establishment economic religion, not only in Australia but throughout the Anglo-Saxon world. Its power has been such that anybody who wanted to be a serious player in the socio-economic debate in English-speaking countries had to pay obeisance to it. . . Economic rationalism dominates the universities, the central or co-ordinating bureaucracies, the privately endowed think-tanks, the business lobbies, and the media.[83]

In most English-speaking countries, conservative think-tanks have been influential in promoting a conservative reform agenda and "widening the parameters of 'respectable' opinion".[84] As a result, free-market ideas have come to dominate all policy issues, including environmental policy. The impact of this development is discussed in the next chapter.

Chapter 6

Think-Tanks and the Environment

Using approaches similar to those of corporate front groups and the Wise Use Movement, think-tanks have sought to cast doubt on the seriousness of environmental problems, to oppose environmental regulations, and to promote free-market remedies to those problems—such as privatization, deregulation and the expanded use of property rights. Corporations that wish to portray themselves in public as being environmentally concerned often fund such think-tanks (with which they are not readily identified) to oppose environmental reforms, just as some corporations privately fund anti-environmental Wise Use groups whilst publicly funding environmental groups.

Think-tanks have themselves supported a number of corporate front groups and Wise Use groups. The Competitive Enterprise Institute (CEI), a think-tank established in 1984 by Fred Smith, Jr, an ex-EPA employee, has worked closely with Wise Use groups. The CEI, based in Washington, calls itself a "pro-market, public policy group committed to advancing the principles of free enterprise and limited government". About a third of its 1994 budget of $2 million came from corporations which appear to approve of the CEI's opposition to environmental legislation, including Dow Chemical, General Motors, Ford, Amoco, Coca-Cola Co, Pfizer Inc, Philip Morris, and Texaco Inc.[1]

As well as publications and media appearances, the CEI is involved in "coalition building, advocacy and litigation", or what its Executive Director Marlo Lewis calls "guerilla actions". For example, the CEI took the National Highway Traffic Safety Administration (NHTSA) to court over its automobile fuel-efficiency standards, arguing that the standards would result in lighter, more dangerous cars. It claimed: "The federal new car fuel economy program imposes a deadly trade-off of blood for oil." The CEI won the Federal court case in 1992, but subsequently lost it after the NHTSA revised its rationale for the standards. The CEI is also involved in grassroots organising, claiming it has a mailing list of 250,000 people it can call on to oppose legislation. It used this list to campaign against a proposal by the Clinton government to impose an energy tax, organising rallies, meetings and media advertisements. The energy tax was defeated.[2]

Casting Doubt on the Urgency of Environmental Problems

Corporations have utilized think-tanks and a few dissident scientists to cast doubt on the existence and magnitude of various environmental problems, including global warming, ozone depletion and species extinction. This strategy is aimed at crippling the impetus for government action to solve these problems, action which might adversely affect corporate profits. Phil Lesly, author of a handbook on public relations and communications, advises corporations:

> People generally do not favor action on a non-alarming situation when arguments seem to be balanced on both sides and there is a clear doubt. . . The weight of impressions on the public must be balanced so people will have doubts and lack motivation to take action. Accordingly, means are needed to get balancing information into the stream from sources that the public will find credible. There is no need for a clear-cut 'victory'. . . Nurturing public doubts by demonstrating that this is not a clear-cut situation in support of the opponents usually is all that is necessary.[3]

Think-tanks have played a key role in providing credible 'experts' who dispute scientific claims of existing or impending environmental degradation and therefore provide enough doubts to ensure that governments 'lack motivation' to act. For example, most conservative think-tanks have argued that global warming is not happening, and that any possible future warming will be slight and may have beneficial effects.

In its *Environmental Briefing Book for Congressional Candidates* the CEI states that "the likeliest global climate change is the creation of a milder, greener, more prosperous world."[4] Likewise, in one of the Heritage Foundation's back-grounders, John Shanahan suggests that nights would become warmer, whilst days would not change, crops would thrive on the increased CO_2 and the world's agricultural belt would be expanded.[5]

Conservative think-tanks have promoted the views of the few scientists who disagree with the vast majority of atmospheric scientists that warming is a likely consequence of increasing levels of greenhouse gases in the atmosphere. They use these dissident scientists—usually not atmospheric scientists—to suggest there is "widespread disagreement within the scientific community". This so-called 'widespread disagreement' is used to make a case against taking 'drastic actions' to reduce greenhouse gases.[6]

One of CEI's publications, entitled *The True State of the Planet*, is an edited collection of papers aimed at putting forward "a Major Challenge to the Environment Movement". The book is the outcome of a project set up by the CEI with funds from the Olin Foundation. In it the authors claim that the "scientific evidence argues against the existence of a greenhouse crisis, against the notion that realistic policies could achieve any meaningful climatic impact, and against the claim that we must act now if we are to reduce the greenhouse threat."[7]

Elsewhere, the CEI uses Gallup polls and a Greenpeace report to support its claim that "there is no scientific consensus to support the proposition that human activity will produce an *apocalyptic warming* of the Earth's atmosphere" [emphasis added].[8] It does not report the consensus amongst the vast majority of scientists that a warming of a few degrees is very likely if humans continue to add greenhouse gases to the atmosphere. Although not 'apocalyptic', the consensus is that one or two degrees is enough to change the climate in ways that are likely to severely affect people in some parts of the world.

Similarly Shanahan argues that there is "enormous uncertainty associated with the scientific methodology used to predict future climate changes".[9] Like the CEI, he claims that global warming is a theory that is widely challenged and that "almost all the scientists agreed that *catastrophic* global warming predictions are unsupported by scientific evidence" [emphasis added]. In each case, these analyses question the most extreme predictions in order to cast doubt on the scientific consensus about more moderate consequences.

Think-tanks in other parts of the world are also seeking to cast doubt on global warming predictions. In Britain, the newly formed Environmental Unit of the Institute of Economic Affairs (IEA) launched *Global Warming: Apocalypse or Hot Air* in 1994.[10] The Australian Institute of Public Affairs (IPA) has also produced articles challenging the greenhouse consensus. An example is *The Greenhouse Panic*, which was reprinted in *Engineering World* magazine. The article, introduced by the magazine editor as "a balanced assessment", argues that "alarmist prejudices of insecure people have been boosted by those who have something to gain from widespread public concern."[11] This article, which would have been more easily dismissed as an IPA publication, has been quoted by Australian engineers at conferences as if it were an authoritative source.

The think-tanks have been so successful at clouding the scientific picture of greenhouse warming and providing an excuse for corporations and the politicians they support that they have managed to thwart the implementation of effective greenhouse reduction strategies by governments in the English-speaking world. According to Greenpeace researcher Andrew Rowell, a 1989 report by the George C. Marshall Institute think-tank on the greenhouse effect "was used by the Bush administration to justify a more lenient approach to CO_2 emissions".[12] The governments of the US and Australia, which produce the world's highest per capita emissions of greenhouse gases, have for many years obstructed international greenhouse gas reduction measures.

Some think-tanks are now trying to repeat this success by challenging the scientific consensus on ozone depletion. CEI argues that the phasing out of CFCs which cause ozone depletion will cost "$44.4 to $99.4 billion over the next decade".[13] The Cato Institute has published *Ecoscam: The False Prophets of Ecological Apocalypse* by Ronald Bailey, the person who edited the CEI's anti-environmentalism book. In *EcoScam* Bailey argues that scientists working for NASA have promoted the ozone depletion theory in order to bolster its budget.[14]

Like the critics of the global warming theory (and usually these are the same people), Bailey and others emphasize the uncertainties surrounding the ozone depletion consensus and the natural fluctuations in ozone levels that occur over time:

> The impact of man-made chlorofluorocarbons (CFCs) on the ozone layer is a complex question that turns on murky evidence, tentative conclusions, conflicting interpretations, and changing predictions. . . it turns out that ozone depletion, like the other environmental dooms analyzed here, is less a crisis than a nuisance. . .[15]

The British Institute of Economic Affairs has published *A Contrarian View of Environmental Problems* by Matt Ridley, which argues that "global temperatures may actually be falling" and "the ozone layer is getting thicker, not thinner, over temperate latitudes".[16] This argument is irrelevant, since the concern is over ozone depletion occurring close to the Earth's poles. A related criticism is that there has been no measured increase in UV radiation detected in cities in the US as a result of ozone depletion. However there is evidence of increases in UV radiation at ground level in Australia (in the Southern hemisphere, where ozone depletion was first observed).[17]

Since around 1993 several publications have come out suggesting that ozone depletion is a scam or a hoax, or at least grossly exaggerated. Most of these are based on the claims of a handful of scientists, perhaps the most quoted of whom is Fred Singer, executive director of a think-tank called the Science and Environmental Policy Project (SEPP). This project was originally set up in 1990 with the help of the Washington Institute for Values in Public Policy (funded by the Rev Sun Myung Moon's Unification Church) which provided it with free office space. (SEPP is no longer affiliated with Moon, and receives its funding from various foundations.)[18]

SEPP argues that global warming, ozone depletion and acid rain are not real but rather are scare tactics used by environmentalists. Singer speaks and writes prolifically on these subjects, and is popular amongst anti-environment groups.[19] Two of the leading Australian conservative think-tanks sponsored him to tour Australia, putting his views on global warming. He has worked for companies such as Exxon, Shell, and Arco.[20] According to the Environmental Research Foundation:

> For years, Singer was a professor at the University of Virginia where he was funded by energy companies to pump out glossy pamphlets pooh-poohing climate change. Singer hasn't published original research on climate change in twenty years and is now an 'independent' consultant, who spends his time writing letters to the editor, and testifying before Congress, claiming that ozone-depletion and global warming aren't real problems.[21]

Another scientist widely quoted in the 'ozone depletion is a hoax' literature is Rogelio Maduro, who has a geology degree. He is an associate editor of 21st Century Science and Technology which, according to the journal *Science*, is published "by supporters of Lyndon LaRouche". Maduro has written a book with writer Ralf Schauerhammer entitled *The Holes in the Ozone Scare: The Scientific Evidence that the Sky Isn't Falling*, published by 21st Century. In it they argue that most chlorine in the stratosphere comes from natural sources such as seawater and volcanoes. Atmospheric scientists, however, point out that the chlorine from these sources is washed out of the air by rain long before it reaches the stratosphere, whereas CFCs are not soluble in water.[22]

Drawing on these few scientific 'experts', who prefer to publish their dissenting views in think-tank and right-wing publications rather than in peer-reviewed scientific journals, conservative and business magazines and radio talk-back hosts such as Rush Limbaugh have been spreading the idea that ozone depletion is not really a problem and that no action needs to be taken. *Business Week* quoted Fred

Singer and Ronald Bailey in an article entitled *What's Flying out the Ozone Hole? Billions of Dollars*, in which it argued that "the propaganda of the Chicken Littles has prevailed over science—and the cost of needlessly replacing cooling equipment will be staggering". Another *Business Week* article a year later quoted Fred Singer as saying that the CFC phaseout was "based mainly on panicky reactions to press releases. . ." The articles were written by Paul Craig Roberts, the chairman of a Washington think-tank and a Distinguished Fellow of the Cato Institute.[23]

This surge of backlash publications has also reached the mainstream press. The *Washington Post* reported that "the problem appears to be heading toward solution before [researchers] can find any solid evidence that serious harm was or is being done."[24] This isn't the first time that the media has serviced those seeking to discredit ozone depletion theories. In the 1970s, when the connection between fluorocarbons from aerosol spray cans and ozone depletion were first made:

> The aerosol industry launched a PR campaign that emphasized 'knowledge gaps' instead of gaps in the Earth's atmospheric shield. Industry press releases formed the basis for articles in numerous newspapers and magazines that questioned the ozone depletion 'theory', enabling aerosol spray manufacturers to buy additional time before their product was banned. In this case, industry profits were deemed more important than the prevention of skin cancer.[25]

This time, think-tanks and their scholars have provided the Republicans in Congress with the rhetoric to oppose a more general CFC phaseout. The Republicans have sought to retract US agreement to the terms of the Montreal Protocol, the international convention aimed at phasing out CFCs worldwide. And a bill was introduced to repeal the provisions of the Clean Air Act relating to production and use of CFCs.[26] *New Scientist* reported in September 1995:

> America's Republicans thumbed their noses at the vast majority of the world's scientists last week by claiming there is no proof that CFCs are destroying the ozone layer. Without proof, they argued, there is no good reason why the US should rush to ban the manufacture of CFCs by the end of the year.[27]

The appropriately named Republican John Doolittle told the House of Representatives Science Committee that ozone depletion was debatable, based on pseudo-science and that "we're not giving Mother Nature enough credit for being able to replenish the ozone layer." He dismissed peer-review as "mumbo jumbo".[28] Also writing in *New Scientist*, Jeff Hecht argued that:

> What the Republicans are doing is playing lawyers' games with science. They demand that theories that they consider inconvenient be proved beyond any doubt—something that is impossible in science. . . The theory is so widely accepted that its originators received a Nobel prize for chemistry. Yet the Republicans don't like this because it implies the need to regulate industrial production of the harmful chemicals that damage the ozone layer. . . If they could find a few scientists who weren't 100 per cent convinced that CFCs depleted ozone, they seemed ready to abandon the Montreal Protocol.[29]

Conservative think-tanks have also challenged other environmental problems. In the CEI's *The True State of the Planet* the authors claim that[30]

• superfund waste sites "pose no real risks to people or the natural environment"
• "following the precautionary principle can lead to greater environmental degradation"
• modern forestry "helps preserve wildlife habitat"
• "commercial logging is not a major cause of deforestation"
• we are "entering an age of increasing and unprecedented natural resources abundance"

The Cato Institute also publishes a number of books which dispute environmental crises such as ozone depletion. These books include *Apocalypse Not*, which argues that much of the environmental movement is a broad-based assault on reason and freedom; *Ecoscam: The False Prophets of Ecological Apocalypse* by Ronald Bailey, mentioned above (in this book Bailey criticizes environmentalists for "their faulty analyses, their wildly inaccurate predictions, their heedless politicization of science, their opportunism, and their courtship of the media"); and *The State of Humanity* edited by Julian Simon, Cato adjunct scholar and well-known critic of those who suggest humans are worse off as a result of environmental degradation.[31]

Julian Simon's optimism is echoed by Jerry Taylor, director of natural resource studies at the Cato Institute, who claims that recycling is unnecessary as resources are infinite and there is no problem burying 1,000 years of US garbage: "We have ten times as much oil as we did in 1950, three times as much forest land as we did in 1920. . . As price incentives increase to find more sources, we will." Recycling, he says, should only be carried out where there is an economic reason to do it; "Recycling is the biggest hoax perpetuated on the American public since the synthetic fuels debacle of the early '80s."[32] In a similar vein, CEI's *Environmental Briefing Book for Congressional Candidates* states: "Recycling can also be a wasteful use of energy, time and money. . . Whether or not to recycle a particular material or product should be determined by the market place, not by government fiat."[33]

In its magazine *Facts*, the Australia Institute for Public Policy also attacks recycling. Drawing on an Industry Commission report, it argues that packaging only accounts for a tenth of the waste stream 'by weight' and that recycling can be costly and produce pollution problems. In the same issue of the magazine, the IPA argues that the amount of pollutants ingested as a result of pesticide use and water pollution are trivial compared with those occurring 'naturally'; that "enhancing the Greenhouse Effect may be necessary for our survival" because nature is not providing enough CO_2; and that the banning of DDT initiated by greens has "been accompanied by a blow out of reported malaria cases to hundreds of thousands" in Sri Lanka.[34]

Most of the conservative think-tanks also attack environmentalism in some way. In its journal *Policy Review*, the Heritage Foundation has labelled the environmental movement as "the greatest single threat to the American economy".

Several equate environmentalism to religious belief. For example Doug Bandow, Senior Policy Analyst with the Cato Institute, talks about the rise of environmental Neo-Paganism.[35] Similarly John Hyde, executive Director of the Australian IPA, says: "Nature worship is not new, and environmentalism is a religion that may currently have a greater following than any church."[36] In 1991 Ron Brunton, Director of the Institute's Environmental Unit in Canberra, gave a paper entitled *Environmentalism and Sorcery*:

> Sorcery beliefs involve the attribution of misfortune to the evil machinations of other humans. These beliefs invariably worsen the problems they are meant to be addressing. They drive people to an obsessive search for scapegoats, to a focus on the wrong causes and the wrong solutions. They create and perpetuate distrust, and so corrode the basis for social co-operation.[37]

Brunton also suggests that 'greens' are, in reality, ambivalent about environmental improvements: "How else can we explain what has happened to John Todd, the director of Ocean Arks International, who developed a process for transforming toxic sludge into drinkable water? Greens are furious with him, and some of his old friends no longer speak to him."[38]

Paralysis by Analysis

Having succeeded in persuading decision-makers that environmental problems are uncertain and not in urgent need of remedy, think-tanks have cleared the path for a challenge to environmental regulations. Nowhere has this challenge been so effective as in the US Congress. The Republicans' 'Contract with America', which was heavily influenced by think-tanks such as the Heritage Foundation, included a number of measures aimed at repealing existing environmental regulations, preventing new ones with a moratorium on new regulations and disabling the authorities that enforce environmental regulations.

For example Congress has passed appropriations riders aimed at inhibiting the ability of government agencies to implement environmental and other regulations, and now the Heritage Foundation is urging the Senate to also pass them:

> The most promising short-term solution is to use the appropriations process to restrict the use of government funds to pursue questionable regulations until a general overhaul of the regulatory process can be achieved. Such riders not only would cool the regulatory zeal of federal agencies, but also encourage the Administration to show more cooperation in negotiating substantive reform.[39]

In an article supporting the anti-environmental legislation, published in the conservative magazine *Insight on the News*, Hank Cox quoted the Heritage Foundation as estimating "the cost of federal regulations to the economy at $500 billion a year, or $5,000 per household". He applauded the legislation as part of a "three-pronged attack from Congress" that would "curtail regulatory activities across the board" and "force staff reductions, impeding the ability of agencies to enforce existing regulations."[40]

Newt Gingrich, leader of the Republicans in Congress, was reported in the *Wall Street Journal* as saying that US environmental policies over the past two decades were "absurdly expensive" and that the US EPA "may well be the biggest job-killing agency in the inner city in America today." Newt and his fellow Republicans have passed the Job Creation and Wage Enhancement Act, its title reflecting Republican assertions that environmental and other regulations inhibit investment and entrepreneurial activity. It too is stalled in the Senate.

Part of the Job Creation and Wage Enhancement Act is the Risk Assessment and Cost-Benefit Act of 1995, which requires that government agencies undertake a full risk assessment and cost benefit analysis before any major rule can be introduced in future. This legislation is aimed at stalling and discouraging environmental regulations, as is the takings legislation (which conservative think-tanks also support—see Chapter Two).

The Act requires that for the introduction of major rules likely to result in an annual cost of $25 million or more a risk assessment should be carried out that discusses all the relevant scientific literature, discusses and explains the differences between them, the methodology used and assumptions made and why they were decided upon, and characterizes the risk. The risk characterisation should include estimates of risk with upper and lower bounds, exposure scenarios and comparisons with other risks that people are familiar with. All this should be carried out even before the cost-benefit analysis is to be done. In some cases, a full peer review would also have to be done.

The Act has been labelled by Carol Browner, head of the US Environmental Protection Agency (EPA), as a "full frontal assault on protecting public health and the environment". Browner estimates that the EPA, one of several agencies affected by the legislation, would need 980 new employees and more than $220 million just to comply with the risk assessment requirements of the Act. The EPA took almost four years and $4 million to produce a risk assessment on dioxin (see Chapter Nine). Peter Montague, from the US Environmental Research Foundation, argues that the Act would "effectively end government regulation of health, safety and environment" because of the magnitude of the work involved. He estimates that under the Act "we can't imagine any regulations passing in less than a decade."

David Michaud, Director of the US Office of Grassroots Action, claims that if the Act had existed twenty years ago, "the federal government could not have banned lead from gasoline, DDT from agriculture or required automobile companies to install seat belts." Former Senator Edmund Muskie, one of the main authors of the original Clean Air and Clean Water Acts, claims the new Act "would halt twenty-five years of accomplishment and turn the clock back to the days when the special interests made the rules and people absorbed the risks."

The legislation has been heavily promoted by the conservative think-tanks. The Competitive Enterprise Institute, for example, has claimed that effective regulatory reform requires "an across-the-board requirement that the benefits of any rule be shown to exceed the risks" and "rules based on hypothetical threats to human health and safety be supported by a preponderance of evidence."[41] In order to do this, it argues, "The EPA should be required to perform a cost/benefit analysis of each and every regulation to ensure that costs of complying with clean water regulation do not outweigh their benefits."

CEI also argues that if the EPA sets standards then it should also provide the money to pay for their implementation and "refrain from imposing unfunded mandates". Additionally, risk assessment would overcome what the CEI sees as the way "regulatory policy has too often evolved in reaction to popular panic to sensational fear stories in the media, not in response to sound science. As a result billions of dollars are wasted every year in battling problems that are not considered dangerous. . ."[42]

Similarly, Shanahan from the Heritage Foundation argues:

> To determine if the world should buy an expensive insurance policy against global warming, the probability of harm occurring must be multiplied by the likely magnitude of the harm. If the resulting expected harm is higher than the economic and social cost, then buying an insurance policy makes sense. If the expected harm is lower than the cost, it does not make sense to do so. Although it is difficult, if not impossible, precisely to quantify the expected harm from global warming, lawmakers must attempt this calculation if they are to develop sensible, cost-effective policies.[43]

In a report entitled *Breach of Faith: How the Contract's Fine Print Undermines America's Environmental Success*, the US National Resources Defense Council (NRDC) found that the new Act would "expressly override the health and environmental protection mandates of the Clean Air Act, the Clean Water Act, the Safe Drinking Water Act, the Endangered Species Act, and virtually all other environmental laws". The NRDC and others are particularly concerned about the bureaucratic requirements of the Act; the Californian-based Global Action and Information Network has labelled it "paralysis by analysis".

Free-Market Environmentalism

Perhaps the most pervasive influence of the ideas promoted by conservative think-tanks in the environmental policy arena has been in the adoption in many countries of elements of free-market environmentalism, particularly market-based approaches to environmental problems. In the name of free-market environmentalism, conservative think-tanks have enabled the conservative, corporate agenda of deregulation, privatization and an unconstrained market to be dressed up as an environmental virtue.

Conservative think-tanks have consistently opposed government regulation and promoted the virtues of a 'free' market unconstrained by a burden of red tape. They have recommended using the market to allocate scarce environmental resources such as wilderness and clean air and replacing legislation with voluntary industry agreements, reinforced or newly created property rights and economic instruments.

They have tried to discredit environmental legislation, giving it the pejorative label 'command and control', and highlighting its deficiencies and ineffectiveness

(ineffectiveness that corporations and some think-tanks have done their best to ensure). The Cato Institute, for example, states that one of its main focuses in the area of natural resources is "dismantling the morass of centralized command-and-control environmental regulation and substituting in its place market-oriented regulatory structures."[44] Anderson and Leal, from the Pacific Research Institute for Public Policy, a San Francisco-based think-tank, say that "free-market environmentalism emphasizes the importance of human institutions that facilitate rather than discourage the evolution of individual rights." They argue that even if legislation improves environmental quality it is at the expense of "individual freedom and liberty".[45]

While legislation is aimed at directly changing the behaviour of polluters by outlawing or limiting certain practices, market-based policies let the polluters decide whether to pollute or not. Polluters are not told what to do; rather, they find it a bit more expensive to continue in their old practices and they have a choice about how and whether they change those practices.

Neoclassical economists have long argued that the "most effective means of dealing with environmental problems is to subject them to the discipline of the market mechanism."[46] They argue that environmental degradation has resulted from the failure of the market system to put any value on the environment, even though it does serve economic functions and does provide economic and other benefits. Some environmental resources—such as timber, fish and minerals—are bought and sold in the market, but their price usually does not reflect the true cost of obtaining them because the damage to the environment has not been included. Other environmental resources such as clean air are not given a price at all, and are therefore viewed by economists as free.

These economists argue that environmental assets tend to be overused or abused because they are too cheap. Their solution is to create a pricing mechanism so that environmental values are internalized by businesses that harm the environment: the extra costs involved in price-based economic instruments such as charges, taxes and subsidies are supposed to provide an incentive to change environmentally damaging behaviour. Such pricing mechanisms are also supposed to prevent the depletion of natural resources. John Hood, a visiting fellow at the Heritage Foundation and Vice-President of the John Locke Foundation, maintains:

> For natural resources over which property rights are relatively easy to establish, such as oil, minerals, or timber, prices serve as an early warning signal to companies about scarcity. If the price is rising, that suggests more demand for the resources than can be met by available supply. Companies then have a financial incentive either to find new supplies or to reduce its need by developing alternatives or ferreting out waste. This market process amounts to a sort of ongoing environmental research project seeking an answer to this question: What is the most efficient and least resource-depleting method of producing the goods and services people need?[47]

Some think-tank economists also argue that there is little incentive to protect environmental resources that are not privately owned; their solution is to create property rights over parts of the environment that are currently free. Rights-based economic instruments such as tradeable pollution rights, for example, "create rights to use environmental resources, or to pollute the environment, up to a predetermined limit" and allow these rights to be traded.[48] Rights-based measures are also a way of providing a pricing mechanism for environmental resources.

A 'proper' price places environmental resources beyond the reach of those who wish to exploit them, or, at the very least, ensures that the social benefits of exploitation exceed the social costs, however these benefits and costs are measured. Accordingly the solution to environmental problems becomes one of 'marketising' the environment through the creation of markets in pollution rights, imposing taxes or subsidies so that prices reflect social costs and awarding quotas of right to pollute.[49]

Both price- and rights-based measures are market-based. In the first case, an economist would say that a price is set and demand determines the quantity of emissions that are released. In the second case, the quantity of emissions is set and demand determines the price to be paid to discharge them.[50]

The preference for market solutions is an ideologically based one:

Its first pillar comes squarely out of a philosophical tradition that grew from Adam Smith's notion that individual pursuit of self-interest would, in a regime of competitive markets, maximize the social good. That tradition is so firmly embedded in economics by now that most economists probably do not realize, unless they venture out into the world of noneconomists, that it is a proposition of moral philosophy. . .[51]

The theory behind the use of economic instruments for pollution control has been present in economic texts for decades, but it is only in recent years that governments of Western nations have come to embrace and promote them. Governments have traditionally favoured legislative instruments over economic instruments for achieving environmental policy. This has been the case because economic instruments were thought to be too indirect and uncertain (aimed at altering conditions in which decisions are made rather than directly prescribing decisions).

Governments have been concerned that additional charges would fuel inflation, and might have the undesirable distributional effect of most severely hitting low-income groups. They have been concerned that the public might see charges as giving companies a 'right to pollute' which they had paid for. Similarly, businesses have preferred direct regulation because of concerns that charges would increase their costs, and also because of perceptions that they would be able to have more influence on legislation through negotiation and delay. For some economic instruments such as carbon or energy taxes, this is still the case; some conservative think-tanks also oppose such taxes, despite their ideological preference for market instruments. The Competitive Enterprise Institute argues that "Energy taxes would weaken US industry and destroy jobs. . .Taxing energy will hurt these industries and compromise America's competitiveness."[52]

During the late 1980s, awareness of global and local environmental problems led to increasing demands from environmental and citizen groups for tightened environmental standards, and for increased government control of private firms and corporations. The market solutions being advocated by conservative think-tanks provided corporations and private firms with an alternative to restrictive legislation, and the rhetoric to make the argument against that legislation in terms that were not obviously self-interested.

Although economists have long advocated economic instruments for environmental regulation, their popularity today owes much to the work of think-tanks, who have effectively marketed and disseminated these policies. Think-tanks have popularized and promoted the work of environmental economists, and many of the leading scholars in this area are associated with them, including Robert Hahn, a resident scholar of the American Enterprise Institute and one of the foremost proponents of tradeable pollution rights; Terry Anderson, who has written for several think-tanks in Australia and the US; Robert Stavins and Bradley Whitehead, authors of a Progressive Policy Institute study; as well as Alan Moran, from the Tasman Institute, an Australian think-tank, and Walter Block from the Fraser Institute, a Canadian think-tank.[53]

Think-tanks have also produced a number of books promoting free-market environmentalism. These include *Free Market Environmentalism*, published by the Pacific Research Institute for Public Policy in 1991; *Reconciling Economics and the Environment*, published by the Australian Institute for Public Policy in 1991; and *Markets, Resources and the Environment*, published by the Tasman Institute in 1991, which argues that "growth, capitalism and markets are fundamental to the achievement of environmental quality."[54] The Australian Centre for Independent Studies has published a book by Barry Maley which "shows how a framework of markets and property rights, and not a top-down command-and-control approach, will best serve human interests" and ensure a healthy environment.[55]

The changing consensus wrought by conservatives has meant that economic instruments, once associated with market economists and conservative bureaucrats, have now been widely accepted. In 1978 Washington-based government officials were interviewed about their attitudes to economic instruments. Their responses indicated that their opinions about economic instruments were based on ideological arguments:

> Proponents of charges were endorsing, in a general ideological way, 'the market', and excoriating government and bureaucrats: opponents of charges were uneasy about or hostile to 'the market' and more convinced of the necessity for the government, bureaucrats and all.[56]

The survey found that Republicans tended to be pro-economic instruments, and Democrats tended to be opposed to them. However the influence of think-tanks has been so pervasive that free-market environmentalism is no longer confined to the Republican party in the US, the Tories in the UK and the Liberal Party in Australia. Prior to becoming President, Democrat Bill Clinton said in 1992 that he believed it was "time for a new era in environmental protection which used the market to help us get our environment on track—to recognize that Adam Smith's invisible hand can have a green thumb. . ."[57]

In 1991 the OECD issued guidelines for applying economic instruments,

and an Economic Incentives Task force was established by the US EPA "to identify new areas in which to apply market-based approaches".[58] Similar units have
been established in regulatory agencies in other countries, including Australia. At
the Earth Summit in Rio in 1992, business groups pushed for the wider use of
economic instruments in conjunction with self-regulation.[59]

The fact is that many environmentalists have been persuaded by the rhetoric
of free-market environmentalism. They have accepted the conservative definition
of the problem, that environmental degradation results from a failure of the
market to attach a price to environmental goods and services, and the argument
that these instruments will work better than outdated 'command-and-control'
type regulations.[60] The US Environmental Defense Fund has been at the forefront
of the push for tradeable pollution rights, and the Natural Resources Defense
Council has also supported them.

Resurrecting the Market and Reinforcing Property Rights

Environmentalists have willingly accepted that "all possible instruments at our
disposal should be considered on their merits in achieving our policy objectives,
without either ideological or neoclassically-inspired theoretical judgement."[61] In
reality, the ideological and political shaping of these instruments has been hidden
behind a mask of neutrality. Stavins and Whitehead have argued that "market-
based environmental policies that focus on the means of achieving policy goals
are largely neutral with respect to the selected goals and provide cost-effective
methods for reaching those goals."[62]

Far from being a neutral tool, the promotion of market-based instruments is
viewed by many of its advocates as a way of resurrecting the role of the market in
the face of environmental failure. They claim that economic instruments provide
a means by which the power of the market can be harnessed to environmental
goals. They serve a political purpose in that they reinforce the role of the 'free
market' at a time when environmentalism most threatens it. For example, publications from the British Institute of Economic Affairs have argued:

> The pursuit of profit in a capitalist economy leads to a husbanding of resources.
> Mature capitalist economies use less resources to produce the equivalent level of
> output and hence do less damage to the environment.[63]

According to the Heritage Foundation's policy analyst John Shanahan, the
free market is a conservation mechanism: "By denying ourselves material wealth
today, by slowing the accumulation of wealth, we are denying our children. You
deny the future by not using resources now."[64] In 1993 Shanahan wrote to
President-elect Clinton urging him to use markets and property rights "where
possible to distribute environmental 'goods' efficiently and equitably", rather
than by using legislation. He argued that "the longer the list of environmental
regulations, the longer the unemployment lines."[65] Similarly, John Hood has
argued in the Heritage Foundation's magazine *Policy Review* that "corporations
pursuing profit have as much chance of generating environmental benefits as

regulators or environmental activists do—particularly when they are faced with prices for waste disposal that are as close to cost as possible."[66]

Market-based measures grant the highest decision-making power over environmental quality to those who currently make production decisions. A market system gives power to those most able to pay. Corporations and firms, rather than citizens or environmentalists, will have the choice about whether to pollute (and pay the charges or buy credits to do so) or clean up. Tradeable pollution rights mean that permission to pollute is auctioned to the highest bidder.[67] Very polluting or dirty industries can stay in business if they can afford the pollution charges or can buy up credits. In this way, companies can choose whether or not to change production processes, introduce innovations to reduce their emissions or just pay to continue polluting.

Anderson and Leal juxtapose the market with the political process as a means of allocating environmental resources and argue that the political process is inefficient, that is it doesn't reach the 'optimal' level of pollution, that is the level of pollution where costs are minimized:

> If markets produce 'too little' clean water because dischargers do not have to pay for its use, then political solutions are equally likely to produce 'too much' clean water because those who enjoy the benefits do not pay the cost. . . Just as pollution externalities can generate too much dirty air, political externalities can generate too much water storage, clear-cutting, wilderness, or water quality. . . Free market environmentalism emphasizes the importance of market processes in determining optimal amounts of resource use.[68]

'Too much' clean water, it seems, is where the company polluting the water has to pay too much to clean up the mess they make. It involves a judgement that costs to the company are somehow synonymous with costs to the community and therefore can be weighed against benefits to the community.

Free market environmentalism and rights-based economic instruments are also promoted by the conservative think-tanks because they reinforce the idea of property rights. The CEI "aggressively promotes free-market environmentalism" because of its belief that "where individual property rights exist in environmental resources, the environment is most likely to be protected."[69]

> America has long been known as a nation where private homes and backyards are beautiful but politically managed parks and streets are a mess. For some the answer is to raise taxes to better support the 'cash starved' public sector. For others the answer will be found in stringent regulations covering every aspect of modern society. A better approach would be to discover what makes homes and backyards beautiful and apply the lessons to problem areas. Rather than bureaucratize the environment, we should privatize our efforts to protect the environment. . . behind every tree should stand a private steward, a private owner, willing and legally enabled to protect that resource.[70]

The British IEA also argues that property rights can help to protect the environment: "The legislation of rhino horn will fail without certain institutional changes, such as greater recognition of private property rights. . . Ideally, most rhinos should be privately owned, and ranched to supply their horn and other products to market."[71]

Economic instruments are being advocated as a technocratic solution to environmental problems, premised on the conservative think-tank's view of the problem—that environmental degradation is caused by a failure to 'value' the environment and a lack of properly defined property rights. By allowing this redefinition of environmental problems, environmentalists and others not only forestall criticism of the market system but in fact implicitly agree that an extension of markets is the only way to solve the problem. As White argues:

> Within this framework of general acceptance of the 'market', the issues of 'capitalist development' and 'ecological sustainability' have tended to congeal around the theme of *environmental costs* and how best to reduce these. The social relations of the market itself are not brought into question; the solution is not seen as involving a major social transformation or radical economic restructuring.[72]

Yet the market, far from being free or operating efficiently to allocate resources in the interests of society, is dominated by a small group of large multinational corporations which aim to maximize their private profit by exploiting nature and human resources.

Chapter 7

The Public Relations Industry

Modern public relations dates back to at least the 1930s, when Edward Bernays "convinced corporate America that changing the public's opinion—using PR techniques—about troublesome social movements and labour unions, was far more effective than hiring goons to club people."[1] Bernays had worked for the wartime propaganda commission in the US, and wrote up his ideas in articles with titles like *Manipulating Public Opinion* and *The Engineering of Consent*, which described the "application of scientific principles and tried practices in the task of getting people to support ideas and programs".[2]

Bernays argued that the essence of democracy was "the freedom to persuade and suggest". He explained that experience during the first World War had shown business people that "the great public could now be harnessed to their cause as it had been harnessed during the war to the national cause, and the same methods could do the job."[3]

One of the early organizations to take advantage of these methods was the National Association of Manufacturers (NAM), the leading US business organization in the earlier part of this century. NAM had already been investigated by a committee of Congress in 1913 for mass dissemination of propaganda aimed at "influencing legislation by influencing public opinion". By the end of the second world war, NAM was able to boast that every day "one or more news stories about NAM appears in newspapers in some part of the country and often in all newspapers in all parts of the country. . ." NAM also spread its pro-business, anti-union and anti-reform message through advertisements and talks, and by the distribution of millions of pamphlets to employees, students and community leaders.[4]

These techniques were also used by individual firms and trade associations; by 1949 *Fortune* magazine was moved to observe: "The daily tonnage output of propaganda and publicity. . . has become an important force in American life. Nearly half of the contents of the best newspapers is derived from publicity releases; nearly all the contents of the lesser papers. . . are directly or indirectly the work of PR departments."[5]

Today public relations is a multi-billion dollar industry. In 1991 the top fifty US-based public relations companies charged over $1,700,000,000 in fees. The industry employs almost 200,000 people in the US; there are more public relations personnel than news reporters. More than 5,400 companies and 500 trade associations have public relations departments, and there are over 5,000 PR agencies in the US alone. The government also employs thousands of people in Public Affairs. PR has gradually replaced advertising in the corporate marketing budget: advertising now makes up less than a third of the money spent on marketing in the US, compared with two-thirds in 1980.[6]

Public relations has also boomed elsewhere in the English-speaking world. The PR industry in the UK, one of the largest outside the US, employs more than 48,000 people, most of them in London. The boundaries between the US and the UK are not clear as some major American PR companies are owned by British companies, and there is increasing partnership between firms in each country. In Australia there are now 2,400 full members of the Public Relations Institute of Australia, membership having increased rapidly over the last three years.[7]

In recent years PR firms have increasingly turned their attention to environmental affairs. Environmental public relations or 'greenwash', as environmentalists call it, dates back to the 1960s. When Rachel Carson's *Silent Spring* was published in 1962, Monsanto responded by distributing to assorted media outlets a parody of Carson's book entitled *The Desolate Year*. Velsicol Chemical Company, manufacturer of DDT, sued Carson's publisher and Bruce Harrison, now owner of a major environmental PR firm with clients such as Monsanto and Dow Chemicals, helped distribute thousands of damning book reviews on behalf of the Agricultural Chemical Association.[8]

By 1990 US firms were spending about $500 million a year on PR advice about how to green their images and deal with environmental opposition. By 1995 that figure had increased to a spend of about $1 billion per year on environmental PR activities. There are now at least forty-two firms in the US specialising in environmental PR, the top fifteen of which collected about $90 million in fees in 1993 for their environmental work.[9] The top seven firms providing environmental PR are shown below:

Net income from environmental PR in 1993	
Burson-Marsteller	$17,959,000
Ketchum PR	15,300,000
Hill and Knowlton	10,000,000
Fleishman-Hillard	9,125,000
Shandwick	6,689,000
E. Bruce Harrison Co.	6,550,991
Edelman PR Worldwide	5,501,000

Source: Bleifuss 1995, p. 4

A survey conducted in 1993 by the Opinion Research Corporation, asking US executives what the key public relations challenges for 1994 would be, found that twenty-three per cent of the 248 respondents named environmental issues (more than any other topic), whereas only twenty-one per cent named the promoting of the company image.[10]

Bruce Harrison, who runs a firm specialising in environmental PR, suggests three reasons for the rise of environmental PR. Firstly he says that "negative images of industrial accidents and environmental disasters coupled with the media's bias toward green advocacy are shaping public perceptions." Secondly, information about companies that used to be kept secret, including emissions data, is now legally required to be made public, which can damage a corporation's reputation. Thirdly, polls show that three-quarters of the population in the US consider themselves environmentalists, and most of these self-proclaimed environmentalists are not prepared to trust business to protect the environment.[11]

PR professionals are being used to counter these negative perceptions of business, caused in most cases by their poor environmental performance. Rather than substantially change business practices so as to earn a better reputation, many firms are turning to PR professionals to create one for them. After all, "It is easier and less costly to change the way people think about reality than it is to change reality."[12]

Good PR can forestall the demand for tough regulation of corporations. An internal General Motors document stated that "GM Public Relations helps to make GM so well-accepted by its various publics that it may pursue its corporate mission unencumbered by public-imposed limitations or regulations." Similarly, Jeff and Marie Blyskal point out in their book on PR that, "because of good image PR, a new DuPont chemical plant would probably be welcomed into a community more warmly than, say, a new plant for Hooker Chemical, whose dark Love Canal reputation precedes it."[13]

The shallowness of green PR became evident when PR professionals rejoiced at the Republicans' gaining control of the US Congress at the end of 1994. The trade publication *O'Dwyer's* suggested that relief was in sight "on the environmental front". One PR expert reportedly said: "There is a new contract on the street. And although the word 'environment' is never mentioned, many observers believe it's less a contract with America than a 'contract on environmental busybodies'." *O'Dwyer's* advised environmental PR people to "ride the Republican-fueled anti-environmental backlash wave as far as possible" but not to overdo it in case the "greenies are again on the rise".[14]

Environmental PR involves the use of the media, educational institutions, community forums, conferences and talk-back radio. These more traditional forums are also being supplemented with many more made possible by emerging technologies:

> Satellite feeds, customized and localized 800-numbers and telemarketing capabilities, computer bulletin boards, advanced mail list merge/purge capabilities, CD ROM publishing, simultaneous multi-location fax transmission, videobrochures, interactive video, electronic couponing, and home shopping networks didn't exist a decade ago. All these technologies represent ways to reach audiences more directly and efficiently than ever before.[15]

Whereas in the past PR used to be mainly about publicity, about a third of environmental PR is nowadays about strategic counselling—shaping public and government perceptions of environmental problems and finding ways to counter environmentalists and environmental regulations. These days, public relations firms perform such diverse tasks as forming grassroots organizations for their clients (see Chapter Two) and gathering information on activists and journalists (see next chapter).

Large Public Relations Firms

Hill and Knowlton and Burson-Marsteller are perhaps the two largest and most influential public relations firms in the world. Hill and Knowlton, with fifty offices in twenty countries, has more than 1,200 employees and works with more than seventy associate companies.[16] Burson-Marsteller has sixty-three offices in thirty-two countries and 1,700 employees worldwide. The services each offers range from public relations to political lobbying, grassroots organising and gathering intelligence on environmental activists. For work such as this they make hundreds of millions of dollars each year.[17]

Hill and Knowlton's clients have included governments from all over the world including Turkey, Peru, Israel, Egypt, Indonesia, Slovenia, the Czech Government, the Duvalier regime in Haiti and the People's Republic of China after Tiananmen Square.[18] Burson-Marsteller has represented national governments including Nigeria during the Biafran War, Romania during the reign of Nicolae Ceausescu, the ruling military junta of Argentina in the late 1970s and the South Korean government.[19]

Each firm advises Wise Use groups in the US and Canada, as well as a range of transnational corporations. Both have been involved in protecting some of the worst industries of our times, downplaying the health effects of smoking on behalf of the Tobacco Institute, keeping public concern at a minimum after the Three Mile Island nuclear accident, and helping to clean up Exxon's image after the Exxon Valdez oil spill.[20]

Hill and Knowlton have helped to keep petrol taxes low on behalf of the American Petroleum Institute, have campaigned for deregulation for the American Truckers Association, been retained by apple growers to fight claims about Alar, worked with the American Association of Advertising Agencies to clean up the image of advertising, helped the National Conference of Catholic Bishops oppose abortion, and advised supporters of the Rev. Sun Myung Moon.[21] Burson-Marsteller has helped corporations out of crises such as the Bhopal disaster (Union Carbide) and the Dalkon Shield IUD controversy (A.H.Robins).[22]

Hill and Knowlton tells potential clients: "If your company or organisation faces a challenge from central, state or local government, you will need to campaign. Hill and Knowlton's worldwide Public Affairs practice organizes campaigns which draw on professional expertise in policy forecasting, media relations, grassroots communications and direct political advocacy." Additionally, Hill and Knowlton helps companies to identify and create sponsorship opportunities in areas such as education, conservation and charity.[23]

Burson-Marsteller claims to be able to help clients all over the world to counteract activist groups. In Australia, its work on behalf of clients such as the National Association of Forest Industries and various developers has raised the ire of environmental activists. Protesters representing several environmental groups occupied their offices at the end of 1995 to draw attention to their "dealings with woodchipping and freeway-building clients".[24]

In preparation for the Earth Summit in 1992, the newly formed Business

Council for Sustainable Development (BCSD), a coalition of about fifty multi-national corporations, hired Burson-Marsteller to "make sure the corporate view-point was well-stated and well received" at the Summit. Burson-Marsteller issued a press release for the BCSD, announcing that the Business Council would be playing a key role in the Rio Summit. It explained that the head of the Council, Stephan Schmidheiny, had been appointed principal adviser for business and industry to Maurice Strong, the Summit's organizer. Strong had no other special advisers and other interest groups had to submit proposals using formal chan-nels.[25] Joyce Nelson, author of the book *Sultans of Sleaze: Public Relations and the Media*, observes:

> With the able assistance of public relations giant Burson-Marsteller, a very élite group of business people (including B-M itself) was seemingly able to plan the agenda for the Earth Summit with little interference from NGOs or government leaders.[26]

Organized business interests such as the Business Council, Burson-Marsteller and the dozens of business lobbyists and trade associations that registered for the summit's preparatory conferences were able to influence the outcomes of the Earth Summit and avoid effective environmental reforms. The Earth Summit agreements support free trade; avoid specific measures such as greenhouse gas emission reductions; avoid any reference to overconsumption by affluent nations; and perhaps of most relevance, avoid mentioning transnational companies, let alone controls over them.[27]

The Earth Summit was a follow-up to the World Commission on Environment and Development, referred to as the Brundtland Commission after its chair Gro Harlem Brundtland. Nelson has pointed to the connections between Burson-Marsteller and the Trilateral Commission, a sort of top level international think-tank founded in 1973 by David Rockefeller and Zbigniew Brzezinski. It has more than 300 élite members made up of former, present and future national leaders including George Bush, and corporation heads, bankers and politicians from the US, Canada, Europe and Japan. Holy Sklar, in her book on Trilateralism, says its purpose is to protect the power of the international ruling class "whose locus of power is the global corporation"; to co-opt the Third World; and to reintegrate communist countries.[28]

Nelson claims that the Trilateral Commission had at least four members in common with the Brundtland Commission, including Maurice Strong, organizer of the Earth Summit, and Jim MacNeill, the principal author of *Our Common Future*, the Brundtland Commission's report on sustainable development. Also, according to Nelson, many transnational corporations that are members of the Business Council for Sustainable Development are also represented on the Trilateral Commission, including Dow, DuPont, Royal Dutch Shell, Browning-Ferris Industries, Mitsubishi, Nippon Steel, Nissan Motor and 3M. Similarly, many of Burson-Marsteller's clients are represented on the Trilateral Commission, and the North American chair of the Trilateral Commission heads up Burson-Marsteller's Canadian operations.[29]

The interest of the Trilateral Commission in sustainable development and the

Earth Summit is clarified in a book published by the Trilateral Commission and written by Jim MacNeill of the Brundtland Commission. In it, MacNeill explains how most urban/industrial regions depend on environmental resources in other places, such as developing countries.

> In essence, the ecological shadow of a country is the environmental resources it draws from other countries and the global commons. If a nation without much geographical resilience had to do without its shadow ecology, even for a short period, its people and economy would suffocate. . . Western nations heavily engaged in global sourcing should be aware of their shadow ecologies and the need to pursue policies that will sustain them.[30]

Nelson also connects the Trilateral Commission with the Wise Use Movement in the US and the Share movement in Canada. She says that Laurance Rockefeller, brother of the founder of the Trilateral Commission David Rockefeller, promoted the multiple-use movement from the early 1960s when he inducted business leaders into it. Some of the key funders of the modern Wise Use Movement are members of the Trilateral Commission and also clients of Burson-Marsteller.[31]

Public Relations and the Media

One of the oldest and most used public relations tools, despite changes in technologies, is still the press release or the news release. These include news, feature stories, bulletins and other announcements which flood media offices. Their purpose is to develop and maintain public goodwill, as well as favourable government policies, for the organization that issues them. The press release was invented by Ivy Lee, one of the earliest of modern public relations experts, whose clients included the Pennsylvania Railway. When there was an accident, instead of trying to cover it up he issued a press release as a way to keep the media on side and to influence the way the accident was reported.[32]

Such press releases were so successful that other railways soon followed suit. By the late 1940s almost half the news was based on press releases from public relations departments and firms. After the war, Bernays supplemented the press release with press conferences, press tours, photo opportunities and pre-arranged interviews, all staged to provide reportable events for the media. These 'pseudo events' make up an increasing proportion of the news today.[33]

Although many news releases do not result in a news story, enough succeed to ensure that much of the news people read or watch on television is manufactured by PR firms rather than discovered by journalists. Most journalists rely on these sources to supply the "raw material of their craft, regular, reliable and useable information".[34] This flow of 'free' information saves the journalist time and effort finding stories to write about. Yet it is very difficult for the public to be able to distinguish real news from PR-generated news.

News stories are frequently copied straight from news releases; at other times they are rephrased and sometimes augmented with additional material. A study of the *Wall Street Journal* found that more than half the *Journal's* news stories were based entirely on press releases. These stories appeared to be written by their own journalists but were hardly changed from the press releases.[35] This practice does not vary much between large and small papers, as larger papers need more stories and smaller papers have fewer staff to write stories. According to various studies, press releases are the basis for forty to fifty per cent of the news content of US newspapers.[36]

The art of PR is to 'create news'; to turn what are essentially advertisements into a form that fits news coverage and makes a journalist's job easier while at the same time promoting the interests of the client. Ironically, this is often far cheaper than paying for expensive television advertisements—that many people 'zap' with their remote controls anyway. Public relations people, many of whom started their careers as journalists, are able to turn their promotional material into a news story that is of interest to journalists, to time it so that it has most impact, and to target it at appropriate journalists. "In other words, behind the media gatekeepers is another whole level of information gatekeepers who are skilled in that most modern of projects, media relations and the making of 'reportable events'."[37]

The reporting of news releases and pre-planned events by the media has three significant advantages to public relations firms. Firstly, it gives credibility and legitimacy to what might otherwise be seen as self-serving publicity or advertising, by giving it the appearance of being news delivered through the agency of an 'independent' third party—the media. While the public will be cautious about what they hear in an advertisement, they put more faith in a news broadcast. In this case the media, with its profile of truth-seeker, serves the role that corporate front groups or think-tanks fulfil for corporations; they put the corporate view while appearing to be independent of the corporations that will gain from it.

Secondly, news releases and packaged news events are advantageous for PR because they displace investigative reporting. The reliance of journalists on sources such as PR personnel and government officials is referred to as source journalism, as opposed to investigative journalism. By providing the news feedstock, they cause reporters to react rather than initiate. Journalists who are fed news stories are less likely to go looking for their own stories, which could bring negative publicity. Even the minority of newspaper stories that are the outcome of investigative journalism are often based on interviews which rely on access to important persons arranged through PR people.

Thirdly, public information officers, corporate spokespeople and PR firms appreciate that "the media set the public agenda of issues by filtering and shaping reality rather than by simply reflecting it."[38] By being the primary source of a journalist's information on a particular story, PR people can influence the way the story is told and who tells it. They also put journalists in touch with 'selected' experts to ensure their viewpoint is backed up by an 'impartial' authority in the news story. PR advice to corporations and industry associations is usually to develop, train and even put on retainer, "credible outside experts to act as 'news sources' for journalists".[39]

What the press release does is to establish lines of control regarding information. It initiates the news-making process, and sets ideal boundaries around what is to be known by emphasizing some information and leaving out other information. . . what the public-relations practitioner must do is establish the framework for the event, the language by which it will be discussed and reported, and the emphasis to be maintained.[40]

Public relations-based news stories are "more likely to reflect positively on the organization providing the information and to reflect its issue agenda" than non PR-based stories.[41] Jeff and Marie Blyskal, in their book *PR: How the Public Relations Industry Writes the News*, explain why:

> Good PR is rather like the placement of a fish-eye lens in front of the reporter. The facts the PR man wants the reporter to see front and center through the lens appear bigger than normal. Other facts, perhaps opposing ones, are pushed to the side by the PR fish-eye lens and appear crowded together, confused, obscured. The reporter's entire field of vision is distorted by the PR lens.[42]

News releases do not necessarily go directly to newspapers. Often a PR service will place it with a wire service first. (Some large agencies have their own wire services.) By 1985, PR Newswire was transmitting 150 stories a day from a pool of 10,000 companies directly into 600 newsrooms belonging to newspapers, radio and television stations. Such stories may be picked up by newsrooms or rewritten by wire services such as AP, Reuters and Dow Jones. In this way the news release becomes a 'legitimate' news story and will be more likely to be taken up by journalists on the newspapers.[43]

An example of a successful public relations campaign conducted largely in the media was that of the aerosol industry which, during the 1970s, managed to forestall a ban on the use of CFC gases for several years. The $3 billion industry sought PR advice after the *New York Times* published an article putting forward the theory that aerosol use could deplete the ozone layer, causing serious public health and environmental impacts.[44]

The PR response began with a press release emphasising that the theory was just a hypothesis and not fact, which was reprinted with little change in the *New York Times*. In the ensuing campaign, many more 'news stories' were 'generated' which were favourable to the industry, in papers such as the *Wall Street Journal*, *Business Week*, *Fortune* magazine and the *Observer* in London. Briefing papers, press releases, transcripts of industry testimony and successfully placed news stories were distributed to aerosol industry people all over the country so they were able to answer media questions. They were also sent a guidebook for testifying at hearings and answering media questions.[45] For example, in answer to a question suggesting the aerosols be banned because there was a chance they would damage the stratosphere, the following answer was suggested:

> There is a slight risk that thousands of different products could be modifying the atmosphere to one degree or another. I do not think it is reasonable or proper to ban products at random to eliminate a threat that many qualified people doubt even exists.[46]

The symbol of children's story book character Chicken Little exclaiming that "The sky is falling!" was used to great effect as part of the PR campaign and reproduced in various newspaper headlines. And the industry front group, the Council on Atmospheric Sciences, retained 'independent' scientists to present their point of view in the media. CFC propellants were eventually banned in the US in 1977. Ken Makovsky, the PR man at the centre of the campaign says: "If we had not taken the offensive in this situation, the ban would have come a lot sooner, and the industry itself would have been unprepared to face market realities. . ."[47] However, in many countries the aerosol industries managed to postpone a ban for several years after this, allowing US and other manufacturers to continue putting CFCs in aerosol cans for non-US markets.

In the 1980s Hill & Knowlton gave their client US Gypsum, which was being sued for installing asbestos in public buildings in Baltimore, advice about how to deal with the media. Its strategy included planting stories in newspapers which were written "by experts sympathetic to the company's point of view", as well as news articles about how safe asbestos was. A company memo following publication of such articles in the *Detroit News* said: "Our consultant, Jack Kinney, very actively fed much of this information to the special writer, Michael Bennet."[48]

Hill & Knowlton also advised Gypsum to set up an industry group to field media inquiries, so that Gypsum wouldn't be immediately associated with media statements and criticism. It suggested that by enlisting 'independent experts' the issue of asbestos, instead of being a public health problem, could be redefined as "a side issue that is being seized on by special interests and those out to further their own causes. . . The media and other audiences important to US Gypsum should ideally say, 'Why is all this furore being raised about this product? We have a non-story here'."[49]

Modern Media Techniques

Satellite connections that enable PR people to arrange live interviews with a client all around the country or even the world are one example of the expanding technological repertoire of public relations firms. Referred to as 'satellite media tours', these enable a person to do interviews with television stations around the country without having to actually travel anywhere. The cost of satellite time used in this way can be cheaper than the cost of travel and accommodation, and TV news directors at local stations like satellite media tours because their own journalists can conduct a one-on-one interview that they can control rather than broadcasting a network distributed interview. It also means that PR firms can go direct to local stations and bypass the national networks.[50]

During the 1980s PR firms began sending out video news releases (VNRs)— fully edited news segments for broadcast as part of television news. Hill and Knowlton established its own fully staffed television production facilities (as did Burson-Marsteller) and by 1985 was already sending video news releases via satellite all over the USA, rather than relying solely on the old-fashioned press release.[51] It is popular nowadays to accompany the fully edited piece ready to be broadcast (A-roll) with unedited footage (B-roll) and a script so the television station crew can put together and edit the story as if they had shot it themselves, inserting their own journalist's voice over, or adding their own material.

Studies showing that the vast majority of Americans get most of their news from television (81% in a 1992 poll) have ensured that VNRs are now widely used by PR companies. They were used by all the presidential candidates in the 1992 elections, but are mainly used by private companies to promote a corporate point of view. Specialists in this area advise customers that a VNR "can help position your company as the authority on a certain topic, issue or industry" and allow them to "take a stance on a controversial issue". Making a VNR is cheaper than making an advertisement—$15,000-$80,000 to produce and distribute, compared with $250,000 for an advertisement—yet like other media releases, they result in news stories that are more credible than commercials because they become part of the news broadcast and are not sourced back to the company that paid for them.[52]

According to *Public Relations Journal*, "VNRs have gone beyond simply selling products and services. They're now about selling ideas, changing and influencing viewer behaviour, and shaping public opinion." Similarly a Hill & Knowlton executive said in 1994 that "We're seeing more people who have a message to get across rather than just selling a product."[53] Lee and Solomon, in their book, *Unreliable Sources*, claim that:

> Every week, hundreds of local TV stations, beset by budget and staff cutbacks, air these free, ready-made news releases, which look increasingly realistic. Even veteran media observers often fail to distinguish between video PR spots and station-produced news.[54]

The production quality of VNRs is now as good as or even better than that of local television stations and most news directors see them as a source of information rather than as a form of propaganda. One of the main distributors of video news releases, MediaLink, found in 1991 that all ninety-two newsrooms it surveyed had used VNRs from PR firms. This was confirmed by a 1993 Nielson study. Another survey in 1992 found that eighty per cent of US news directors use VNRs a few times each month.[55]

VNRs have been slower getting to other countries. At the end of 1991, Adam Shell discussed in *Public Relations Journal* whether Europe would be the next frontier for VNRs. Distribution costs were the main barrier, although even then European television producers were using them occasionally. By 1994, however, a MediaLink survey found that eighty-seven per cent of European broadcasters thought VNRs helpful, and thirty per cent broadcast more than ten per month; in addition, sixty per cent of European PR people wanted pan-European VNRs and thirty per cent wanted US distribution.[56]

When the Australian Liberal Party used them for regional television stations in its 1996 election campaign, they were fairly new to Australia. Jonathan Raymond from MediaLink in Australia told ABC Radio that there was already a tradition of sending background video information to television stations and that video news releases merely took this one step further. He explained that with the intense competition for groups to get media attention, video news releases gave his corporate customers extra leverage.[57]

As far as the television viewer is concerned, a VNR piece is done by the station's reporters and is no different from the rest of the news. However there are important differences. Pre-packaged interviews can be edited to give the best possible impression, and they avoid the possibility of probing or follow-up questions from a journalist, or impromptu and perhaps more frank responses from the interviewee. With a video release, the person being interviewed can be coached to give the 'best' answers and any 'mistakes' can be edited out before the news room sees it.

VNRs allow the corporation to influence the agenda of the news by providing footage that may otherwise be difficult to obtain (including archival, on-location and aerial footage), and all free of charge. Even if the station doesn't use the footage it is a powerful way of suggesting how the story could be put together. Stephen Claney from the Australian company Interface argues that his company assists newsrooms overcome logistical problems. He says of one instance when he sent a video news release containing interview footage:

> The newsroom simply went and re-interviewed the person, asked similar questions to ours, and then ran it in the story, using our overlay footage. So we assisted them in constructing the story, we gave them an example of someone who was worth speaking to, and showed them how it could be used. And I think that's a great result all around.[58]

However, according to Granville Williams in *Journalist*, it was the use of VNRs by Greenpeace in its campaign against the ocean disposal of the Brent Spar, Shell's oil drilling platform, that prompted British journalists to question the way that VNRs might be manipulating them. He quotes the BBC News Editor as admitting that Greenpeace was able to provide "better, more compelling and more frequent footage than we can ourselves" but that "Greenpeace exploit our thirst for a good story (particularly in the summer) and for dramatic pictures, and they play on the traditional news values of conflict and confrontation."[59]

The BBC has guidelines on use of VNRs which include the following:

• Use of material shot or supplied by a pressure group must be clearly labelled and if it is supplied in an edited form we should consider making that clear
• We should not broadcast interviews from VNRs
• We must avoid promoting a particular product or supplier[60]

Both the BBC and its rival network ITN subsequently labelled Greenpeace VNRs covering their Muroroa campaign against French nuclear testing. Yet ITN and Burson-Marsteller jointly own Corporate Television Networks (CTN), which produces VNRs for corporate and government clients such as Glaxo, Unilever and the Department of Transport.[61]

Corporate videos are seldom labelled, for example by an on-screen credit to the effect that "this video footage has been provided by company X." Such labelling has been rejected by PR people, who say their clients would not like it because they would lose the "third party endorsement a news report normally carries". Says one VNR producer, "The public could possibly misconstrue the VNR as an infomercial."[62]

Public Relations and Government

Public relations can be aimed at the general public (grassroots propaganda) or at influential members of the society such as politicians, top bureaucrats, media executives and commentators (treetops propaganda). It is the latter group which sets the terms of the debate and the political agenda. Treetops propaganda has been important in ensuring that the debate over pollution, for example, is not discussed in terms of rights to clean air, but rather in terms of the costs to the polluters of cleaning up the air and, given these costs, how clean we can reasonably expect the air to be.[63]

Government relations or lobbying is a form of PR targeted at politicians and/or bureaucrats which aims to influence the passing of legislation, its implementation, and the setting of public policy. Lobbyists can influence decision-makers by making themselves useful to them as a reliable source of information, by being the conduit for donations and favours (referred to colloquially as 'booze, blondes and bribes') or as a result of past working relationships and friendships.

In the 1970s, US public relations firms started to move into lobbying, which had previously been the province of Washington law firms. In order to do so they hired people on the basis of their political connections—who they knew and who their friends were. For this reason we find the same revolving door pattern between public relations and lobbying firms and government as we found between think-tanks and government in Chapter Five.

When the Republicans lost office in 1992 there was a mass movement of government officials to the lobbying and PR firms. Ralph Nader's group, Congress Watch, tracked 300 of them: over half moved to Washington DC lobbying and PR firms.[64] The door swings both ways, and former lobbyists often become part of government, where they have a unique opportunity to help their former clients.

Hill and Knowlton's lobbying efforts are aided by its employment of former government officials who have good access to government. Frank Mankiewicz of Hill and Knowlton says that one of his firm's strengths is being able to "get half an hour of somebody's time". One of the best known Washington lobbyists, Robert Gray, was Appointment Secretary and subsequently Cabinet Secretary for President Eisenhower before being hired by Hill and Knowlton. There he established Hill and Knowlton's lobbying operations in the 1960s at a time when public relations was seen as quite a separate activity to lobbying.[65]

When Ronald Reagan was campaigning for the Presidency in 1980, Hill and Knowlton paid Gray while he took part in the campaign, in the hope that this would provide invaluable lobbying access if Reagan was elected. As it happened Gray did not go back to work for Hill and Knowlton, but set up his own PR and lobbying firm to take advantage of the access he now had to the Reagan government. Later his firm was integrated into Hill and Knowlton's operations. It was

Gray who rehabilitated Richard Nixon from disgrace to respected 'Elder Statesman'.[66]

Apart from Gray, Hill and Knowlton is full of former government officials. A former chief of staff to George Bush was appointed head of Hill and Knowlton's US operations before leaving to become Senior Vice-President of Philip Morris. One of Hill and Knowlton's vice presidents had been a general policy adviser to Bill Clinton. Sir Bernard Ingham, Margaret Thatcher's Press Secretary from 1979-1990, is now a director of Hill and Knowlton UK. When Hill and Knowlton established a European affairs senior adviser they hired Stanley Clinton Davis, who had been a member of both the European Commission and the British Parliament.[67]

Howard Paster, who was head of Hill and Knowlton's Washington office, became one of Bill Clinton's top appointments as Director of Intergovernmental Affairs for the White House. Paster was replaced in Hill and Knowlton by Thomas Hood, one of Clinton's aides.[68] Less than a year later Paster went back to work for Hill and Knowlton as Chairman, at twice his original salary. Clinton replaced Paster with a former employee of Griffin Johnson and Associates, whose clients include the American Nuclear Council, the American Petroleum Institute, CBS, Waste Management Inc (now WMI) and the Tobacco Institute.[69] In Australia, one of former Prime Minister Bob Hawke's advisers was appointed to head Hill & Knowlton's Canberra office.[70]

Burson-Marsteller's offices, like Hill and Knowlton's, are full of ex-government officials who now lobby their former colleagues. In the 1980s they hired a number of such people, including a former press secretary to Nancy Reagan, a former press secretary to the Carter White House and a former secretary to the Senate's Democratic minority. In its publicity material, Burson-Marsteller boasts that it can target decision-makers and ensure that they are "aware not only of the *logic* in a client's point of view, but also the *political power* behind the client's position" [emphasis in original].[71]

As can be seen by Burson-Marsteller's claim, lobbying and public relations are not separate activities. Generating community support can put pressure on an undecided politician. Gray has described how he would send his people to a politician's home districts to generate public support that would influence their vote. "We can land in Topeka, Kansas, and in thirty minutes we'd be able to find and make contact with the key media people there: editors, talkback show producers, TV and radio news directors."[72] A series of newspaper editorials and statements by opinion leaders has an impact, even if the politician suspects it is generated by public relations.

Well-placed 'news' stories in the right papers such as the *Washington Post* also influence Congress. Says one PR expert: "It makes them aware of an issue. It sensitizes them to the importance of an issue, so when a PR person or lobbyist calls upon them, the Congressman knows he's being called upon for something important enough to be in the newspaper."[73]

Another means of influencing a politician, as described by John Stauber and Sheldon Rampton in their book *Toxic Sludge is Good for You!*, is to "create an artificial bubble of peer influence surrounding the targeted politician, so that the 'legislator will get the feel of total community support for an issue'." This is done by hiring one of his friends or business colleagues, someone with media contacts who is influential in the politician's electorate, to gather together a group of key business and community leaders well-connected to the politician. These people, chosen because they are sympathetic to the goals of the client for business or other reasons, then lobby the politician who gets the impression that anyone who is anyone must favour this outcome.[74]

If a politician has been persuaded in some other way to vote in a corporation's interests, he or she may still need to have some public support or at least seem to be acting in the public interest, rather than be seen to be voting on the basis of campaign donations. "You have to give your guy the ammunition to show the press that the issue he's backing is inherently something the public—specifically your target's constituents—wants," says Frank Mankiewicz from Hill & Knowlton. He suggests the easiest way to do this is with a favourable poll.[75] As shown in Chapter Two, grassroots organising can also achieve this.

And just as public relations is an important element of lobbying, lobbying is an increasingly important element of public relations.

> "The real work today is done behind the scenes on issues," says a former H&K executive. "You have people of substance going to regulators and assistant secretaries," he explains. "Then you notify the press in advance that the government is taking a certain action, and why, and who you represent, and why your client deserved to have this regulation changed. . . You make your client's story a government story, showing how the government action—by now a quiet fait accompli—has not only helped your client, but is good for the people. That's how your get the story out the right way in the media," he says smiling. . .[76]

One example of a large, concerted public relations/lobbying campaign was that conducted by the Mexican Government and US businesses to get approval for the North American Free Trade Agreement (NAFTA). These groups spent well over $25 million to promote NAFTA, "hiring a phalanx of Washington law firms, lobbyists, public relations companies and consultants" such as Burson-Marsteller. They were aided by the conservative think-tanks, the Business Roundtable, the National Association of Manufacturers and the Chamber of Commerce, as well as major and regional media outlets. Opponents included environmental groups such as Greenpeace, Friends of the Earth and the Sierra Club, who were concerned that US corporations would move to Mexico to avoid US environmental regulations.[77] Yet the opposition was never taken very seriously by the US government in the face of such well-financed and coordinated lobbying.

Another example was the campaign waged against President Clinton's health care plan by health insurance firms, conservative think-tanks and others. Between $100 million and $300 million was spent opposing the reforms to a health care system which is one of the most inequitable and wasteful in the industrialized world. This was far more money than the total spent by all the presidential candidates in 1992 in the US (or in any previous year), and in many ways resembled a presidential campaign. It was spent on lobbyists, television advertisements and a massive grassroots effort which "generated more than 450,000 personal contacts with Congress—phone calls, visits or letters—more than a thousand for every member of the House."[78]

When environmental activist Ken Saro-Wiwa and eight fellow Ogoni activists were hanged by the Nigerian government in 1995, the Nigerian government launched a public relations/lobbying campaign in the US to avoid sanctions being applied. One of the major issues about which the Ogonis were protesting was the environmental degradation caused by Shell Oil's activities in their country, which they claimed had ruined their land. According to Ron Nixon in the *Nation*, Maurice Dawkins, a paid lobbyist for the Nigerian government, played a key role in the formation and organization of three US front groups formed to support the Nigerian government—the National Coalition for Fairness to Nigeria, the National Coalition for Fairness in African Policy and Americans for Democracy in Africa. These groups paid for 'advertorials' in key newspapers such as the *New York Times* and courted the black American press.[79]

Public Relations or Propaganda?

Propaganda is often associated with dictatorships. However in a 'free society', where official bans on free speech are not tolerated, it is necessary for those who would rule to use subtle means to silence threatening ideas and suppress inconvenient facts. Public relations and propaganda play a "more covert and sophisticated role" in technologically advanced democratic countries "where the maintenance of the existing power and privileges are vulnerable to popular opinion".[80] These activities are most advanced in the United States, where advertising and manipulation of public opinion has been researched and practised more than anywhere else.

The public relations industry describes its own activities as being based on two premises:

• That in a modern democracy every organisation, from the national government to the corner store, survives ultimately only by public consent
• That the consent of the public cannot exist in a communications vacuum[81]

Early PR experts were not afraid to use the term propaganda to describe what they did. George Fitzpatrick, thought to be the first Australian PR professional, was listed in the Sydney telephone directory before the second World War as "Registered practitioner in Public persuasion, propaganda, publicity".[82]

Alex Carey, author of *Taking the Risk out of Democracy*, defines propaganda as communications aimed at getting a target audience to adopt particular attitudes and beliefs. Nowadays such activities are referred to as public relations, although even that term is becoming tarnished and some practitioners prefer to refer to their jobs using labels such as public affairs, corporate communications, media relations, issues management or even public education. But the aims have not changed. Fraser P. Seitel, in his textbook on Public Relations, says that "much

more than customers for their products, managers today desperately need constituents for their beliefs and values." Public relations provides publicity for products and services but it also sells corporate images, goals and philosophies,
political programmes, and social ideas.[83]

Propaganda aims to "persuade not through the give-and-take of argument
and debate, but through the manipulation of symbols and of our most basic
human emotions".[84] There are a number of basic propaganda techniques identified by the Institute of Propaganda Analysis, many of which are used in public
relations. Two examples of these are 'name-calling' and 'glittering generalities'.[85]

'Name-calling' involves labelling an idea or group of people so as to get others
to reject them or treat them negatively without evidence being put forward to
support such a label. For example, labelling radical environmentalists as 'ecoter-
rorists' or environmental ideas as 'communist inspired'. Alternatively, negatively
charged words like 'coercion', 'waste' or 'radical' are used to describe an idea. A
classic name-calling device used against residents protesting about the siting of an
unwanted facility in their neighbourhood is to call them NIMBY's—Not In My
Back Yard, thereby labelling them as merely self-interested. A newer acronym
used against environmental activists is Going BANANA—Build Absolutely
Nothing Anywhere Near Anything.[86]

Such labels not only seek to harm the reputation and therefore the effectiveness of opponents but they also "may convince local citizens, who fear being stig-
matized, to refrain from asking any questions. Moreover, labelling long-time
residents and neighbours who pose questions makes them appear as outsiders,
lacking authority, and easy to marginalize."[87]

'Glittering generalities' involve the use of "vague, abstract, positive terms"
such as 'common sense', 'commitment', 'democracy' and 'scientific' to win
approval for something without recourse to any evidence. It is the reverse of
name-calling. For example, the identification of the market with 'freedom of
choice' and polluting activities with 'job creation'.

Labelling and stereotyping is part of the art of propaganda, which works at a
subconscious level through symbols and dichotomies of good and evil, sacred and
satanic. Terms such as the American Way of Life come to symbolize the sacred;
propaganda seeks to associate ideas such as free enterprise with the American Way
of Life whilst labels such as communist and radical are used to conjure up notions
of evil and threats to the American Way of Life.

In an article on the internet from Public Relations Management Ltd, those
doing battle with environmentalists are advised to "find symbols around which to
wrap the message. . . The value and power of symbols can't be overstated."
Symbols suggested include "more government, higher taxes, lost jobs, ghost
towns, abandoned farmers, less individual freedom, family breakdowns, disinte-
grating social values".[88]

In Newt Gingrich's pamphlet *Language, A Key Mechanism of Control*, he
advises Republican candidates to use "positive, governing words" for themselves
and negative words for their opponents and he gives lists of such words. Positive
words include: challenge, choice, dream, family, hard work, incentive, initiative,

pride, reform, vision etc. Name-calling words include: betray, collapse, crisis, decay, endanger, greed, hypocrisy, incompetent, self-serving, shallow etc.[89]

The use of propaganda techniques such as these by PR people will be discussed in the next chapter, which outlines some of the strategies that are used to improve the environmental credentials and public image of corporations whilst discrediting environmentalists and environmental regulations.

Chapter 8

Public Relations Strategies

In an article addressed to the chemical industry, James Lindheim, director of Public Affairs Worldwide at Burson-Marsteller in London, described how various industries such as oil and forestry had suffered major declines in public opinion but had successfully managed to remedy them through public relations. In the 1970s, environmentalists drew public attention to the clear-cut forests and the image of environmental degradation was a compelling one. In response, the forest products industry launched a massive PR campaign ($7-10 million million per year for five years) promoting the message that "We love the forest and protect it. When we cut trees, we plant them. We are not rapers of the hillside, we are farmers of trees; we grow them and reap them and plant them."[1] Lindheim pointed out that:

> The forest products industry could have tried to explain clear-cutting for its economic efficiency, and pointed out that the prices of paper and houses would go up if they were not allowed to continue to cut ugly swatches out of the forest. But they didn't try to explain what they were doing in their own terms. They explained it in the public's terms, and connected themselves to powerful positive images in the public's mind: protection of the forests and farming.[2]

Lindheim explained the rationale behind this sort of strategy in terms of a psychiatrist's relationship with an irrational patient:

> There is, for instance, a very interesting technique that psychiatrists use to deal with irrational and distressed patients. They call it the therapeutic alliance. When an anxious patient first arrives, the psychiatrist will be a very sympathetic listener. The whole time that his mind is telling him that he has a raving lunatic on his hands, his mouth will be telling the patient that his problems are indeed quite impressive, and that he the psychiatrist is amazed at how well the patient is coping, given the enormity of the situation. . .Once that bond of trust is established, true therapy can begin and factual information can be transmitted.[3]

Lindheim advised the chemical industry to do the same: to build a therapeutic alliance with the public, which has an irrational and emotion-based reaction to chemical risks. He said that scientists and engineers should avoid the temptation to try to explain to the public how safe pesticides and plastics and food additives are. "Obviously, people don't understand. If they did, they wouldn't worry and they certainly wouldn't be hostile."[4] Since the public is so concerned with protecting the environment, the chemical industry "must use its communications resources to demonstrate its commitment to solving environmental problems, and making environmental improvements".

> The industry must convince people that it cares, not by giving them facts about the true risks and benefits of chemical products but by creating a therapeutic alliance. It must accept the legitimacy of their concern, although some may see these concerns as misguided and irrational. . . The industry must be like the psychiatrist: rationally figuring out how it can help the public put things in perspective. . .[5]

What is essential for good public relations, according to Lindheim, is trust. But trust "is built on emotion, not on facts" so increasing public understanding will not be helpful. Similarly, Bill Brody, Professor of Public Relations at Memphis State University, argues that "people are likely to respond to ideas, objects, persons, and events as much by what they think and feel about them as by what they know about them."[6]

Communicating and Cultivating Trust

There is a growing literature on risk communications, much of which is aimed at advising corporations on how to deal with the fears that their operations engender in the community. In the magazine *Cash Flow*, David Katz writes that risk communication consultants are increasingly needed by companies with "existing or potential pollution liabilities. . . to help cool down the furore and thus curb their risks." The risks he is talking about here are not the health and environmental risks to the community, but the risks to the company of regulation and law suits. He suggests that risk communicators could help such companies "to communicate with the press and public to sway the government and to develop strategic plans to deal with pollution regulators".[7]

Many risk communicators concentrate on developing ways to effectively explain findings of the risk assessments done by company experts, and therefore to reassure the public:

> The self-imposed task of risk communicators is to disseminate various truths to an audience that is deficient in some fundamental and obstructive way, beyond 'ignorance of the facts'. Those to whom risk assessments need to be communicated are perceived to lack reason or be hampered by an assortment of psychological and political disabilities—bias, special interest, ideological commitment, and so forth.[8]

Joe Epley, past president of the Public Relations Society of America, writes of the need for international public relations because "public opinion, fueled by hysteria, a desire to live in a risk-free environment, and unfounded perceptions of the industrial world, is making it difficult for many manufacturers to operate on either a local or global basis."[9]

Risk communication aims to correct the public's 'false' view of risk. Some risk communicators acknowledge that many of the factors influencing a person's perception of risk are quite rational, for example whether the risk is imposed or voluntary. Nonetheless they seek to change perceptions rather than reduce risks. For example, Peter Sandman's well-used formula, Risk = Hazard + Outrage, is used by companies and government agencies trying to get community acceptance for hazardous facilities to work out ways to reduce outrage rather than to reduce the hazard. This is done by concentrating on communicating the concern, honesty and trustworthiness of the organization proposing the additional risks.

Stuart Price, a communications consultant who has worked for Westinghouse Electric Corporation, advises in an article on *Learning to Remove Fear from Radioactive Waste* that "bringing concerned citizens into the decision-making process, rather than just launching one-way information packets in their direction, is a technique that can build good will and resolve many fears". He recommends the use of advisory boards with local residents, environmentalists and workers on them, and regulators and waste generators present to provide expert advice and explain the 'reality' behind the newspaper headlines.[10]

These are all suggestions that have been taken up by the Responsible Care programme which was thought up by the Canadian Chemical Producers Association and is now subscribed to by chemical industries in many countries including the UK, USA and Australia. Responsible Care is aimed at restoring the declining image of the chemical industry, rebuilding trust and avoiding more regulation. It uses voluntary codes of practice, open days and public advisory panels to achieve these ends.[11]

Of course, when something does go wrong there is a whole new generation of public relations experts, called 'crisis communicators', ready to swing into action. Crisis PR manages public perception following industrial accidents, the public uncovering of adverse effects of a product, and corporate mistakes. In their literature, these crisis experts frequently cite the aftermath of the Exxon Valdez shipwreck, which spewed tons of oil over pristine arctic wilderness, as a prime example of PR gone wrong. The aftermath they refer to is Exxon's fallen reputation rather than the oil-soaked coastline and damage to marine life. In the world of PR, problems arise from the failure to communicate strategically, not from wrongful activity. The hundreds of articles in PR magazines and books that cover the Exxon Valdez accident almost invariably focus on how Exxon could have handled their PR better. However, as journalist Craig Mellow points out; "For all the stress on strategic counseling, no one talked about whether Exxon should have had better hiring or emergency-response policies beforehand."[12]

The advice that crisis communicators give is therefore aimed at restoring reputation rather than preventing reoccurrences or fixing the physical consequences of the disaster: the problem is not reality but the perception of reality. The sort of advice that is given to companies for dealing with a major incident includes firstly ensuring the top company executive goes to the scene of the accident immediately to show that she or he cares: "Images of strong emotional responses must be captured (for which the chief will be trained by a crisis communicator). Executive hands and shoes must be soiled for the camera."[13]

Corporations are also advised that television cameras should be kept away from meetings between the company and the aggrieved community, to avoid mass broadcasts of angry citizens. Company representatives should dress to identify with the community and, if at all possible, the company should be portrayed

as a victim, suffering as a result of an accident it could not prevent.[14] Harold
Burson of Burson-Marsteller also advises that is important to 'control' media coverage and arrange employee interviews: "Failing to make witnesses available will
lead to media efforts to obtain interviews on their own, either outside the gates
or at the local watering hole. Control is the important element here."[15]

Emphasising the Positive

One of the ways PR experts enhance the image of their clients and show that they
care is by emphasising their positive actions, no matter how trivial, and downplaying any negative aspects, no matter how significant. According to Robert
Gray, former chairman of Hill and Knowlton Worldwide, "Our job is not to
make white black or to cover the truth, but to tell the positive side regardless of
who the client is."[16] Sometimes this involves putting a positive spin or interpre-
tation on the available information:

> Did this year's fines levied by the Environmental Protection Agency (or the state
> equivalent) drop to 'only' $5 million? Then celebrate the company's 'continued pos-
> itive trend in compliance.' Was there no improvement from last year's release of toxic
> chemicals? Then report on the 'levelling off of emissions.'[17]

One public relations expert advised companies in *Public Relations Journal*:
"To report bad news, state the problem, then focus on the actions you are taking
to reduce the risk and improve the situation."[18] She also advised that it is important to get in first, "in hostile situations" in order to "shape the message". One
firm that was required by Californian regulations to disclose their emissions and
their health effects (including cancer risks) sent a letter to local residents in
advance.

> By getting their letter to residents prior to the agency letter [containing their emis-
> sions details], the company was able to take control of the message and reinforce its
> proactive stance. . . Opening a dialogue with the neighbourhood gave the manufac-
> turer a forum to communicate the positive elements of the plant.[19]

Some companies make the most out of measures they have been forced to
take by the government, making it seem that they have undertaken the improvements because they care about the environment. Companies that have poor environmental records can also improve their image and increase their sales merely by
using recycled paper in their products or making similar token adjustments. Peter
Dykstra, media director of Greenpeace USA, says, "They depict five per cent of
environmental virtue to mask the ninety-five per cent of environmental vice."[20]

Jolyon Jenkins, writing in the *New Statesman and Society*, claimed that BP, a
company responsible for the clearing of large areas of rainforest in Brazil,
responded to the rise in environmental consciousness in the late 1980s with "a
£20 million 're-imaging campaign' in which it daubed all its property in green
paint, and advertised its annual report under the slogan 'Now We're Greener
Than Ever'."[21] Greenpeace campaigners Dadd and Carothers claim that the

multinational oil company Chevron spends about five times as much publicising its environmental actions as it does on the actions themselves.[22]

The nuclear industry has stressed its lack of air pollution and carbon dioxide emissions as an environmental benefit, whilst not discussing the environmental and health problems surrounding extraction of uranium, nuclear accidents or disposal of nuclear wastes. Hill and Knowlton has helped the nuclear industry to come up with statements such as "Nuclear protects the public against an unacceptable level of peril from air pollution." The American Nuclear Society's Publicity Director argued that the nuclear industry needed to "paint itself green" and try to be identified with the environmental movement. The Canadian Nuclear Association also launched a three year, C$6 million campaign in the late 1980s which portrayed nuclear energy as 'clean' and 'safe' and the solution to global warming and acid rain problems.[23] In the UK, the name of the location of a nuclear reprocessing plant was changed from Windscale to Sellafield in an obvious attempt to acquire a better public image.

Every year Earth Day provides another opportunity for firms to get environmental credentials, deserved or otherwise. One US PR consultant observed: "There's a virtual feeding frenzy among corporations about what roles they will play on Earth Day." On the same topic, the Public Affairs Director for the Monsanto Chemical Company has said: "There's a mad scramble for many companies to project an 'I am greener than thou' attitude." The Chemical Manufacturers Association encourages its members to get involved, and public relations firms help their clients to "shape and publicize their pro-environment messages."[24] Corporate funding and sponsorship has turned Earth Day into a multi-million dollar event that is marketed with slick glossy brochures and Earth Day merchandise. It provides corporations with a means to green their image and, according to *Public Relations Journal*, to play "a key role in defining the future direction of the environmental movement".[25] Associated events, such as fairs where firms can showcase their 'green' credentials and Clean Up campaigns are common in the mid-nineties. These clean-ups "offer a chance to 'bond' with the community over an environmental cause and to foster 'camaraderie among employees' who are often compensated for their time."[26]

The attempt to provide a 'green' and caring persona for a corporation is a public relations strategy aimed at promising reform and heading off demands for more substantial and fundamental changes.[27] A PR expert advised in *Public Relations Journal*:

> There really are no solid solutions to many environmental problems other than ceasing to partake in the activity that causes the environmental hazard. Therefore, the key to devising successful solution ideas is to show that your client cares about the environmental issue at hand.[28]

The Council on Economic Priorities has studied the environmental claims of a large number of corporations and found that "many of them are using 'green' public relations programs as a pro-environmental smokescreen while they continue to pollute." Examples they gave in 1992 included Dow Chemical, which "received favorable publicity for a $3 million wetlands protection program, while downstream from its factories birds were turning up with dioxin-related deformities"; and Mobil, which claimed that "so-called biodegradable plastic bags would not disintegrate in landfills and that their use should not be encouraged. Then they went ahead and introduced biodegradable plastics with an enormous advertising campaign."[29]

3M is perhaps one of the most successful companies when it comes to attaining a green image. Although it is the 13th-worst US corporation when it comes to emissions of toxic chemicals into the environment,[30] the name 3M is almost synonymous with the idea of pollution prevention through its much-publicized 3P (Pollution Prevention Pays) scheme. Indeed 3M's 3P programme, implemented in the 1970s by two engineers and an 'environmental communications specialist', has saved $500 million for a very small monetary expenditure, earned a Silver Anvil Award from the Public Relations Society of America, brought much welcome media publicity and helped "soften regulatory attitudes toward the industry".[31]

Corporate philanthropy is another means of showing that a company cares. The Puget Sound Bank found that it increased its number of customers by setting up the Puget Sound Fund. The name of the fund was chosen purposely to "cement the identification" between the bank and the environmental fund. Each time a customer made a transaction at one of their automatic teller machines the bank would donate a small amount of money to the Fund, which would be used to give grants to environmental groups. Cheques were produced with scenes of Puget Sound on them. The aim was to make the public feel that in supporting the bank they were also supporting an environmental cause.[32]

The strategy worked better than the bank had hoped. Between 1988 and 1990 cash withdrawals through the machines increased fifty-six per cent and the bank retained its market share despite increased competition. The fund raised $30,000 in 1990, which was dispersed to thirty-two environmental groups. It was far cheaper than an advertising campaign, and attracted favourable media coverage worth more than could have been bought with conventional publicity. "It's free advertising and of the best type. That's press you can't buy!" The bank's marketing director pointed out that "Banking is a business in which the perception is often the reality."[33]

Getting Environmentalists on Side

One way for corporations to show they care about the environment, even if they don't care enough to make major changes to their business practices, is for them to donate money to an environmental group or sponsor an environmental project. Companies which fund cash-starved environmental groups believe "the imprimatur of activists will go a long way in improving their reputation among environmentally aware consumers."[34] However they do not necessarily support the aims of the groups they fund.

Companies which have sponsored US environmental groups such as the World Wildlife Fund (WWF), Nature Conservancy, Defenders of Wildlife,

Natural Resources Defense Council, Environmental Defense Fund, Audubon Society and the National Wildlife Federation have also been sponsoring several anti-environmental groups.[35] The mining multinational RTZ, which operates polluting mines in Third World countries, donates money to the National Trust, the British Trust for Conservation Volunteers, and the Council for Environmental Conservation (the Environment Council). Shell, which manufactured the pesticide Aldrin that is now banned in the US, was subject to an international boycott when it planned to dump the Brent Spar oil drilling platform into the sea, and which has operated controversial oil operations in Nigeria, gives about £200,000 to environmental organizations each year.[36]

Many environmental groups accept the money because they believe that "private sector cash can increase an organization's clout and bankroll membership building programs."[37] However, such arrangements also enable corporations to get valuable information about environmental groups and how they work and think; information that will help them oppose the environmental groups' goals.[38]

Such donations can also have the additional benefit of co-opting and corrupting environmentalists. Public relations practitioners have observed that environmental groups are "favoring cooperation rather than confrontation" more and more.[39] *O'Dwyer's PR Service Report* explains how wealthy companies can co-opt environmental groups with donations and job offers. Corporations can win approval from environmental organizations, or at the very least a blind eye, through donations to these organizations.

Consultancies and perks for individual environmentalists also work wonders for getting a favourable hearing. In 1993 *Public Relations Journal* reported how Ciba-Geigy had arranged a tour of Europe for US environmentalists, academics, journalists and others to study European industrial waste management programmes. Environmentalists were recruited from the ten largest environmental groups in the US as well as from state and grassroots groups. The stated aim of the study tour was to bring together the various stakeholders, provide them with up-to-date information and encourage a dialogue between them and Ciba-Geigy. "To avoid the perception that the tour was biased in any way", Ciba arranged for it to be funded by non-industry sources as well as itself, and for others to be involved in its organising and planning. For Ciba-Geigy the tour successfully improved relations with the environmentalists and others.[40]

In Sydney Australia, a besieged water and sewerage authority attempted to improve its image by funding environmentalists to review its operations and plans. The funds were sufficient to employ a number of people full-time, and it even paid these groups to prepare a formal application for the funds. Four groups were funded: Friends of the Earth, the National Parks Association, the Nature Conservation Council of NSW, and the Total Environment Centre.

The groups involved were assured that they were free to say whatever they wanted in their reports and that they would have free access to Water Board documents. In October 1994 the groups, under the umbrella name of The Sydney Water Project, published a series of leaflets for comment by the public. These leaflets had a striking resemblance to Water Board fact sheets (produced in earlier years) in tone and style, albeit that they were now printed on recycled paper. They were bland, and criticisms of the Board were weak and tentative.

Increasingly, business people are seeing the advantages of working out deals with environmental groups. James Harris, a Vice-President of Hill and Knowlton and also a member of the Sierra Club's national Public Affairs Advisory Committee puts it this way:

> For the environmental groups, working with corporations offers a ready source of funds and a chance to influence their behaviour. For corporations, environmental groups offer the opportunity to obtain positive publicity and gain access to group members, who tend to be better educated and more affluent than the general public. They also provide credibility, which can be particularly valuable. . . In political coalitions, environmental groups can provide substantial clout, with their large memberships and lobbying expertise.[41]

Bruce Harrison, in his book *Going Green: How to Communicate your Company's Environmental Commitment*, advises companies that "choosing green partners at the community level is without doubt the best strategy to improve your standing."[42] Such relationships certainly pay off for industry. McDonald's now has one of the best environmental 'images' of any US corporation after forming a partnership with the Environmental Defense Fund. The Audubon Society approved of Mobil drilling for oil under an Audubon bird sanctuary, their representative explaining: "Conservationists have just got to learn to work with industry."[43]

One employee of Hill and Knowlton gives advice to corporations: "Help them raise money. . . Offer to sit on their board of directors". He also suggests hiring staff from environmental groups, who are available "at very reasonable rates". Top environmentalists may be more expensive. When Burson-Marsteller hired Des Wilson, former chairman of Friends of the Earth in the UK, as director of public affairs and crisis management, he was "reckoned to be one of the highest paid people in PR".[44]

PR consultant Philip Lesly argues that activists are people who are "disappointed with their small roles [in society]; so they have the time, the inclination and the opportunity to attack the structure."[45] He suggests that the best way to deal with such people is to give them a role:

> If a group has legitimate arguments and shows it has a sound approach, enlist its leaders. Often they will make great contributions as employees. They might be retained as consultants. Or they may become active in a new working group you set up jointly.[46]

Stauber and Rampton, who edit *PR Watch*, point out that hiring activists is a "crude but effective way to derail potentially meddlesome activists".[47] There are numerous examples of activists who now work for the industries they once opposed. For example Paul Gilding, formerly executive director of Greenpeace International, does consultancy work for big business and bodies such as the Queensland Timber Board.[48]

Another tactic, called 'cross-pollination', enables PR firms to get strategic alliances going between different clients who might otherwise be opposed to each other. This can be done by donating public relations work to charities in order to be able to pressure them into supporting other clients later on. An example is where the PR firm Porter/Novelli, which represented a number of produce growers and pesticide manufacturers, was able to call in favours from the American Cancer Society, to which it had provided free services for decades (presumably to enhance its own reputation). When a documentary claiming that pesticides caused cancer in children was about to be screened, the PR firm managed to get the Cancer Society to issue a memo criticising the documentary, which was then used by the pesticide industry to lobby against the broadcasting of the documentary.[49]

Porter/Novelli seems to have made an art form of this sort of cross-pollination. Many of its early clients were government departments; this made Porter/Novelli attractive to corporate clients who wanted to lobby these departments. The firm soon had a long list of corporate clients as well as its government clients. "We began to see that there were synergies and opportunities to bring these two together," says Novelli. One example is that its previous PR work for a government department puts Porter/Novelli in a good position to represent the interests of a corporate client to that same government department.[50]

Porter/Novelli also specializes in providing "*pro bono* work for health-related charities whose endorsements can help its corporate clients". Its brochure reads:

> One of our specialties is aligning our clients with diet, health, and consumer groups to create dynamic partnerships for public education, cause-related marketing. . . and corporate-image enhancement.[51]

Another example of cross-pollination is the way Hill and Knowlton set up a coalition of environmental groups to publicize the dangers of unprotected sun exposure resulting from ozone layer depletion. Unbeknownst to at least some of the environmentalists, this was funded by one of Hill and Knowlton's clients, which produced sun screen lotion.[52]

In some cases cross-pollination happens through membership of boards. For example Frank Boren, a board member of ARCO Petroleum, served as president of the Nature Conservancy. He argued that such cooperation was advantageous for industry: "One good thing about that is that while we're working with them, they don't have time to sue us."[53]

Dealing with Uncooperative Environmentalists

Not all environmentalists are so willing to capitulate to corporate agendas; it is usually the more conservative groups that will cooperate. In dealing with activists, public relations firms generally employ a 'divide and conquer' strategy which exploits differences in the environment movement between moderates and radicals.[54] Various public relations experts have attempted to categorize environmentalists in order to devise a strategy to deal with them.

Lesly divides activists into five personality classifications:

- advocates who argue for what they believe in
- dissidents who are against many things because of their character
- activists who want to get something done or changed
- zealots who are overridingly singleminded, and
- fanatics who are "zealots with their stabilizers removed"[55]

He suggests that reasonable people can be dealt with using reason, but zealots and fanatics have to be dealt with by withering away their power base and support.[56]

Ronald Duchin, from the PR firm Mongoven, Biscoe and Duchin, categorizes activists as either radicals, opportunists, idealists or realists:

> [The] activists we are concerned about here are the ones who want to change the way your industry does business—either for good or bad reasons: environmentalists, churches, Public Interest Research Groups, campus organizations, civic groups, teachers unions, and 'Naderites'.[57]

Duchin describes 'radicals' as those who want to change the system and have underlying socio-economic/political motives. They are anti-corporations and multinationals and are the hardest to deal with because they won't compromise. 'Opportunists', according to Duchin, are activists who oppose corporations because they want power, attention, and employment. The key to dealing with them is to offer them the appearance of a victory.[58]

'Idealists' are altruistic, highly credible, with a sense of justice. "They must be educated. . .Once the idealist is made fully aware of the long-term consequences or the wide ranging ramifications of his/her position in terms of other issues of justice and society, she/he can be made into a realist."[59] 'Realists' are pragmatic and willing to compromise and work within the system. Duchin recommends concentrating any public relations activities on realists and seeking to cooperate with them. A solution forged with the realists will generally become the accepted solution, he says.

Duchin's formula is therefore to isolate the radicals, turn the idealists into realists, co-opt the realists to support industry solutions and the opportunists will go along with the final agreement. The radicals, he says, need the support of the idealists and realists to have credibility. Without them they are marginalized and "seen to be shallow and self-serving".[60]

The isolation of radicals was also the strategy of Ketchum Communications Public Relations when it was advising its client Clorox Corporation in 1991 on how to deal with an expected anti-chlorine campaign. It recommended labelling protesters as 'terrorists' and suing critical journalists for defamation.[61] Labels such as 'extremist' and 'terrorist' are an example of the propaganda technique of name-calling described in the previous chapter. It is, according to Penny Cass, an attempt to activate preconceptions and stereotypes already held by the public. "Category-based expectancies define a group in such a way as to predict future behaviour and to interpret ambiguous information in the shadow of pre-existing stereotypes."[62]

Cass argues that this is particularly effective in environmental disputes, where people are willing to believe such things of people they disagree with and where environmentalists are often bearers of bad news. People who tell of extreme consequences are more easily labelled as extreme. Thus if a NASA scientist concludes that global warming is underway and another scientist questions this, the NASA scientist is seen to be the more extreme of the two, even if her assumptions are more conservative, because her conclusion "deviates from normative expectancies".[63]

This attempt to brand environmentalists as extremists and terrorists has been aided by various dirty tricks campaigns that have attempted to falsely pin violent actions on environmentalists. David Helvarg cites an example where Hill and Knowlton, on behalf of their clients Pacific Lumber, distributed fake photocopies of material purportedly produced by the group Earth First! calling for violence.[64]

Isolating radicals also requires managing the media and ensuring the radicals don't get much coverage. Lesly outlines various strategies for this, including:

• becoming "the key reliable source on the subject"
• holding media people responsible for what they report
• providing information early before an issue takes off
• preventing the opposition from setting the agenda
• "innoculat[ing] the channels of influence against readily accepting what the activists will charge", and
• "spell[ing] out the consequences of allowing the activists' position to prevail"[65]

Gathering Intelligence

Techniques for dealing with environmental activists and the media depend on knowing who they are and how they operate. Several public relations firms specialize in supplying this sort of information. The firm Mongoven, Biscoe and Duchin (MBD) maintains extensive files on organizations such as Greenpeace and Friends of the Earth, which detail their strategies, methods and priorities. This information is used to assist their corporate clients, who are almost all members of the Fortune 100, to resolve "public policy conflicts between corporations and activist groups". Activist groups are characterized as radical, realistic or idealistic and assessments made of their potential impact, anticipated initiatives, relations with other groups and potential for industry relationships. Profiles of key staff are included.[66]

The services that MBD provides for clients include the reviewing of lists of those registered to attend a company's annual meeting so as to anticipate possible disruptions; analysing the public record of a leading activist to anticipate style and content of the campaign he or she will conduct against the client; and proposing environmentalists who would be suitable candidates for corporate Boards of Directors and advisory boards.[67]

This sort of information is sometimes gathered through misrepresentation by staff who pose as journalists or friends of friends. Journalist John Dillon has documented two cases where Burson-Marsteller employees have disguised themselves, one as working for a consumer council and the other as an employee of a television programme, in order to get information for a client. Staff from another firm, National Grassroots and Communications, pretending to be the executors of an old lady's estate who wanted to find a suitable organization to donate money to, obtained the financial records of an activist group and then used those records to oppose that group.[68]

PR Watch alleges that MBD has spied on and undermined consumer activists and family dairy farmers opposing Monsanto's bovine growth hormone (BGH) on behalf of clients Monsanto and Philip Morris/Kraft/General Foods. Kaufman Public Relations also resorted to spy tactics when it was hired by the National Dairy Board to promote BGH. It put together a team that recruited local residents to attend a New York city activist conference posing as housewives.[69] Their brief was to:

> attend the event, monitor developments, ask questions, and provide other support as appropriate. Each attendee must be able to articulate the basic [pro-BGH] arguments on the issue and cite one or more substantive reasons for supporting the Dairy Board's position.[70]

Kaufman PR was caught out after a Freedom of Information inquiry, and the National Dairy Board severed its contract with them following the bad publicity.

Another organization which gathers 'intelligence' on activists is the Foundation for Public Affairs, which is funded by hundreds of corporations such as Dow Chemical, Exxon, Philip Morris, Mobil and Shell Oil. This foundation monitors over seventy-five activist publications and compiles information on over 1,300 groups and organizations. It publishes *Public Interest Profiles*, a directory of 250 major US public interest groups which includes funding sources, methods of operation, budgets and boards of directors.[71]

Public relations firms also collect information about journalists. One boasts:

> Let us be your eyes and ears when the environmental media convene. . . Gather vital information on key journalists. . . Who's the boss?. . . Age and Tenure. . . How do you break the ice? . . . Not only will you find news on journalists, we'll tell you what they want from you and what strategies you can employ with them to generate more positive stories and better manage negative situations.[72]

Another, TJFR Publishing, has biographical data on about 6,000 journalists which enables it to offer useful information to clients when they are approached by a journalist. It can provide the client with background information on the journalist, and advise them on strategies to use with that particular individual to ensure a positive story or at least to minimize negative reporting.[73]

PR firms also employ devices such as experiments involving reporters to see how they think. One journalist, Vicky Hutchings, wrote about her experience in a strange meeting with assorted other people invited by a PR consultant representing a multinational oil company. During this meeting they took part in various brainstorming and word association exercises, for which Hutchings got paid $50.[74] Another journalist outlined in *Environment Writer* the way DuPont's PR people invited journalists to take part in an exercise during which they were asked to develop storylines based on various sentences such as "DuPont makes very wonderful chemicals, and no one needs to worry." The journalists were watched by hidden DuPont researchers and paid $250 for their participation.[75]

Polling is an important public relations tool for researching public opinion: finding out who is opposed to a company and who are potential allies. It is also a way of testing what will work in a PR campaign. Questions are given such as "If you knew such and such, how would you feel about X company?", with follow-up questions depending on the answers. In this way the company can work out what are the right triggers to get people on their side. And in a similar vein, they can test public opinion before a trial or some event and get it postponed, for example, if they find that they are unlikely to win over a jury in the prevailing social climate.[76]

A Hill & Knowlton subsidiary, Group Attitudes Corporation, conducts opinion research surveys for its clients but also uses researchers who "infiltrate a community and live there undercover for a week or so" so that they can "identify leaders, assess the scope of a particular problem and find out who is creating the problem". Where a client is trying to site an unwanted facility, such researchers can work out what compromises the community is willing to make before any formal community consultation begins.[77]

Prior to the Gulf War, Hill & Knowlton used opinion polling to work out its strategy for persuading the American people, on behalf of a Kuwaiti coalition, that the US should go to war to defend Kuwait. It commissioned a million-dollar public survey, finding out that Iraqi atrocities against Kuwaitis would be an effective way to achieve this. Hill and Knowlton then produced commercials, radio shows and video news releases designed to convince people that Iraqis were committing such atrocities.[78]

Dealing with Local Residents

Public relations firms often classify local residents, as they do environmentalists, into various publics so that they can concentrate on targeting those likely to be persuaded of the benefits of a proposed project and marginalizing those who are likely to oppose it. Desmond Connor, a Canadian PR consultant, advises against holding a public meeting early on before the various publics can be approached separately. He says:

> The proponent typically calls a public meeting in order to explain the project to them, confident that their opposition will then disappear. In fact, the public meeting usually crystallizes a more informed, organized and articulate opposition and generates widespread negative publicity for the proponent and the project.[79]

Instead, he advises companies to identify "the latent and secondary beneficiaries of the project (the five volt positive people, compared with the 220 volt negative opponents)". These are people who "stand to benefit in small and indirect ways" from the project. These people should be kept informed and involved in a "joint problem solving process. As people work together, informed peer group pressure usually results in workable compromise solutions—not ideal from anyone's point of view, but acceptable to all or nearly all."[80]

In 1989 an Australian Joint Taskforce on Intractable Waste engaged the public relations firm Community Projects Ltd to develop a community consultation strategy to prepare the way for the establishment of a high temperature incinerator in Australia to burn hazardous wastes.[81] Several attempts had already been made to site an incinerator for hazardous wastes but none had been successful, usually because of the strength of local opposition to such a facility.

With the help of Community Projects Ltd, the Taskforce attempted to get broad 'in principle' acceptance for the high temperature incinerator before a location for it was chosen. The aim was to ensure that a detached, 'rational' debate took place before the emotions of concerned local residents clouded the issue and before the community living near the proposed incinerator site could muster support from the broader community. Environmental groups were contacted to procure their commitment to the project before they could be approached and influenced by the local community once the site had been chosen. Some environmental groups supported the incinerator, while others opposed it.

The consultation process did not seek to find out what the community wanted done with hazardous wastes, as that had been decided even before the Taskforce was appointed. Its aim was to win acceptance for a high-temperature incinerator. The Taskforce and their PR consultants sought to "achieve active public recognition that the proposal is in the public interest".[82] Having studied various technological controversies, Dorothy Nelkin and Michael Pollak found this was a typical approach:

> Mechanisms for public involvement may increase direct public influence on the formation of policy, or may merely inform policy-makers about public concerns. More often they are a means to manipulate public opinion, to win acceptance of decisions already made, and to facilitate the implementation of these decisions.[83]

Like others involved in such siting controversies, the Taskforce assumed that most opposition "is based upon ignorance that can be overcome" if the appropriate information is supplied. It therefore supplied reassuring information to the groups whose support it sought. However the most fervent opponents to the incinerator were among the best informed about the issue, a point the Taskforce admitted in one of its reports, stating that supporters or potential supporters "tend to be less well-informed on the issues involved than are the opponents".[84]

The Task Force was advised not to waste its persuasive efforts on that part of the environment movement opposed to the incinerator because they were unlikely to change their position. Community Projects interviewed opposition groups in order to distinguish "opposition likely to thwart a desired outcome ('effect') from that which is likely to be ineffective even if it is discomforting ('noise')".[85] The reason for needing to do this was that the Taskforce wanted to manage and control the debate or, as it put it, "limit destructive conflict". It stated:

> Unstructured public involvement is likely to be chaotic and potentially destructive to a proposal. In the absence of a structure for public involvement, individuals and

groups will create their own mechanisms. . . By providing a framework for public involvement, the form and direction of this involvement can be managed in the public interest. Under these circumstances public involvement in the development of a proposal is more likely to be productive and creative, and the scope for destructive conflict is significantly reduced. . . [86]

Of course the terms 'productive', 'creative' and 'destructive' are all defined in terms of achieving the goal of establishing a hazardous waste facility.

Allies from within the environment movement were enlisted to help get the incinerator accepted in Australia. Remaining opponents were categorized and dismissed as either ignorant, having vested interests, or, in the case of those stubborn yet well-informed environmentalists who could not be co-opted, the Taskforce stated that they showed "clear signs of wishing to assume the role of champions".[87] The use of the term 'champions' was a way of implying that opponents are not concerned about the public interest. The Taskforce stated:

Champions are those who see some benefits for themselves in adopting one position or another in a potential conflict. They are sometimes more concerned with the opportunity to enhance their reputation than with the details of the case.[88]

The Taskforce was unsuccessful in its efforts[89] and to date no hazardous waste incinerator has been established in Australia. Instead, various parts of the waste stream are to be treated with more specific technologies, some currently being developed for the purpose.

Often a public consultation exercise is little more than a public relations exercise, undertaken for the primary purpose of winning public accceptance for an unwanted facility. The process of consultation provides an opportunity for the developer to show a caring, open approach and to cultivate trust in the face of community concerns. Yet more often than not corporations (and governments) are unwilling to reduce or eliminate the hazards that give rise to those concerns; their public relations advisers help them to mould and manage public opinion instead of responding to it.

Public relations shapes the interaction between corporations and their 'publics' in a way that is designed to mould public opinion and win acceptance of corporate goals and ideologies. Yet that influence only works while it is hidden. The exposure of public relations strategies, their messages and sources undermines their strength and persuasive power.

Chapter 9

Scientific Controversy: Dioxin

The health and environmental effects of dioxin have been the subject of fierce debate for more than twenty years. Dioxin earned a reputation as "one of the most toxic substances know to humans" as a result of tests on animals which found that one form of the compound, 2,3,7,8-TCDD, was "the most potent carcinogen ever tested". There are seventy-five other dioxin compounds besides 2,3,7,8-TCDD, of varying toxicity.[1]

Dioxins are by-products of many industrial processes including waste incineration, chemical manufacturing, chlorine bleaching of pulp and paper, and smelting. In fact any process in which chlorine and organic matter are brought together at high temperatures can create dioxin.[2] It is for this reason that Greenpeace and other environmental groups have called for phasing out of the chlorine industry.

Between the 1950s, when dioxin was discovered to be a contaminant in herbicides, and 1995, when the EPA concluded that the general population may be exposed to unacceptably high levels of dioxins, corporations have set out to confuse the public and influence governmental regulation of dioxin. They have used all the mechanisms described in this book to achieve this: corporate front groups, grassroots organising, strategic lawsuits against public participation, conservative think-tanks, public relations firms, 'educational' materials and the media. This chapter describes how they have done this.

In their introduction to *Dying from Dioxin*, Lois Marie Gibbs and Stephen Lester describe the dioxin story as one that "includes cover-ups, lies, and deception; data manipulation by corporations and government as well as fraudulent claims and faked studies. . . It's a story of money and power; of how corporations influence government actions and how this collusion affects the public."[3]

One of the key players in this story has been Dow Chemical. It is a major manufacturer of chlorine, producing forty million tons of it each year, much of which is used to make plastics, solvents, pesticides and other chemicals. In 1965 a Dow researcher warned in an internal company document that dioxin "is extremely toxic",[4] but Dow has always publicly claimed it is not. It is of vital importance to Dow that the dangers of dioxin are minimized and tough regulation of the chlorine industry is avoided. Dow uses lobbying firms and trade associations such as the Chemical Manufacturers Association, the National Association of Manufactures and the US Chamber of Commerce, to influence politicians to vote against increased regulation of the chlorine industry.[5]

Each of these is armed with lawyers and lobbyists who daily stroll the corridors of Congress, the EPA and the White House, influencing public policy in ways

unimaginable, and inaccessible, to ordinary citizens. Each of these has a public relations budget, and staff to write op eds, testify before Congress or the EPA, appear on
news shows as 'experts', speak to civic groups.[6]

Dow Chemical alone has spent more than a million dollars over the last ten
years on donations to politicians running for national office. In the 1992 election
Dow, together with other chlorine producers, donated more than $1.4 million to
people running for Congress. In 1995 Dow provided the services of one of its
lobbyists, free of charge, to the House of Representatives Commerce Committee,
which has attacked the EPA and environmental protection laws.[7]

Dow executives are given public speaking training so they can take part in
various forums as effective and persuasive speakers. In recognition that scientists
have more credibility than other company employees, Dow's 'Visible Scientist
Program' gives Dow scientists special training to be able to "communicate
through talk shows, citizen groups, and newspaper editorial-board briefings about
such issues as hazardous-waste management and chemical plant safety".[8]

Dow also supports and finances corporate front groups such as the Alliance
to Keep Americans Working, the Alliance for Responsible CFC Policy, the
American Council on Science & Health and Citizens for a Sound Economy.
Additionally, the company uses firms specialising in manufacturing
"groundswells of carefully orchestrated 'citizen' support for Dow's point of view."[9]

Industry-Funded Research

Throughout the 1980s the only generally agreed effect of dioxin on humans was
chloracne (a skin disease that can be disfiguring but is not generally fatal), despite
hundreds of studies undertaken during the late 1970s and 1980s indicating otherwise. A handful of studies funded by Monsanto and BASF, which purported to
show no health effects from dioxin exposure apart from chloracne, proved dis-
proportionately influential, notwithstanding their dubious methodology.

Dioxins have been studied more than any other chemical.[10] They have been
found to be toxic to all of the animals tested. However, the assumption that these
tests can be extrapolated to humans is hotly contested. In this context the
Monsanto and BASF studies were used to support the case that effects on humans
were quite different to the effects being observed in laboratory animals. Michael
Fumento, who is associated with the conservative think-tank the Competitive
Enterprise Institute, argues in his book *Science Under Siege* that:

> The assumption that dioxin is the most deadly chemical created by man—an assump-
> tion that is taken by most people to mean 'most deadly to *me*'—would only be true if
> we weighed about a pound and were small stout-bodied, short-eared, nearly tailless
> domesticated rodents. . . But let's say that you are not a guinea pig, but rather are con-
> siderably smaller and have a little stub of a tail. That is, you are a hamster. Well, in that
> case you could practically season your porridge with dioxin, because tested hamsters
> required a dose about 1,900 times as high as the guinea pigs' to kill half the test
> group. . . Rabbits, mice, and monkeys cluster somewhere in the middle. . .[11]

The reliance on animal experiments was necessitated by the inability to experiment on humans, which was thought by most to be unethical. However this did not stop Dow from doing experiments on prisoners at a Pennsylvania prison in 1965, applying dioxin to their skin and observing that they developed chloracne. No follow up was done on these prisoners.[12] Apart from these experiments, the only human data available is where humans have been exposed to large doses of dioxin through their occupation or by accident, and these are the people on whom most human studies concentrate.

Chemical companies have studied workers accidentally exposed to dioxin, in an effort to prove that they do not have any more cancers than those not exposed. Monsanto has been involved in a number of such studies that have since been discredited. In the mid-1980s it conducted epidemiological studies of workers exposed to dioxin in a 1949 accident at a Monsanto plant where herbicides were being manufactured. At the time the studies were conducted, Monsanto faced having to pay out millions of dollars in lawsuits to Vietnam veterans and to its factory workers, who claimed that they were suffering ill effects from exposure to dioxin.[13]

Monsanto claimed that their studies showed that exposure to dioxin caused no ill-effects apart from an increased risk of getting chloracne. Three of its studies were reported on or published in major prestigious scientific journals such as *Scientific American*, *Science* and the *Journal of the American Medical Association* (*JAMA*). However Monsanto's studies were later discredited during a court case, when the corporation's medical director admitted that Monsanto scientists:

> had knowingly omitted five deaths from the exposed study group and had further reclassified four exposed workers as unexposed, in order to equalize the death rates in the exposed and unexposed workers. The exposed workers, Dr. Roush admitted, had eighteen cancer deaths instead of the nine deaths reported by Monsanto, an overall cancer death rate 65% higher than the normal population rate.[14]

When Peter Montague, editor of *Rachel's Hazardous Waste News*, reported these allegations in his newsletter in 1991, Bill Gaffey, one of the Monsanto scientists, sued him for $4 million for libel. The scientist, then retired, was being represented by a law firm that regularly represents Monsanto. It was a classic SLAPP case intended to intimidate and therefore silence Montague. The lawsuit successfully silenced others from discussing the fraud, including the media: "Press coverage in the US and abroad dried up once the libel case was brought against Montague." Gaffey died before the case could be tried but not before admitting "under oath that he knew he had been hired in 1979 partly to help defend Monsanto against lawsuits over dioxin."[15]

Medical records, obtained by Greenpeace, of thirty-seven of the exposed Monsanto workers studied for four years following the accident show that the workers suffered "aches, pain, fatigue, nervousness, loss of libido, irritability and other symptoms. . . active skin lesions, [and] definite patterns of psychological disorders", but the study officially reported only the skin lesions.[16]

A BASF study of workers exposed to dioxin in an industrial accident at a

BASF chemical plant in Germany in 1953 was found to have "presented the data in a way that disguised the cancers". An epidemiologist hired by the workers found that two workers suffering from chloracne were placed in the low-exposure or non-exposed group whilst twenty plant supervisors, whom he claims were not exposed, were included in the exposed group to dilute the results. If those twenty people had not been included in the exposed group, the study would have demonstrated a high incidence of cancer among the workers.[17]

Doubts have also been cast over studies undertaken by the US Centers for Disease Control (CDC) of Vietnam War veterans exposed to dioxin when Agent Orange was sprayed in areas where they were on duty. About 200,000 veterans claimed that they were suffering health problems ranging from cancer and birth defects in their children, to skin rashes, numbness, infertility and radical mood swings as a result of that exposure.[18] At stake was the reputation of the US government as well as the potential for billions of dollars in lawsuits against chemical companies such as Dow, and the government itself.

Having spent millions of dollars carrying out the study over a three-year period, the CDC, headed by Vernon Houk, announced that because of difficulties in identifying who had been sprayed and who hadn't, the study had been abandoned. This was despite an assessment by the National Academy of Sciences, as requested by the CDC, which showed that there was sufficient data available to do a credible epidemiological study. The CDC later reported that many of the health problems experienced by veterans, which were more than veterans of other wars, were due to the 'increased stress' involved in the Vietnam War.[19]

A Congressional inquiry into the CDC studies later found they were "flawed and perhaps designed to fail". Admiral Zumwalt, who now regrets ordering the spraying of Agent Orange when he was in charge of US Naval Forces in Vietnam, has accused the CDC of manipulating data on Agent Orange as a result of political interference, "in an effort to deny the link between Agent Orange exposure and health effects".[20]

A court case filed in 1979 by veterans and their families against Dow Chemical and other chemical manufacturers was settled out of court in 1984 after the chemical companies tendered evidence from the Monsanto and BASF industry studies, which they claimed showed exposure to dioxin caused no long-term health effects apart from chloracne.[21] Seven chemical companies agreed to pay $180 million to the veterans whilst denying that Agent Orange had caused their health complaints.

Industry and EPA Get Together

In 1985, following a risk assessment, the US EPA classified dioxin as a "probable, highly potent human carcinogen" based on animal data. According to EPA scientists: "When the current data do not resolve the issue, EPA assessments employ the assumption basic to all toxicological evaluation that effects observed in animals may occur in humans and that effects observed at high doses may occur at low doses, albeit to a lesser extent."[22] Because the action of dioxin in the human body was not understood, the EPA assumed that there was no safe level of exposure to dioxin and that its carcinogeneity was directly proportional to the dose a person was exposed to. Standards were set on this basis and resulted in extremely small levels of dioxin being deemed unsafe. Other countries such as Canada and some European countries took a less cautious approach and allowed standards to be less stringent by 170 to 1700 times.[23]

Following the setting of standards in 1985, the EPA came under intense pressure from the industry to revise them. This pressure was stepped up when, in 1985, dioxin was accidentally found in the discharges from pulp and paper mills that used chlorine for bleaching the paper white. Fish downstream from those mills were also found to be contaminated and tests showed that dioxin was present in the manufactured paper goods. These tests were part of ongoing research for the National Dioxin Study.

The American Paper Institute set up a 'crisis management team' to deal with the situation. Leaked documents obtained by Greenpeace show that the administrator of the EPA met with representatives of the pulp and paper industry and promised that the EPA would revise downward its risk assessment of dioxin to ease the problem for the industry. He also agreed to notify the industry as soon as the EPA received any requests for information about the study under the Freedom of Information Act (FOIA) and that it would not release any results of testing before publication of the final report on the study. The EPA would then send the American Paper Institute a letter saying that testing data was preliminary and meaningless.[24]

Attempts by environmental activists Paul Merrell and Carol Van Strum to get results of these tests from the EPA in 1986 through the Freedom of Information Act (FOIA) were initially fruitless; later Greenpeace obtained the leaked documents and Merrell and Van Strum used them in court. "Suddenly the EPA found thousands of pages of documents responsive to our FOIA request that they had previously denied even existed."[25]

In 1987 the EPA released its National Dioxin Study, following the publication of a Greenpeace report alleging an EPA cover-up and collusion between the EPA and the paper industry. By this time the Paper Institute was well prepared with a public relations strategy. It used PR firm Burson-Marsteller to publicize the EPA letter saying the pulp and paper mill data in the report was meaningless. The Institute also advised members approached by the media to behave as if it was "old news" and to "suggest that this is a story that was covered way-back-when. . ."[26]

I would suggest we use the background statement we already have prepared because it is written in a tone that suggests that what is going on has been going on for a long time. I also would include the article from *Scientific American* which suggests that dioxin may not be all that serious a health problem. . .We might not want to include the above material in a *formal* kit. That might give the appearance we consider this a major event. Instead we might send some material, only when asked, in a regular API envelope.[27]

True to its word, the EPA stated in 1987 that it may have overestimated the risks of dioxin,[28] citing the Monsanto and BASF studies as key evidence. A second EPA risk assessment was done in 1988, which suggested that dioxin could be less potent than its 1985 assessment indicated. In the 1985 assessment, it had assumed that dioxin was a complete carcinogen which both initiated genetic change in cells and promoted the proliferation of damaged cells causing cancer. Industry scientists argued that dioxin was only a promoter of cancer and not a complete carcinogen. Among those putting this argument were Syntex scientists. Syntex Agribusiness was responsible for cleaning up a dioxin contaminated town—Times Beach, Missouri—and estimated that "relaxing the cleanup standard from one part per billion (ppb) to ten ppb would reduce cleanup costs by sixty-five per cent."[29]

Animal studies seemed to indicate that dioxin was a complete carcinogen, but it did not behave like either an initiator nor a promoter. Rather than question the initiator-promoter model, which has since been found to be inappropriate to dioxin, the EPA decided to base its risk assessment on a mid-point between the risk of a promoter and that of a complete carcinogen, which would have resulted in the 'safe' standard being loosened sixteen-fold.[30]

However this move was thwarted when evidence of the manipulation of the industry studies was presented to the EPA's Scientific Assessment Board by an EPA project manager and chemist, Cate Jenkins. The Board subsequently argued that there was no scientific justification for changing the dioxin standards. Meanwhile the allegation that the industry studies had been fraudulent was investigated by the EPA's Office of Criminal Investigations, which concluded that this was "immaterial to the regulatory process" and "beyond the statute of limitation".[31]

According to William Sanjour, an EPA policy analyst:

> One gets the impression, on reviewing the record, that as soon as the criminal investigation began, a whole bunch of wet blankets were thrown over it. . . . None of the scientific groups in the EPA, it seems, wanted to touch this hot potato, and no one in position of authority was instructing them to do so.[32]

Instead Cate Jenkins, whose memo prompted the investigation, was herself investigated for two years. She was transferred to "an unimportant position with nothing to do" and spent a few years fighting her employer, the EPA, in the courts before she was vindicated and reinstated.[33]

Renewed Industry Public Relations Efforts

When the EPA failed to adjust their standards for dioxin following the 1988 reassessment, the various interests concerned continued to apply pressure to downgrade the standards and to convince the public that dioxin wasn't really dangerous. A loosening of dioxin standards could mean that pulp and paper mills would not have to install expensive new equipment to reduce or eliminate the dioxin being discharged into waterways.

A reappraisal of how dangerous dioxin was could also save dioxin producers billions of dollars in legal claims from those exposed to it. In October 1990 the papermaking company Georgia Pacific had lost a court case in Mississippi for alleged dioxin pollution and had $1 million in punitive damages awarded against it. This was expected to trigger many other similar suits against other paper mills in various states, involving thousands of people and worth billions of dollars.[34] Other industries were facing similar legal actions.

In a concerted PR effort between 1990 and 1991, the industry was largely successful in changing dioxin's public image from being "one of the most toxic substances known" into that of an innocent victim of scaremongering by environmentalists and overzealous bureaucrats. Vernon Houk of the CDC, speaking at a conference sponsored by Syntex, which was being sued in over 350 dioxin-related lawsuits, argued that EPA standards for dioxin should be relaxed. His statements were influential as he had been the public official who had called for the permanent evacuation of 2,000 residents of Times Beach, Missouri, after dioxin-contaminated oil had been sprayed there as a dust suppressant in the 1970s. At the time seventy-five horses and several cats and dogs had died.[35] Now Houk was saying that those people had been evacuated needlessly:

> In summary, with the exception of chloracne. . . there are no convincing data for the association of dioxin exposure in humans, with early mortality, adverse reproductive outcomes, or chronic diseases of the liver or of the immune, cardiovascular, or neurologic systems. The overall cancer question is not settled, but if dioxin is a human carcinogen, it is, in my view, a weak one that is associated only with high-dose exposures.[36]

Houk was quoted and cited extensively in the media. However, when he was called before a congressional subcommittee to answer allegations of "improperly aiding the paper industry's campaign to loosen restrictions on dioxin pollution in water", he admitted that his proposals to relax dioxin standards were "taken practically verbatim from paper industry documents".[37] This did little damage to his credibility in the media, which had its own links with the paper industry (see Chapter Thirteen).

The paper industry also set out to cast doubt on the scientific basis of EPA's dioxin standards. It hired five scientists in 1990 to re-examine a 1978 study showing that dioxin caused cancer in rats. This study had been influential, and was reputed to have been the real basis for the EPA's tough line on dioxin. The rat slides from that study were re-examined by the five scientists and tumours recounted. The paper industry's scientists counted fifty per cent fewer tumours than had been originally counted. Although the new count still showed that dioxin was a more potent carcinogen at low doses than other chemicals, the paper industry used their recount to push the EPA to loosen their dioxin standards.[38]

The Chlorine Institute also attempted to shift the scientific consensus concerning dioxin. In 1990 the Institute, a chlorine industry trade group with members such as Dow Chemical, DuPont, Georgia-Pacific, International Paper, and Exxon Chemical Co, organized a conference of dioxin scientists at the Banbury Center. The Chlorine Institute believed that scientists were coming to perceive that dioxin was not as dangerous as once thought and they hoped that the conference would be "beneficial to our interests, particularly our interest in the paper industry". It appointed three scientists as organizers and they in turn picked the thirty-eight participants: scientists and regulators from the US and Europe. Also in attendance was George Carlo, consultant to the Institute. The Institute hired Edelman Medical Communications to publicize any conference outcome that was to the Institute's advantage.[39]

Conference attendees agreed that dioxin affects cells by binding to and activating a receptor which then acts on the nucleus of the cell, interacting with the DNA and causing problems. This is similar to the way that steroid hormones act. Some of those attending concluded that this implied that, as a number of molecules of dioxin had to bind to the receptor before toxic effects would occur, low doses of dioxin could be safe and therefore there was a threshold or safe level of exposure. This, they argued, would imply that the EPA's no threshold, linear model had overestimated the dangers of dioxin.[40]

Following the conference, the Institute's PR firm Edelman Medical Communications sent out a press packet with a background paper put together by Carlo, Edelman and the Institute, claiming that the conference had reached a consensus that dioxin was "much less toxic to humans than originally believed". This outraged some of the scientists present who had not reached this conclusion and who felt that they had been manipulated by the Chlorine Institute.[41]

According to the magazine *Chemistry and Industry*, the Institute was merely coordinating a "public outreach program" to "capitalize [sic] on the outcome" of the conference. Indeed the industry was able to use the supposed Banbury conference consensus together with the rat tumour re-count to get some states in the US to loosen dioxin standards for discharge of wastes into waterways below those set by the EPA. (They are technically able to do this if they can support their standards scientifically.)[42]

In January 1991 a comprehensive study of US chemical workers exposed to dioxin in the course of their work at least twenty years earlier was published in *The New England Journal of Medicine*. The thirteen-year study was carried out by Marilyn Fingerhut and her colleagues at the National Institute for Occupational Health and Safety, covering over 5,000 men who worked at twelve different factories between 1942 and 1984. It found that the workers had a fifteen per cent higher death rate from cancer than the US average. Those exposed to low levels of dioxin (about ninety times background levels) had no statistically significant increase in cancers, whilst those exposed to high levels (about 500 times background levels) were fifty per cent more likely to die of cancer.[43]

In an editorial for the issue of *The New England Journal of Medicine* in which the study was published, John Bailar predicted that "parties on both sides of the continuing debate about the regulation of dioxin exposure will no doubt cite this work in support of their positions"[44]—which indeed they did.

The chlorine and paper industries cited the Banbury conference, the Fingerhut study and the recount of tumours from the earlier rat study in a major public-relations campaign to show that dioxin was safer than previously thought. They lobbied the EPA to reassess its regulation of dioxin. Emerging evidence that dioxin could cause a range of effects on health, besides cancer, was ignored. The National Chamber Foundation, an affiliate of the US Chamber of Commerce, released a report claiming that "new studies reveal cancer risks from exposure to dioxin are greatly exaggerated" and dioxin "poses no threat to humans, at either normal exposure levels or elevated exposure levels caused by occupational practices or industrial accidents."[45]

In early 1991, executives from four major paper companies visited William Reilly, the EPA's director, to convince him to reassess dioxin in the light of the new evidence. In a memo following the meeting they thanked Reilly for his receptiveness to their ideas, pointing out that their industry was subject to unwarranted "public fears about risk associated with dioxin which bears no relationship to scientific evidence. A consequence of this atmosphere is that our companies are now the subject of groundless class action toxic tort suits seeking billions of dollars in damages."[46]

According to the EPA's Cate Jenkins, the industry pressure to reassess dioxin represented a "last-ditch effort to win litigation that's currently pending in the court system". The assessment would take a few years, during which the industry could win several law suits by arguing that risk from dioxin was low. The paper companies told the EPA: "Reasoned public statements can help calm the needless public alarm that has, in turn, stimulated a proliferation of unjustified legal action against so many companies in our industry."[47]

Reilly seems to have obliged. The EPA began its third assessment of the risks of dioxin within a few months of the meeting, and in August that year William Reilly told the *New York Times*: "I don't want to prejudge the issue, but we are seeing new information on dioxin that suggests a lower risk assessment . . . should be applied."[48] This contrasted sharply with the views of many of the EPA's own scientists. However it was widely reported in the media that the EPA thought that dioxin dangers were exaggerated.

In an editorial the *New York Times* praised the EPA for "sensibly considering new evidence that could lead to relaxation of the current strict and costly regulatory standards" for dioxin, and a few days later it ran a front page story beginning: "Dioxin, once thought of as the most toxic chemical known, does not deserve that reputation, according to many scientists"—who were not named.[49]

The media generally downplayed the dangers of dioxins during the early 1990s (see Chapter Thirteen), despite emerging evidence that indicated that it was in fact just as dangerous as had previously been thought. Between 1990 and 1993 several studies highlighted that reproductive and immune-system effects of dioxin could in fact be more devastating for human health than the cancer caused by dioxin. One study accidentally found that monkeys exposed to low levels of dioxin every day developed endometriosis, and that the severity of the disease increased with increased exposure. Scientists also found that the immune system of mice was suppressed when exposed to relatively low levels of dioxin. "Mice pretreated with dioxin readily die after exposure to a quantity of virus that rarely kills healthy mice." The amount of dioxin required to cause this affect was far lower than the amount required to cause dioxin's other effects in animals.[50]

Latest EPA Dioxin Reassessment

The EPA's third and most recent reassessment study took almost four years and cost $4 million. Because of the way that dioxin was thought to mimic hormones in binding to receptors in the cells, the EPA considered a range of chemicals that act in this way including the family of dioxins, dibenzofurans (or furans) and PCB, calling them 'dioxin-like' chemicals.

The study involved about 100 scientists, including non-EPA scientists used to peer-review each chapter as it developed. EPA management decided that:

> since the question of dioxin's risk had been marked by considerable controversy for more than a decade, we should pursue a process that would achieve scientific consensus on this issue. . . As a first step, it would be conducted as a cooperative effort, written by both EPA scientists and external scientists and peer-reviewed by scientists outside the Agency who were experts on dioxin. We hoped this would help ensure not only that the most current, most scientifically accepted information was used, but also that all scientific views would be heard and debated.[51]

Public comments were invited, three peer-review workshops were held and the drafts of each chapter, most of which were authored or co-authored by outside scientists, were reviewed and revised by a panel of scientists from other government agencies.

In 1994 a draft report was released and open to public comment, and in 1995 the final report was published. The report stated that:

> There is adequate evidence from studies in human populations as well as in laboratory animals and from ancillary experimental data to support the inference that humans are likely to respond with a plethora of effects from exposure to dioxin and related compounds.[52]

> Most significant in this analysis is the heightened concern about noncancer effects in humans, including disruption of the endocrine, reproductive, and immune systems, as well as dioxin's impact on the developing fetus, which may occur in some cases at or near background levels.[53]

The report referred to studies that had found "decreased sperm count in men, higher probability of endometriosis in women, weakened immune systems, and other health problems" as a result of dioxin exposure in the general population at levels already found in the food supply. The report claimed that current background levels of dioxins could be posing a risk of one additional death in every thousand or one in every ten thousand, even though as little as thirty pounds of dioxin may be released in the US each year.[54]

The EPA study also examined the sources of dioxin in the environment and the ways in which people are exposed. It concluded: "The presence of dioxin-like compounds in the environment has occurred primarily as a result of anthropogenic practices", i.e. human activities. It based this conclusion on the sampling of tissue of ancient humans and sediments in lakes near industrial centres in the

US, which showed low levels of dioxins prior to 1920.[55]

The study found that most dioxin is carried through the air and taken up by plants, which are in turn eaten by fish and animals which bioaccumulate the dioxin in their fatty tissues. By the time humans eat the fish, beef, dairy products etc, the dioxin is far more concentrated than it originally had been in the environment and it accumulates in the fatty tissues of humans. Ingestion of dioxin via food is a far more significant means of exposure than breathing in polluted air. The report noted that the major source of dioxin was incinerators, and that sources such as chemical manufacturing could be significant but that there was insufficient data on them.[56]

The Chlorine Industry and Its Allies

Whilst the new risk assessment was being put together by the EPA, the new scientific studies being published were causing alarm in industry groups. The Chemical Manufacturers Association established the Chlorine Chemistry Council in 1993 "to handle public relations, political lobbying, and 'scientific initiatives' on all issues for the chlorine industry". By 1994 the Council was receiving an estimated $12 million annual funding plus another $120 million of in-kind support from member companies. It hired two public relations firms to augment its own public relations staff.[57]

The Chlorine Chemistry Council works with other like-minded organizations in other countries, including Euro Chlor, and coordinates the International Group of Chlorine Chemistry Associations. It is supported in its public relations efforts by various corporate front groups such as the American Council on Science and Health, conservative think-tanks such as the Competitive Enterprise Institute and the Heartland Institute, as well as the Wise Use Movement. The industry is also supported by a number of workers groups. The Alliance for the Responsible Use of Chlorine Chemistry (ARCC) is an alliance of unions and chemical companies that "recognizes the significant society and economic benefits provided by chlorine chemistry". The Chlorophiles, a group of workers in Belgium and the Netherlands, describe themselves as "an independent non-profit organization of workers in the chlorine and PVC industry who want to react against allegations against their work."[58]

The chlorine industry and its allies have five main arguments:

1. Dioxin occurs naturally and has nothing to do with the chlorine industry.
2. Calls for a phase-out of the industrial use of chlorine amount to banning the element chlorine from the planet.
3. Chlorine-based products bring great benefits and are indispensable to modern life.
4. The case against dioxin is based on emotion rather than science.
5. Nature produces many substances that behave like dioxin.

Each of these arguments is discussed below.

1. Dioxin occurs naturally

The chlorine industry has attempted to attribute much of the dioxin in the environment to natural sources and to everyday familiar processes, in an attempt to
rid it of its image as a synthetic, man-made toxin. The idea is to present it as a
natural part of modern life and to disassociate it from chlorine. The argument
was first introduced by Dow in 1978 and is still used today. The British Plastics
Federation argues: "The stark fact is that dioxins have been present in the atmosphere since man first created fire."[59] Arnold and Gottlieb, founders of the Wise
Use Movement, argued in *Trashing the Economy* that dioxin "is now widely recognized as a naturally occurring substance created whenever combustion of
natural substances occurs".[60] The Chlorine Chemistry Council says:

> Among the natural sources of dioxin are forest fires, volcanoes, and compost piles.
> Man-made sources of dioxin include municipal, hospital and hazardous waste incin-
> erators, motor vehicles, residential wood burning and a variety of chemical manufac-
> turing process. With so many sources, it is not surprising that scientists have detected
> dioxins virtually everywhere they have looked.[61]

In contrast, environmental groups such as Greenpeace are keen to point out
that dioxin is a byproduct of the chlorine industry and that dioxin is ubiquitous
because chlorine products are ubiquitous. They say that motor vehicles emit dioxin
because chlorinated chemicals are added to petrol, wood-burning releases dioxin
because of the use of chlorine-based wood preservatives and that incinerators are a
major source of dioxin because of the chlorine-containing wastes burnt in them—
PVC plastics in medical waste incinerators, chlorinated solvents and pesticides in
hazardous waste incinerators, and PVC plastics, chlorine-bleached paper, chlorine-
containing paints, pesticides and cleaners in municipal incinerators:[62]

> Dioxin in the environment at levels that potentially threaten human health is neither
> natural nor unavoidable; it is the necessary result of the production, distribution and
> disposal of the products of chlorine chemistry. Eliminating dioxin generation will
> require that humans stop making the chlorine-based chemicals that inevitably lead to
> dioxin formation.[63]

2. Banning the element chlorine from the planet

The Competitive Enterprise Institute, a think-tank which has received funds from
the Chemical Manufacturers Association, put out an essay subtitled "The End of
Chlorine" which claimed: "There is a mounting campaign, led by environmental
activists in wealthy industrialized nations, to eliminate every last man-made chlorine molecule from the face of the earth."[64] Such an idea is ridiculed by pointing
out that "Mother Nature manufactures at least 1,500 chlorine-containing chemicals" including common table salt.[65] The Alliance for the Responsible Use of
Chlorine Chemistry says "Groups like Greenpeace want to rid the world of chlorine. . . hundreds of animals and organisms manufacture chlorine compounds. . ."[66]

Greenpeace's calls for a gradual phase out of the industrial use of chlorine,
initially seen as radical, were backed by more respected mainstream organizations
as the effects of dioxin emerged during the 1990s. In 1992 the Science Advisory

Board of the International Joint Commission on the Great Lakes (IJC) concluded that organochlorines were a public health threat and that the use of chlorine as an industrial feedstock should be phased out:

> We conclude that persistent toxic substances are too dangerous to the biosphere and to humans to permit their release in *any* quantity. . .We know that when chlorine is used as a feedstock in a manufacturing process, one cannot necessarily predict or control which chlorinated organics will result, and in what quantity. Accordingly, the Commission concludes that the use of chlorine and its compounds should be avoided in the manufacturing process.[67]

In the following year (1993) the Governing Council of the American Public Health Association, one of the leading scientific and medical associations in the US, unanimously endorsed a resolution urging US industries to stop using chlorine. It stated "the only feasible and prudent approach to eliminating the release and discharge of chlorinated organic chemicals and consequent exposure is to avoid the use of chlorine and its compounds in manufacturing processes."[68]

3. Chlorine-based products bring great benefits
In Britain, leading chlorine manufacturers were reported in *The Financial Times* to be "mounting an unprecedented public relations drive to trumpet chlorine's merits".[69] In the US, the Competitive Enterprise Institute and other chlorine industry supporters say that banning chlorine would mean that millions of people in the third world would die from want of disinfected water:

> Even more daunting, a chlorine phase-out would halt the production of most plastics, pesticides and chlorine-containing drugs. . . From safe drinking water, clean swimming pools, pest-free crops, to flame retardants and food packaging, quality white paper and bright socks, Saran wrap, plastic bottles, garden hoses, window frames and sturdy plumbing pipes, the end of chlorine would spell the end of modern civilization itself.[70]

This is also the line taken by a Chlorine Chemistry Council news release which used National Health Week to point out how "chlorine is an important contributor to public health protection and disease prevention. . . virtually eliminating waterborne diseases such as cholera and typhoid in the US" and is used in eighty-five per cent of drugs. And on the internet the Council explains how chlorine "works for the environment". Three examples are given: by enabling the production of materials for automobiles that make them lighter and therefore more fuel-efficient; through "crop protection chemicals" (a euphemism for pesticides) that result in higher crop yields and therefore less pressure to convert rainforests for agriculture; and in purifying silicon for use in solar panel chips.[71]

The Council claims "almost forty per cent of US jobs and income are in some way dependent on chlorine", and the Alliance for the Responsible Use of Chlorine Chemistry argues that "chlorine-related industries provide some five million jobs worldwide and direct capital investment in the hundreds of billions of dollars". The alliance therefore resolves to "undertake programs of education

and advocacy regarding the responsible applications of chlorine chemistry."[72]
A writer in the *Texas Observer* noted:

> The CCC and its allies are quick to characterize any attempt to point out the con-
> nection between dioxin, organochlorines and chlorine production as part of a sinis-
> ter campaign to 'ban chlorine' immediately, so that they can conjure up the
> catastrophic effects and costs of an abrupt elimination of chlorine—as if it were to
> happen overnight, without transition or alternatives.[73]

Indeed, the Council argues that chlorine is "irreplacable in our economy"
and "it's hard to envision life without it." However, as well-known environmental scientist Barry Commoner pointed out to a Citizen's Conference on Dioxin,
chlorine-based products have permeated the modern world "not so much by creating new industries as by taking over existing forms of production. . . It grew
through a virulent form of industrial imperialism." He suggests that there are and
have been alternatives to these chemicals.[74]

Gordon Durnil, chair of the International Joint Commission which had recommended a phasing out of the industrial use of chlorine (and a conservative
Republican Bush appointee), wrote in his book *The Making of a Conservative
Environmentalist* that the Commissioners had discussed how long a phase-out
would take, thinking that it might take fifty years. They were amazed when
"Industry came to us and told us how stupid we were" for suggesting a phase out
of chlorine because "finding a suitable alternative might take thirty years. Later
they reduced that to twenty years."[75]

4. The case against dioxin is based on emotion rather than science
The chlorine industry and its allies present their opponents' arguments as coming
from environmentalists, such as Greenpeace, rather than from scientists. In this
way they maintain that the argument that dioxin is dangerous is based on fear
and emotion, but that their own view is based on science. Gordon Gribble,
writing for the Heartland Institute think-tank, says: "Numerous reports in the
media have ascribed possible detrimental health effects to chlorine, dioxin and
other chlorinated chemicals. . . Greenpeace. . . has led the attack. . . Greenpeace's
claims face formidable opposition from the scientific community." He and others
in the industry continue to insist that "The only documented adverse health
effect of exposure to dioxin is the skin disease chloracne."[76] The issue of other
health effects is never presented as being supported by scientific evidence nor
even as a scientific controversy.

The Chlorophiles say they are concerned that 'mankind' will be excluded
from the benefits of chlorine because of "prejudices and false or erroneous information".[77] The Wise Use leaders Arnold and Gottlieb go so far as to claim that
"a $400 million government study has concluded that dioxin is everywhere and
has been doing no detectable harm. . . However, environmental groups still try
to peddle fear of dioxin as a fund-raising gimmick and press for more government studies, hoping that one will someday come up with the politically correct
result."[78]

The Managing Director of the Chlorine Chemistry Council, C. T. Howlett, told a UN working party:

> Rather than being guided by what we know—the scientific facts about chlorine and chlorinated compounds and the many benefits they have brought to society—the debate is revolving around what we don't know and the fears that spring from a lack of understanding and rush to judgement.[79]

He called for the debate to move from "Greenpeace's slanderous characterization of 'Absolute Death' to the scientific reality of 'Absolute Necessity'. . ." and that common sense would show that chlorine chemistry's benefits more than outweighed its "hypothetical risks". He even suggested that dioxin "may ironically help provide a cure for breast cancer" by providing, at certain exposure levels, "a form of chemoprotection".[80]

In 1995 Howlett addressed the American Chemical Society, stressing "the role that you, as scientists, can help play in setting the record straight". He said that "the scientific data to support a chlorine ban or restrictions on its uses are sketchy or non-existent" and that the chlorine issue was being driven by "perception, sprinkled with a strong dose of politics":

> To the public, dioxin is the most toxic chemical known to mankind. This belief persists despite a preponderance of scientific evidence that dioxin does not cause adverse human health effects other than chloracne, a condition that results only from extremely high levels of dioxin exposure. . . Rather than advancing public knowledge about dioxin—and perhaps, calming some fears, the EPA's draft reassessment, failed to differentiate its regulatory policy on dioxin from matters of scientific fact.[81]

5. Nature produces many substances that behave like dioxin

Another line taken by the Competitive Enterprise Institute and the Alliance for the Responsible Use of Chlorine Chemistry is that synthetic oestrogens such as dioxin that act as endocrine disrupters are dwarfed by the phytoestrogens produced by hundreds of plants that "appear to produce endocrine disrupters. . . The estrogenic effects from the phytoestrogens in our diets are an estimated forty million times greater than those from synthetic chemicals. . . To date, however, there is no concrete evidence that either pose a risk to human health."[82]

A similar line has been used in Australia by the head of the Environmental Health and Safety Unit of the Commonwealth government who has said that while most of the focus has been on man-made chemicals, naturally occurring oestrogens and those produced for therapeutic use "are produced or ingested in much larger amounts than environmental pollutants". He said that there is "no definite proof for any connection between environmental exposure of humans to oestrogenic substances and increasing cancer incidences or decreasing male fertility" and that the emphasis should be on the need for further research.[83]

The British Plastics Federation also refers to the "presence of naturally-occurring oestrogenic chemicals in foodstuffs such as soya, peas, beans etc." And the Chlorophiles have argued that "plants give natural oestrogen mimics in our food." They suggested that we ingest so many 'natural carcinogens' in our food that we should not be concerned about minute amounts of carcinogens caused by chlorine products.[84]

Chlorine Industry Public Relations

In the face of the threat to chlorine, the Chlorine Chemistry Council hired PR firm Mongoven, Biscoe & Duchin (MBD), who analysed the EPA reassessment report and its public relations implications. As we saw in the previous chapter, MBD specializes in gathering intelligence on environmental activists; in this case it keeps the Chemistry Council up to date on "anti-chlorine activists" and their strategies, and advises on ways to counter them.

MBD warned the Chemistry Council that environmental activists would use "children and their need for protection to compel stricter regulation of toxic substances" and that "this would reduce all exposure standards to the lowest possible levels. . ." They also warned that the use of the 'precautionary principle' would be pushed by activists; therefore the industry should fight against the precautionary principle and "assist the public in understanding the damage it [the principle] inflicts on the role of science in modern development and production. . ."[85] According to Peter Montague:

> Mongoven's long-term strategy is to characterize the 'phase out chlorine' position as 'a rejection of accepted scientific method,' as a violation of the chlorine industry's Constitutional right to 'have the liberty to do what they choose,' and in that sense as a threat to fundamental American values.[86]

MBD recommended a series of steps the Chlorine Chemistry Council should take, including:[87]

- taking "advantage of the schisms" within the US government administration such as within the EPA and between the EPA and other government agencies
- hiring Ketchum Public Relations to "reach out to editorial boards to highlight flaws in the risk assessment portion of the dioxin reassessment"
- enlisting "legitimate scientists. . . willing to ask pointed questions" at forthcoming conferences
- building alliances on the PVC issue, "beginning with those with an obvious economic stake, e.g. home builders, realtors, product manufacturers, hospitals and others. . ."
- taking steps "to discredit the precautionary principle within the more moderate environmental groups as well as within the scientific and medical communities. . ."
- directing a programme to "pediatric groups throughout the country and to counter activist claims of chlorine-related health problems in children. . ."
- getting medical associations on side by getting a panel of eminent physicians to emphasize the role of chlorine "as a key chemical in pharmaceuticals and medical devises" and by stimulating peer-reviewed articles in medical journals on "the role of chlorine chemistry in treating disease. . ."

• making alliances with environmental groups such as INFORM: "The organization has a solid history of working with corporations, citizen groups, major environmental organizations and governments at all levels."

The Chlorine Chemistry Council has developed classroom materials to "improve the way science and environmental issues are discussed in the classroom". These include a newsletter for teachers, curriculum materials, and a module for ninth and tenth graders on *Understanding Environmental Health Risks* that encourages children to "weigh risks and benefits so they can make sound decisions about environmental hazards."[88] A package entitled *Welcome to Building Block City!* has been described by a Consumers Union study of environmental materials as "Commercial and incomplete with several inaccuracies and strong bias for chlorine compounds. . . Fosters false sense of how safe chlorinated chemicals are."[89]

The Council also has teaching materials on the internet which stress the benefits of chlorine and ask students to list all the products that they use at home and at school which use chlorine. They are given a check list of such items to start with. In discussing risk on its internet pages, the Council presents taking risks as an everyday part of life, such as driving a car or flying in a plane: "Risk accompanies virtually everything we do. Even seemingly 'safe' activities, such as taking a bath or climbing stairs, sometimes result in injury or death."[90] The implied message is: "Why even bother about the risk of chlorine products when the benefits are so obvious?"

The Chlorophiles have undertaken a number of actions on behalf of the industry, including a protest at Greenpeace headquarters in Brussels against their anti-chlorine campaign; a petition; and a letter-writing campaign directed at advertisers who use the terms 'chlorine-free' or 'PVC-free' as a selling point.[91] In 1994 they lodged an unsuccessful complaint against a Greenpeace leaflet with the Dutch Advertising Code Council.[92]

When the Clinton administration proposed that the EPA investigate chlorinated organic chemicals the Chlorine Chemistry Council suggested to its members, their employees and customers that Clinton intended to ban chlorine. It called on them to write to Clinton and to members of Congress and was able to generate, it claims, a million letters to Congress, as well as getting industry executives to contact members of congress, cabinet members and executive branch appointees.[93] *Plastics World* proclaimed "Industry officials are aghast that the Clinton Administration would even contemplate a ban on chlorine, given its enormous role in our society, both in industry and in public health. . . Behind all the fuss is a mere thirty pounds or less of dioxins produced annually. . . That's not even a needle in a haystack."[94] The Chemical Manufacturers Association met with cabinet members and the proposed study was never carried out.

An example of how the Chlorine Chemistry Council has been operating at the local level is the battle over anti-dioxin resolutions at a Texas Parent Teacher Association (PTA) convention in 1995. A number of local PTAs had passed such resolutions without too much fuss prior to the state convention. Then, less than two weeks before the convention, a number of industry groups, including the

Chlorine Chemistry Council, the Texas Chemical Council, the Texas Association of Business and Chambers of Commerce and various others became involved in a pre-convention battle to thwart the resolutions.[95] One of the resolutions stated that the PTA "supports legislation and actions that decrease, phase-out and eliminate the creation, release and exposure of dioxins... .[and] the use of alternative processes, technologies, and products that avoid exposure to Dioxin, especially those that are chlorine-free."[96]

A front group of six PTA members who posed as 'concerned parents' sent a letter with a package of information "from leading citizen and business organizations, academic scientists and public officials" to PTA members and convention delegates. In the letter they labelled the resolutions as "one-sided. . . inaccurate and misleading". They described the resolution calling for the elimination of dioxin as a ban on chlorine and chlorine-derived products. The second resolution, which opposed the use of hazardous waste as fuel in a local cement kiln run by TXI, was characterized as a threat to legitimate business. Three of these 'ordinary parents' were members of the Chemical Council, one of them an employee of DuPont; a fourth parent was TXI's director of communications; and a fifth was a "government affairs consultant" for mining companies and married to the director of the front group Texas Citizens for a Sound Economy.[97]

Parents also received a letter from the President of the Texas Institute for the Advancement of Chemical Technology which claimed that "the use of waste-derived fuel by cement kilns has been proven safe by state and federal studies" and that "no scientific evidence exists connecting the process with any negative effects". The letter also cited the beneficial uses of chlorine and the jobs the chlorine industry provided.[98]

Before the convention, five professional chemical industry representatives met with the proposer of the motion for three days, persuading her to change the wording of the anti-dioxin resolution. In the end she accepted their reworded resolution which avoided all mention of chlorine and called for further research and "voluntary reductions" of dioxin. That resolution was passed, but the second resolution on the cement kiln was postponed indefinitely in a procedural motion before discussion could take place.[99]

Reassessment Responses

The industry response to the EPA draft reassessment report was a coordinated one, with various industry representatives meeting to discuss strategies and divide up tasks. The agricultural industry groups, affected because their products had been labelled as being contaminated with dioxins, formed the Dioxin Working Group, coordinated by the National Cattlemen's Association, to lobby Washington officials about the reassessment report and make use of their strong relations with the Agriculture department to apply pressure to the EPA to water down its conclusions before the final report was published.[100]

Advice to the chlorine industry from a consultant with the PR firm E. Bruce Harrison was to emphasize the "gaps in science" and "highlight uncertainties".

The National Cattlemen's Association hired scientists to write a critique of the reassessment. The dioxin-source industries such as the chemical industry and the incinerator industry questioned the toxicology in the report. The American Forest and Paper Association hired the ENVIRON Corporation to put together an expert panel to review the EPA's reassessment. This panel argued there was not enough scientific information to support the EPA's conclusions that "adverse human health effects should be expected at near current background body burdens." It argued that although developmental and immunological effects were found in animals, no such effects have been found in humans, and cancer was inconclusive because workers had been exposed to other chemicals at the same time.[101]

The Chlorine Chemistry Council attempted to undermine the EPA's findings, using scientific consultants to attack them at the EPA's hearings in Washington and by influencing the EPA's Scientific Advisory Board (SAB) panel which was undertaking a review of the reassessment. According to a Greenpeace report, two of the most vocal opponents to the report on the SAB panel were scientists who had received funding from the chlorine industry. One had received several million dollars worth of grants from the American Forest and Paper Association to study dioxin, and gifts for research from the Chemical Manufacturers Association and Dow Chemical. The other had received grants from Dow Chemical several years running and his Center had received grants from companies with an interest in dioxin regulation such as Ciba-Geigy, DuPont, General Electric, Georgia-Pacific, ICI, Monsanto and others.[102]

The Scientific Advisory Board met in May 1995. Its recommendations mainly addressed "refinements, corrections, and clarifications, not substantive revisions". It agreed with the EPA position that "current levels of dioxin-like compounds in the environment" are derived from human activities. It also concurred that their estimate of average dioxin exposure was reasonable. "Virtually all of the committee" believed that dioxin and dioxin-like materials should be classified as a probable human carcinogen.[103]

The Board was less happy with the final concluding chapter of the health document. Some of the committee felt that the chapter tended to overstate the possibility for danger, whilst others thought the chapter was "appropriately conservative within the context of public health protection".[104] In the face of criticisms by the Board that this chapter of the Reassessment had not been adequately peer-reviewed, the main authors of the concluding chapter published it in a peer-reviewed journal in September 1995.[105]

According to the Citizen's Clearinghouse for Hazardous Waste:

> When the May 1995 meeting of the SAB's committee on the reassessment failed to produce any significant challenge to the findings of the reassessment, the CCC and its allies from the American Forest and Paper Association (AFPA) made up their own story of what happened at the panel's meeting and spun their own story to the *Wall Street Journal* and other media outlets.[106]

At the end of 1995 the Congress's Subcommittee on Energy & Environment held a public hearing on "Scientific Integrity and Federal Policies and Mandates: Case Study 1—EPA's Dioxin Reassessment". Prior to the hearings, Peter Montague of the Environmental Research Foundation claimed: "It is widely understood in Washington that this hearing is going to be a 'witch hunt' aimed at punishing the EPA for reaching conclusions that the paper industry and other industrial poisoners don't like."[107] The Citizen's Clearing House pointed out that in 1993-1994 twenty-four out of the twenty-eight members of the House Subcommittee which was holding the hearings had received money from the Political Action Committees representing the forest and paper industries, the chemical industry and waste management industries.[108]

Prior to the hearing, environmentalists, including the Citizen's Clearinghouse, complained that the witnesses who would give evidence at the hearing were "hand-picked by the Republican majority to downplay the health risks from dioxin". They asked why scientists who argued that dioxin was dangerous, such as Linda Birnbaum, principal author of the concluding chapter, were not being allowed to testify whilst industry experts were invited to do so.[109] A group of forty-six scientists also wrote a joint letter to the committee stating:

> The subcommittee's current list of non-governmental witnesses is composed exclusively of individuals whose scientific integrity is compromised by the funding of their work; by dioxin-polluting industries such as incinerator, chemical, and pulp and paper corporations.[110]

Whilst the final outcome of the dioxin battle remains to be seen, it is clear from this account that corporations have engaged in a concerted and lengthy public relations campaign to portray dioxin as relatively safe. They have been able to do this through their use of third parties to put their case as well as through direct lobbying and public relations tactics. These efforts have often been concealed from the public, which must rely on the media for their information. Media coverage of the dioxin issue will be further considered in Chapter Thirteen.

Chapter 10

Advertisers: Getting Them Young

Our enormously productive economy. . . demands that we make consumption our way of life, that we convert the buying and use of goods into rituals, that we seek spiritual satisfaction, our ego satisfaction, in consumption. We need things consumed, burned up, worn out, replaced, and discarded at an ever increasing rate.

Victor Lebow, Retailing Analyst[1]

Advertisers spend hundreds of billions of dollars a year worldwide encouraging, persuading and manipulating people into a consumer lifestyle that has devastating consequences for the environment through its extravagance and wastefulness.[2] In his book *Earth in the Balance*, Vice-President Al Gore wrote:

Our civilization is holding ever more tightly to its habit of consuming larger and larger quantities every year of coal, oil, fresh air and water, trees, topsoil, and the thousand other substances we rip from the crust of the earth, transforming them into not just the sustenance and shelter we need but much more that we don't need: huge quantities of pollution, products for which we spend billions on advertising to convince ourselves we want, massive surpluses of products that depress prices while the products themselves go to waste, and diversions and distractions of every kind.[3]

Advertising expenditure has multiplied seven times since the 1950s. It has grown faster than the world economy and three times faster than global population. And almost half of that expenditure is targeted at Americans: the average American is exposed to about three thousand advertisements each day. More money is spent persuading Americans to be consumers than is spent on higher education or Medicare.[4]

Whilst each advertisement may be outwardly aimed at selling a particular product, it is also promoting "the interests and ideology of its corporate sponsors".[5] And the persistent avalanche of advertisements that television watchers and others are exposed to sells a consumerist way of life that offers personal fulfilment through the acquisition and accumulation of commodities.

Even if they fail to sell a particular product, they sell consumerism itself by ceaselessly reiterating the idea that there is a product to solve each of life's problems, indeed that existence would be satisfying and complete if only we bought the right things. Advertisers thus cultivate needs by hitching their wares to the infinite existential yearnings of the human soul.[6]

Most advertisements tell little about the product they are selling; rather, they seek to create an impression. They attempt to associate their product with the unarticulated desires of their audience. Advertising exploits individual insecurities, creates false needs and offers counterfeit solutions. It fosters dissatisfaction that leads to consumption: "Consumers are taught personal incompetence and dependence on mass-market producers." They are taught that being a citizen "means no more than being a consumer".[7]

Targeting Children

By the time most US children start school they will have spent more hours watching television than they will spend in class for their entire schooling. Television tends to be used as a *de facto* babysitter and is often a focal point for family life. But a child's exposure to the consumer ethic does not stop at the school gates: a massive infusion of corporate messages bombards school students everyday. Billboards in school hallways carry advertisements, sports events are sponsored, commercial radio is piped in and an 'educational' television channel carries commercial advertisements. Corporate logos and advertisements appear on buses, scoreboards, posters, book covers and videos, and corporations sponsor contests, literacy programmes, reading projects and communications skills training which use their products.[8]

The phenomenon of corporate sponsorship permeates the English-speaking world. In Australia it is a growing but contentious area and "sponsorship is being actively sought as a replacement for Government funding and support."[9] Currently, less is spent on school education in Australia than any other OECD country. Corporate logos are appearing on school reports and letterheads—even McDonald's logos on school uniforms in one school.[10] A number of US-style advertising and sales promotion schemes have already infected the Australian schools system, including:

- Apple providing schools with computers in exchange for numbers of receipts from the Coles supermarket chain. This turned children into promoters for Coles and resulted in them harassing shoppers for their dockets in the stores and their car parks: "We are making beggars of our children," noted an official of the NSW Teachers Federation. Nevertheless this scheme was so successful for Coles sales (with over 6,000 schools taking part) that five other Australian companies have introduced similar schemes.[11]
- McDonald's and Domino's Pizzas giving schools a portion of profits from fast food sales thereby encouraging students to coerce parents and others to buy pizzas or hamburgers in order to raise money for their schools.[12]
- Pizza Hut's 'Book It' program where free pizzas are provided as learning incentives. Winning a free pizza usually means the whole family has to go to Pizza Hut and buy pizzas to keep the child company. Moreover, instead of teaching children the joy of reading they are being bribed to read: "Perhaps we are giving a subliminal message to children that these things are not worth doing for their own sakes. . .?" (In 1992 over 400,000 primary school students took part in this scheme in Australia; 58,000 schools in the US also participate in this scheme, and it also operates in Canada.)[13]

Public relations firms and advertisers have targeted school education in a big way. They recognize that brand loyalties and consumer habits formed when children are young and vulnerable will be carried through to adulthood. According to a senior vice president of Grey Advertising: "It isn't enough to just advertise on television. . . You've got to reach kids throughout their day—in school, as they're shopping at the mall. . . or at the movies. You've got to become part of the fabric of their lives."[14] The British advertising firm Saatchi and Saatchi formed a Kids division in 1992 to sell products to children between two and fourteen years of age. In 1995 it was paid over $100 million for this service.[15]

Children are increasingly the target of advertisements because of the amount of money they spend themselves, the influence they have on their parents' spending (the nag factor) and because they are trainee consumers. According to the CEO of Prism Communications, "They aren't children so much as what I like to call 'evolving consumers'."[16] In the US there are over fifty-seven million school age children and teenagers who spend about $100 billion each year on sweets, food, drinks, video and electronic products, toys, games, movies, sports, clothes and shoes. Additionally they influence family spending decisions worth another $130 billion on food, vacations, the family car and other spending.[17]

Similar trends are evident in Canada, where 4.4 million children up to twelve years of age spend $1.5 billion dollars annually and influence a further $15 billion spending.[18] In Australia, advertisers attending a conference on *Marketing to Kids and Youth* were told that children and teenagers between the ages of ten and seventeen spent $3.3 billion every year. Another conference, on the subject of *Consumer Kids*, was told that Australian children under eighteen had an average A$31.60 to spend each week and that they influenced more than seventy per cent of their parents' clothes and fast food purchases.[19]

The US Consumers Union estimates that 30,000 commercial messages are targeted at American children each year. By the age of seventeen, each teenager will have been exposed to hundreds of thousands of advertisements. Increasingly, younger children are being targeted. Advertisers spent $500 million in 1990 on marketing aimed at US children under twelve years compared with $100 million in 1980.[20]

According to *Direct Marketing* magazine, by the age of eight children make most of their own buying decisions: "Children start at a very early age to develop brand loyalty."[21] Indeed, advertising research indicates that children as young as three or four years old recognize and ask for particular brands. Selina Guber from Children's Market Research says that children brought up since 1980 "are aware of brands and status items even before they can read." Kids 'R' Us president, Mike Searles, says "If you own this child at an early age. . . you can own this child for years to come."[22]

Yet there are questions about the ability of children so young to understand advertising and its intent, and not be deceived and manipulated by it. Experts say that children don't understand persuasive intent until they are eight or nine years old and that it is unethical to advertise to them before then.[23] According to Karpatkin and Holmes from the Consumers Union, "Young children, in particular, have difficulty in distinguishing between advertising and reality in ads, and ads can distort their view of the world."[24] At the same time, Richard Mizerski, an Australian professor of marketing, observes: "Their cognitive structures are beginning to form and they are most sensitive to external influences."[25] This is especially a problem when advertisements appear on school walls, posters and book covers, and gain legitimacy from the supposed endorsement of the school such that children think they must be true.

Older children pay less attention to advertisements and are more able to differentiate between the ads and TV programmes, but they are still easy prey for advertisers. Around puberty, in their early teens, children are forming their own identities and they are "highly vulnerable to pressure to conform to group standards and mores". At this age they feel insecure and want to feel that they belong to their peer group. Advertising manipulates them through their insecurities, seeking to define normality for them, influencing the way they "view and obtain appropriate models for the adult world", and undermining "fundamental human values in the development of the identity of children". Advertisements actively encourage them to seek happiness and esteem through consumption.[26]

The British Code of Advertising and Sales Promotion recognizes that children are more vulnerable than adults to the hidden messages of advertising and states that advertisements aimed at children "should not exploit their credulity, loyalty, vulnerability or lack of experience". In particular, "they should not be made to feel inferior or unpopular for not buying the advertised product" nor to be "lacking in courage, duty or loyalty". In 1995 the UK Advertising Standards Authority (ASA) received 175 complaints about advertisements aimed at children and upheld sixteen of these.

In the late 1980s Chris Whittle realized that teenagers were "the new pipeline into American households". To take advantage of this, Whittle Communications founded Channel One. From 1990 it loaned schools VCRs, televisions and a satellite dish "in exchange for students' minds for twelve minutes each day". Today, 350,000 classrooms (forty per cent of classrooms in the US) with eight million students between the ages of thirteen and eighteen have accepted the Channel One deal. It requires ninety per cent of the students at a school to watch the twelve-minute program ninety per cent of the time, from beginning to end and without interruption.[27]

That twelve minutes includes two minutes of advertising in the middle of it, paid for by companies selling products like snack and fast foods, who are eager to reach the children at a formative age when brand loyalty and consumer habits can be established. These advertisements are thought to be so effective that Channel One is able to charge twice as much for an advertisement as a network television station charges for a prime-time news spot—in 1994, about $200,000 for thirty seconds.[28]

> Students in schools with *Channel One* are required to attend to the television screen in a fashion unprecedented in the history of the medium, they watch ads in a structured environment with an authority figure demanding their attention. They watch in an environment of peer influence.[29]

The deal is quite coercive for schools that sign up for a three-year contract. If they break the contract, for example by not requiring ninety per cent of students to watch the twelve-minute broadcast, then they are "financially liable for the cost of cabling school buildings and for the removal of video equipment".[30] Teachers are not supposed to interrupt or turn off the broadcast whilst it is being aired.[31]

Channel One facilities are found mainly in poorer areas where schools cannot afford to buy the equipment themselves. A study by researchers at the University of Massachusetts found that the schools that spent least on educational materials were most likely to receive Channel One, whilst those that could afford their own video equipment tended to reject the deal. Channel One has been banned in high schools in the states of California and New York.[32]

In a study investigating the effects of advertising on Channel One, researchers at Michigan State University found that children exposed to Channel One "expressed more consumer-oriented attitudes than non-viewers" and had more materialistic attitudes. Whilst children often watch ads on television at home it has been found that discussing the ads with parents negates the effect of the ads to some extent, and reduces the subsequent materialism in children, whereas Channel One precludes that. The researchers concluded that "advertising to school students is harmful to their value system."[33]

Another study, by a researcher at the University of Missouri-Columbia, found that most teenagers were quite naive about the advertisements they saw on Channel One and did not view them as an attempt to sell a product or service. They were not always able to distinguish between advertisements and news items. One Pepsi advertisement, which less than half the students identified as a real advertisement, even confused the student teacher. A study of 3,000 Channel One viewing students in North Carolina found that most of them thought the products advertised would be good for them because they were being shown the advertisements at school.[34]

Other researchers have found that the news content of Channel One's broadcast also leaves a lot to be desired. It is made up of three minutes of world and national news and seven minutes of "news magazine features of interest to adolescents". It is "too fast-paced and fragmented to deepen students' understanding of current events", and many of the news features promote the interests of the owners of the Channel, including Phillips and Time Warner; for example stories on a new light bulb and on Warner Brothers' movies. Other features promote products such as an item on how Nike shoes are made or one on the popularity of Ninja Turtles.[35]

The whole broadcast is produced with techniques normally used for video clips. Speech is twice as fast as normal for both news and advertisements, and news items are very short—in fact shorter than the advertisements. Mark Crispin Miller, a professor of journalism, observed: "I found that the outright commercials were less worrisome than the so-called news segments themselves, which were more often than not pro-business propaganda."[36]

A new arena for advertising is the internet. It is estimated that about a million children are using the internet world-wide, a figure that is bound to

increase dramatically over the next few years.[37] According to the Director of
Saatchi & Saatchi Interactive, "This is a medium for advertisers that is unprecedented. . . there's probably no other product or service that we can think of that
is like it in terms of capturing kids' interest."[38] In their advertising material
Saatchi and Saatchi explain their Kid Connection service:

> We at KID CONNECTION are committed to understanding kids: their motiva-
> tions, their feelings, and their influences. In keeping with our mission to connect our
> clients to the kid market with programs that match our clients' business objectives
> with the needs, drives and desires of kids. . . Interactive technology is at the forefront
> of kid culture, allowing us to enter into contemporary kid life and communicate with
> them in an environment they call their own.[39]

Children as young as four are being targeted by advertisers on the internet,
and often these interactions with children are unmediated by parents or teachers.
These advertisers elicit personal information from the children by getting them
to fill out surveys before they can play and offering prizes such as T-shirts for
filling in "lengthy profiles that ask for purchasing behavior, preferences and information on other family members". Advertisers then use this information to "craft
individualized messages and ads" targeted at each child. The ads are integrated
with the other content of the internet site, which is designed to keep the children
engrossed in play for hours at a time. There are even product "spokescharacters"
to interact with the children and develop relationships with them so that long-
lasting brand loyalties can be developed.[40]

Targeting Education: Infiltrating School Lessons

Teachers are being overwhelmed with free and unsolicited curriculum material
from public relations firms, corporations and industry associations. The corporate stampede to get their messages into schools through 'educational' resources
whilst their customers are very young is a recent phenomenon. In 1993 corporations spent $381 million in the US on school education, which accounted for
15% of all corporate donations.[41]

Lifetime Learning Systems is one of the companies which compiles educa-
tional materials on behalf of corporations and trade associations. It services more
than 350 corporations in the US alone, as well as associations such as the
American Nuclear Society, and claims to reach almost one hundred per cent of
US schools—sixty-three million young people every year.[42] According to Lifetime
Learning Systems' promotional literature:

> Kids spend forty per cent of each day in the classroom where traditional advertising
> can't reach them. . . Now you can enter the classroom through custom-made learn-
> ing materials created with your specific marketing objectives in mind. Communicate
> with young spenders directly and, through them, their teachers and families as well.[43]

> Let Lifetime Learning Systems bring your message to the classroom, where young
> people are forming attitudes that will last a lifetime.[44]

Coming from school, all these materials carry an extra measure of credibility that gives your message added weight.[45]

IMAGINE millions of students discussing your product in class. IMAGINE their teachers presenting your organization's point of view.[46]

The great advantage of embedding corporate messages in sponsored learning materials over more direct means of advertising is that any residual scepticism with which conventional advertisements might be treated disappears altogether when it comes to advertisements and public relations material secreted within school lessons. As one writer points out: "Imagine—your target market not only reads your ads—they get tested on them."[47] One kit put out by Teacher Support Software, which is used in many kindergartens in Texas, includes test questions such as "Taco Bell has [blank] and burritos."[48]

More often the corporate message is more subtle—sometimes so subtle that the teachers don't even notice it. If they do, they may turn a blind eye so that they can use the materials, which are hard for them to resist, particularly for teachers in poorly resourced schools. The materials, professionally produced with lots of colour and games, prepared homework assignments and even computers that automatically grade the students' work, are generally offered for free.[49]

In the US, as in Australia and Canada, school education receives inadequate government funding and teachers have inadequate teaching resources available to help them. In Canada, the Ontario Secondary School Teachers' Federation has prepared and distributed a pamphlet on the commercialisation of schools in Canada, noting that budget cuts by provincial governments in the 1990s have made the school system a major target for business interests, who seek to fill the resource gap.[50]

Some say that corporations are "taking advantage of schools short on funds by feeding them materials, filled with company logos, that are designed to encourage consumption."[51] It is almost as if underfunding of schools is part of a corporate strategy to enable advertisers better access. At the very least, corporate sponsorship of school resources enables the underfunding of schools by governments to continue.[52]

Corporations eager to enhance their public image, increase product visibility and establish consumer lifestyles are responding to America's education crisis *en masse*. Just about every major company or trade association now markets flashy, bright education books, brochures, posters and videos, many of which focus on the environment. Curricula, product logos and even advertisements on subjects ranging from recycling and math to financial planning and poetry have found their way into most public school systems across the country.[53]

In most cases, the so-called educational materials give students a distorted picture of environmental issues and other problems, social choices and tradeoffs. They present a corporate view as 'fact' and report the results of corporate-funded studies without saying who financed them. They often fail to "acknowledge the sponsor's own financial interest, or to disclose conditions and information that affect the accuracy of what they teach".[54]

There is not really any competition from non-corporate views, because environmental groups and others don't have the funding that is necessary to develop and distribute such an array of professionally produced materials and distribute them widely. And teachers do not have the resources or knowledge to balance the material with differing viewpoints.

> Corporate influence on what children learn doesn't end with ads for products and services. American students are introduced to environmental issues as they use materials supplied by corporations who pollute the soil, air, and water. . . And there is a good chance that they'll be taught the virtues of corporate-supported economic initiatives, such as the North American Free Trade Agreement, with handouts on "critical thinking" bankrolled by Mobil Oil, a supporter of the pact.[55]

Sometimes teachers are trained to use these materials. Every year hundreds of thousands of teachers in the US attend workshops run by corporations in conjunction with their educational materials. These materials are sent directly to teachers, bypassing official curriculum review committees, so that they are not subject to any scrutiny apart from that of the teachers themselves, who may not be able to judge the accuracy or bias in the materials. Advertisers at a Toronto conference on "Kid Power: Creative Kid-Targeted Marketing Strategies" were told how to bypass the 'gate-keepers' so that their messages could be transmitted directly to the children.[56]

Environmental Education

Project Learning Tree is an environmental educational programme for schools sponsored by the Forestry industry. It claims to be "one of the premier environmental education programs in the world". It is used in the US, Canada, Mexico, Japan, Sweden, Finland and Brazil, and has been going for over twenty years, during which time it has reached about twenty million students. In the US alone about 60,000 teachers attend its workshops each year where they learn how to "use the program with young people".[57]

The programme claims to train children from kindergarten through to 8th grade how to "investigate environmental issues, and encourages them to make informed, responsible decisions".[58] According to one of its critics, the Institute for Earth Education, *Project Learning Tree* promotes "the idea that the forest's primary purpose is that of a resource for human use, not a community of life for a variety of plants and animals."[59]

Project Learning Tree says that its goal is "helping students to learn HOW to think, not WHAT to think."[60] It follows in the tradition of earlier efforts by industrialists to train the masses to be consumers. Edward Filene, a spokesperson for industrialists in the 1920s and 30s, spoke frankly about the need to create a consumer culture where industry could "sell to the masses all that it employs the masses to create". "The time has come," he argued, "when all our educational institutions. . . must concentrate on the great social task of teaching the masses not what to think but *how to think*, and thus to find out how to behave like human beings in the machine age."[61]

Many corporate-sponsored packages seek to teach children to be consumers and to passively accept the corporate viewpoint on environmental issues. Public relations professionals have recognized that environmental education in schools can lead to children who campaign against polluters and influence decisions made by their parents about environmental matters. Most children are interested in the environment: research undertaken by World Wide Fund for Nature (WWF), which has formed a partnership with Eastman Kodak to produce educational materials on biodiversity, found that seventy-one per cent of children were interested in the environment and seventy-four per cent of those would willingly spend an hour outside school hours each week to learn more about it.[62]

The potential to shape environmental perceptions and improve corporate images at the same time has attracted many customers to the firms designing educational materials for corporations. The American Nuclear Society has a kit which tells children about the beneficial uses of nuclear technology and attempts to describe the problem of waste disposal in harmless terms: "Anything we produce results in some 'leftovers' that are either recycled or disposed of—whether we're making electricity from coal or nuclear, or making scrambled eggs!"[63]

Caretakers All, curriculum material designed by the Beef Industry Council, was developed for PR purposes to reverse a trend of declining meat consumption. The package, which won a Public Relations award at the 1993 National Agri-Marketing Association's advertising and communications competition, aimed to marry "the concepts of agriculture and environmental stewardship in students' minds". It set out to show how farmers and ranchers look after the environment, and to counter what environmentalists were saying about how farmers and ranchers cause erosion and habitat destruction through overgrazing, as well as polluting waterways above and below ground with manure from feed lots.[64]

The kits consist of study prints depicting farming scenes, such as bedding for dairy cattle made of shredded newspaper, and also a clean-up day in a park. Each print has activities associated with it, such as experiments with salt water and plants and helping to clean up the school. The US Consumers Union describes *Caretakers All* as "pure one-sided image-building for farmers and ranchers, disguised as lessons on land conservation".[65]

Twenty thousand kits were distributed free to teachers. Barbara Selover, Director of the Meat Board Education Programs, says that for an investment of $425,000 those kits will reach about two million young children over the next few years: "That comes to about 21 cents per child, which we feel is a pretty cost-effective investment."[66] She is reported in the journal *Agri Marketing* as citing four reasons why the kit worked well as a public relations tool for the beef industry:

> First, the subject matter—taking care of the environment is a serious issue that merits attention in schools. Next, the materials reach children at an age when they are very impressionable. It also is an in-depth learning tool that delivers a consistent message over a period of time from a trusted source—their teacher. Finally it reaches large numbers of teachers and students directly.[67]

Georgia-Pacific, a corporation with forestry interests, produces elementary school materials that claim that forestry saves forests because: "When no one harvests, trees grow old and are more likely to be killed by disease rot, and the elements. Very old trees will not support many kinds of wildlife because the forest floor is too shaded to grow the ground plants animals need."[68]

The American Coal Foundation's materials manage to avoid mention of global warming and acid rain when they claim, in the module on *Coal and Our Environment*, that "To keep coal from harming our land, air and water: coal is cleaned before it's burned. 'Scrubbers' take out most of the harmful gases; Soil is replaced. Grass and trees are planted after surface mining." Exxon has also produced a kit that portrays fossil fuels as being environmentally friendly and having no practical rivals. The Council for Wildlife Conservation & Education, an affiliate of the National Shooting Sports Association, has produced *Wildlife for Tomorrow: The Story of Our Un-Endangered Species.*[69]

The chemical industry has concentrated on science education. It has expanded its role to an active one of "helping to train teachers, encouraging employee volunteers to teach courses, and guiding school curricula" with the stated aim of improving science comprehension, giving "kids a balanced view of how science improves our daily lives", producing "well-rounded students, who, one day, may be decision makers affecting industry policy". The chemical industry has also targeted university students, science and non-science, with its Responsible Care Curriculum Program. Responsible Care, a code of practice for the chemical industry, was introduced to improve the public image of the chemical industry and to promote self-regulation as an alternative to increased government regulation of the industry. The Curriculum Program aims to "increase university faculties' awareness of Responsible Care, as well as to erode stereotypes of the industry".[70]

The chemical industry, including companies such as ICI, which operates in the UK and Australia, has been active in providing curriculum materials outside the US—as has the mining industry. The petroleum industry has also been active in both Australia and New Zealand, hoping to "provide a more balanced account" of their operations. BP Oil New Zealand provides various curriculum materials to New Zealand schools on issues ranging from dealing with oil spills to global warming and ozone depletion. The Australian Institute of Petroleum and the Australian Petroleum Exploration Association provide project materials, classroom speakers, and site visits for Australian schools. Also glass, aluminium and plastics companies and industry groupings provide materials to both Australian and New Zealand schools.[71]

In Australia, state government education departments have worked together with business groups. In Western Australia the Ministry of Education has prepared curriculum materials sponsored by Woodside Petroleum, BHP, BP, Shell, Mitsui, Mitsubishi and Cal Asiatic for all secondary schools in the state. The Employer's Education Consortium of Victoria, a coalition of nine of Victoria's largest companies, has had a major input into the state's high school curriculum with the introduction of a compulsory Australian studies unit on the *World of Work.*[72]

In Canada, corporate-sponsored teaching materials have also been a cause for concern, and in 1995 the Ontario Secondary School Teachers' Federation did a study of commercialization in Ontario schools which raised a number of questions about the alliance between business and schools in the light of funding cutbacks by government. Examples of this sort of relationship in Canada include the provision of educational materials and speakers by the Canadian Nuclear Association, Ontario Hydro and the BC Council of Forest Industries. The latter ran an essay competition for high school students on 'Why Clearcut Logging is Beneficial for British Columbia'.[73]

In a report entitled *Captive Kids*, the US Consumers Union analysed 111 different sets of educational materials sponsored by commercial enterprises, trade organizations and corporate-backed nonprofit organizations, twenty-one of which were on environmental topics. It found that the four sets of materials on energy issues presented "lopsided views" and six of the eight sets of materials on solid waste issues were sponsored by companies that "produce disposable products, make packaging or packaging materials, use a great deal of packaging, or are providers of recycling services". As a result of the sponsor's vested interests in how solid waste problems are resolved, these learning materials tended to avoid discussion of reduced consumption or product reuse as serious alternatives, instead emphasising recycling. They presented "a distorted picture of the problems, choices, and trade-offs". The Consumers Union described a McDonald's package called *The Rain Forest Imperative* as "self-serving" and one by the Polystyrene Packaging Council, *The Plastics and the Environment Sourcebook*, as "highly commercial and incomplete with strong bias toward polystyrene packaging".[74]

The Consumers Union found that nearly eighty per cent of the sponsored educational materials it analysed "contained biased or incomplete information, promoting a viewpoint that favors consumption of the sponsor's product or service or a position that favors the company or its economic agenda". It concluded that the commercialisation of education, arising from advertisements and sponsored educational material containing "biased, self-serving and promotional information" posed a "significant and growing threat to the integrity of education in America".[75]

> In-school commercialism is at its worst, we believe, when it masquerades as educational materials or programs and offers half-truths or misstatements that favor the sponsor of the materials. It may be difficult if not impossible for most teachers to correctly judge the objectivity and accuracy of such materials. . . Unfortunately, a teacher's use of a sponsor's materials or products implies an endorsement, and any benefits of such use may come at the cost of teaching children to scrutinize marketing messages objectively.[76]

At the same time as corporate materials are flooding schools and bypassing curriculum review committees, non-corporate environmental education materials are coming under attack from communities dependent on the extraction industries, conservative Christian groups and conservative think-tanks such as the Heritage Foundation and the Competitive Enterprise Institute.[77]

Conservatives recognize the power of genuine environmental education to foster environmental concern and values in the next generation, and are threatened by it. Some conservative Christians have even labelled non-corporate environmental education materials as paganistic, satanistic, anti-Christian and anti-business: "The growing 'environmental education' movement is a recruitment drive intended to conscript young students into a pagan children's campaign."[78] They argue that "the constant depiction of a planet on the brink of environmental catastrophe is frightening children and turning them into eco-warriors at home."[79] According to one Republican State politician:

> This cloudy mixture of New Age mysticism, Native American folklore and primitive Earth worship is being promoted and enforced by the Clinton administration. It is driving the nation's regulatory scheme, and workers, small businessmen and property owners are becoming [its] victims.[80]

Each year the group People for the American Way reports on hundreds of attempts to restrict books in schools, and the numbers of such attempts are increasing each year. For example, a high school text entitled *Environmental Science: Ecology and Human Impact* was withdrawn from one school after a manager of a Monsanto chemical plant, an employer in the area, called for it to be banned as the book was said to be anti-industry. Dr Seuss's *The Lorax* was subjected to a parents' campaign in the timber town of Laytonville, California, because it depicts a character that defends the trees. Another book, *Earth Child*, which uses activities to help students appreciate the beauty of nature and learn about the stars, has also come under attack as satanic and containing "subliminal messages to brainwash our children".[81]

Conservatives are concerned about text books that teach about global warming, acid rain and ozone depletion—all theories they dispute—or which promote activism such as letter-writing and petition-signing. Jonathan Adler from the Competitive Enterprise Institute, who argues that acid rain is beneficial for the eastern forests because it provides nitrogen which is a nutrient, was one of a team who put together *A Parent's Primer on the Environment*, which critiques environmental textbooks.[82]

Environmental education is a required part of the curriculum in public primary and secondary schools in thirty states in the US, but in Arizona this was reversed in 1990 after a campaign led by a State Republican who labelled the curriculum guide as "ecocultism". In Meridian, Idaho, the school board issued teaching guidelines which stated: "Discussion should not reflect negative attitudes against business or industry who do the best job under present regulations considering economic realities."[83]

> In Boise, Idaho, fish and game biologist Jon Rachael used to visit schools to present wildlife programs. State law, however, forbids him to discuss a topic that's anathema to the state's powerful ranchers: reintroduction of the wolf into Idaho and Yellowstone National Park.[84]

Clearly the infiltration of school curricula through banning some texts and offering corporate-based curriculum material and lesson plans in their place can conflict with educational objectives, and also with the attainment of an undistorted understanding of environmental problems. Unfortunately children are usually not able to discriminate between genuine education and the manipulative messages of corporations. Many assume that what they are taught in the classroom must be the truth.[85]

Commercialism in Education

Chris Whittle intended to extend his Channel One concept much further, with the opening of hundreds of profit-making schools in partnership with Time Warner and UK-based Associated Newspapers. The schools would charge fees, offer scholarships and reduce the need for teachers by using computerized instruction and classroom helpers. Although this project has not gone ahead, Burger King has established 'Burger King Academies' in fourteen cities in the US and they are intending to expand into the UK. These schools are "fully accredited quasi-private high schools". IBM and Apple are also considering getting into the market of for-profit schools.[86]

In Baltimore, the management of nine public schools has been handed over to a private company, Educational Alternatives Inc, which is receiving $27 million of public funds over five years for the task. Similar schemes have been promoted in Australia for "poorly-performing public schools", and 'partnerships' between business and schools have been growing. The international marketing company Amway offers work experience to students of an Australian high school and gives lectures in subjects including agriculture, history and business studies. Petroleum industry personnel give lectures in Australian schools, and teachers are invited to gain experience of the petroleum industry through secondment for twenty or forty weeks, with the hope that they will take back what they have learnt to the classroom.[87]

Jane Coulter, from the University of New South Wales Public Sector Research Centre, notes that Australian schools "are being actively canvassed by corporate and multinational organisations to enter into sponsorship arrangements where the distinction between pedagogy, promotion, and marketing is not clear."[88] The International Organization of Consumers Unions says the corporate sector is using education to:

- counter perceived anti-business culture (particularly in response to political pressure groups)
- privatize public education systems by stealth
- promote free-market ideology
- use schools as a market for their commercial activities and propaganda[89]

Educators worldwide are concerned that "corporate involvement supplants public schools' mission of preparing students for participation in civic life with that of preparing students for life as workers in the free-market enterprise system."[90] Or, as Marianne Manilov of UNPLUG!, a youth group that campaigns against commercialized education, says: "Students aren't learning how to be thinkers or citizens, but rather consumers."[91] Writing in *New Internationalist*, Jonathan Kozol says: "When business enters education, therefore, it sells something more important than the brand names of its products. It sells a way of looking at the world and at oneself. It sells predictability instead of critical capacities. It sells a circumscribed, job-specific utility."[92]

In any curriculum, the more business- or consumer-oriented material there is, the less alternative material there will be. Moreover, the more dependent a school is on corporate funds the less likely it will be to teach students "to question the means and motivations of business".[93] Alex Molnar, professor of education at the University of Wisconsin-Milwaukee, who has written a book on the commercialisation of US schools, says that unless current trends change, "by the end of the century, the link between public education and school's ability to deliver corporate profits may be impossible to sever. And if that happens, the substitution of market values for democratic values in public education will largely be accomplished."[94]

There is some evidence that this is already happening. Surveys show that high school students are less interested in a meaningful life and more interested in making money, when compared with those of previous generations. Alan Durning reports that "Between 1967 and 1990, the share of Americans entering college who believed it essential to be 'very well-off financially' rose from forty-four per cent to seventy-four per cent. The share who believed it essential to develop a meaningful philosophy of life dropped from eighty-three per cent to forty-three per cent."[95]

Chapter 11

Advertisers: Influence and Strategies

The pervasiveness of advertising is nothing new. In 1947 *Fortune* magazine noted that no corner of the globe was beyond the reach of advertisers, and that Americans in particular were saturated in advertising:

> The American citizen lives in a state of siege from dawn till bedtime. Nearly every-thing he sees, hears, tastes, touches, and smells is an attempt to sell him something. Luckily for his sanity he becomes calloused shortly after diaperhood; now, to break through his protective shell the advertisers must continuously shock, tease, tickle, or irritate him, or wear him down by the drip-drip-drip of Chinese water torture method of endless repetition.[1]

Vance Packard, in his classic 1960 book *The Waste Makers*, documented the various strategies US retailers were using to promote consumerism and increase sales. After the post-war spending boom, manufacturers were faced with the "spectre of satiation" where most homes had the requirements of modern living. In such circumstances it was hard to see why people should keep buying goods—such as furniture, fridges, toasters, vacuum cleaners and cars—that they already possessed.[2]

A recession in the late 1950s drove this problem home; politicians and busi-ness people began urging people to consume for the good of their country. At a press conference President Eishenhower told the public that in order to remedy the recession they should buy. When asked what people should buy, he replied "Anything". Marketers used slogans like "Buy now—the job you save may be your own," and "Buy, buy, buy; it's your patriotic duty."[3]

> The central problem was to stimulate greater desire and to create new wants. And this was becoming a little more difficult each year. . . Old fashioned selling methods based on offering goods to fill an obvious need in a straightforward manner were no longer enough. Even the use of status appeals and sly appeals to the subconscious needs and anxieties of the public. . . would not move goods in the mountainous dimensions desired. . . What was needed was strategies that would make Americans in large numbers into voracious, wasteful, compulsive consumers. . .[4]

Packard outlined some of the strategies used for this purpose, including the production of throwaway single-use items, the introduction of credit, the manipulation of the consumer through 'bargains', 'sales' and 'trade-ins' and the introduction of planned obsolescence: when an item breaks in a short period of time, when new models outperform old ones, or when fashion changes make per-fectly serviceable and functional items undesirable.

'Loyal' Americans were again being asked to spend money in mid-1990 to get the US out of recession. Today, as in the 1950s, sales figures over the Christmas period are a major indicator of economic buoyancy that are reported in national news programmes. Capitalist economies depend on consumers spending more and more each year to help the economy grow. The continuing reliance on obsolescence for promoting sales means that economic growth and the viability of many companies are, in essence, dependent on waste.[5]

Green Marketing

The word 'consumer' comes from the Latin *consumere* which means "to take up wholly, to consume, waste, squander or destroy".[6] Planetary protection via consumerism would therefore seem to be a major contradiction. However the damage that consumerism is doing to the environment is not a message that corporations want to be spread. It is not surprising that the 1990s saw the rise of green marketing, which was aimed at increasing consumption, not reducing it. Many firms sought to capitalize on new markets created by rising environmental consciousness. "If we made a lot of money destroying this planet, we sure can make money cleaning it up," said one Vice-President for Environmental Affairs of a major Canadian food distributor, who has written a handbook on environmental marketing called "Green is Gold".[7]

Surveys showed that a significant proportion of consumers, particularly young mothers in high-income countries, made an effort to buy green products such as unbleached papers and items made of recycled paper. About twenty-eight per cent of all consumers said they were willing to pay more for safe aerosols and biodegradable plastic products, and thirty-five per cent were willing to pay more for natural foods that were not produced using pesticides.

These trends prompted a surge of advertisements and labels claiming environmental benefits. Green imagery was used to sell products, and caring for the environment became a marketing strategy. One survey conducted in conjunction with Stanford University Graduate School of Business found that forty-five per cent of US businesses believed that environmental issues were 'critical', most thought they would increase in importance, and thirty-one per cent had undertaken environmental promotions or marketing exercises.[8]

Green marketing was a way of redirecting a willingness to spend less into a willingness to buy green products. In 1989, at the height of public environmental consciousness around the world, a North American poll found that eighty-four per cent of people surveyed "would opt for a lower standard of living" if this would help the environment.[9] However, as Joyce Nelson points out:

> The spectre of a wide majority of citizenry choosing a lower standard of living is not something that brings joy to the power-breakfast. Voluntary simplicity combined with stringent regulation of polluters is a lifestyle scenario whose possible wide-scale adoption triggers a gag-reflex in boardrooms across the continent.[10]

Green marketing not only ensured that markets would not shrink but boosted sales of products that were labelled green. Sally White, in a report advising manufacturers, argued:

> In an affluent society such as ours, environmental problems are unlikely to be solved by heavy-handed attempts to make people consume less. The solution lies in redirecting many consumer choices towards environmentally friendly products. The answer is not necessarily reduced consumption but with more thoughtful consumption.[11]

Green advertising encourages people to buy more by suggesting they should buy a certain product because it is good for the environment. It implies environmental problems can be solved through purchasing the right products and perpetuates the logic of consumerism that "human fulfilment is still defined largely in terms of the purchase of commodities."[12]

Green marketing can take advantage of the very devices that promote consumerism and waste, such as fashion. A Sears clothing advertisement said: "Now helping the environment can really help you look good."[13] According to Paul Hawken, author of *The Ecology of Commerce*, "Green marketing by definition is a fraud. The leopard's new spots will wash off in the first acid rain, because green marketing is based on a view of the customer that's just as demeaning as the one that got us into this situation in the first place."[14]

Green marketing encourages customers to replace goods they already have with environmentally sound ones, or buy products they didn't know they needed. In marketing jargon this is called "repositioning", which involves "taking the same old stuff and repackaging it according to the latest taste."[15] As Packard observed:

> If you are a producer and most families already own your product, you are left with three possibilities for making further sales. You sell replacements; you sell more than one item to each family; or you dream up a new or improved product—or one that at least seems new or improved—that will enchant families that already own an 'old' model of your product.[16]

By marketing a 'green' version of an existing product, manufacturers are able to take up extra shelf space and offer an extra choice for consumers. In this way they can expand their market share to include consumers that want green products. Since manufacturers still make environmentally damaging products and retailers still sell non-green products on the shelves next to green ones, it is evident that green marketing is merely a way of expanding sales. If they were genuinely concerned to protect the environment they would replace the unsound products with sound ones, not just augment their existing lines.[17]

In the late 1980s and early 1990s various green toys were marketed to capitalize on the budding environmental consciences of children. For example Toxic Crusaders, Eco-Warriors and the Trash Bag Bunch were dolls that fought against polluting villains. These toys not only promoted the idea that environmental damage was caused by individual villains "displaying a mean and nasty streak" rather than corporations, but also boosted toy sales. For example, Toxic Crusaders were released by Playmates after sales of Teenage Mutant Ninja Turtles were declining because the market was saturated.[18]

Green marketing does not necessarily mean green products, but false and misleading claims can be hard for the consumer to detect. Products that have not been changed can be advertised as having an environmental aspect that they always had and that is typical of all such products. One example is the claim that laundry detergents are not being tested on animals—when they never have been. John Winward, in his study of consumer preferences, identified three types of environmental labelling which are of concern even though "they are unlikely to be judged sufficiently inaccurate to fall foul of the British Trade Descriptions Act: unjustified optimism, spurious distinctions, and excessive claims."[19]

The British Code of Advertising and Sales Promotion states that:

> Claims such as 'environmentally friendly' or 'wholly biodegradable' should not be used without qualification unless advertisers can provide convincing evidence that their product will cause no environmental damage. Qualified claims and comparisons such as 'greener' or 'friendlier' may be acceptable if advertisers can substantiate that their product provides an overall improvement in environmental terms either against their competitors' or their own previous products.

If a complaint is upheld, the UK Advertising Standards Authority can ask for the advertisement to be withdrawn or amended. If the advertiser refuses, the ASA can give it adverse publicity or in the extreme case of a "persistent or deliberate offender" refer the case to the Office of Fair Trading for an injunction. However a disproportionate number of complaints in 1996 and 1997 were made against advertisements by environmental groups rather than against false green claims by corporations.

For example, in May 1996 Shell International Petroleum successfully complained about a joint advertisement by the Body Shop, Friends of the Earth and Greenpeace which criticized Shell's activities in Ogoniland, Nigeria. The advertisement was ruled to be misleading as it implied that Shell was currently operating in Ogoniland. A later complaint (July 1996) by Friends of the Earth about a Shell International advertisement, which also referred to Shell's activities in Ogoniland, was partially successful. The ASA agreed that Shell's claims that sixty per cent of oil spills were caused by sabotage could not be adequately supported.

Another complaint, by the Timber Trade Federation against Friends of the Earth, was also upheld. The FOE advertisement stated that rainforests would disappear in forty years "unless we act now". Although FOE had research to support their claim, the Authority argued that "readers would infer from the claim that it was a generally accepted prediction" and asked them to change the advertisement to "make clear that the claim was their rough estimate".

In contrast, the Authority was more willing to accept the research claims made by British Nuclear Fuels in its advertisements. The Campaign for Nuclear Disarmament Cymru (the Welsh CND) complained about claims made by British Nuclear Fuels that 97% of reactor fuel could be recycled "into clean uranium and plutonium for re-use". Research furnished by British Nuclear Fuels showed that this was "theoretically" possible and so the claim was accepted. In another case, Greenpeace complained about a British Nuclear Fuels advertisement that claimed that investments had been designed to minimize environmental impact and that the result would be "safe" beaches at Sellafield and "clean, non-polluting energy". The ASA did not uphold these complaints, arguing that "readers would take the claim [of minimized impact] to mean only economically feasible efforts were made to prevent environmental damage"; that the claim about safe beaches would be understood by readers not to mean "a guarantee of absolute safety"; and that the claim of "clean and non-polluting energy" was acceptable as "the emissions from the plant were within all safety limits".

The most cynical marketers simply use environmental imagery to conjure up the impression that a product is good for the environment without making any real claims at all; this is what Paul Gilding, formerly of Greenpeace, has referred to as "bung a dolphin on the label and we'll be right."[20] Consumers are becoming quite cynical about product labels that claim environmental credentials. One survey by the Roper Organisation found that most Americans no longer believe green claims on labels. Although the claims are not "deliberately dishonest", they are misleading.[21]

Plastics, once advertised for their throw-away convenience, are now touted as recyclable. However there are various technical reasons why the recyclability of plastics is limited to what the plastics industry calls 'linear recycling'; that is, they cannot be recycled for the same use again.[22] JoAnn Gutin attended a conference on *Reducing Plastics in the Wastestream* where the Oui-Oui Skreen, "a spongy, blue plastic doily, saturated with an overpowering bubble-gum scent" designed to be placed in urinals, was launched as a great breakthrough in recycling. She described it as:

> the perfect metaphor for everything that's wrong with the idea of recycling plastics. It's ugly as sin, the world doesn't need it, and it's disposable. . . what would have gone to the landfill as a plastic bottle in January would instead go as a urine-soaked plastic doily in May. Did I miss something?[23]

It is easy for people to fall for what Juliet Kellner calls the 'bit-less-bad' trap. An example is that of unleaded fuel. People might feel righteous using unleaded fuel. But overuse of private motor vehicles, even using unleaded fuel, is still harmful to the environment.[24] Advertisers targeting 'would-be green' motorists do not suggest that people do not buy cars or drive less. In 1993 Saab advertised:

> Our cars actually clean the air. Amazing but true. An independent test found that when a standard Saab was driven in London's traffic, hydrocarbon and nitrogen oxide levels in the car's exhaust were found to be lower, remarkably, than in the surrounding air. In other words, our car's engine removed these pollutants from the environment![25]

Businesses such as The Body Shop have been heralded around the world for their green products. Yet some environmentalists question the need for cosmetics at all and point out that producing products in an environmentally sound way might be encouraging consumerism. In 1991 the *Economist* reported that cosmetics sales were declining, partly because of the rise of the healthy natural look, and that to "convince sceptical consumers that they should spend more, not less, on their looks, the big cosmetics companies are in turn spending an ever-bigger chunk of their profits on marketing."[26] The fact that The Body Shop was going against the trend of declining sales because of its emphasis on biodegradable, non-animal-tested products was not missed. The following year, aggregate cosmetic sales were up and it was reported in *Drug & Cosmetic Industry* that the industry was exploiting environmental concerns to boost sales.[27]

Green marketing provides a profitable outlet of expression for guilty consciences. Those who do the right thing in the supermarket alleviate their concerns and may even believe that their actions are all that is required to protect the environment. "At its worst, green consumerism is a palliative for the conscience of the consumer class, allowing us to continue business as usual while feeling like we are doing our part."[28] The need to change attitudes towards consumption, values and institutional structures is ignored. "Consumers, finally satisfied that they can 'do something', may seek no further than their shopping trolleys to help the planet."[29]

Patricia Hynes, a US academic, argues that green consumerism reduces people to consumers.[30] Their power to influence society is reduced to their purchasing power, and the value of goods is reduced to people's willingness to buy them. In their book *Green Business: Hope or Hoax*, Christopher and Judith Plant point out that green consuming does not deal with issues such as economic growth on a finite planet, the power of transnational corporations, and the way power is structured in our society.

> Because the commodity spectacle is so all-engaging, 'light' green business tends to merely perpetuate the colonization of the mind, sapping our visions of an alternative and giving the idea that our salvation can be gained through shopping rather than through social struggle and transformation. In this respect, green business at worst is a danger and a trap.[31]

Influence of Advertisers on the Media

Commercial television and radio stations receive most if not all of their income from advertisers. Tens of billions of dollars are spent every year just on television advertising, and the media does its best to create a product that suits those advertisers. Whilst audiences may consider advertisements as an unwelcome interruption to their news and entertainment, that news and entertainment is a way of attracting people to the medium so they will be exposed to the advertisements—a way of delivering audiences for advertisers.[32] "TV works like a Trojan horse: it gains entry into our homes with promises of entertainment and novelty, then delivers its true cargo of commercial messages."[33]

Throughout this century, newspapers' income has depended less and less on sales to readers, and more and more on advertising. Between 1950 and 1980 they had a forty per cent drop in sales whilst profits skyrocketed. During this same period control of newspapers became more corporate, "hastening the conversion of newspapers to primarily carriers of advertising". This has inevitably meant that newspapers have become less responsive to their readers and more responsive to their advertisers.[34] Indeed, the modern newspaper has been shaped by the demands of advertisers:

> You name it: the appearance of ads throughout the pages, the 'jump' or continuation of a story from page to page, the rise of sectionalization (as with news, cartoons, sports, financial, living, real estate), common page size, halftone images, process engraving, the use of black-and-white photography, then color, sweepstakes, and finally discounted subscriptions were all forced on publishers by advertisers hoping to find target audiences.[35]

The influence of corporate advertisers on news content—as opposed to style—is both indirect (in that the media shapes its content to attract an audience that will suit its advertisers), and direct (in that media outlets edit material that is likely to offend advertisers, especially with news stories). In terms of direct pressure from advertisers, a 1992 US study of 150 newspaper editors found that ninety per cent said that advertisers tried to interfere with newspaper content, and seventy per cent said that advertisers tried to stop news stories altogether. Forty per cent admitted that advertisers had in fact influenced a story.[36] According to Laurie Ann Mazur, co-author of *Marketing Madness*, in 1993 Mercedes Benz told thirty different magazines that it would withdraw its advertisements from any issue that contained articles critical of Mercedes, German products or Germany.[37]

An editorial in *Industry Week* in 1994 exhorted advertisers to exert more influence over the television and radio programmes that their ads were associated with: "It's time for managements to examine exactly what their ad dollars promote." It suggested that captains of industry "determine carefully what they want their organisations to stand for—and against—and then direct their marketing colleagues to use those beliefs to help guide their advertising decisions. . . Advertising—or the lack thereof—can be a powerful weapon in our marketplace of ideas."[38]

In Australia, Rural Press, with 126 print publications and twenty-seven radio stations, is one of the largest media organizations operating in rural areas of the country; it combines news with support for advertisers. One of its managers has stated in the company's internal newsletter:

> Concern continues to be expressed about our failure to lend editorial support to our major clients. I've expressed frustration on numerous occasions about the lack of support for clients at some sites, and I've recently had complaints from ICI, CropCare and Elders. A failure to enforce commercial awareness, whether it be in the journalists or sub editors, will not be tolerated.[39]

Former *Washington Post* editor Ben Bagdikan argues that advertising "deeply influences the subjects dealt with in the nonadvertising sections of newspapers and broadcast programs." For example, the car industry is a big advertiser in the *New York Times*, and "Times publisher and CEO Arthur Sulzberger admitted that he leaned on his editors to present the auto industry's position because it 'would affect advertising'."[40] The group Fairness and Accuracy in Reporting (FAIR) has told how *Forbes* magazine, anxious to attract and maintain insurance company advertising (which in 1990 made up seven per cent of its advertising income), criticized personal injury lawyers for winning money off "outnumbered" insurance companies and attempted to bring Ralph Nader, a thorn in the side of the insurance industry, into disrepute.[41]

Corporations can also use sponsorship, a more indirect form of advertising, to influence the content of the media. The US Public Broadcasting Service (PBS) and National Public Radio are heavily dependent on corporate sponsors for their broadcasting because their government funding is insufficient. By 1981, oil companies were subsidising almost three quarters of prime-time shows on PBS. Projects that are unlikely to attract corporate sponsorship are much less likely to go ahead.[42] According to the host of one of PBS's shows: "You cannot get a TV or a radio show on the air in America these days unless it targets an audience that corporations are interested in targeting and unless it carries a message that is acceptable to corporations."[43] The inevitable result is that conservative current affairs programmes get funded, whilst those critical of corporate activities do not.

In the US there is enough business for at least one advertising agency to specialize in producing commercials for public broadcasting. In Australia the Australian Broadcasting Commission (ABC) is not legally able to screen advertisements, nor to obtain sponsorship. However an ABC journalist who spoke out about 'back door' sponsorships and financial influence over programming was victimized and lost his job, despite an unblemished employment record and several journalism awards. (He was later reinstated following an investigation.) Recent government cuts to the ABC by the Howard conservative government have reopened the question of sponsorship and advertising as an alternative source of funds, although the public clearly does not want advertisements on the ABC.[44]

Programmes that displease advertisers or sponsors can cause problems for their media outlets. WNET, a public TV station in New York, lost its corporate underwriting from Gulf & Western after showing a documentary called *Hunger from Profit* about the activities of multinationals in the Third World. Gulf & Western said the documentary was "virulently anti-business, if not anti-American".[45]

In 1989 Turner Broadcasting decided to broadcast *Rage Over Trees*, a documentary produced by the Audubon Society. Even before it was screened, the broadcaster and its advertisers were bombarded by letters, telephone calls and faxes from the Wise Use Movement complaining about the film. As a result all the programme sponsors withdrew, causing Turner to lose $100,000 in revenue. Another Audubon documentary, *The New Range Wars*, was broadcast in 1991 by PBS. The film, which accused cattle ranchers of overgrazing fragile grasslands and threatening endangered species whilst being subsidized by public taxes, was considered "too controversial" by Ford, which withdrew its PBS sponsorship.[46]

> Prospective shows are often discussed with major advertisers, who review script treatments and suggest changes when necessary. Adjustments are sometimes made to please sponsors. . . corporate sponsors figure they are entitled to call the shots since they foot the bill—an assumption shared by network executives, who quickly learn to internalize the desires of their well-endowed patrons.[47]

The indirect influence of advertising on media content is more pervasive. Since the media depend on advertisers and sponsors for revenue, they seek to maximize those audiences that will attract advertisers—not just any audience will do. Papers that attract large numbers of low-consuming working-class people have often failed through lack of advertiser support. In Britain the *Daily Herald* and *Daily Sketch* failed financially despite daily circulations above a million, whereas papers with much smaller circulations that are read by affluent people whom advertisers want to reach, such as *The Financial Times*, have thrived.[48]

In television, a one percentage point loss on the ratings can represent a loss of $100 million a year in advertising, so producers of television entertainment try to avoid material that would scare advertisers and audiences away. The result is, according to Jacobson and Mazur in their book *Marketing Madness*, "TV programs that flow seamlessly into commercials, avoiding controversy, lulling us into submission like an electronic tranquilizer."[49]

Television: Promoting Consumerism

Although media outlets avoid controversial material, they do not want to bore their audiences. This has brought about an increase in non-news content, or 'fluff', aimed at entertaining consumers and creating "a buying mood as bait for more advertising". Television shows tend to promote consumerism, portray a positive image of business in general—with bad business people being an obvious deviation from the norm—attract affluent audiences, and aim at light entertainment rather than examination of complex and controversial subjects. Today's television "projects an ethos of materialism through its programming as well as its advertising", with images of happy consumers whose problems are solved through their purchases and through "proper social behaviour" as seen on television shows. Programmes that appeal to people who don't buy much, the poor and the old, don't tend to last long. Nor do those that promote social awareness.[50]

James Twitchell, Professor of English and author of *Adcult USA: The Triumph of Advertising in America* predicts that cable and remote control mean that "commercials will disappear. They will become the programming."[51] Already channels such as MTV and home-shopping channels are made up of programmes that are little more than advertisements. This tendency has meant increased competition for advertising dollars from cable television. One advertising executive rejoiced at the ability this influence gave advertisers to "create programming environments that heighten our clients' messages."[52]

There is also an increasing creep of advertising materials into regular programmes, especially games and talk shows. In the 1980s a new marketing strategy was introduced: the programme-length commercial or 'infomercial', which is dressed up to look like a regular television show with theme music, credits, paid studio audiences and celebrity hosts, and is listed in television guides as a regular programme. An example is McDonalds' *The Mac Report*, which has all the appearance of a business news programme.[53]

In the US today ninety per cent of television stations show infomercials, generating $400 million per year for those stations and providing relatively cheap advertising for the sponsors. "Knowing that consumers view ads with skepticism, marketers sneak through our defenses by blurring the lines between advertising, news, and entertainment." A version of the infomercial aimed at children is the television show whose main characters are modelled after toys. By 1988 sixty-four per cent of television toy advertisements were for toys related to children's television programmes. Often cartoon characters would be launched as movies, be followed up by television series and then be merchandised on hundreds of products from t-shirts to toys.[54] The head of Disney explained to *Advertising Age* in 1989 how the Disney Corporation's activities all reinforced each other: "The Disney Stores promote the consumer products which promote the [theme] parks which promote the television shows. The television shows promote the company."[55]

One particularly successful marketing venture has been the Teenage Mutant Ninja Turtles, which was dreamed up in an advertising agency and has spawned various television programmes, movies, a range of toys and accessories and a billion-dollar industry in licensed products which feature the creatures. Toy manufacturers have found that it is more profitable for television shows to feature several characters needing various accessories so as to maximize the product lines that can be sold.[56]

Watching television is the major activity, apart from sleeping and working, for most people in the US, the UK and an increasing number of other countries. In many homes in the US, television is on seven hours a day, "issuing a stream of soap operas, situation comedies, music videos, and sales spiels. . . commercial television promotes the restless craving for more by portraying the high consumption life-style as a model to be emulated."[57]

And it is not only in the US that this high consumption life-style is portrayed and emulated: US television has a huge impact on television programming all over the world and has been an effective way of spreading American consumerist culture. CBS alone distributes its programmes to over 100 countries. By 1984 "US programs accounted for seventy-five per cent of the $400 million international marketplace."[58] Additionally, US movies, music and videos have carried the consumer culture to other lands:

> The penetration of foreign countries by US, or other imported, television constitutes a new form of cultural imperialism. Although there is some extraction of profit from television sales, many European countries give so-called underdeveloped countries free television, and the United States charges very low rates in order to acclimate the country to consumer capitalist media forms and ideology. This form of imperialism destroys traditional culture and values (under the code of 'modernization') and imposes a new kind of transnational, global consumer culture on the entire world.[59]

As the chief executive of H.J. Heinz says; "Once television is there, people of whatever shade, culture, or origin want roughly the same things."[60]

Advocacy Advertising

The consumerist messages of advertisers and the media they support are sometimes supplemented by specially placed advertisements that promote corporate values: about a third of corporate advertising is devoted to purposes other than promoting products. In the US, around one billion dollars per year is currently spent on 'advocacy advertising'. "Unlike conventional advertising that pushes either a product or a corporate image, advocacy advertising sells political beliefs and thus appeals to the public as citizens rather than as consumers."[62]

According to Prakash Sethi, who has written a book on the subject, advocacy advertising "attempts to change or sustain public opinion and social policy on specific short-term issues as well as on the values that underlie our social and political institutions."[63] Advocacy advertising variously aims to:

- counter public hostility to corporate activities
- counter critics of corporate activities
- promote free-enterprise values
- make up for inadequate access to and perceived bias in the media
- influence government policy
- motivate individual behaviour in some way[64]

Such ads have been used by the advertising industry itself. In 1991 the World President of the International Association of Advertisers (IAA) described how the association was "working hard" to promote the value of advertising—to advertise advertising. He asked an audience of fellow advertisers: "How can we change the climate in which advertising is perceived and debated—from one that presents it as an easy, natural target for regulation, restriction and even prohibition, to one in which its vital role is recognized, understood, respected, and is treated accordingly?" He recommended that the following argument be put: "Advertising is the voice of the free enterprise system and the foundation of a free media" and that therefore there is an "inextricable link between advertising and democracy".[65]

> Advertising, like market institutions in general, is an enabling device for individual choice. It facilitates choice in the lives of consumers. And for that reason, critics and opponents of advertising are also critics and opponents of individual choice. . . commercial expression should be defended as a form of freedom of expression, no different in any important qualitative aspect from any other form of expression, such as political, religious, cultural or artistic expression.[66]

Advertisements for advertising appeared on CNN in Europe in 1995, featuring two children selling lemonade at nearby stalls. They argued that advertising brought competition and therefore lowered prices and improved products. A series of similar advertisements on CNN in 1997 argued that the media and various sponsored activities such as sports would be dramatically curtailed without advertisements to pay for them.

In advocacy ads, associations, corporations and industry groups try to claim "social legitimacy via identification with widely held social beliefs or representation of the public interest".[67] For example, advertising is identified in the above quotation with individual choice and freedom of expression.

> The sociocultural environment of the advocacy ads is that of American values or widely held beliefs. By suggesting that the underlying rationale of a given advocacy message emanates from and is supported by traditional American values, the sponsor of the message expects to insulate himself from critical attack, for his adversaries must implicitly criticize these values in order to raise objections to the ad message.[68]

Pioneered by Mobil Oil, advocacy advertisements allow corporations to editorialise.[69] Mobil spends millions of dollars a year on this form of advertising. Take, for example, the following Mobil ad:

> Business, generally, is a good neighbour, and most communities recognize this fact. . . From time to time, out of political motivations or for reasons of radical chic, individuals try to chill the business climate. On such occasions we try to set the record straight. . . And the American system, of which business is an integral part, usually adapts. . . So when it comes to the business climate, we're glad that most people recognize there's little need to tinker with the American system.[70]

Many other companies use advocacy ads, including Union Carbide, the Chase Manhattan Bank, W. R. Grace and Co. and Bethlehem Steel. During the 1970s oil, chemical and steel companies actively campaigned through advertisements on the themes of environmentalism, energy or "explanations of the capitalistic system". Electric Power System, proclaiming themselves to be "environmentalists long before it was popular", ran a series of ads which opposed tightened air quality standards, mandatory stack gas scrubbers and monitoring of emissions at the top of the stack rather than at ground level. "Strict adherence to unreasonable regulations that are not necessary to protect health, would only jeopardize the nation's electric power supply," the ads said.[71]

Joyce Nelson reports in *Sultans of Sleaze* that by 1980 "US corporate PR departments were spending an estimated $1 billion per year on such advocacy advertising . . . devoted to bypassing reporters by buying newspaper and magazine space to present the corporate point of view." Around this time, Canadian papers began selling advocacy advertising space, representing it as "freedom to advocate a point of view through the use of corporate advertising".[72] This prompted one media critic to respond that advocacy advertising "gave people who have money more freedom of speech than people who don't have money".[73]

Environmentalism is still a major theme of advocacy advertising. Such advertising generally espouses much environmental concern, avoids specific information, and tends to be inaccurate about the company's role in creating environmental problems.[74] Advocacy ads on environmental issues have, according to Sethi, taken one of three forms:

> • exaggerating the meager efforts of the industry in controlling pollution, projecting them as voluntary while in fact they may have been undertaken under threat of government prosecution

• downplaying the adverse consequences of pollution and publicizing adverse economic consequences on jobs and incomes, and

• implying that voluntary individual action will largely solve the problem[75]

Mobil's advertisement on Earth Day 1996 proclaimed how much better the American environment was, and how the oil industry had played a role in those improvements (largely as a result of complying with legislation).[76] In another ad, Mobil deplored the move towards legally binding international greenhouse emission standards arguing that "such an approach is likely to cause severe economic dislocations" and is premature.[77] Another defends cars:

Today, cars are being targeted by some as an environmental concern. Perhaps we should ask ourselves, 'Where would we be without them?' And, 'Can we do without them?' The answers are probably, 'Not very far,' and 'Not very likely.' The combined economic contribution of the automotive industry and the ancillary industries that support it are mind-boggling: trillions of dollars in sales, billions in profits and millions of jobs. . . As to their environmental record, today's cars with today's fuels are hardly the threat some portray them to be.[78]

The chemical industry has also made wide use of advocacy advertising. One television ad, paid for by the Iberville Chemical Council (including Dow Chemical, Ashland Chemical, Ciba-Geigy and ICI Americas), which showed chemical workers turning over a giant leaf, was reinforced with print and billboard ads and followed up with opinion surveys. The percentage of people surveyed in the small town of Iberville who agreed that "chemical companies are concerned about the health of people in the community" increased from fifty-three per cent to sixty-seven per cent after the ad, and those who thought that plant emissions were decreasing went from nineteen per cent to twenty-eight per cent. This encouraged the Chemical Manufacturers Association to initiate a $10 million per year national advertising campaign over five years.[79]

In the US, advocacy advertisements are treated differently from other advertisements by the Federal Trade Commission. Normally, ads are regulated to ensure their content is not deceptive nor false, but advocacy advertisements are considered to be political statements and so are considered to be beyond the power of these regulations, as the Supreme Court has ruled that falsehood is inevitable in political debate.[80]

The advantage of advocacy advertising for corporations, as opposed to relying on media releases and coverage, is that the content and timing of what appears in the media can be completely controlled. Sometimes the ads are even covered in the media, as in the case of health care ads placed by the Health Insurance Association of America opposing President Clinton's health reforms: "Almost every leading newspaper and television network in the country ran stories about the ads, including a front page story in the New York Times." Following the ad campaign, support for the reforms had fallen from sixty-seven per cent to forty-four per cent. The perceived success of these ads in defeating health care reform has provided an additional encouragement for advocacy advertising, which has grown rapidly recently.[81]

It is estimated that three-quarters of all advocacy advertising is paid for by corporations. In his book on *Advocacy Advertising*, Sethi notes that whilst individual advertisements can be countered by public interest groups, a large number of corporations pushing "common themes in advocacy campaigns dealing with pollution, consumerism, government regulation, economic growth, the energy crisis, and the virtues of the free enterprise system" can have a considerable effect:[82]

> There are indeed reasonable grounds for concern that advocacy advertising campaigns, when pursued by a significantly large number of corporations, over a period of time, can overwhelm the information mix available to the public and thereby squeeze out or sharply reduce the expression of alternative viewpoints on important issues affecting society.[83]

Procter and Gamble

Procter & Gamble (P&G) has been active in all the areas of advertiser influence discussed in this and previous chapters; green marketing, environmental education for schools, advocacy advertising through its membership of various coalitions and associations, and influencing media content. Procter and Gamble funds corporate front groups, utilises grassroots organising specialists and is associated with conservative think-tanks.[84]

P&G is the largest advertiser in the world, spending five billion dollars a year on advertising. In the US it spends well over a billion dollars just on television advertising, including syndicated and cable television. It sells its consumer products (300 brands) in 140 countries, operates in fifty-seven countries, and its annual sales of cosmetics, health care, food, beverage, cleaning and paper products are over $35 billion, half of which are made outside the US. It employs almost 100,000 people worldwide. P&G has appeared on *Fortune* magazine's "America's Most Admired US Corporation" list for the past decade.[85]

Advertising and marketing are central to P&G's success. According to a company report by Prudential Securities Inc, "Procter continues to gain market share over time in important categories such as detergents, diapers, hair care, and feminine care on a global basis. . . [as] a result of an unsurpassed new product portfolio supported by extensive research efforts and superior marketing skills." And another report, by Morgan Stanley & Co Inc, says that Procter & Gamble is in their opinion "the most savvy packaged-goods marketer in the world."[86]

In the 1920s P&G boosted soap sales by over twenty-five per cent with a series of newspaper advertisements which featured a family that used Ivory soap and a villain that used coloured and scented soaps. Following this success, P&G tried radio shows which also featured stories that aimed to sell soap. These stories became known as 'soap operas' or 'washboard weepers'. One series, *Ma Perkins*, advertised Oxydol soap, mentioning the brand twenty to twenty-five times in each fifteen-minute episode. It was aired five days a week and, although five thousand people complained about it in the first week, was a great commercial success. Soap sales doubled within a year and the show ran from 1932 to 1960.[87]

When television arrived, Procter & Gamble was quick to utilize the new medium for its advertising, sponsoring sports, games shows and fashion shows. In 1949 it formed P&G Productions to "produce or buy television programs and motion pictures". By the mid 1950s, thirteen different Procter & Gamble soap operas were being broadcast on television. P&G has recently joined up with the Paramount Television Group to produce television shows and series targeted at young mothers who are potential consumers for their diapers, washing products, etc.; a television sitcom resulting from the partnership has already screened on the CBS television network. The partnership is also hoping to produce interactive TV, internet services and CD-ROMs. P&G chief executive Ed Artzt is reported to have urged advertisers at a meeting of the American Association of Advertising Agencies in 1994 to "take steps to ensure that advertising is a part of programming in a new media world".[88]

Procter and Gamble has also produced environmental education materials for school children. One of its educational packages, *Decision Earth*, was distributed to almost 75,000 schools in the US. It included worksheets, overhead transparencies and other materials.[89] The aim of this package was "to raise student awareness of the complex consumer product choices they face and help them make informed choices based on the product's ability to meet their needs as consumers".[90]

The package contained some highly controversial claims on waste disposal, mining and forestry issues. For example, P&G argued in their package that disposable diapers (nappies) are no worse for the environment than cloth diapers. The company just happens to be the world's largest manufacturer of disposable nappies—although this wasn't mentioned in the package. (It claims to have invented disposable diapers in 1961.) The package described garbage-fuelled incineration processes where energy is recovered as "thermal recycling", and didn't mention the toxic ash or emissions that result.[91] In defence of its clear-cut forestry practices, the package stated:

> Clear cutting removes all trees within a stand of a few species to create new habitat for wildlife. Procter & Gamble uses this economically and environmentally sound method because it most closely mimics nature's own processes. . . Clear cutting also opens the forest floor to sunshine, thus stimulating growth and providing food for animals."[92]

Decision Earth was subject to various complaints and is no longer distributed in the US, although P&G continue to distribute it free to Canadian schools. Another package currently distributed by Procter & Gamble is *Planet Patrol*, aimed at grades four to six, which teaches students "how to be part of the solution to America's growing solid waste crisis". The materials have been evaluated by the Consumers Union, which found them to be "highly commercial and incomplete with strong bias in presenting issues related to its products and packaging".[93]

Procter and Gamble Educational Services have produced a variety of other educational materials. Its unit on *Advertising & the Economy* promotes the benefits of advertising, using P&G products and advertisements as examples; it was described by the Consumers Union as "commercial and biased. . . in essence a book of P&G product ads". It also has a unit on labour issues in the nineteenth century: entitled *Coping with Growth*, it asks students to put themselves in the place of William Cooper Procter in 1886, trying to get the workers to cooperate in a time of industrial turmoil. The text asks the students to consider how the workers can be persuaded "that their overall interests are truly inseparable from those of Procter and Gamble".[94]

P&G has been applauded by industry commentators for its initiatives in greening its products; in 1991 and 1993 it was ranked third in Roper's polls for environmental reputation amongst consumers (McDonald's ranked first). Its green initiatives include using recycled plastics and paperboard in packaging, producing refill packages, producing concentrated versions of products such as laundry detergents (less volume to transport), making disposable diapers less bulky and selling deodorants without cartons. CEO Ed Artzt said in 1992 that environmental issues were Procter & Gamble's "greatest global challenge. . . It's more than just the right thing to do, it's essential if we are to continue to maintain the leadership positions we enjoy in our product categories."[95]

Yet when the US EPA produced an Environmental Consumer's Handbook, Procter & Gamble and Scott Paper complained about the handbook's recommendations to decrease use of disposable paper cups and replace household cleaners with baking soda and vinegar solutions. The handbook was subsequently revised.[96]

Until it was reformulated in 1994, Procter & Gamble's *Tide with Bleach* was the only remaining laundry powder on the US market still containing phosphates. Other companies had substituted zeolites in earlier years because of environmental concerns while Procter and Gamble, with the help of PR firm Hill and Knowlton, made the case against the need for such substitution. When several states in the US banned detergents with phosphates it became uneconomic for Procter & Gamble to continue to resist the trend. However P&G continued to claim that "there is no science indicating that elimination of phosphates from detergent would have a significant impact on the environment."[97]

The modesty of P&G's environmental efforts have been made up for by the enthusiastic marketing that goes with them. Before it launched or even tested its Downy Refill package—a demonstration it was doing something about the landfill crisis—it sent its lobbyists and PR people to Washington to explain the innovation to members of Congress and their staff. It held a press conference, packed with experts and company executives, to explain how the packaging of the fabric softener in a plastic-coated milk-type carton would be better for the environment. This all occurred just before a congressional debate on the re-authorization of the Solid Waste Disposal Act, which opened up the potential for mandatory recycling and packaging reforms. "By introducing Downy Refill in Washington, the company's lobbyists gained much-needed ammo in their advocacy of a cautious private-sector approach to the solid waste problem."[98]

Some of Procter & Gamble's green marketing claims have been disputed, however. Its claim that Pampers disposable diapers (marketed with the logo of WWF on the package) have no worse environmental impact than cloth diapers was challenged by the Women's Environmental Network in Britain which argued that such claims are "limited in scientific credibility, dishonest, manipulative and biased". It cited a report that found disposable nappies use five times more energy, require twenty times more raw material inputs and create seventy times more solid waste than cloth nappies. The Advertising Standards Authority (ASA) upheld the complaint finding that the claims were indeed "misleading".[99]

Author Paul Hawken, advocate for the greening of business, is another critic of Procter & Gamble's green marketing methods:

> I recently saw an advertisement for Procter and Gamble showing a disposable plastic diaper and a great mound of rich, black compost, the kind of compost I have not been able to make in twenty-five years as a gardener. And the ad implied this compost was made of disposable diapers. But when you read the fine print, you find out this hasn't been done yet, that Procter and Gamble is offering money to municipalities to start pilot programs for composting. . . This is the same Procter and Gamble that has fought proposals in Wisconsin, Connecticut, and Kentucky to tax disposable diapers to pay for environmental cleanup. In Kentucky it was a penny a diaper. . .Which Procter and Gamble do you want me to believe? When we see this manipulation of our needs as customers, we know we're being flimflammed. We're not just being taken for a ride. Our intelligence is being taken for granted.[100]

Procter & Gamble has opposed efforts to regulate green marketing claims in the US. It has also opposed green labelling systems saying they "are a disincentive to those companies that excel environmentally, especially those denied ecolabels based on shortsighted and unscientific criteria".[101] It fought Californian legislation to mandate stringent definitions of terms such as 'recycled' and 'biodegradable' in green marketing. The legislation was upheld by a federal appeals court in 1994. *Advertising Age* greeted the decision with the prediction that this could spell the end for green marketing. However, advertisers, including P&G, vowed to fight the decision all the way to the Supreme Court if they had to.[102]

Partly as a result of its green marketing efforts, Procter & Gamble has won a number of environmental awards, including the Chemical Industries Responsible Care Award in 1995, DuPont's Award for Innovation (for a reduced plastic use container) in 1994, the Thomas Edison Award for global leadership in environmental quality management in 1993, and the President's Environment and Conservation Challenge Award in 1991 and 1992. In 1992 it received a Gold Medal for International Corporate Environment Achievement from the World Environment Centre and in 1991 P&G was selected as most environmentally conscious company in the US in a 1991 *Advertising Age*/Gallup Poll Survey. In 1995 *Marketing Week* reported that the UK Labour Party had praised the environmental marketing efforts of companies like Procter & Gamble.[103]

Yet Alecia Swasy, in her book *Soap Opera: The Inside Story of Procter and Gamble*, documents how the company has polluted groundwater and the Fernholloway River with its pulp mill waste and intimidated people who campaigned to have the river cleaned up. At the same time as Procter & Gamble was being hailed as an environmental hero:

> Residents living near the river were told not drink their water. Even as P&G disputed scientific evidence, the company was recommending its own managers drink

bottled water. And the company eventually began giving away free bottled water to residents. . . They still shower in the water, but it leaves a film on the skin.[104]

Swasy describes the way the Fernholloway was transformed from "a fishing paradise" to the most polluted river in the country's Southeast: "black as motor oil. . . laced with dangerous chemicals from the pulp mill" where "female fish have developed male characteristics because pollution causes hormonal changes in fish". According to Swasy, the company has been able to get away with this gross pollution because of its lobbying power in Florida.[105]

Procter & Gamble is also the subject of an ongoing consumer boycott by animal rights groups who claim that the company is responsible for fifty thousand animal deaths per year in the US alone. P&G, which uses animals to test its products, say they are "committed to eliminating the use of animals for safety testing as soon as good science permits", but its critics argue that testing products on animals does not tell how humans will react to those substances and that "such testing protects the company but not the consumer". They also point out that other companies produce similar products without the need to test them on animals.[106]

In 1986, lawyer Tom Riley wrote a book entitled *The Price of Life* about his battle to win a lawsuit against Procter & Gamble for the death of a woman from toxic shock syndrome. The woman had died after using Rely tampons, manufactured and marketed by Procter & Gamble. According to Swasy, many previous cases had been settled out of court, sometimes for as much as $1 million, with confidentiality clauses as P&G attempted to prevent publicity of its role in the toxic shock syndrome deaths.[107] She says that, on publication of his book, Riley

> received offers to appear on talk shows, but all bookings were mysteriously cancelled at the last minute. As the country's largest advertiser, P&G wields tremendous clout with the media. An appearance by Riley might have cost a program untold dollars in P&G commercials. Apparently no one was willing to take that risk.[108]

Indeed, Procter and Gamble seems to take its influence over media content seriously. According to Martin Lee and Norman Solomon in their book *Unreliable Sources*, P&G once stated in a memo on broadcasting policy that "There will be no material that will give offense, either directly or indirectly to any commercial organization of any sort." Gloria Steinem, feminist and editor of *Ms* magazine, says that Procter & Gamble has made it clear that "its products were not to be placed in *any* issue that included *any* material on gun control, abortion, the occult, cults, or the disparagement of religion". *Ms* magazine decided to do without advertising because of such demands by advertisers.[109]

P&G spends $284 million a year on television advertising, much of it on day-time television talk shows, and has openly talked about its efforts to influence the content of these shows. Talk shows have come under criticism from some conservative sectors of society because of their explicit sexual content and "mainstreaming of deviance and assaultive behaviour". Although they have good ratings, they have a potential to alienate some of P&G's more puritan customers.[110] Procter & Gamble has described how it uses its financial muscle to change the content of those shows, "bankrolling the content they support and pulling dollars from topics they do not".[111] R.L Wehling, their Senior Vice President-Advertising, wrote:

> We outlined what we consider to be appropriate content and we made it clear only those shows that live up to these standards will receive our advertising support. . . And over the past year, we declined to advertise on nearly a thousand individual episodes we felt didn't measure up to our standards.[112]

P&G withdrew advertising worth millions of dollars from four of these shows after producers refused to change their content. Other talk shows, according to a P&G spokeswoman, "were definitely willing to work with us". The more recalcitrant talk shows had been given the chance to change their content "within a reasonable time frame".[113]

Consumer Culture

Procter and Gamble may be the largest advertiser in the world, but it is only one of them. We live in a world where the best minds of our times are put to work finding ways to persuade us that we need things we don't really need. The product of their labours is highly effective, as Alan Durning, author of the Worldwatch book *How Much is Enough?*, notes: "From an anthropological perspective, ads are among the supreme creations of this era. . . combining stunning imagery, bracing speed, and compelling language to touch our innermost fears and fancies. Prime-time television commercials in the industrial countries pack more suggestion into a minute than anything previously devised."[114]

The proliferation of products in modern society gives the illusion of more choice and better living standards. Yet often it is only the advertising, the brand names and the packaging that differentiates the rows of products on the supermarket shelf. Does all this choice really enrich our lives? Or does it gradually erode the quality of our lives by degrading the environment that sustains us?

Paul Ekins, a British economist, defines a consumerist society as one where "the possession and use of an increasing number and variety of goods and services is the principal cultural aspiration and the surest perceived route to personal happiness, social status and national success." Yet despite the promise of the advertisements, consumption is not a major determinant of happiness, and there is no evidence that either Britons or Americans are any happier now than they were forty years ago when consumption levels were much lower.[115]

In reality, the pressures to earn enough money to compete in a consumer race undermines some of the major factors determining happiness, such as leisure time and social relations. On average, modern Americans spend more time working than they did thirty years ago (or even ten years ago), and less time with their children, so as to be able to afford the consumer items that advertisers persuade them they need. Most Americans today say they would be happier if they could spend more time with their friends and family and about a third, according to a Gallup poll, would take a twenty per cent cut in income if they or their spouses could have more free time.[116]

The consumer culture is so all-consuming that people spend nearly all their waking hours involved with it: working for the money to spend on consumer goods, commuting to and from work, watching televised advertisements and television programs that promote the consumer lifestyle, and shopping for the things they discovered they wanted whilst watching television. But the escalating production and consumption is degrading the environment at rates that undercut improvements achieved through technological and legislative change.

Advertisements and commercial sponsorship subsidize the delivery of news, entertainment and education, but we all pay the price in the end, not only through buying goods we don't necessarily need (whose price includes the cost of advertising), but also through being socialized into a consumer culture which the planet cannot support indefinitely.[117] Durning says:

> Stripped to its essentials, contemporary advertising has three salient characteristics. It preys on the weaknesses of its host. It creates an insatiable hunger. And it leads to debilitating over-consumption. In the biological realm, things of that nature are called parasites.[118]

Advertising—on television, in newspapers and magazines, on billboards and in school education—is now so pervasive, its message of consumerism so overwhelming, that alternative voices and messages don't get heard: "Commercial speech is so powerful that it drowns out all other sounds."[119]

Chapter 12

The Media: Corporate Influences

Corporate executives and conservative leaders attributed the surge of regulation and the distrust of business of the late 1960s and early 1970s in part to the media and what they perceived as its liberal bias. As part of the political resurgence of conservative ideas, they sought to build their own reliable media outlets and to have more influence over existing media organizations. Robert Parry, author of *Fooling America*, a book about the Reagan/Bush era, describes a well-financed plan to build a conservative press, conceived by Richard Nixon:

> In the twenty-five years since Nixon started 'pushing' this project, the conservatives have constructed a truly intimidating media machine. It ranges from nationwide radio talkshows by Rush Limbaugh and scores of Limbaugh-wannabes, to dozens of attack magazines, newspapers, newsletters and right-wing opinion columns, to national cable television networks propagating hard-line conservative values and viewpoints, to documentary producers who specialize in slick character assassination, to mega-buck publishing houses that add footnotes to white-supremacist theories and a veneer of respectability to journalistic fabrications, and even to narrowly focused organizations that exist simply to hurt the surviving mainstream journalists who still won't toe the line.[1]

Every conservative organization, from think-tank to front group, had its own publication or media programme. The Wise Use Movement's Center for the Defense of Free Enterprise owns radio stations and interests in television stations. Think-tanks and PR firms recruited journalists from the mainstream media to their own staffs. Conservative student newspapers were financed, as was conservative television programming such as Milton Friedman's series *Free to Choose*, which was broadcast on the Public Broadcasting Service (PBS). So much oil company money went into sponsoring PBS programmes that it was nicknamed the Petroleum Broadcasting Service.[2]

Many conservative journals have benefited from the millions of dollars ploughed into them by wealthy conservative foundations and corporations. In contrast, progressive publications have to survive on readers' subscriptions and donations. Beth Schulman, associate publisher of *In These Times*, documents the $2.7 million in grants going to the conservative magazines *The American Spectator*, *The National Interest*, *The Public Interest* and *The New Criterion*, whilst the top progressive magazines *The Nation*, *Mother Jones*, *The Progressive* and *In These Times* received a total of $269,500 in grants over the same period.[3]

Conservative columnists were encouraged and nurtured, while progressive journalists and their editors were pestered and subjected to complaints. Various conservative media-watch organizations were set up for this purpose, such as Accuracy in Media (AIM), founded to "expose liberal bias in the media", and the Media Institute, which included executives from major corporations such as Procter and Gamble and Mobil Oil on its national advisory board.[4]

Perhaps the most significant development, however, was the rise of the conservative talk show. Since the early 1980s the number of talk radio stations in the US has quadrupled to over 800. The abolition of the 'fairness doctrine' in 1987, which "required broadcasters to present fair coverage of opposing views on major public issues", helped in the evolution of the more strident, right-wing stations.[5] "Talk radio has become a potent conservative marketing tool," says Howard Kurtz, author of *Hot Air*, a book on talk shows.[6]

An example of their use to defeat a bill occurred at the end of 1994. A bill to prevent politicians from accepting perks and gifts from paid lobbyists, and requiring paid lobbyists to disclose activities such as organising 'grassroots' protests, passed in the House. But then, according to Kurtz, Newt Gingrich managed to get well-known radio host Rush Limbaugh to oppose the bill in his shows, labelling the bill as 'anti-American' and 'unconstitutional'. He told his listeners the bill would require citizen groups to disclose membership lists (which the bill's sponsors denied). The members of the Senate were swamped with phone calls, and forty-four senators changed their votes, defeating the bill.[7]

Talk radio has been used in this way to defeat other regulatory measures:

> There was no easy antidote to the misinformation and distortion that often accompanied lobbying campaigns and could now be broadcast coast to coast. The creaky machinery of Congress always made it easier to block some piece of legislation than to forge a consensus, and the conservatives now had a powerful weapon at their disposal. When enough radio hosts lined up behind them, they could talk a bill to death.[8]

Recently in *Rolling Stone* Eric Alterman revealed a 1991 'Communications Plan' by Newt Gingrich and his colleagues to "create our own propaganda machine for the widespread distribution of broadcast, print and computer communications to supply our activists and potential followers with ideas, information and rhetoric."[9] According to Robert Parry, this has become a "right-wing media machine" which sets the agenda for much of the national media "deciding which ideas and individuals are accepted and which are marginalized". This media machine is credited with playing a major role in the 1994 Republican takeover in Congress.[10]

Becoming the Major Source of the News

While the conservatives have been building their own media machine they have also been honing their skills at influencing the mainstream media, which is also corporate-owned (see next chapter). In previous chapters we saw that the majority of news items are based on information provided by PR people via press releases, news conferences and staged events. News is also shaped by the choice of people whom journalists interview for research, quotes and on-air appearances. A major focus of the new corporate activism has been to ensure that corporate-funded people are the ones that the media turn to for comment, be they scientists, think-tank 'experts' or front group spokespeople. Corporations have become especially adept at making the best use of television talk shows:

> In recent years, the dramatic growth of talk radio has been accompanied by an increasingly elaborate and sophisticated apparatus aimed at influencing what is said on the air. Political parties, think-tanks, and advocacy groups use so-called burst fax technology to inundate hosts with their talking points. Savvy publicists steer prominent guests to the most sympathetic shows.[11]

The success of this strategy can be seen in the wide use of conservative think-tank personnel by the mass media. In 1995 a study of major newspapers, radio and television transcripts found that the media referred to the Heritage Foundation more than any other think-tank. Altogether there were 7,792 citations of conservative think-tanks, 6,361 of centrist think-tanks and 1,152 of progressive or left-leaning think-tanks. Often think-tanks are cited without any indication of their ideological basis or funding sources and their personnel are treated as independent experts. The think-tanks themselves are seldom investigated by the media.[12]

Most cited think-tanks in 1995, by media[13]

Think-Tank	Political Orientation	No. of Citations
Heritage Foundation	conservative	2,268
Brookings Institution	centrist	2,192
American Enterprise Institute	conservative	1,163
Cato Institute	conservative/libertarian	1,163
RAND Corporation	centre-right	795

The editor of the Heritage Foundation's journal observed that by the end of the 1980s, editorial pages were dominated by conservatives. Media commentator and progressive columnist Norman Solomon also notes that the mainstream media in the 1990s tends to offer either experts who support the status quo or "populists of the right-wing variety". He points out that nowadays it is unusual for media forums to include "unabashedly progressive critiques of the negative effects of corporate power".[14]

A study by Lawrence Soley in his book *The News Shapers* found that the evening news broadcasts by the three major television networks tended to have a centre-right bias—using ex-government officials, conservative think-tank experts and corporate consultants as analysts rather than left-wing activists or progressive think-tank experts. Economist Dean Baker says news stories on trade, for example, almost always rely on sources in government and business, without questioning the vested interests that these sources might have in the issues. This is supported by a 1993 study, which found that "leading newspapers overwhelmingly used pro-NAFTA sources" when reporting on the North American Free Trade Agreement. This was despite the opposition to the Agreement from environmental and labour groups.[15]

A 1989 study of the highly regarded US ABC television current affairs show *Nightline,* conducted by media monitoring group Fairness & Accuracy in Reporting (FAIR), found that eighty per cent of its US guests were professionals, government officials or corporate representatives. Five per cent represented public interest groups and less than two per cent represented labour or ethnic groups; eighty-nine per cent were male and ninety-two per cent were white. The study concluded that "*Nightline* serves as an electronic soapbox from which white, male, élite representatives of the status quo can present their case."[16] (*Nightline* also influences who is used as a source by other journalists.[17])

FAIR's study of the Public Broadcasting Service (PBS), often criticized by conservatives for its liberal bias, also found that the majority of programming on PBS stations used conservative sources (mainly corporate) and government spokespersons, and rarely used activists such as environmentalists.[18]

> The leading talkshows on public TV are either hosted by conservatives. . . or feature inside-the-Beltway centrists. . . Most public TV stations feature one daily . . . and two weekly. . . programs that serve a business/investor audience, while most stations lack a regular series on labor or consumer issues.[19]

Even on public television, experts used for economic coverage were mainly corporate representatives. For all public television coverage, eighteen per cent of sources were corporate representatives, compared with six per cent who were activists of all persuasions. Environmentalists made up 0.6 per cent of sources. The researchers concluded: "While there were exceptions. . . public television did little to highlight the voices of organized citizens, relegating activists along with members of the general public to the margins of political discourse." Even the documentaries, although having more diversity of voices, still relied on the usual news sources. Nevertheless, the constant complaints from conservatives about the liberal bias of public broadcasting tends to exert an ongoing pressure towards conservatism.[20]

FAIR also studied US media coverage of environmental issues from April 1990 to April 1991, including the three main television networks, seven major newspapers and three national newsweeklies—in all almost 900 print articles and over 100 network news stories. It concluded: "Mainstream environmental reporting took its cue not from press-hungry environmentalists, but from the government, corporate and (often non-science) academic establishments."[21]

The increasing trend for corporations to use front groups and friendly scientists as their mouthpieces has further distorted media reporting on environmental issues, since the media often do not differentiate between corporate front groups and genuine citizen groups, and industry-funded scientists are often treated as independent scientists. Because of the myth of scientific objectivity journalists tend to have an uncritical trust in scientists; few "question the motivation of the scientists whose research is quoted, rarely attributing a study's funding source or institution's political slant."[22] Nor do the mainstream media generally cover the phenomenon of front groups, think-tanks and artificially generated grassroots campaigns, which would serve to undermine their operation by exposing the manipulation and propaganda on which they depend.

Corporations are aided in their bid to dominate news sources by the tendency of most journalists to use, as sources, people from the mainstream establishment, whom they believe have more credibility with their audience. Highly placed government and corporate spokespeople are the safest and easiest sources, in terms of giving stories legitimacy. When environmentalists are used as sources, they tend to be leaders of the 'mainstream' environmental groups, which are regarded as more moderate. Those without power, prestige and position have difficulty establishing their credibility as a source of news, and tend to be marginalized.[23] According to Charlotte Ryan, in her book *Prime Time Activism*:

> Using institutional affiliation and famous faces to measure an issue's importance has an interesting overall effect: the criteria implicitly reinforce the stability of government or other powerful institutions while at the same time providing spice via the drama of shifting faces and activities. This is truly novelty without change.[24]

Journalists who have access to highly placed government and corporate sources have to keep them on side by not reporting anything adverse about them or their organizations, as otherwise they risk losing them as sources of information. In return for this loyalty, their sources occasionally give them good stories, leaks and access to special interviews. Unofficial information, or leaks, give the impression of investigative journalism, but are often strategic manoeuvres on the part of those with position or power.[25] "It is a bitter irony of source journalism . . . that the most esteemed journalists are precisely the most servile. For it is by making themselves useful to the powerful that they gain access to the 'best' sources."[26]

> Contrary to all the hype, journalists who gain renown for breaking torrid stories about the federal government may be among those most enmeshed in a mutually-reinforcing web connecting them with power brokers on the inside.[27]

Winning Over the Journalists

Corporations, and the conservative organizations they fund, have employed a deliberate policy of nurturing and rewarding conservative journalists. In the US, promising journalists have been provided with internships by the Institute for Educational Affairs, which is funded by conservative foundations. Corporations offer awards and prizes to journalists who report business in the way they like; these rewards are sought by journalists, who want the prestige and career enhancement they offer.[28] Corporations also offer perks such as meals, gifts, and travel to seduce journalists and ensure favourable stories. Howard Kurtz describes how, when he was with the *Washington Post*, he "was inundated with mail dangling the prospect of freebies" such as hotel stays, meals, entertainment and cruises on ships.[29]

Journalists who can internalize the value system of their employers will climb the career ladder.[30] Top reporters are wooed by those with money and powerful connections. In recent years, high-profile journalists have been getting lecture fees of up to $50,000 for a single speech to a business audience. And, according to Kurtz, "the bulk of that money comes from corporations and lobbying organizations with more than a passing interest in the issues the journalists write about and yak about for a living."[31]

Since 1990, US politicians have been unable to accept speaking fees from interest groups because of the clear conflict of interest, but journalists are often unable to recognize that their own situation is similarly compromised, arguing that it does not mean they would give favourable coverage to the corporation providing the fees. However Alan Murray, *Wall Street Journal* bureau chief, pointed out:

> You tell me what is the difference between somebody who works full time for the National Association of Realtors and somebody who takes $40,000 a year in speaking fees from realtor groups. It's not clear to me there's a big distinction.[32]

Journalists are generally prohibited by their employers from giving paid speeches to groups they are likely to be covering directly,[33] and controversy over speaking fees has led the three major television networks to impose restrictions on when their journalists can accept them. But influence is often more subtle than favourable reporting to a particular corporation or association that has paid the fees. It may subconsciously influence the way journalists report on corporate affairs in general and on matters that affect corporate interests, especially since they may be earning as much from such fees as they do from their salary.

From the point of view of corporations and trade associations paying these fees, what they are getting for their money, apart from the entertainment and glamour that television 'celebrities' offer, is the establishment of a good relationship. They figure that by the time the journalist has supped and socialized with their executives and their wives, they are less likely to be subject to hostile reporting and more likely to gain access to the journalist to put their side of a story.[34]

Such fees also provide an example to all journalists of how profitable reporting that is favourable to corporations can be. Bud Ward, in *American Journalism Review*, described how John Stossel, once "the scourge of US corporations when he worked as a TV consumer reporter" is now "winning an ardent following in these same circles" doing television programmes such as a special on *Are We Scaring Ourselves to Death?* (watched by sixteen million people), which downplayed environmental and health risks and questioned efforts to regulate those risks. Stossel, who now advocates the elimination of agencies such as the EPA "because they interfere with the market", has become a star speaker, receiving large speaking fees from organisations such as the American Industrial Health Council.[35]

Indeed, paying a trusted journalist to narrate a documentary that promotes a corporate view point is a means of buying credibility for it. Walter Cronkite from the CBS network, once labelled 'the most trusted man in America', accepted a fee of $25,000 from the industry front group American Council on Science and Health to narrate a documentary entitled *Big Fears, Little Risks* which dismissed fears about pesticides.[36]

Jeff Cohen and Norman Solomon write in their book *Through the Media*

Looking Glass that before becoming White House counsellor to President Clinton in 1993, "pundit David Gergen dispensed pro-corporate views on PBS's *MacNeil/Lehrer NewsHour*. Most of Gergen's income came from speeches— $700,000 from 171 talks in sixteen months."[37] Gergen is one of many examples of the revolving door between government and the media. Earlier in his career Gergen had written speeches for Nixon, been Director of Communications for Gerald Ford, and helped with the Reagan election campaign.[38] "The well-oiled revolving door between the news business and the political world enables reporters to become press secretaries and political hacks to be reborn as enlightened pundits", says Kurtz.[39]

In other instances, Pat Buchanan used the US television programme *Crossfire* as a refuelling stop between his Republican presidential campaigns; Ross Perot became a radio talk show host after his presidential campaign; John Sununu made the transition from being George Bush's chief of staff to being simultaneously a lobbyist and consultant to the multinational chemical company W.R. Grace & Co. and host of CNN's *Crossfire* program.[40] Ronald Reagan's White House spokesperson became an editor of *US News & World Report*, and various speech writers and press secretaries for past presidents have moved into the media. George Will, a member of Reagan's campaign team who helped Reagan prepare for his debates with Carter in 1980, went on to praise Reagan's performance in the debates when he was subsequently an ABC News commentator and columnist for *Newsweek* and the *Washington Post*.[41]

In Australia there is also a long tradition of journalists becoming press secretaries to politicians, and various members of the former Labour government have gone into media jobs, including John Button, former Industry Minister, and Graham Richardson. Richardson, who once held the posts of Environment Minister and Communications Minister, drawing up the rules for Pay TV, is now a newspaper columnist, Channel 9 executive and top level advisor to media mogul Kerry Packer. Even former Prime Minister Bob Hawke has tried his hand with guest spots on the Australian *60 Minutes* programme.[42]

As a result of this revolving door between the media and government and also between the media and public relations firms, the élite journalists and frontpeople in the media are often drawn from the ranks of those whose previous jobs were to present the best possible image of corporations, politicians and past presidents. How critical can we expect them to be of the establishment?[43] Yet when the media broadcasts its news it rarely reveals its own interests, nor the backgrounds or even the current connections of its journalists, reporters and supposedly objective commentators.

Former US Vice-President Dan Quayle claims: "One of the strengths of democracy is diversity, but there is an amazing lack of it at the top levels of the national media. The best-known journalists are rich, travel in élite circles and share a common ideology. They are far removed from the great working-class traditions of American political journalism."[44] Top journalists receive very high salaries—television news personalities get millions of dollars per year and network correspondents get over $100,000—which gives them a very privileged view of the world: "They are part of the moneyed class, just like the people they report on." They are happy to support the status quo, because they themselves are doing well out of it.[45]

Many of those who haven't reached the top yet are also fairly well-off. Big city reporters have incomes only "slightly lower than those of their neighbours the lawyers and corporate middle managers".[46] Modern journalists are fed a continual diet of corporate ideology from their college days, where courses in journalism schools are now endowed by corporations and foundations, and in their jobs they are bombarded daily with propaganda from conservative think-tanks.[47]

Some commentators have suggested that journalists have a social bias arising from their middle-class background, which manifests in the sorts of topics they are interested in and therefore report on. For example, Elizabeth Martínez and Louis Head argue that the media have neglected the issue of environmental racism. Environmental racism is a term that describes the tendency to site hazardous and undesirable facilities in Latino, African, Asian, Native American and other 'minority' communities; Martinez and Head suggest journalists are not generally interested in such communities. Environmental racism was nominated as one of the top twenty-five censored stories in 1991 by the staff of Project Censored at Sonoma State University in California.[48]

Similarly, academic Dorothy Nelkin notes that, despite all its coverage of chemical carcinogens and contaminated sites, journalists have seldom covered the workers in the chemical industry and how they are affected. Occupational health is generally avoided by journalists, and when they do cover it they tend to use official sources rather than workers themselves.[49]

Journalistic Objectivity

Journalists often claim that their own biases and the pressures from advertisers and media owners do not affect their work, because of their professional norm of 'objectivity'. Journalistic objectivity has two components. The first is 'depersonalisation', which means that journalists should not overtly express their own views, evaluations, or beliefs. The second is 'balance', which involves presenting the views of representatives of both sides of a controversy without favouring one side.[50] Associated conventions include:

> *Authoritative* sources, such as politicians, must be quoted (in this way the journalist is seen to distance him- or herself from the views reported, by establishing that they are someone else's opinions); 'fact' must be separated from 'opinion', and 'hard news' from 'editorial comment'; and the presentation of information must be structured pyramidically, with the most important bits coming first, at the 'top' of the story.[51]

Any journalistic comment comes from 'specialist' correspondents who are quoted as experts by the reporter, in the same way that a scientist might be. The news reporter refrains from such comment.[52] These conventions perpetuate the impression that reporters are simply conveying the 'facts' and not trying to influence how people interpret them. The ideal of objectivity gives journalists legitimacy as independent and credible sources of information.

The rhetoric of journalistic objectivity supplies a mask for the inevitable subjectivity that is involved in news reporting, and reassures audiences who might otherwise be wary of the power of the media. It also ensures a certain degree of autonomy to journalists, and freedom from regulation to media corporations.[53] However, news reporting involves judgements about what is a good story, who will be interviewed for it, what questions will be asked, which parts of those interviews will be printed or broadcast, what facts are relevant and how the story is written.

> Value judgements infuse everything in the news media. . . Which of the infinite observations confronting the reporter will be ignored? Which of the facts noted will be included in the story? Which of the reported events will become the first paragraph? Which story will be prominently displayed on page 1 and which buried inside or discarded? . . .Mass media not only report the news—they also literally *make* the news.[54]

Objectivity in journalism has nothing to do with seeking out the truth, except in so much as truth is a matter of accurately reporting what others have said. This contrasts with the concept of scientific objectivity, where views are supposed to be verified with empirical evidence in a search for the truth.[55] Ironically, journalistic objectivity discourages a search for evidence: the balancing of opinions often replaces journalistic investigation altogether. FAIR's survey of environmental reporting found that it tended to be "limited to discussion of clashing opinions, rather than facts gathered by the reporters themselves".[56]

1. Balance

The conventions of objectivity, depersonalisation and balance tend to transform the news into a series of quotes and comments from a remarkably small number of sources. Balance means ensuring that statements by those challenging the establishment are balanced with statements by those whom they are criticising, though not necessarily the other way round.[57] For example, despite claims by the nuclear industry of anti-nuclear media bias, a FAIR study of news clippings collected by the Nuclear Regulatory Commission over a five-month period found that no news articles cited anti-nuclear views without also citing a pro-nuclear response, whereas twenty-seven per cent of articles cited only pro-nuclear views. (It also found that seventy-two per cent of editorials and fifty-six per cent of opinion columns were pro-nuclear.)[58]

Balance means getting opinions from both sides (where the journalist recognizes that there are two sides) but not necessarily covering the spectrum of opinion. More radical opinions are generally left out. The US EPA is sometimes used as an environmental source in one story and as an anti-environmentalist source in another. Nor are opposing opinions always treated equally in terms of space, positioning and framing.[59] Balance does not guarantee neutrality even when sources are treated fairly, since the choice of balancing sources can be distorted. FAIR gives the example of a *Nightline* show where radio talk show host Rush Limbaugh argued that volcanoes are the main cause of ozone depletion.

(This is an example of a growing talk show tradition of featuring right-wing ideologues as experts on scientific questions.) Limbaugh was 'balanced' with then
Senator Al Gore "who argued that the answer to ecological problems was more
'capitalism'."[60]

In practice, objectivity means journalists have to interview legitimate élites
on all major sides of a dispute, and this gives the powerful guaranteed access to
the media no matter how flimsy their argument or how transparently self-interested. In their attempts to be balanced on a scientific story, journalists may use
any opposing view "no matter how little credence it may get from the larger scientific community".[61] But giving equal treatment to two sides of an argument can
often provide a misleading impression. Phil Shabecoff, former environment
reporter for the *New York Times*, gives the example of views on climate change:

> The findings of the International Panel on Climate Change—a body of some 200
> eminent scientists named by the World Meteorological Organization of the United
> Nations Environment Program—is generally considered to be the consensus posi-
> tion. But I have seen a number of stories where its conclusions are given equal or less
> weight than those of a single scientist who has done little or no significant peer-review
> research in the field, is rarely, if ever, cited on those issues in the scientific literature,
> and whose publication is funded by a fossil-fuel industry group with an obvious axe
> to grind. . . for a reporter, at this stage of the debate, to give equal or even more
> weight to that lonely scientist with suspect credentials is, in my view, taking sides in
> the debate.[62]

In the environmental magazine, *Sierra*, Paul Rauber gave another example of
how equal treatment can give a misleading impression:

> Hundreds, maybe thousands of people gather to call for the factory to stop polluting
> or for the clearcutting to end. In one little corner, half a dozen loggers or millwork-
> ers hold a counter-demonstration on company time. That night on the evening news,
> both sides get equal coverage.[63]

2. Depersonalisation

The requirements of objectivity often lead journalists to leave out interpretations
and analysis which might be construed as personal views, to play it safe by reporting events without explaining their meaning, and to keep stories light and superficial so as not to offend anyone.[64] Bagdikian relates how:

> News became neutralized both in selection of items and in nature of writing. American
> journalism began to strain out ideas and ideology from public affairs, except for the
> safest and most stereotyped assumptions about patriotism and business enterprise. It
> adopted what two generations of newspeople have incorrectly called 'objectivity'.[65]

Journalists who accurately report what their sources say can effectively
remove responsibility for their stories onto their sources. The ideal of objectivity
therefore encourages uncritical reporting of official statements and those of
authority figures. In this way, the individual biases of individual journalists are
avoided but institutional biases are reinforced.[66]

Professional codes ensure that what is considered important is that which is said and done by important people. And important people are people in power. TV news thus privileges holders of power. . . Its focus on individual authority figures as privileged spokespersons reflects the ideologies of individualism and élite authority.[67]

The occasional environmental journalist finds the pretence of objectivity goes against their conscience. Teya Ryan, producer of CNN's program *Network Earth*, wrote: "As the air in Los Angeles grew browner, more debilitating. . . as the destruction of the world's rain forests became widely known; and as everyone wondered where to put the trash—particularly the plutonium—I wondered if 'balanced' reporting was still appropriate."[68] Others see it as necessary for their credibility: "The peril is that if readers perceive journalists as having become advocates rather than reporters, then they won't trust anything they read or say."[69]

The appearance of objectivity is so important that some media outlets don't even let their journalists take part in public political activity, such as marches and demonstrations, even as individual citizens in their own time. Journalists at the *Washington Post*, for example, received a memo stating: "It is unprofessional for you. . . to take part in political or issue demonstrations, no matter on which side or how seemingly worthy the cause."[70]

3. Sphere of Objectivity
The rules of objectivity only apply to a recognized sphere of controversy. If two sides are not recognized, there is no perceived need for balance. Some ideological assumptions are "so taken for granted" by the mainstream media that they don't even recognize them as being ideological.[71] Jeff Cohen, executive director of FAIR, points out that journalists recognize a propaganda of the left and a propaganda of the right but not a propaganda of the centre. "Being in the center—being a centrist—is somehow not having an ideology at all. Somehow centrism is not an "ism" carrying with it values, opinions and beliefs."[72] Michael Parenti, author of *Inventing Reality: The Politics of the Mass Media*, says:

Journalists (like social scientists and others) rarely doubt their own objectivity even as they faithfully echo the established political vocabularies and the prevailing politico-economic orthodoxy. Since they do not cross any forbidden lines, they are not reined in. So they are likely to have no awareness they are on an ideological leash.[73]

Journalists are free to write what they like if they produce well-written stories "free of any politically discordant tones"; that is, if what they write fits the ideology of those above them in the hierarchy. A story that supports the status quo is generally considered to be neutral and is not questioned in terms of its objectivity, while one that challenges the status quo tends to be perceived as having a "point of view" and therefore biased. Statements and assumptions that support the existing power structure are regarded as 'facts' whilst those that are critical of it tend to be rejected as 'opinions'.[74] For example, one study of environmental stories found that: "While the media were willing to dispute dire environmental predictions, they were more accepting of dire economic projections—citing enormous anticipated job losses while rarely asking how the figures were derived, or if plant closings and layoffs were the only options."[75]

Some questions also remain outside the realm of contested territory. *Village Voice* journalist Daniel Lazare points out that media reports on energy consumption in the US consistently ignore the cheap and easy availability of fuel, and the subsidies and tax concessions supporting oil production and energy consumption in the US as being a factor that encourages wasteful consumption. Lazare blames this on the fact that "taxes remain a dirty word inside Washington" and also on "political conformism and cultural insularity" in most newsrooms: "Cheap gas, cars and highways are—unquestionably—the American way."[76]

Objectivity not only stops short of the centre; it also doesn't go too far away from the centre. Although the media in countries such as Britain and the US are fairly impartial when it comes to the spectrum covered by the established political parties they have been much less fair to views outside this establishment consensus: "Impartiality and objectivity, in this sense, stop at the point where political consensus ends—and the more radical the dissent, the less impartial and objective the media."[77]

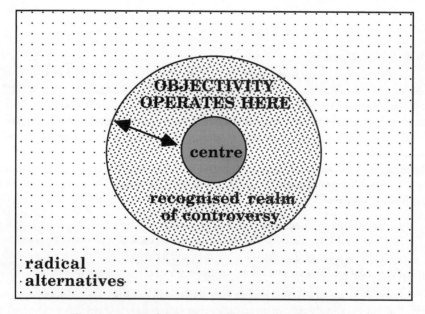

Figure 1: Limited Operation of Objectivity Conventions

Framing and Presenting the News

The environmental movement relies extensively on the mass media to get its message across to the general public, but doing so has its costs.

In the late twentieth century, political movements feel called upon to rely on large-scale communications in order to *matter*, to say who they are and what they intend to publics they want to sway; but in the process they become 'newsworthy' only by submitting to the implicit rules of newsmaking, by conforming to journalistic notions (themselves embedded in history) of what a 'story' is, what an 'event' is, what a 'protest' is. The processed image then tends to become 'the movement' for wider publics. . .[78]

In his analysis of how the media treated the new left student movement of the 1960s and 70s, Todd Gitlin observes that the movement was at first trivialized and marginalized through images that emphasized frivolity, youth, outlandishness, militancy and deviance whilst understating numbers and effectiveness, and neglecting the content of the movement's statements and the causes of the students' protests.[79] "Thus the protesters were made the issue rather than the things about which they were protesting."[80] Such media images and symbols are powerful, not only in shaping the public perception of a movement but also the movement's perception of itself.

The media tends to present images and style, rather than meaning and content: "The media intervene to label these activities as deviant or illegitimate, marginalizing them and diverting public attention away from the root causes of social conflict towards its epiphenomenal forms."[81] Protest actions and events are described as theatre spectacles rather than as "part of a democratic struggle over vital issues".[82] It is the style that is copied and multiplied, whilst the radical message of the protesters is diluted and ignored. Kellner argues that "when television portrays social change or oppositional movements, it often blunts the radical edge of new social forces, values, or changes. Moreover, it tries to absorb, co-opt, and defuse any challenges to the existing organization of society."[83]

Environmental problems are poorly reported in the media because of the need to provide entertainment rather than political awareness, to attract audiences for advertisers, even in news and current affairs programmes. This occasionally affects a specific item of news but more generally affects the kinds of stories that are covered and the way they are covered. News editors are reluctant to deal with controversial political and social issues that might alienate potential consumers. As a result news has become bland and neutral, and ignores issues that concern large portions of the population who are not considered to have or exercise much buying power (see Chapter One).[84]

Yet bland news can be boring, so the lack of controversy and social significance is made up for by making the news entertaining and interesting. Intellectual and political interest is replaced by 'human interest', conflict, novelty, emotion and drama, or as one feature writer put it "currency, celebrity, proximity, impact and oddity"—the elements of newsworthiness.[85] In his book *The Media*, Keith Windschuttle claims that each news outlet has a 'news formula' which aims to attract a loyal, predictable audience for advertisers. The 'news formula' is a way of selecting 'good stories' for this purpose; an "unwritten hierarchy of favoured news". He says that "the formula of the popular, or down-market, press [is] based on stories about celebrities, disasters, monsters, politics and deviance".[86]

Another way of maintaining interest on television is to have constantly changing images. Academic Kiko Adatto has documented in her book *Picture Perfect* the decreasing length of the sound bite in the US, which had fallen from

42.3 seconds in 1968 to 9.8 seconds in 1988. "Politics, in other words, was being shot and edited to the rhythms of a Coca-Cola advertisement. Forget about hearing a whole paragraph on a policy decision; a politician was now lucky to finish a sentence." This trend has also been observed in Australia, where John Henningham, a Professor of Journalism, has studied news bulletins on Channel 9. He found that each shot lasts an average of less than five seconds, and that there are up to thirty-three shots in reports that last little more than a minute. He agrees that "news bulletins are striving for the visual excitement of the commercial or rock clip."[87]

Entertainment merges with current affairs, producing 'infotainment' which, as Philip Gold notes in the conservative magazine *Insight on the News*, blends "trivial amusement with the address of serious issues", reduces "serious reportage into fragmented coverage of the latest 'shocking developments'" and squeezes out "more serious discourse". Television news producers prefer very short stories with good visuals, and action stories that add excitement to the news. They are very good at providing drama and emotion but poor at giving in-depth information on complex issues.[88] News stories are presented very quickly, in rapid succession and with little explanation. "The typical anchor delivers more than two hundred words a minute." As a result, people who rely on television to get their news tend to be "the least-informed members of the public".[89]

The need to entertain turns social processes and events into stories, "with some unfolding built into the action, starting somewhere and leading to somewhere else".[90] Stories that "elicit strong emotions" are best:

> Every news story should, without any sacrifice of probity or responsibility, display the attributes of fiction, or drama. It should have structure and conflict, problem and denouement, rising action and falling action, a beginning, a middle and an end.[91]

Stories that take longer than a day to unfold are told as a series of climaxes.[92] Says one editor: "Acid rain, hazardous waste. . . they're the kind of big bureaucratic stories that make people's eyes glaze over. There's no clear solution, no clear impact. They're not sexy."[93] The news media are poor at dealing with slow-moving changes and "indeterminate or fluid situations". The news "is characteristically about events rather than processes, and effects rather than causes". As a result, environmental reporting tends to concentrate on events such as the Earth Summit or various Earth Days, accidents and disasters such as oil tanker spills, and official announcements.[94]

Media outlets stress immediate events; they do not back track on past events because they want their audiences to tune in or buy their newspapers every day. They want to give the impression that they will miss out on something if they don't. "The focus on what just happened, the emphasis on getting scoops and beating the opposition to a story that everyone would have reported anyway in a day, says that knowing what just happened is the crucial thing." This means journalists have to work to very tight deadlines and don't have the time to investigate properly and consult a wide range of sources.[95] Each story competes for priority and an emphasis on 'breaking news' doesn't encourage coverage of long-term issues.

The journalistic tendency to balance stories with two opposing views leads to a tendency to "build stories around a confrontation between protagonists and antagonists".[96] Despite their importance, issues such as garbage and sewage sludge only get coverage when there is a fight over the siting of a landfill or incinerator, and then the coverage is on the "anger and anguish of affected citizens, or the conflicting claims of corporate spokesmen, government regulators and environmental activists" rather than the issues and technical background to them. A survey of media coverage in the US in 1991 commissioned by the American Society of Mechanical Engineers found that independent experts were seldom used as sources: "The news was not oriented toward describing or explaining the problem, but rather toward disputes over what should be done about it."[97]

In one story by ABC's *Nightline*, for example, Nebraskan residents opposing a 'low-level' radioactive waste dump in their neighbourhood attempted to present, with the help of an EPA expert Hugh Kaufman, rational arguments involving discussion of various technical issues. However, according to Kaufman, the TV crew wanted emotional material and in the end used archive footage of heated meetings to get the emotional content they wanted:

> They defined the issue this way: The public are a bunch of emotional misfits who think about Chernobyl and aren't doing their homework, while proponents are these brilliant technical experts. In other words they walked in with a predetermined story when, in fact, what they had seen in Nebraska was just the opposite.[98]

This is a feature of many news stories about local controversies. The intelligence and research of local residents is downplayed, and they are presented as passionate, self-interested and inexpert. This tends to discourage wider support for their cause from the viewing public and to disempower other citizens by depriving them of attractive models of political activism.

Stories need characters, so personalities become important in television news and celebrities are created. The focus on individuals also means that the way that individual examples and actions fit into a broader social context is left out.[99] David Ricci, in his book *The Transformation of American Politics*, says:

> In the case of politics, it is usually a tale of individuals. . . where one dramatis persona struggles against another for power and personal gain. Such 'horse race' journalism tends to slight the importance of political parties and social issues because, after all, they are less exciting, more difficult to film, and almost impossible to describe without longer verbal expositions than television ordinarily cares to provide.[100]

Having to fit with media imperatives also influences politicians and the policies they pursue: policies that can be explained in simple terms and converted into positive media symbols are preferred. As journalist Howard Kurtz points out, the television format, with its need to keep things moving and avoid the audience becoming bored and switching channels, favours the status quo because "the case for reform is always more complicated" and takes time to explain.[101]

Talk show campaign spots have revealed that the questions that ordinary callers ask of politicians are quite different from those asked by reporters. Citizens are interested in policies and how they will be affected by them, whereas reporters want to know about political strategies and power plays. Media coverage of politics tends to focus on strategies rather than issues, and avoids discussion of policies which would require journalists having to actually read legislation and analyse its implications. "Since each question tends to be framed around the never-ending battles between the White House and Congress," writes Kurtz, "the debate is circumscribed in a way that excludes unorthodox or unpopular notions."[102]

This is by no means a unique feature of US politics. Writing in the British magazine *New Statesman & Society,* Steven Barnett observes: "It is now universally acknowledged that the conduct of politics is increasingly dictated by modern techniques of publicity and media exploitation. Proper political dialogue takes second place to the sharpness of the suit, the succinctness of the sound-bite, the control of interviews and the use of advertising techniques."[103]

Similarly Warwick Beutler, a former political reporter for the Australian Broadcasting Corporation, ABC, says that until the mid-1980s journalists focused much more on the substance of parliamentary bills, but now they report the power struggles. Former Labor MP Fred Daly agreed, saying that most media coverage concentrates on the mistakes and manoeuvres of politicians rather than the parliamentary debate.[104]

James Fallows, the Washington editor of *The Atlantic Monthly,* says in his book *Breaking the News: How the Media Undermine Democracy* that in their efforts to entertain, journalists have been "concentrating on conflict and spectacle, building up celebrities and tearing them down, presenting a crisis or issue with the volume turned all the way up, only to drop that issue and turn to the next emergency".[105] And Simon Hoggart, writing in *New Statesman & Society,* observes that the tendency of some US newspapers and tabloid TV shows to offer "'News McNuggets', events chopped up, stuffed with artificial flavouring, and served in bite-sized portions", is heading towards Britain, where "news is becoming increasingly a ready-processed product designed to make no call on understanding or imagination." Hoggart describes the tendency to turn all news into a human interest story, and if it is not amenable to that, not to cover it. This involves picturing victims and heroes, and not bothering with the social analysis and historical background.[106]

News stories are told as "self-contained, isolated happenings". Events from wars to union strikes are presented without historical or social context, which would take too much time or space. Reporting of environmental problems tends to be superficial, narrowing the focus to specific events in isolation rather than looking at systemic problems that caused them, such as the international monetary system or the unregulated power of corporations, and concentrating on the costs of environmental measures. Environmental problems become a series of events that emphasize individual action rather than social forces and issues.[107]

Current affairs programmes do expose corporate misdeeds, accidents and environmental and health problems resulting from unsafe products and production processes, but in a way that does not call into question "fundamental political or economic structures and institutions".[108]

By treating business wrongdoings as isolated deviations from the socially beneficial system of 'responsible capitalism', the media overlook the systemic features that produce such abuses and the regularity with which they occur. Business 'abuse' is presented in the national press as an occasional aberration, rather than as a predictable and common outcome of corporate power and the business system. The exposé *that treats the event as an isolated and atypical incident implicitly affirms the legitimacy of the system. . .*[109]

Environmental disasters are rarely followed up, and environmental revelations that are uncovered by journalists are "seldom incorporated into the body of knowledge and perspective" that environmental journalists draw on in their work. Miranda Spencer, writing in *Extra!,* gives the example of the exposé in *Christian Science Monitor* that air pollution reductions reported by corporations were "based on paperwork tricks" which failed to inform later reporting of the Clean Air Act.[110]

Former *Boston Globe* journalist Dianne Dumanoski admits, with reference to environmental reporting, "Our coverage is all too often driven by our business's appetite for novelty and conflict. We often don't do a good job of reporting on the science of complicated issues, and we generally do a lousy job of helping our audience understand uncertainty, which is the central dilemma faced in making environmental policy."[111]

Lack of Diversity in News Reporting

Clearly journalists and their editors are only one of the filters through which news stories must pass. While individual journalists may have left leanings, this is not reflected in national news coverage. This is because "the news is not what reporters report but what editors and owners decide to print" or broadcast.[112] Editors are free to cut, edit or drop stories without consulting the journalists who wrote them. There is seldom a need for direct intervention by owners to ensure a corporate or conservative slant to the news. "Rather, managers in business, government, and the media share a common mindset which informs and prioritizes news coverage."[113]

Most journalists learn which stories are likely to be run and which are not, and internalize this so it becomes a form of self-censorship that many are unaware of.[114] Those that don't self-censor do not get very far. Anthony Bevins, who worked on a number of 'quality' British papers, wrote in the *British Journalism Review.*

> It is daft to suggest that individuals can buck the system, ignore the pre-set 'taste' of their newspapers, use their own news sense in reporting the truth of any event, and survive. Dissident reporters who do not deliver the goods suffer professional death. They are ridden by newsdesks and backbench executives, they have their stories spiked on a systematic basis, they face the worst sort of newspaper punishment—byline deprivation.[115]

Indeed, various former environmental writers claim to have been victimized or lost their jobs for investigating stories that their employers would rather not have investigated or for their perceived environmental bias. Bruce Selcraig, in *Sierra*, gives examples of several environmental journalists in the West of the US who "were reassigned or simply made so miserable they left". He quotes Jim Detjen, President of the rapidly growing Society of Environmental Journalists: "Virtually every veteran environmental writer I know, has been threatened with the loss of his or her job at one time or another."[116]

The influence of editors, owners and advertisers as well as journalistic conventions are clearly more important to the final result of journalism than the differences between individual journalists, as otherwise there would be more difference between the way various media outlets report the news. The mass media are extremely homogenous in the news it delivers. In the US, most national news is reported from Washington, DC by an ever-increasing number of journalists (more than 10,000 in the 1990s) who "track the same individuals, institutions, and events" in a similar way.[117] Kurtz claims that the chorus of voices fails to "challenge the underlying assumptions of official Washington" so that "any argument that lacks significant support in Congress is blown off the radar screen as irrelevant."[118] Even reporting of local happenings tends to be shaped by a general approach and framework set at a national level and local newspapers often take their lead from national newspapers.[119]

> As mainstream journalism has centralized its focus and its personnel, it has developed a commonality in perspective that reinforces its own dominant beliefs and messages, in sharp contrast to the older system of competition among newspapers of differing ideologies. By and large, those journalists who remain geographically outside Washington look to their on-scene counterparts for raw information and, increasingly, opinion and analysis. . . it is not so very misleading to speak of 'the news media' as a singular entity, replete with its own rules, norms, beliefs, leaders, and its own independent ability to shape events.[120]

The difference between network television stations is minimal. Well-known media critic Edward Herman explains the reason that the news is reported the same way on every channel, and indeed all over the English-speaking world:

> The media's frequently homogenous behaviour arises 'naturally' out of industry structure, common sources, ideology, patriotism and the power of the government and top media sources to define newsworthiness and frameworks of discourse. Self-censorship, market forces, and the norms of news practices may produce and maintain a particular viewpoint as effectively as formal state censorship.[121]

Chapter 13

Reporting on the Environment

Media reporting of environmental problems increased at the end of the 1980s, reaching a peak in 1989-90 in many countries around the world and declining steadily after that. Studies of media content in the US show that environmental coverage in the early 1990s was less than two per cent, despite the high level of concern amongst the public.[1]

One study by Michael Nitz and Sharon Jarvis at the University of Arizona found that television news stories tended to "underemphasize risks and overdramatize spins on disputes" and that "coverage is largely episodic, full of isolated dramatic vignettes of conflict and jeopardy in which animals play the starring roles".[2] Environmental stories, which were seldom lead stories, lacked background information and only included technical or scientific information twenty-two per cent of the time. Large corporations that tend to sponsor newscasts and run green advertising campaigns were almost never examined for their environmental record.[3]

Coverage of former communist countries at this time concentrated on the pollution and environmental degradation in these countries, implying it was far worse than anything in the West and "an inevitable by-product of a centralized, totalitarian system".[4] This treatment of environmental degradation as being the result of the prevailing political system contrasted with the way it is usually treated in the West, where rather than being the inevitable result of a capitalist system that puts profit before environmental protection it tends to be treated as the result of isolated accidents and misdemeanours of individual companies.

In the US, for example, Love Canal, Times Beach and the thousands of other Superfund sites represent exceptional circumstances, whereas sites such as these in the East are 'symptomatic' of a socio-economic system. Also the role of West Germany in exporting ten million tons of toxic waste to East Germany was neglected. As Peter Dykstra of Greenpeace has pointed out, this highlights a double standard where "under Marxism, the environment is 'sacrificed' to production goals; under capitalism, the environment is 'balanced' with production goals." This sort of reporting enables corporate funded think-tanks to claim that pollution in Communist countries proves that the free market was necessary to prevent environmental degradation.[5]

Whilst environmental degradation in the East was being played up, the media began to play down the degradation in the West. After the initial flurry of crisis reports around 1989-90, the media settled into a phase that has been variously referred to by environmentalists as 'revisionist' and 'backlash'. Environmental stories in the 1990s cast doubt on the crisis stories that the media had featured earlier. The stories now tended to have an economic framing, focusing on the costs of regulation in terms of jobs and money.[6]

When the 1990 Clean Air Act was debated in the US, the media "generally let government and business frame the discussion". And that discussion focused on whether Americans could afford better air standards, rather than on the health and environmental effects of polluted air. "Almost no scientists or public health specialists were quoted." Instead the costs and job losses cited by business and free-market economists were generally reported without question.[7]

Economics professor Richard Du Boff argues that economists quoted within this prevailing economic framework "are overwhelmingly those from the free market and neoconservative right".[8] He observes:

> In general, coverage of the anti-regulation campaign has followed ground rules established by the right wing: Free market arguments set the tone and are then treated with careful respect if not absolute deference. The pro-regulation case is rarely given a comprehensive airing, and its advocates appear at irregular intervals, as figurative snipers. . . Emphasis is on the costs of regulation—frequently exaggerated—and references to the benefits that accrue to the public are omitted altogether.[9]

This cost-benefit framework does not consider who gets the benefits—the public—and who pays the costs—corporations. Nor does it consider that money spent by these corporations in cleaning up their act is paid to other businesses and often provides jobs and promotes economic activity. A recent OECD report found that there was no evidence that spending on environmental protection had affected US national growth nor the competitiveness of American firms and that, in fact, it had created some four million jobs and was likely to create another million by the year 2000. In contrast, federal energy subsidies that encouraged wasteful energy use were costing billions each year.[10]

In *Canadian Dimension*, Doug Smith observed the transition in reporting styles from the late 1980s to the 1990s:

> When the environment got a second chance for fifteen minutes of fame, we all found ourselves subjected to endless lectures on the new three Rs, reuse, recycle reduce. . . we also saw the emergence of green consumer reporting. Any entrepreneur who claimed that his product was environmentally friendly won his fifteen minutes of public acclaim. At times the media's main interest in the environment seemed to be marrying the shopping craze of the eighties with saving the planet. . . Then came the fourth R, the recession. The phrase 'It isn't easy being green' headlined innumerable stories on the high cost of saving the earth. . . In short, environmentalism was being restored to its status as a fringe concern, one that would have to be ignored while the tough decisions were made about the economy.[11]

The media has also "played a decisive role in publicizing and spreading anti-environmental initiatives", giving plenty of coverage to the Wise Use Movement and ignoring the obvious part played by corporate interests in mobilising loggers and others for maximum media impact.[12] Those who have sought to cast doubt on global warming and ozone depletion have found a ready audience in environmental journalists at some of the top newspapers. The environmental journalist Kevin Carmody observed that "by 1994, the *Los Angeles Times*, ABC News and the *Chicago Sun-Times*, among others, were taking the iconoclastic position that Americans were being unnecessarily frightened about everything from street crime to pollution. . ."[13]

In the *Los Angeles Times*, David Shaw argued in an article headed "Living Scared: Why Do the Media Make Life Seem so Risky?" that people today are less likely to die from cancer (except lung cancer) and therefore the dangers posed by environmental pollutants are exaggerated. He neglected to point out that a major reason why death rates have fallen is not that people are exposed to fewer carcinogens, but that they seek treatment earlier and get better treatments for some types of cancers.[14]

Keith Schneider, at the *New York Times*, became notorious in the early 1990s for his revisionist stories which argued that environmental hazards such as contaminated sites are not as dangerous as once thought: "Many experts. . . question the wisdom of spending billions of dollars to protect people from traces of toxic compounds. . . [M]any scientists, economists, and government officials have reached the dismaying conclusion that much of America's environmental program has gone seriously awry."[15]

Schneider saw himself as a pioneer of a new type of environmental reporting: "We look [at] and view all sides equally skeptically, and that we come to conclusions based on data, not the frantic ravings of one side or another." He suggested that the press had been a captive of environmental groups who did not necessarily tell the truth: "Environmental journalists have to regard environmental groups with as much skepticism as we have traditionally regarded polluters."[16]

Schneider's reports, which suggested that environmental regulations are not based on sound science, cited very few scientists by name, preferring to refer to unspecified scientists and studies, along with politicians, bureaucrats, economists and industry people, to back his assertions. Those scientists he did name were not identified as consultants to industry, where that was the case.[17]

> What sources were left out? Nearly everyone concerned with matters other than money and deregulation, be they independent scientists, ordinary citizens (particularly pollution victims) and environmentalists. Indeed, the series was notable for the absence of dissent, lacking even a superficial effort to seem 'objective' or 'balanced'.[18]

According to journalist Miranda Spencer, Schneider has described the Wise Use Movement as "one of the most important and interesting movements to arrive in environmentalism in a long time". However others have argued that the Wise Use movement is to some extent a media-enhanced phenomenon. Journalist Tim Eagan, Seattle correspondent for the *New York Times*, who travels extensively to small towns and rural communities, claims he has not seen much evidence of the Wise Use Movement, and says of the media: "We've elevated Wise Use to this large alternative movement, which I really don't see on the ground."[19]

The new emphasis on the costs of environmentalism at the *Times* was no accident. Schneider was appointed to the position of environmental reporter to replace Phil Shabecoff, who covered the environment on the *Times* for fourteen years. Shabecoff was transferred to reporting on the Internal Revenue Service after he was told that he "wrote too much about environmental problems, and not enough about the economic problems that environmentalism was causing."[20]

Schneider is not an isolated phenomenon in environmental reporting. *Newsweek* writer and *Atlanta Monthly* columnist Greg Easterbrook produced the classic good news book on the environment with his *A Moment on the Earth: The Coming Age of Environmental Optimism*, which was immediately used by conservative interests, corporate PR departments and lobbyists as well as the media to argue the case against the need for environmental legislation.[21]

Two British journalists have also published revisionist books on the environment. Matt Ridley, a *Sunday Telegraph* columnist, has had his book *Down to Earth: A Contrarian View of Environmental Problems* published by the Institute of Economic Affairs; and Richard North, formerly an environment writer with the *Independent*, has published *Life on a Modern Planet: A Manifesto for Progress*. The multinational chemical corporation ICI funded research for North's book.[22]

Boyce Rensberger at the *Washington Post* has also caused much controversy, including a rebuttal from the American Chemical Society, with his claims that ozone depletion is being solved "before they can find any solid evidence that serious harm was or is being done", and with his favourable and extensive coverage of Patrick Michaels' claims that global warming could be beneficial. Michaels publishes a magazine funded by coal companies and his research is funded by organizations such as the Edison Electric Institute. Needless to say, these connections were not mentioned in Boyce's article,[23] nor in a more balanced 1997 article in the UK-based *New Scientist* magazine entitled 'Greenhouse Wars: Why the Rebels have a Cause'.

In this way the media have given the doubts raised by industry scientists a status above and beyond that given to them within the scientific community. This exaggerates the uncertainty associated with these environmental hazards which "can be parlayed into paralysis of Congress".[24] In an article in *Sierra*, Paul Rauber says:

> Most reporters don't know much about science, and are unable to distinguish legitimate scientific dispute from bogus posturing. . . fewer than a dozen scientists, many of them on the payroll of coal and energy companies, say not to worry. On the evening news, both sides get equal time. . . No matter how thoroughly their charges were debunked, however, the skeptics and the fossil-fuel industry got what they were after: a shadow of a doubt far larger than the facts warrant, and a ready-made excuse for timid legislators to stick with the status quo.[25]

When the Earth Summit came around in 1992, the media coverage was massive. The media contingent at the conference in Rio numbered in the thousands and came from all over the world. However the mass media coverage of the Summit in the US was patchy, according to two different accounts by freelance journalists covering the event. William Ryan, a former editor of the *Guardian* newsweekly, claimed the US media focused on negotiations over the global warming treaty, Bush's veto of specific greenhouse gas targets and vanishing rain forests, but gave little examination to the "vastly differing Northern and Southern perspectives on who is responsible for destroying the environment, what needs to be done, and who should pay for it."[26]

J. A Savage, covering the conference for the *San Francisco Bay Guardian*, *Ms* magazine and *Focus* magazine, noted that the Global Forum, the conference for non-government organizations that was held in conjunction with the Summit, was scarcely covered; environmentalists quoted were almost always from well-funded US environmental groups; and many issues were neglected. For example the controversial use of the World Bank's Global Environmental Facility to control and distribute money raised to help poorer countries achieve sustainable development was hardly discussed.[27]

The environmental movement is often characterized in the media as "just another special-interest group" looking after its own "economic and institutional well-being" rather than a broad-based social movement.[28] The more radical environmental groups are sometimes treated as fringe loonies. Earth First! took exception when ABC's *World News Tonight* suggested that the so-called Unabomber was linked with their organization. According to Earth First!, the "top level" meeting of Earth First! that the Unabomber was supposed to have attended was actually a public conference which 400 people attended. (The FBI apparently obtained a list of attendees.) Earth First! also claim that a hit list, on which two of the Unabomber's victims were supposed to be, was in fact produced by an underground anarchist publication not connected with Earth First!.[29]

Whilst mainstream media outlets have been downplaying environmental problems, others have been taking the opportunity to make money out of audiences that are concerned about them. Three new environmentally oriented television channels were being set up in 1995 in response to the twenty per cent of US citizens who are active environmentalists and the thirty-five per cent who care enough about the environment to change their shopping decisions.[30] These people represent a market opportunity rather than an information gap. The founder of Ecology Channel, Eric McLamb, apparently "has no qualms about saying the venture's primary purpose is to provide entertainment and make money".[31]

> I don't know about the survivability of a 24-hour station that does nothing but bash corporations. . . Do you want to see hour after hour that shows destruction and environmental catastrophe? Hour after hour saying you've got to change?. . . It turns off so many people and turns off corporations, and that's your money source.[32]

The channel is using PR firm E. Bruce Harrison for public relations and to "help us develop educational material for schools to make sure the right message goes out that everyone agrees on". McLamb said the channel will show "a happy, prosperous lifestyle in harmony with the environment" with programmes such as The Jungle Book and The Home Gardening Club. "Ours is a feel-good show," says McLamb.[33]

Another new cable channel is Planet Central Television, which aims to cover social and environmental issues as well as having "lots of entertainment". It hopes to get "a revenue stream impelled by 'infomercials'," advertising and commercial sponsorship: "We are going after a trillion dollars worth of business that is not in television right now."[34]

Reporting on Dioxin

The media played a major role in the early 1990s in changing public perceptions of dioxin from deadly poison to misunderstood and maligned chemical. The *New York Times* has been one of the leading papers to downplay the dangers of dioxin. In 1991 it devoted an editorial and two front-page articles by Keith Schneider to government official Vernon Houk's claims. One article, headlined *US Officials Say Dangers of Dioxin Were Exaggerated*, stated that "exposure to the chemical, once thought to be much more hazardous than chain smoking, is now considered by some experts to be no more risky than spending a week sunbathing." The other article called for relaxation of "the current strict and costly standards" for dioxin.[35]

Schneider's stories were reprinted in more than twenty other major newspapers, and the claims that dioxin was no longer dangerous were repeated by dozens of other media outlets. Headlines in other papers included "The Deadliness of Dioxin put in Doubt by New Data" (*Los Angeles Times*), "On 2nd thought, toxic nightmares might be unpleasant dreams" (*Chicago Tribune*) and "The Double Take on Dioxin" (*Time* magazine). No journalists bothered to contact the CDC to see what they thought of Houk's claim that the CDC had made a mistake in evacuating Times Beach. If they had, they would have found the same action would still have been taken twenty years later, based on the most up-to-date scientific evidence.[36]

The comparison with sunbathing, which Schneider admits he thought up himself, was repeated in many media outlets variously attributed to "top federal scientists" (*Arizona Republic*), "some health specialists" (*Newark Star-Ledger*), "a widening group of scientists" (*Sacramento Bee*) and "some studies" (AAP and *Dallas Morning News*).[37] The sunbathing comparison was also repeated in a 1994 book entitled *Environmental Overkill*, by Wise Use Movement hero, scientist and former governor of Washington state, Dixy Lee Ray:

> Exposure to dioxin, once thought to be much more hazardous than chain smoking, is now considered to be no more risky than spending a week sunbathing. The difference between these two beliefs—less than ten years apart—is that the first one was based on unsubstantiated statements, hearsay, and hype with no data to back it up, while the second rests solidly on years of carefully gathered evidence corroborated by independent experts.[38]

Whilst some newspapers reported the dioxin controversy well, most notably the *Wall Street Journal*, which exposed the public relations efforts behind the Banbury conference, many followed the *Times'* lead, ignoring new evidence that was emerging that in fact dioxin was more harmful than previously thought because of its non-cancer effects.[39] David Lapp, writing in *Multinational Monitor*, says that:

The media's failure to report on developments that contradict industry's dioxin message while giving so much attention to Houk and others' questionable beliefs indicates the power of the forces confronting environmentalists and their allies.[40]

New studies indicating the danger of dioxin was in fact worse than previously realized (see Chapter Nine), were hardly reported in the US press. In fact, the *New York Times* and other papers continued to push the line that scientists no longer thought dioxin was so dangerous after all and gave the impression that the controversy over dioxin had in fact been resolved. Schneider wrote in 1993 that: "billions of dollars are wasted each year in battling problems that are no longer considered especially dangerous," such as dioxin.[41]

However, the rehabilitation of dioxin was not the sole preserve of the newspapers. One 1991 report on dioxin by National Public Radio (NPR) was examined by Charlotte Ryan. On the face of it, it appeared as if the coverage of the issue, which had included two government scientists, two environmental activists and an independent consultant, had been balanced and fair. But as Ryan points out, one of the two government scientists—who were treated as neutral experts— was Michael Gough, whose questioning of the toxicity of dioxin was based on industry funded studies, "one of which was written by Gough himself while on sabbatical from his government job."[42]

The other government scientist was Linda Birnbaum, an EPA scientist who had been temporarily convinced by the Banbury Conference that the EPA's dioxin assessment might be wrong. The independent consultant was George Carlo, consultant to the Chlorine Institute. Only one of the two environmental activists was identified as a scientist, although both were. And the whole piece was introduced with a statement that "recent studies suggest the dangers of dioxin may be overrated."[43] Ryan concludes:

> While appearing to reflect diversity of opinion, NPR's report on dioxin fell prey to. . . a "well-financed public relations campaign by the paper and chlorine industries". Buying into mainstream journalistic assumptions about scientific objectivity and government neutrality, NPR did not help its listeners understand how federal government regulation and environmental research have been politicized.[44]

Even after the EPA's draft reassessment was leaked to the media in 1994, reaffirming that dioxin is a probable carcinogen but also concluding that other, noncancer health effects of dioxin and dioxin-like chemicals were far greater than previously thought,[45] media coverage tended to suggest that the dangers of dioxin had all been exaggerated by emotional environmentalists.

In an article in *Time* magazine, Madeleine Nash makes no acknowledgment of any scientific basis for the hazards of dioxin. She states: "Now environmentalists say dioxin and scores of other chemicals pose a threat to human fertility" and that "with the escalating rhetoric, many professionals in the risk-assessment business are worried that once again emotion rather than common sense will drive the political process." She quotes a risk analyst who "suggests that people should strive to keep the perils posed by dioxin in perspective and remember other threats that are more easily averted."[46]

"Phantom risks and real risks compete not only for our resources but also for our attention," Graham observes. "It's a shame when a mother worries about toxic chemicals, and yet her kids are running around unvaccinated and without bicycle helmets."[47]

Reporter Gina Kolata, who had replaced Schneider at the *Times,* wrote a series of articles stating that the theory that chlorine-based chemicals might interfere with hormones has been "refuted by careful studies", which she did not name. The *Times* declined to publish letters to the editor by scientists refuting this allegation, and a group of scientists actually paid for an advertisement so as to be able to point out the 'inaccuracies' in Kolata's article.[48]

In one article reviewing the book *Our Stolen Future*—which was written by three people, two of whom are scientists—Kolata suggested that the claims in the book had no scientific basis, despite the mountain of evidence cited in the EPA dioxin reassessment report, and were merely a trendy expression of political correctness: "In a warning supported by allies who include Robert Redford and Vice-President Al Gore, some environmentalists are asserting that humans and wildlife are facing a new and serious threat from synthetic chemicals."[49]

The reporting on this issue is not altogether surprising. All newspapers depend on large quantities of paper produced at pulp and paper mills that discharge dioxin-contaminated waste. The newspapers benefit from the cheaper paper prices that result from paper mills not having to install new equipment to eliminate dioxins nor pay out large sums as a result of lawsuits over dioxin pollution. Moreover, many newspapers also own shares in these mills: for example, the *New York Times* recently had major interests in four paper mills. At the time of the 1991 series on the harmlessness of dioxin, one of the mills partly owned by the *Times* was the subject of a Canadian law suit claiming C$1.3 billion for polluting three rivers with dioxin.[50]

Other papers also have financial interests in paper and timber companies and "have taken editorial positions supporting relaxed dioxin standards without disclosing their ties to the industry". Vicki Monks, writing in the *American Journalism Review,* points to Central Newspapers ("owned by former Vice-President Dan Quayle's family"), which partly owns a newsprint mill and also owns the *Arizona Republic* and *Indianapolis Star,* both of which have downplayed dioxin's dangers in editorials. In a similar position is the Times Mirror Co and its paper the *Los Angeles Times,* as well as the *Chicago Tribune* and the *Washington Post.* None have declared their conflict of interest in reporting on dioxin issues.[51]

Ownership of the Media

Most media organizations are owned by multinational multi-billion dollar corporations that are involved in a number of businesses apart from the media, such as forestry, pulp and paper mills, defence, real estate, oil wells, agriculture, steel production, railways, water and power utilities.[52] Such conglomerates not only create potential conflicts of interest in reporting the news, but also ensure that the makers of the news take a corporate view.

The boards of these media companies typically include representatives of international banks, multinational oil companies, car manufacturers and other corporations. Take for example the board of the *New York Times*: it shares board members with Merck, Morgan Guaranty Trust, Charter Oil, American Express, Bethlehem Steel, IBM, Scott paper, Sun Oil, First Boston Corporation, Ford Motor Company and Manville Corporation.[53] And during the 1980s, as a result of the spate of corporate takeovers, many media organizations "lost some of their limited autonomy to bankers, institutional investors, and large individual investors whom they have had to solicit as potential 'white knights'."[54]

Noam Chomsky, who has documented a number of biases in the US media's treatment of foreign affairs, points out that media corporations "are closely integrated with even larger conglomerates" and like other businesses they sell a product (audiences) to buyers (advertisers).[55]

> In short, the major media—particularly, the élite media that set the agenda that others generally follow—are corporations 'selling' privileged audiences to other businesses. It would hardly come as a surprise if the picture of the world they present were to reflect the perspectives and interests of the sellers, the buyers, and the product. . .[56]

The owners of the media influence the selection, shaping and framing of the news to attract advertisers—"Proprietors determine the target audience and general editorial approach to that audience"[57]—but also to ensure a favourable political climate for their media and other business concerns. In a survey by the American Society of Newspaper Editors, about a third of newspaper chain editors admitted that they "would not feel free to run a news story that was damaging to their parent firm."[58]

Windschuttle cites several examples of interventions by Australian media owners Keith Murdoch, Rupert Murdoch, Frank Packer and Warwick Fairfax. Rupert Murdoch is well-known for this. He controls two-thirds of the newspaper market in Australia, as well as one-third of the market in Britain through ownership of three of Britain's largest daily national newspapers and two of its largest circulation Sunday papers. He also controls extensive satellite broadcasting in dozens of countries: his Star satellite service beams television to 220 million people in Asia. His Fox network in the US is fast becoming a fourth major commercial television network, and Fox is moving into cable television with a news service that it hopes will rival CNN, which Murdoch is reported to consider "too liberal". Murdoch's media empire also includes book publishing companies in Australia and the US, Festival Records, 20th Century Fox as well as interests in computer software, offshore oil and gas and air transport.[59]

According to journalist Sasha Abramsky, Murdoch "has—and uses—the power to make British politicians, and to break them unless they toe his line". Murdoch papers gave Margaret Thatcher "glowing press" throughout her rule, and Murdoch eventually received a knighthood—one of the few non-British citizens to do so. Thatcher received a "lucrative" book contract from Murdoch's book publishing firm HarperCollins (as did Newt Gingrich, whose contract was for $4.5 million). His papers, says Abramsky, "have consistently opposed the

peace movement, trade unions, progressive social programs. . . while supporting
the death penalty, lower taxes at any cost and hawkish foreign policies."[60]

Murdoch's power is indicative of the highly concentrated media ownership in
the UK, where control lies in the hands of a few "proprietors with explicit conservative views".[61] About eighty per cent of the press in Britain is controlled by
only four corporations, and the situation is similar for broadcast media. Robert
Maxwell was also an interventionist owner who, according to Brian McNair,
"boasted that his ownership of national newspapers gave him the power 'to raise
issues effectively. In simple terms, it's a megaphone.'" McNair, author of *News
and Journalism in the UK*, argues that in Britain "the economic interests and political preferences of the proprietor continue to be the most important determinant
of a news outlet's editorial line."[62]

The pattern of media concentration in Australia and Britain is repeated in
Europe, where Murdoch's News International is only the fifteenth largest media
conglomerate. Robert Hersant, imprisoned for collaborating with the Nazis,
owns newspapers whose combined circulations include one-third of France's
readers of national papers and two-fifths of Poland's readers. In Italy, Silvio
Berlusconi owns three television channels and three pay TV channels, as well as
newspaper and magazines. Berlusconi used his media empire to win political
leadership in Italy but was forced out of government in controversial circumstances. The trend in media ownership is not only towards concentration within
countries but also towards the creation of 'global media empires' that include
newspapers, television stations, magazines, movie studios and publishing
houses.[63]

The majority of US media outlets, including newspapers, magazines, radio,
television, books and movies are controlled by less than twenty huge corporations
(compared with forty-six in 1983).[64] "Ninety-eight per cent of US cities have daily
papers without competition. Ten newspaper chains control almost half the daily
newspaper circulation. And even the remaining independently owned papers are
dependent on the wire services and generally follow the nation's newspapers of
record."[65] Recent mergers include those of the CBS network with Westinghouse,
Capital Cities/ABC with Disney, and Ted Turner's media interests (including
CNN) with Time-Warner. The entry of Westinghouse into the television world
means that two of the major commercial networks are directly affiliated with the
nuclear industry, as General Electric owns television network NBC.[66]

Even cable television, which was supposed to be a means of providing diversity to television content, has ended up becoming an interconnected network of
channels, "most of them owned by an interlocking set of a half-dozen or so giant
corporations" including Disney, Time Warner, and General Electric. Those cable
stations that aren't connected to the big cable owners, like the small independent
TV and radio stations, need to be well-funded, and often have corporate or
wealthy conservative sponsors.[67]

The mechanism of control usually exercised by media proprietors is through
the appointment of editors "who become the proprietor's 'voice' within the news-
room, ensuring that journalistic 'independence' conforms to the preferred editorial

line."[68] The power of the media is not just through its editorial line but also in covering some issues rather than others, some views but not others. It is this power that makes politicians so reluctant to cross the large media moguls and to regulate the industry in the public interest:

> In this sense, the media have enormous power over national elections. . . those candidates who are placed on the media's agenda have a chance to win; those that are ignored languish. Those issues—either policy or personal—which the media spotlight become the yardsticks for measuring candidates. When candidates receive heavy (and favourable) publicity, their campaigns flourish. . .[69]

They also have power to influence the policies that elected governments implement, and plenty of reason to exercise that power. "In recent years, media companies have been among the most profitable businesses" in the US.[70] Chomsky points out:

> What is at issue is not the honesty of the opinions expressed or the integrity of those who seek the facts but rather the choice of topics and highlighting of issues, the range of opinion permitted expression, the unquestioned premises that guide reporting and commentary, and the general framework imposed for the presentation of a certain view of the world.[71]

General Electric and NBC

General Electric's ownership of NBC is a good example of the way a corporation can influence television content. NBC is a television network which broadcasts to over 200 affiliated stations, reaching almost all homes in the US. Additionally, NBC owns and operates six televisions stations and is in the process of purchasing three more. NBC claims that its news programmes "represent a primary source of global news for a significant portion of the public". The company also owns two cable stations, CNBC (Consumer News and Business Channel) and *America's Talking,* and has ownership stakes in seventeen others. "NBC has moved aggressively to take the NBC brand to new markets around the world." In 1983 it acquired Super Channel, "Europe's largest general-programming service", offering programmes to seventy million homes and 350,000 hotel rooms in forty-four countries. It has a Spanish-language news service reaching twenty-one countries in Latin America and is about to launch an Asian Service. Advertising revenue is NBC's primary source of income.[72]

General Electric (GE) is itself one of the largest and most diverse corporations in the world, with annual revenue for 1996 of $79.2 billion (more than forty per cent from outside the US) covering "light bulbs and locomotives, jet engines and nuclear bombs, TV broadcasting and nuclear power plants and financial services". It has $191 billion in assets, 506,000 stockholders, 216,000 employees worldwide, 177 plants in the US and over 100 outside the US, and makes billions of dollars of profits each year ($7.28 billion in 1996). GE is the largest manufacturer of jet engines in the world, the largest supplier of electric motors, one of the largest manufacturers of major appliances, the second-largest plastics manufacturer in the US, and the second largest supplier of electronics to the US Defense Department.[73]

GE is by no means a hands-off owner of NBC. Lee and Solomon, in their book *Unreliable Sources*, have detailed how GE insisted on the removal of references to itself in an NBC programme on substandard products. They also point out that NBC journalists have not been particularly keen to expose GE's environmental record and that TV commercials by a group called INFACT, urging a boycott of GE products, were banned by NBC as well as other television stations. NBC did however briefly report GE's indictment for cheating the Department of Defense, which was reported more extensively in other media outlets. Former NBC News Chief Lawrence Grossman claims that the head of GE, Jack Welch, made it clear to him that he worked for GE and told him not to use terms such as 'Black Monday' to describe the stock market crash in 1987 because it depressed share prices such as GE's.[74]

Todd Putnam, editor of *National Boycott News*, tells of how he was approached by the NBC's *Today Show* to do an interview about consumer boycotts. Their biggest boycott at the time was against General Electric and its nuclear defense contracts, but the show wouldn't let him talk about it; it was reluctant to have him mention boycotts against any large corporation, preferring him to talk about "a boycott that was 'small', 'local' and 'sexy'."[75] Mark Gunther, writing in *American Journalism Review*, claims that in an NBC *Today Show* on the subject of defective bolts in planes, bridges and nuclear plants, references to General Electric's use of defective bolts were edited out and only mentioned in a follow-up segment after criticism of the omission.[76]

In 1990 *NBC Nightly News* ran fourteen minutes of coverage over three days of a breast cancer detection machine produced by GE, without mentioning that it was made by NBC's owners. The other two major television networks didn't bother to cover it at all.[77] Helen Caldicott, who had been featured on the *Today Show* previously, found that when she wrote her book *If You Love This Planet*, which used GE as a case study of an environmentally damaging company, her scheduled appearance was mysteriously cancelled.[78]

In 1987, one year after GE took over NBC, NBC broadcast a special documentary promoting nuclear power, using France as a model. The promotion for the programme proclaimed that "French townspeople welcome each new reactor with open arms." The documentary won a Westinghouse-sponsored prize for science journalism. (Westinghouse Electric Company also builds nuclear power stations.) Shortly after the documentary was screened, when there were a couple of accidents at French power stations and there was significant opposition to nuclear power amongst the French population (polls showed about one-third opposed it), NBC did not report the story although some US newspapers did.[79]

Karl Grossman documents in *Extra!* how the programme *What Happened?*, broadcast on NBC in 1993, gave a one-sided account of the Three Mile Island nuclear accident and its aftermath. It showed local resident Debbie Baker saying that she was not as afraid of the nuclear plant as she used to be. Yet according to

Grossman, Baker, whose son was born with Down's Syndrome nine months after the accident, and who has received $1.1 million in a settlement arising from the accident, was shocked at how the programme had been edited to imply her acceptance of the plant. She said she was still extremely uncomfortable with the plant and that what she had said was she felt safer since her groups set up a network of radiation monitors around the plant. Neither Baker's settlement nor the two hundred or so others made to families who have suffered injury, birth defects and death following the 1979 accident were mentioned. Instead a nuclear power industry expert was featured, saying that the plant's back-up safety systems worked successfully.[80]

> When *Extra!* pointed out that no scientists critical of nuclear power appeared in the program, Jaffe [executive producer of the show] responded, 'That is correct. Maybe there is some misunderstanding. That show is not a journalistic show but an entertainment show to look into and to find out the reason and cause of various accidents and incidents.'[81]

NBC has not been alone in putting a positive spin on the Three Mile Island nuclear accident. On the tenth anniversary of the accident, the *New York Times* ran an anniversary article opposite the editorial page headlined *Three Mile Island: The Good News*, which argued that the accident had been good for the nuclear power industry, prompting better management and emergency planning. The paper did not report the fact that 2,000 residents living near the plant had filed claims for cancer and other health problems they blamed on the accident, nor the 280 personal-injury settlements paid out to such claimants, nor the unusual clusters of leukemia, birth defects and hypothyroidism around the plant.[82]

This was not the first time *Times* reporting had fitted in with GE's views. In 1986 the *Times* reported on the use of humans as subjects in tritium absorption experiments (tritium is routinely handled by nuclear power plant workers). An early edition of the paper said: "The tritium study was financed by the Atomic Energy Commission and conducted by the General Electric Company at Richland, which abuts the Hanford [nuclear weapons] reservation." In the late edition the sentence ended after Commission and no longer named GE.[83]

General Electric influences other media outlets through its advertising and sponsorship. It ceased its multi-million dollar funding of a *World of Audubon* TV series when specials on ranching and logging prompted a Wise Use Movement-generated fax and letter campaign threatening a boycott of GE products. Charles Cushman claims he organized 35,000 letters and faxes, but General Electric says it did not renew its sponsorship of the series because of budget cutbacks.[84] The Public Broadcasting Service was a beneficiary of sponsorship by General Electric when it decided not to screen the Oscar award-winning documentary *Deadly Deception: General Electric, Nuclear Weapons, and Our Environment*. The reason given by PBS was that the film had been partly financed by INFACT, which was boycotting GE: "We do not permit the producer of the programme to be the subject of the programme."[85]

GE's interests are not limited to nuclear power: indeed they are so extensive that it would be hard to find many political subjects in which GE doesn't have an interest. GE has a "permanent team of two dozen lobbyists with a large support staff" in Washington, and also hires lawyers and lobbyists for particular projects. In its lobbying GE claims to represent the interests of millions of people—its employees, suppliers and customers—not to mention the public interest.[86]

Although GE contributes to politicians from both political parties and its top executives include some Democrats, the corporation is a staunch supporter of the Republican Party. It employed Ronald Reagan in 1954 when his acting career was 'floundering', giving him a TV career and sending him on a lecture circuit around the country pushing GE causes such as deregulation, lower corporate taxes, and attacking communism, labour unions and social welfare. This period working with GE in the 1950s and 60s marked the start of Reagan's political career.[87]

GE's support of Reagan and the Republicans began to pay off in a big way after Reagan was elected president. He introduced tax cuts which resulted in a windfall for GE: in the years 1981-83, GE made a profit of $6.5 billion but received a tax rebate of hundreds of millions of dollars.[88]

> Its tax burden went from $330 million a year to minus $90 million a year—money the government now owed GE. By rough estimate, the 1981 tax legislation yielded as much as $1.3 billion for General Electric over several years and probably much more in the long run. . . GE's windfall did not, however, create any new jobs for Americans. On the contrary, the company was in the process of drastically shrinking its US workforce—eliminating nearly fifty thousand people from its payroll through layoffs, attrition and the sell-off of subsidiaries. The tax windfall, however, did help GE finance its aggressive campaign of corporate acquisitions. . .[89]

One of these occurred in 1986 when GE bought RCA, which owned the television network NBC, for $6.28 billion. A previous similar attempt by ITT to buy the ABC network (1966-7) had been prevented by the Justice Department after a public outcry on the grounds that it "could compromise the independence of the ABC's news coverage of political events in countries where ITT has interests". However no such objection was made in the case of GE, and the then US Attorney General later joined GE's board of directors.[90] Douglas Kellner, in his book on *Television and the Crisis of Democracy*, argues:

> The fact that this corporation—one of the major producers of nuclear weapons and energy, a top defense contractor, and a key player in the military-industrial complex. . . was allowed to take over a major television network and use it to advance its corporate goals makes a mockery of the antitrust laws, the public utility status of broadcasting, and the federal regulatory apparatus.[91]

General Electric as a Responsible Corporate Citizen

GE is a leading member of the Business Roundtable, and supports a range of corporate front groups including the American Council on Science & Health, Citizens for a Sound Economy, and the Council for Energy Awareness (which promotes nuclear power).[92]

> GE's board is a conservative cross-section of the power élite—corporate executives, bankers, retired cabinet members and generals, an Ivy League president and several Ivy boardmembers. There are multiple ties with the Morgan bank, Citicorp, Manufacturers Hanover. GE boardmembers also serve on several media industry boards—Harper & Row, Reuters, the Washington Post. They are well-represented in the branches of the permanent government, too. . .[93]

GE funds various conservative think-tanks, including the Institute for International Economics, the American Enterprise Institute and the Center for Strategic and International Studies.[94] These conservative think-tanks funded by GE provide 'independent' experts to give comment on media outlets owned and funded (through advertising and sponsorship) by GE. "Not surprisingly these well-paid sluggers go to bat for the big business and national security state, confirming biases already deeply ingrained in US media." Nor is it surprising that think-tank experts are used so much by a media whose owners help to fund them.[95]

Despite its control of the NBC network, its interlocking board of directors with other media outlets and its ownership of the cable channel CNBC, GE spends millions on commercials and sponsorship of television programmes on other networks including ABC, CNN and PBS to improve its image. It spends $40 million per year on image ads.[96]

GE likes to portray itself as a good citizen providing 'the good things in life', giving large donations for schools, scholarships for the underprivileged and local community projects. However its history reveals its priority remains with corporate profits. During the Depression, GE introduced planned obsolescence into the life of light bulbs so as to boost sales, and during the War that followed GE was found guilty by the courts of collaborating with a key German company, Krupp. After the war it was found guilty of price-fixing and bid-rigging (in 1961 and again in 1978) and recently (in 1985 and again in 1988, 1990 and 1991) it has also been caught defrauding the US government in defense contracts. According to a 1994 report of the Project on Government Oversight GE was guilty of "sixteen instances of fraudulent activity" against the government between 1990 and 1994—more than any other company.[97]

In 1981 GE executives went to jail for bribing a Puerto Rican official on a power-plant contract, and in 1989 GE was fined for discriminating against low-income consumers. Other complaints against GE, such as insider trading and employment discrimination, have been settled out of court.[98] GE has also been sued by three Midwest utility companies for "knowingly installing unsafe systems" after attempts by GE to keep secret an internal report "critical of its faulty nuclear reactor design" were exposed.[99] In 1992 the *Washington Post* reported that GE had "pleaded guilty to charges of fraud, money laundering and corrupt business practices in connection with its sale of military jet engines to Israel."[100]

In theory, all these convictions and accusations could be cause for the US Federal Communications Commission (FCC) to rule that GE was unfit to hold

a broadcasting license. In fact the day before GE announced its intention to buy
NBC, the Commission relaxed its character qualifications, "declaring that a large
corporation could be held responsible for felonies only if the heads of the corporations or those directly involved in the broadcasting aspect were wrongdoers."
Under the new rules, the Commission decided in 1986 that GE had rehabilitated
itself and should be able to hold NBC's broadcasting licenses.[101]

In 1995 two environmental groups, Ozone Action and the Environmental
Law Foundation, sued several major refrigerator manufacturers and retailers,
including General Electric, for advertising refrigerators as 'ozone safe' or 'CFC
free', although they were using the ozone-depleting chemical hydrochlorofluorocarbons (HCFCs). Also in 1995 the firm Electric Mutual Liability, whose sole
business was insuring General Electric's asbestos and environmental liabilities,
filed for bankruptcy.[102]

GE makes pollution control equipment but also creates its own pollution:
four of its factories are "on the EPA's list of the most dangerous industrial sources
of toxic air pollution". It has been sued over the contamination of land and
groundwater at a bomb-making plant in Washington. Toxic and radioactive
wastes have also been found in the sewage system and nearby bay at a plant in
Florida where GE manufactured triggers for hydrogen bombs. In Alabama, the
state won an out-of-court settlement from GE for dumping PCBs in the Coosa
River. New York state officials have been less successful in a fight over PCBs in
the Hudson River, where fishing had to be banned, although they did get GE to
pay for the clean-up of ground water contaminated with organochlorines near
one of their plants.[103]

In 1992, state and federal authorities closed down a GE processing plant in
Anaheim, California. The EPA had suspended its PCB-handling license because
ongoing operations posed "an unreasonable risk to human health and the environment". The EPA later fined GE $353,000, "one of the highest PCB fines ever
levied by the agency". In the meantime Steve Sandberg, an employee of the plant,
is suing GE, claiming he was told that PCBs were harmless by his employers
when they knew otherwise. Sandberg was given the job of cleaning out exploded,
burned-up PCB transformers and suffered health problems including chloracne,
which is associated with dioxin contamination. Sandberg is one of many suing
GE and other companies across the US over the effects of PCB.[104]

Yet despite its environmental record, and perhaps because of its media clout,
General Electric managed to be one of the top ten companies in terms of environmental reputation amongst consumers in 1991, according to a Roper Poll.
However, it lost its position in 1993, which may be due to its being identified in
several magazines as one of the most environmentally unsound companies.

In a 1993 *Fortune* magazine article entitled 'Who Scores Best on the
Environment', GE were listed as one of ten most 'laggard' companies (out of 130
of America's largest manufacturing companies) for the following reasons:

> Admits being a potentially responsible party at more than seventy Superfund sites; a
> 1992 ruling by thirty-two state attorneys general forced a change in the efficiency
> claims for its Energy Choice light bulbs and imposed a hand-slapping $165,000 fine.

Its fines for OSHA [Occupational Health and Safety Administration] violations were 150% higher than any other company's in the electronics industry. Though it has made progress in reducing total toxic chemical releases, GE consistently remains on most green groups' worst lists.[105]

The *Fortune* article also notes General Electric's reluctance to adopt the Coalition for Environmentally Responsible Economies (CERES) principles, otherwise known as the Valdez principles, a voluntary code of conduct for environmental protection. This was despite shareholders' resolutions in favour of their adoption.[106]

Similarly, GE was named one of the worst eight toxic polluters in America by the Council on Economic Priorities in 1992 and 1993. The reasons:

> This Fairfield, Connecticut-based giant designed Mexico's only nuclear power plant, which has dumped 2.5 million gallons of radioactive waste water into the Gulf of Mexico. Several American utility companies have charged that GE sold them deficient nuclear-containment vessels. The EPA has named GE as a potentially responsible party at more Superfund sites than any other company. Over a thirty-year period, GE plants dumped 500,000 pounds of polychlorinated biphenyls (PCBs) into the Hudson River. . .[107]

GE took part in the corporate fight against the Superfund legislation enacted in 1986, which sought to pay for the clean-up of toxic sites through charging the companies that created them. This legislation was a response to public outrage, but once the legislation had been passed the public had been placated and the corporations went into action. GE hired Stephen Ramsey, who had "developed the liability rules for enforcing the Superfund law" whilst Assistant Attorney General for Environmental Enforcement in the Reagan government, and who had later worked for a private firm that helped corporations avoid the billions of dollars that the law could potentially cost them.[108]

Together with Dow, DuPont, Union Carbide and Monsanto, GE formed a coalition to work towards the overturn of the Superfund legislation when it came up for renewal. According to William Greider, author of *Who Will Tell the People*, this coalition sought to persuade the public that the legislation was not working. To do this, the Superfund Coalition used lobbyists Charles E. Walker Associates and environmental consultants William D. Ruckelshaus Associates. (Ruckelshaus had been head of the US EPA under both Nixon and Reagan.)[109]

The coalition looked for allies amongst environmentalists, and funded the Conservation Foundation, headed by William Reilly, to undertake a major research project for them. Other groups approached included the Sierra Club, the Natural Resources Defense Council, the Environmental Defense Fund and the Audubon Society, but none of these wished to be involved. When, later, the corporate coalition sought to distance itself from the project to make it seem to be more independent of vested interests, Ruckelshaus was able to persuade the EPA to fund the project to the tune of $2.5 million in 1988 whilst the corporations played a less visible role.[110] Greider says:

The Superfund law, it is true, wasn't working—partly because the affected corporations were stubbornly resisting their financial liabilities and partly because EPA was
itself quite slothful, cleaning up only a handful of hazardous sites each year from the
backlog of thousands. Now, the two main delinquents—EPA and the corporations—
were teaming up to ask what the problem was.[111]

The strategy worked well for all involved. By 1991 William Reilly had
become the new head of the EPA, appointed by George Bush on recommenda-
tion of William Ruckelshaus, and Ruckelshaus had become Chief Executive
Officer of one of the major waste-disposal companies, Browning-Ferris
Industries.[112] Most importantly, the media was reporting the failure of Superfund
and its huge costs.

A *New York Times* front-page article that year began: "A decade after
Washington declared war on businesses that expose the public to hazardous
wastes, environmental experts are questioning the unquestionable: Is it worth
spending a staggering $300 billion to $700 billion to restore waste sites to pristine condition?"[113] The article quoted expert sources such as an employee of
General Electric and a so-called 'environmentalist' from the group Clean Sites, a
corporate front group that highlights the costs of toxic clean-ups to its sponsors.[114]
This 'environmentalist' later wrote to the *Times* saying: "We. . . do not represent
an 'environmentalist' constituency. . . Our financing comes from reimbursements
for services, and grants from corporations, foundations and government." The
article also quoted an "expert" from the "environmental research group"
Resources for the Future, a group described by *In These Times* as "an industry-
funded organization promot[ing] the idea that dangers from toxic contamination
have been vastly overrated".[115]

Once in office as head of the EPA, Reilly's approach was to get corporations
to clean up their own sites and pay for it themselves rather than getting the EPA
to clean them up and charge industry. However, according to the Office of
Technology Assessment, OTA, this meant the clean-up was often not adequate,
because companies wanted to save money. In fact, in one year corporations saved
"perhaps as much as $1 billion" by OTA estimates, compared to the cost of
having to do the job properly.[116]

The way the environment is reported is clearly influenced by the corporate
ownership of the media, especially when it comes to issues such as dioxin which
have such large and immediate financial ramifications for media owners. Whilst
the media are also influenced by news sources and advertisers, the corporate
agenda of the large media moguls is not so different from that of their corporate
advertisers.[117] Bagdikian argues: "Since media owners are now so large and deeply
involved in the highest levels of the economy, the news and other public information become heavily weighted in favor of all corporate values."[118]

News is defined firstly by those who have privileged access to the media as
sources and interpreters—public relations people, government officials and
accredited experts. It is then shaped according to journalistic conventions, aimed
at attracting and entertaining an audience for advertisers, and fitted into a
general framework and approach that suits corporate owners. All these influences

determine the news output that most people depend on for information about the world beyond their personal experience.

Douglas Kellner, in his book *Television and the Crisis of Democracy*, argues:

> Democracy presupposes the existence of a public sphere in which vigorous debate on issues of public importance takes place so that decisions can be made on complex and controversial issues. In a system of commercial broadcasting, however, profit imperatives limit the amount of time given to political debate. . . corporate control severely compromises the democratic functions of television and renders it, first and foremost, an instrument of social control and legitimization rather than a medium of information and democratic debate.[119]

Chapter 14
Conclusion: Declining Democracy

Surveys show that the majority of people in most countries are not only concerned about the environment: they think environmental protection should be regulated by governments and given priority over economic growth.[1] Yet this widespread public concern is not translating into government action because of the activities of large corporations that are seeking to subvert or manipulate the popular will.

A recent *ABC News/ Washington Post* survey, for instance, found that nearly three-quarters of people in the US didn't think government was doing enough to protect the environment; an *NBC News/ Wall Street Journal* survey found that a majority of respondents wanted environmental regulations strengthened (compared to less than one in five people who thought they should be weakened). Similarly, a *Time/*CNN poll found that a majority of people wanted environmental expenditure by government increased, with only sixteen per cent wanting it reduced. A Harris survey found that most people would be willing to pay more taxes and higher prices if the money was spent "to protect and restore endangered species". And a Gallup poll in 1995 found that two-thirds of people agreed that "protection of the environment should be given a priority, even at the risk of curbing economic growth", a result mirrored in a 1994 *Times Mirror* Magazines survey.[2]

Despite such public opinion, the Republican-dominated Congress has actually been dismantling and weakening existing environmental regulations, with devastating consequences for the environment. *The Economist* recently reported an OECD study that found the environment was deteriorating in the US:

> Wetlands, good for wildlife, are being mopped up by developers; extinctions are increasing. . . Municipal waste accumulates: each American now jettisons 2kg of rubbish a day, more than any other people on earth. Nuclear waste and used nuclear fuel pile up in temporary stores. The number of vehicles on the roads has doubled since 1970, and drivers cover twice as many miles. . . Some 15% of rivers and 10% of lakes are still too grubby for people to swim or fish in. Some 59m people still live in areas where the air is dirtier than the government thinks safe. And the United States remains the world's largest producer of carbon dioxide, which may be causing global warming.[3]

Yet the corporate-generated Congressional attack on environmental legislation goes on relentlessly. Industry groups have used their lobbyists, their political contributions, their coalitions and front groups to achieve this result.

Lobbyists for the coalitions have provided staff to Republican lawmakers, drafted parts of bills, and sat on the dais with congressmembers during committee meetings; they even set up an office adjacent to the House floor to write amendments during the floor debate last March. . . 267 political action committees (dubbed the Dirty Water PACs because of their anti-environmental agenda) contributed $57 million to political candidates between 1989 and 1994.[4]

The pattern of public concern and government inaction is repeated in other countries. For example, whilst Australians are amongst the world's most environmentally concerned people, their government's environmental record is one of the worst for OECD countries. A 1994 *Sydney Morning Herald* Saulwick poll found that fifty-seven per cent of people surveyed thought environmental protection should have a higher priority than economic growth,[5] while a NSW EPA survey, which also found high levels of environmental concern, discovered a "strong community perception that the politicians are out of touch with voters on environmental issues".[6]

The London-based New Economics Foundation, in comparing the environmental performance of twenty-one OECD countries, found that Australia, Canada and the US were at the bottom of the list, with Australia at number eighteen, Canada at twenty and the US last at twenty-one (the UK was at number ten). Australians rivalled Americans in terms of garbage production and carbon dioxide emissions per head. Australia also scored badly, as did the US, on energy efficiency, species extinctions and private vehicle use.[7] The influence of the industrial lobby in Australia is clearest on the greenhouse issue, where the government relies on coal and mining industry-funded studies in its decision-making. This led to the situation where the Australian government lobbied (unsuccessfully) to obstruct an international climate agreement in Berlin in 1995, even after the US supported it.[8] In 1997 Australia continued to lobby Japan and other countries to oppose European proposals for uniform international greenhouse gas reductions.

The media can give a distorted impression of public opinion on environmental and other issues. Michael Parenti, in his book *Inventing Reality: The Politics of the Mass Media*, argues:

> Public opinion is not just an expression of sentiment; it is a democratic power resource that sometimes constrains and directs policymakers who otherwise spend their time responding to the demands and enticements of moneyed interests. . . The media short-circuit the process by which public preference may otherwise be translated into government policy.[9]

The gap between what the majority wants and what government delivers would seem to indicate a failure of democracy. Yet, ironically, the corporate subversion of the green movement described in this book has been a response to the effective exercise of democratic power by citizen and environmental activists two decades earlier. Although robber barons of a much earlier era like William Vanderbilt could declare "The public be damned!",[10] modern corporate executives cannot afford to take this attitude.

Alex Carey, author of *Taking the Risk out of Democracy*, argued that the twentieth century has seen three related developments: "the growth of democracy, the growth of corporate power, and the growth of corporate propaganda as a means of protecting corporate power against democracy."[11] Similarly, Noam Chomsky argued in his book *Necessary Illusions*:

> In the democratic system, the necessary illusions cannot be imposed by force. Rather, they must be instilled in the public mind by more subtle means. A totalitarian state can be satisfied with lesser degrees of allegiance to required truths. It is sufficient that people obey; what they think is of secondary concern. But in a democratic political order, there is always the danger that independent thought might be translated into political action, so it is important to eliminate the threat at its root.[12]

Corporate Power

Corporate power has various dimensions. Traditionally, it has been institutionalized in government decision-making structures as a result of the importance of corporate investment to economic growth and the provision of employment. Individual companies can threaten to withdraw that investment if they do not get their way. It is therefore in the interests of government to negotiate and consult extensively with corporate representatives on all policy matters that may affect them. This gives corporations privileged access to government policy-making. In many countries, such as Britain and Australia, "policy-making occurs not so much in parliament or indeed even in cabinet, but in a more decentralized pattern of *policy communities* involving institutionalized interaction between key departments, relevant statutory authorities, advisory committees and a range of select, client interest groups."[13]

Clearly the bargaining power that any particular company can exercise will depend on its size, the number of people it employs, its ability to move offshore and the state of the economy in the country where the company is exercising that power.[14] The more that corporations can cooperate and present a coherent and united political agenda, the more power they will have. The degree of corporate influence can fluctuate over time, and in the late 1960s and 1970s corporate power was particularly weak. However since that time corporations have consciously built coalitions, set aside individual differences and become more politically active and consequently more powerful.

Another traditional form of influence has been through financial contributions to parties and candidates; it costs millions of dollars just to run for office in the USA, and most of that comes from corporations, including seventy per cent of contributions to the Democrat and the Republican parties.[15] In the UK, corporate donations seem to account for over half of all donations to the Conservative Party (£4.3 million out of £7.3 million in 1992/3). But donations don't have to be made public; almost two-thirds of donations received between 1987 and 1991 cannot be traced to their donors by outsiders to the Party. According to Paul Anderson and Nyta Mann in *The New Statesman & Society* in 1994:

> The Tories' finances are one of the great unsolved mysteries of British politics. . . What is known about the Tories is that they have received substantial sums from companies

and individuals with commercial interests in government spending and policy decisions. The big corporate donors of the past fifteen years include defence, engineering
and construction companies that have benefited from large government contracts,
tobacco companies that want to prevent legal constraints on advertising their products, and privatized utilities.[16]

In Australia, business directly sponsors political party campaigns rather than
individual candidates, and the major parties, Labor, Liberal and National, receive
the majority of their financial support in this way.[17]

However, politicians are concerned with getting re-elected, and this means
that public opinion matters. Citizens generally do not like the idea that government is run to suit those with economic power and resources. With the rise of
public interest groups in the 1960s and 70s, the closed policy-making arrangements between industry and government were 'forced open' and governments
had to listen to other voices. Environmental groups and others gathered their
own information, some of it from government files using Freedom of
Information Acts. This information could be effectively used in hearings and in
the media, and decision-makers learned to take account of a greater range of
interests and to justify their decisions on rational grounds.[18]

This need for 'rational' decisions meant bureaucrats "churned out an endless
stream of statistics, reports, hearings, bulletins, journals, rulings, proposals, statements, press reports, and other forms of information" on every issue.[19] Politicians
were now exposed to a far greater range of information from more sources and had
to appear to be making informed decisions. A new market was thus created for a
particular kind of information which enabled politicians to justify decisions that
were often still being influenced by financial donations and corporate pressure.[20]

In response, the major corporations opened up public affairs offices. Public
relations firms, lobbyists and think-tanks proliferated, shaping and moulding
information and manufacturing expertise on behalf of their clients and offering
it to the politicians. Although caught somewhat off-guard at first, in many ways
the move towards information-based decisions has suited business interests
because of their ability to hire experts—scientists, economists and statisticians—
and their fear of losing the 'emotional' battle.

Clearly not all interest groups have equal resources at their disposal, and in
their efforts to persuade government some groups have more bargaining power,
time, resources and energy.[21] As William Greider asks in his book *Who Will Tell
the People: The Betrayal of American Democracy*: "Who can afford to show up at
all these public hearings? Who will be able to deploy their own lawyers or scientists or economists to testify expertly on behalf of their agenda? Who is going to
hire the lobbyists to track the legislative debate at every laborious stage? Most citizens do not qualify."[22] Public-interest groups, such as environmental groups, find
it impossible to keep up with all the public hearings and submissions.

Corporations clearly have far greater financial resources at their disposal. As
pressure groups, they can invest millions of dollars into grassroots organising,
polls, lawyers, computer and satellite technology, video news releases, and professional advice to put their case directly to politicians and government officials and

to garner public support.

The greater power of corporations in a democratic system has long been recognized. In 1978 an effort to regulate the amount of money that corporations could spend on propaganda was defeated in the US Supreme Court. A dissenting judge observed:

> Corporations are artificial entities created by law for the purpose of furthering certain economic goals. It has long been recognized, however, that the special status of corporations has placed them in a position to control vast amounts of economic power which may, if not regulated, dominate not only the economy but also the very heart of our democracy, the electoral process.[23]

Since that time, corporations have indeed set out to use their economic power to dominate the machinery of democracy. Greider argues that a new industry has emerged in Washington that he calls "democracy for hire". He says this involves the packaging and sale of democratic expression, and "guarantees the exclusion of most Americans from the debate."[24] He points out that:

> Only those who have accumulated lots of money are free to play in this version of democracy. . . Modern methodologies of persuasion have created a new hierarchy of influence over government decisions—a new way in which organized money dominates the action while the unorganized voices of citizens are inhibited from speaking.[25]

The traditional pluralist account of competing interest groups gives a veneer of democratic respectability to what is in reality a corporate rout: "The steady diffusion of authority has simply multiplied the opportunities for power to work its will. . . pluralist deal-making continues in the guise of governing—but now the entrenched monied interests are back in charge of the marketplace, running the tables in the grand bazaar."[26] Governments, rather than weighing the demands of various interests, are less and less responsive to public opinion and more and more influenced by these corporations and monied interests.

A primary assumption of democracy is that there is no collusion of interests between government and the groups trying to lobby them, but in practice this is not the case. During the 1980s a close and at times unethical relationship developed in the US between lobbyists and the Reagan administration:

> Members of Congress worked in tandem with lobbyists to generate 'grassroots' support for pet issues. Lobbyists formed coalitions to support the White House's favorite issues. The White House recruited lobbyists to help with controversial appointees needing Senate confirmation. The Congressional committees or the White House Commissions that were supposed to be looking out for the people's interests, who were to oversee the agencies, who were to clean up the 'messes' when discovered, worked with and were often comprised of lobbyists and publicists. The very organizations designed to protect America from an abusive system had become part of the system.[27]

Yet despite their huge influence, or perhaps because of it, there is almost no government scrutiny or regulation of lobbying activities.[28] John Stauber, editor of

PR Watch, says: "The corporate flacks, hacks, lobbyists and influence peddlers, the practitioners of modern PR. . . have become a kind of occupation army in our democracy."[29]

The revolving door syndrome further weakens the separation between government and corporate interests. The creation of a senior executive service in the US and in countries like Australia has enabled business people and those whom they have funded in think-tanks to penetrate the top layers of government bureaucracy. Each new administration appoints the top levels of the agencies and departments such as State, Defense and Treasury. These appointments often come from the corporate sector, "corporate leaders who sever their numerous directorships to serve in government for two or three years, then return to the corporate community in a same or different capacity."[30] In Australia they retain their corporate shareholdings whilst in government unless there is an obvious conflict of interest with their ministerial duties. In any case, it is unlikely that they lose their corporate perspective during their period of office.

Similarly, senior bureaucrats and politicians are often employed by corporations, think-tanks, the media and lobbying firms when they lose office or retire from it. In Australia, key politicians from the previous Labor Government have moved into organizations such as the Plastics Industry trade association, and into consultancies which help developers gain government approval for environmentally damaging projects. To have this opportunity, these former government officials need to service corporate interests whilst in office. The same is true of top public servants. Similarly, in the US, as has been documented earlier in this book, there is a regular flow of personnel between government administrations and think-tanks, the media and public relations firms. Some think-tanks, such as the Heritage Foundation, actively select and train young people with this in mind. Robert Sherrill, in the fifth edition of his well-used university text *Why They Call it Politics: A Guide to America's Government*, points out:

> The revolving door between government and industry is oiled by money. Former high-level bureaucrats and politicians leave government to become well-paid lobbyists for big business—often the same big-business elements that they were allegedly regulating when they entered government. (Many were alumni of big business at the time they entered government; revolving doors, after all, do go in a circle.)[31]

The shareholdings of politicians provide another mechanism by which corporate interests are protected. In 1996 there was a major controversy in Australia over the shareholdings of the newly elected Liberal government[32] and their potential to create conflicts of interest. However this seems to be accepted practice in the UK where, in 1995, 389 out of 566 MPs had registered financial interests "in outside bodies, directly related to being an MP".[33] Liberal Democrat MP David Alton noted:

> Prime Ministers soon find solace in directorships and consultancies outside government. On the backbenches the same holds true. One hundred and thirty-five Conservative MPs hold 287 directorships and 146 consultancies between them, and the other parties are not immune. Twenty-nine Labour members share sixty

directorships and forty-three consultancies; while Liberal Democrats hold a total of fifteen."[34]

The UK adds another dimension to the relationship between business and government by enabling big corporate donors to have their directors knighted; they may subsequently be placed in the House of Lords, where they become part of the legislative system. According to Alton, a donation of more than £500,000 has a fifty per cent chance of earning a knighthood for a company director.[35]

Close relationships between politicians and industry executives can affect environmental legislation in other ways. Not only do politicians find their way onto corporate boards during and after their terms in government, but industry executives are also often placed on government committees, where they can help make and implement government policy. In 1995 Sir Ron Dearing, director of the corporation IMI, which donated £30,000 to the Tories in 1993, was appointed chairman of the National Curriculum Council; he was recently responsible for a report into higher education in the UK.[36]

In 1995 the UK committee which set pollution limits for the cement industry had a membership that included people from the British Cement Association, the British Association of Cement Manufacturers, British Pre-Cast Concrete Federation, ARC Southern, Castle Cement, Pioneer Aggregates and the British Ready Mixed Concrete Association.[37] Two years later a House of Commons Select Committee, set up following public concerns about the increased use by cement kilns of industrial waste as a fuel source, found that the control of cement kiln emissions by the Environment Agency had been, according to *New Scientist*, "lax and secretive".[38]

The close relationship between corporations and governments is especially important when it comes to the implementation of laws. Once a law is enacted, politicians feel satisfied that they have been seen to be doing something, and the media spotlight tends to be removed. Yet it is then that the real negotiations begin. In Washington, for example, tens of thousands of lawyers, lobbyists, trade associations, consultants and business people then engage in a struggle "over the content of federal regulations—the precise meaning that will flow from the laws that Congress has enacted."[39]

Covert Power

The structural power of corporations through their ownership and control of a large part of any modern nation's economy, and their power as a highly resourced and powerful pressure group with close ties to government, are supplemented by a third form of power which is far more covert: the power to set the political agenda and shape perceptions.[40] Corporations seek not only to influence legislation and regulation but also to define the agenda—what it is legitimate for government to consider and what can be discussed in the political arena—thereby rendering those groups who have other agendas ineffective. "Everybody is compelled to work within a system of values and institutional rules which restricts the formal political process to making the current system work, even though the

system only benefits the few."[41] Even the defeats suffered by individual corporations can be seen as "set within a wider political context—an outer framework—
which invariably serves the system needs of capitalism."[42]

Setting the agenda means deciding not only what will be discussed but also
what won't be. Covert power covers the area of 'non-decisions' as well as decisions.[43] For example, environmental issues can be debated so long as the system
of decision-making that gives autonomy to corporations to decide what they
produce and how they produce it is maintained. Decision-making and political
debate is therefore confined to the relatively safe areas of waste discharge, packaging, and product safety. So effective is the manufacture of the new corporate
consensus that many have accepted the assumption that unless corporations are
happy then the economy will suffer and the working and the poor will be worse
off. "For the homeless in the streets, then, the highest priority must be to ensure
that the dwellers in the mansions are reasonably content."[44]

Corporations use their economic power and resources to shape public
opinion through the think-tanks, public relations and propaganda. But this
shaping is designed to go unnoticed, "to alter perception, reshape reality and
manufacture consent"[45] without their targets being even aware that it is happening. Says one PR executive: "You never know when a PR agency is being effective; you'll just find your views slowly shifting."[46]

Corporations also use institutions such as the media to shape cultural understandings, meanings and values and "if not usurping the whole of ideological
space, still significantly limiting what is thought throughout the society."[47] True
democracy would require easy access for all points of view to be communicated
with mass audiences on topics of debate, but the media portrays a very restricted
range of views. 'Photo opportunities' and spectacles replace lively political debate.[48]

Education is another obvious arena in which to shape public perceptions and
cultural expectations. Through pervasive advertising on television and in schools,
and through specially designed educational materials distributed to schools, corporations have quite consciously set about ensuring that future generations are
big consumers, share corporate values and view environmental problems from a
corporate point of view. Advertising and the television programming it supports
also reinforce the idea that personal, social and environmental problems can be
solved through purchasing corporate products and services.

Democracy has become dominated by a vast information industry aimed at
attaining the consent of the public to the goals and values of those who can best
afford the experts.

> The ascendancy of the PR industry and the collapse of American participatory
> democracy are the same phenomenon. The growing concentration of economic
> power in fewer and fewer hands, combined with sophisticated marketing techniques
> and radical new electronic technologies, have come together in the past decade to
> fundamentally re-shape our social and political landscape. . .[49]

The aim is not to eliminate debate or prevent controversy, because controversy reinforces the perception of a healthy democracy. What is important is the

power to limit the subject, scope and boundaries of the controversy.[50]

This results in—and is reinforced by—minimal differences between major political parties. In the US, Britain and Australia there has been a merging of agendas and a decline in difference between parties.[51] The sameness of the parties, the emptiness of the campaign rituals and commercials, and the feeling that their votes don't count for much, has contributed to massive voter apathy in the US and Britain, where voting is voluntary.

At a time of rising citizen participation in environmental and public interest groups, less than half US citizens even bother to vote. At the regional and local level a candidate usually only needs twenty to thirty per cent of the votes of the eligible electorate to get elected. At the 1994 Congressional elections when the Republicans gained a majority, only a third of those eligible to vote did so. Even amongst those who vote, apathy is high. One survey found that only ten per cent of those who voted thought their vote made a difference and only seventeen per cent thought the election was important.[52]

In the UK, participation in general elections tends to be higher, generally between seventy and eighty per cent. However *Freedom's Children*, a 1995 study by Helen Wilkison and Geoff Mulgan of UK voters between eighteen and thirty-five years old, found that young people are increasingly alienated from party politics. They are less likely to register to vote than older people, "less likely to vote for or join a political party, and less likely to be politically active."

> The overwhelming story emerging from our research, both quantitative and qualitative, is of an historic political disconnection. In effect, an entire generation has opted out of party politics.[53]

Whilst they are concerned about particular issues, including the environment, they do not see that voting for a particular party will do much to address them.

The Media and Democracy

The media's bland diet of superficial material does not encourage participation in the political process, but rather depoliticizes the audience. Political Scientist Lance Bennett argues that the "parade of disjointed spectacles" that fill news programmes "relegate citizens to spectator roles, leaving a residue of powerlessness after the drama and entertainment of the moment have faded."[54] This is done by avoiding larger questions of power and institutional reform, by focusing on individual actors, appealing to the "concerns of individual viewers" and severing the connection between political information (as received from the media) and political organization and participation.[55] The media present politics "as a depressing spectacle rather than as a vital activity in which citizens can and should be engaged."[56]

Television, in particular, tends to depoliticize its viewers by filling their time with mindless passive entertainment which portrays the existing system of free enterprise and consumption as generally beneficial, and gives only limited air play to protest groups, usually the more moderate of these. The TV entertainment format tends to shorten viewers' attention spans, so that they have less patience for listening to ideas that take a while to explain.[57]

Joe Saltzman, an editor of *USA Today*, argues that the media practice of replacing complex information with symbols, images and catchwords, has trained the audience to want nothing else, and that this threatens democracy:

> Citizens become conditioned to respond to the facile stereotype, to the symbols they trust or fear, and they become incapable of understanding and acting on real debate and questioning. They even grow to resent such discussion, wanting instead a quick fix, a fast image, an easy-to-grasp phrase.[58]

"The overwhelming conclusion is that the media generally operate in ways that promote apathy, cynicism, and quiescence, rather than active citizenship and participation."[59] Writing about the British media in his book *Packaging Politics*, Bob Franklin notes that most citizens glean their political knowledge from the media, but at the same time the media packaging of politics has emphasized "image and appearance" and the reduction of political discourse to sound bites. Audiences have therefore grown "increasingly sceptical, uninterested and cynical about media presentations of politics". This has resulted in "an increasingly widespread lack of interest in politics".[60]

> In media democracy, politics (like football) has become an armchair activity. Watching the match from a ringside seat at home has replaced the need to play the game. Participation in a media democracy is essentially ersatz and vicarious.[61]

Similarly Jacobson and Mazur, from the Centre for the Study of Commercialism, argue that television undermines democracy:

> Democracy demands an informed citizenry; TV reduces information to oversimplified factoids. Democracy demands involvement; television keeps us glued to the couch. Democracy depends on the freedom of the press; television is controlled by a handful of private interests. Democracy thrives in strong communities; television keeps us isolated in our separate living rooms.[62]

At the same time that the media are turning the public away from politics, politicians are increasingly using the media, rather than the public, "as a source of issues and as a source of support". The media have become the most significant audience for politicians.[63] Noam Chomsky divides the media into 'mass popular' and 'élite'. The latter, for example the *New York Times* and the *Washington Post*, are aimed at decision-makers—the "more educated, wealthy, articulate part of the population".[64] Of the mass popular media, Chomsky says:

> For the large mass of the population, I suspect that the main impact of television comes not through the news but through mechanisms to divert their attention. That means network programming—everything from sports to sitcoms to fanciful pictures of the way life is 'supposed' to be. Anything that has the effect of isolating people— keeping them separated from one another and focused on the tube—will make people passive observers. . . The role of the public, then, is to be spectators, not participants; their role is just to watch and occasionally to ratify.[65]

Implications for Environmentalism

Nevertheless, the media plays a part in creating mass movements through its ability to present images of protest and alternative lifestyles to masses of people. No matter how negatively it portrays such groups and their leaders, it cannot prevent people from being attracted to the values and lifestyles of those being portrayed. In the 1960s, television "might have inadvertently advanced counter-cultural and radical values."[66]

The periodic emergence of counter-cultural movements and strong public activism is a sign that even the underlying realm of cultural understandings and meanings is fluid and changeable. This fluidity and changeability means that the opportunity to break free from corporate definitions of what is possible and feasible is always there. John Stauber and Sheldon Rampton, in their book *Toxic Sludge is Good For You!: Lies, Damn Lies and the Public Relations Industry*, put their faith for the future in the emergence of a new genuine democratic movement. They say that the existence of such a vast public relations industry "proves it *is* possible. The fact that corporations and governments feel compelled to spend billions of dollars every year manipulating the public is a perverse tribute to human nature and our own moral values."[67]

But to influence the covert realm of cultural constructions and ideology requires going beyond the superficial jockeying for influence that occurs in the realm of policy debate. Environmentalists, particularly those in the major environmental groups, tend to concentrate their efforts in the public realm of pressure group politics and ignore the ideological sphere where corporations set the agenda. It is in this ideological sphere that environmentalists need to devote their energies if they want to win.

Jim Hightower argues in *Earth Island Journal* that environmentalists are not doing much good as lobbyists in Washington, where the boundaries of the debate and its rules of etiquette are already clearly drawn:

> We've simply got to get the hogs out of the creek. As Aunt Eula knew, this is not a chore to undertake in your best trousers, politely pleading: 'Here hog, here hog. . . pretty please.' To get hogs out of the creek, you have to put your shoulders to them—and shove. . . Yet most national environmental organisations today are indeed dressed in their Sunday trousers, engaged in the soft-hands work of lawyers and lobbyists in Washington, sincerely but futilely attempting to negotiate the relative positions of hogs. . .[68]

A new wave of environmentalism is now called for: one that will engage in the task of exposing corporate myths and methods of manipulation. One that opens up new areas and ideas to public debate rather than following an old agenda set by corporations.

References

Chapter 1

1 Vogel 1989, p.65.
2 Parenti 1986, p.67.
3 Vogel 1989, pp.70, 98.
4 Vogel 1989, p.59.
5 Vogel 1989, p.112.
6 Grefe and Linsky 1995, p.2.
7 Quoted in Vogel 1989, p.194.
8 Vogel 1989, pp.10-11.
9 Grefe and Linski 1995, p.3.
10 Blyskal and Blyskal 1985, p.153.
11 Saloma 1984, p.67; Vogel 1989, pp.195-7.
12 Vogel 1989, p.197.
13 Vogel 1989, p.198.
14 Vogel 1989, p.200.
15 Himmelstein 1990, p.132; Ricci 1993, p.156; Sherrill 1990, p.374.
16 Bell and Warhurst 1992, pp.58-9; Wanna 1992, p.73.
17 Wanna 1992, p.74.
18 Vogel 1989, p.204.
19 Sale 1993, p.49.
20 Vogel 1989, p.217.
21 Parenti 1986, p.73; Sethi 1977, p.61.
22 Carey 1995, pp.87-88, 105, 112, 114.
23 Vogel 1989, p.221.
24 Himmelstein 1990, pp.146, 149-50.
25 Vogel 1989, p.223; Saloma 1984, p.74; Himmelstein 1990, p.140.
26 Carey 1995, pp.112-3.
27 Carey 1995, pp.113, 116-7.
28 Carey 1995, pp.88, 119, 125.
29 Alterman 1994, p.59.
30 Himmelstein 1990, pp.129, 146.
31 Parenti 1986, pp.91, 93.
32 Entman 1989, p.86.

33 Vogel 1989, p.193.
34 Carey 1995, p.89; Parenti 1986, p.74.
35 Sale 1993, pp.49-51; Ricci 1993, p.43.
36 Rowell 1996, p.22; Winward 1991, p.107; Doern and Conway 1994, p.118; Peter Perkins 1990, p.34.
37 McIntosh 1990.
38 O'Keefe and Daley 1993.
39 Harrison 1993, p.6.
40 Quoted in Rowell 1996, p.71.
41 O'Callaghan 1992, p.86.
42 Quoted in Greider 1992, p.24.
43 Silas 1990, p.34.
44 Quoted in Nelson 1993, p.27.
45 Bovet 1994b.
46 Grefe and Linsky 1995, p.244.
47 Levathes 1995, p.18.
48 Levathes 1995, p.19; Megalli and Friedman 1991, p.184.
49 Gardner 1991.
50 Rowell 1996, p.22.
51 Rowell 1996, p.320
52 Raghavan 1995, p.31.
53 Anon. 1993, p.18.

Chapter 2

1 Rose 1991.
2 Megalli and Friedman 1991, p.4; Stapleton 1992, p.35.
3 Megalli and Friedman 1991, pp.184-5.
4 Poole 1992, p.61.
5 Megalli and Friedman 1991, p.3.
6 Bleifuss 1995c, p.11; Anon. 1994i, p.319; Anon. 1987b; Anon. 1987a.
7 Bleifuss 1995c, p.11.

8 Megalli and Friedman 1991, p.3.
9 Anon. 1994a; Hileman 1993; Anon. 1993a; Deal 1993, p.56.
10 Megalli and Friedman 1991, p.6.
11 Megalli and Friedman 1991, pp.3-4; Pope 1995, p.14; Anon 1994i, p.317.
12 Megalli and Friedman 1991, p.6; Deal 1993, p.62; Bleifuss 1995a, pp.6-7; Rosenberger 1996.
13 Deal 1993, pp.62-3; Parenti 1986, p.73l; Rosenberger 1996.
14 Poole 1992, p.61; Burke 1994, p.7; Kuipers 1994, p.18.
15 Megalli and Friedman 1991, pp.3, 148; Ruben 1992, p.29.
16 Megalli and Friedman 1991, pp.80-81.
17 Anon. 1996i.
18 Anon 1994i, p.317.
19 Megalli and Friedman 1991, pp.70-73; Ruben 1992, p.29; Rowell 1996, p.84.
20 Rowell 1996, p.240.
21 Burton 1994, pp.17-18; Rowell 1996, pp.238-240.
22 Burton 1996.
23 Faucheux 1995, pp.20-1, 26-30.
24 Carney 1992, p.281.
25 Quoted in Stauber and Rampton 1995/96, p.23.
26 Anon 1994i, p.318.
27 Cooper 1993-4.
28 Anon 1994i, p.317.
29 Stauber and Rampton 1995c, p.84.
30 Greider 1993, p.8; Faucheux 1995, p.24.
31 Greider 1992, p.37.
32 Grefe and Linsky 1995, pp.214-5.

Chapter 2 continued

33 Greider 1992, p.39.
34 Quoted in Stauber and Rampton 1995/96, p.18.
35 Stauber and Rampton 1995/96, p.23-24.
36 Sherrill 1990, p.376.
37 Auerbach 1985, p.19; Bleifuss 1995a, pp.2, 6; Nelson 1993 , p.9.
38 Stauber and Rampton 1995b; Stone 1996.
39 Dillon 1993, p.38.
40 CLEAR 1996, p.18.
41 Lord 1995; Keim 1996.
42 Cooper 1993/94.
43 Cooper 1993/94.
44 Quoted in Stauber and Rampton 1995c, p.91.
45 deButts 1995.
46 Rampton and Stauber 1995b, p.8; Stauber and Rampton 1995c, p.85; Faucheux 1995, p.21.
47 Rampton and Stauber 1995a, pp.1-2.
48 Keim 1996.
49 Faucheux 1995, p.53.
50 Faucheux 1995.
51 Grefe and Linsky 1995, p.148.
52 Faucheux 1995.
53 Lord 1995.
54 Anon 1994i, p.318.
55 Irvine 1993.
56 Irvine 1993.
57 Grefe and Linsky 1995, pp.239-9.
58 Stauber and Rampton 1995/96, p.24.
59 Price 1992, p.546.
60 Faucheux 1995, pp.22, 25.
61 Grefe and Linsky 1995, p.138.
62 Lindheim 1989, p.494.
63 Grefe and Linsky 1995, pp.87-89.
64 Grefe and Linsky 1995, pp.87-89, 134, 92.
65 Grefe and Linsky 1995, pp.134, 143, 147.
66 Grefe and Linsky 1995, p.143.
67 Stauber and Rampton 1995c, p.88.
68 Keim 1996.

69 Keim 1996.
70 Grefe and Linsky 1995, pp.143-4.
71 Quoted in Grefe and Linsky 1995, p.92.
72 Patterson 1996, p.24.
73 Grefe and Linsky 1995, pp.145, 249.
74 Holzinger 1994.
75 Faucheux 1995, pp.21, 24.
76 Johnson 1993, p.14.
77 Seitel 1995, p.383.
78 Harrison 1993, p.186.
79 Grefe and Linsky 1995, p.94.
80 Lesly 1992.
81 Crowley 1992.
82 Crowley 1992.
83 Bleifuss 1995a, pp.5-6; Arnstein 1994, p.29.
84 Baker 1995.
85 Baker 1995.
86 Beder 1989.
87 Vandervoot 1991, p.15.
88 Quoted in Tokar 1995, p.151.
89 Quoted in Brick 1995, p.36.
90 Ron Arnold quoted in Stapleton 1992, p.35.
91 O'Callaghan 1992, p.84; Burton 1994, p.17.
92 Arnold 1992.
93 Stapleton 1992, pp.32-3; Burke 1994, p.5.
94 Arnold 1992; Burke 1994, p.5.
95 Tokar 1995, p.150; Stapleton 1992, p.34; Goldberg 1994.

Chapter 3

1 Baum 1991; Gottlieb 1989, p.158.
2 O'Callaghan 1992, p.84; Helvarg 1994a, p.649; O'Keefe and Daley 1993; Rowell 1996, p.29.
3 O'Callaghan 1992, pp.84-6; Gottlieb 1989, pp.86-7; Poole 1992, p.88; Helvarg 1994c, p.126.
4 Burke 1994, p.5; Gottlieb 1989, pp.5-6.
5 Gottlieb 1989, pp.6, 12.
6 Roush 1995, p.2.

7 Tokar 1995, p.156.
8 Helvarg 1995, pp.18, 20.
9 Maughan and Nilson 1994.
10 Collins 1995.
11 Arnold and Gottlieb 1993, p.10; Gottlieb 1989, p.xviii.
12 Gottlieb 1989, p.xix.
13 Quoted in Harding 1993, p.3 and in Tokar 1995, p.151.
14 Helvarg 1994a, p.12.
15 Charles Cushman, Multiple-Use Land Alliance, quoted in Satchell 1991, p.75; Arnold and Gottlieb 1993, p.7.
16 Arnold 1992.
17 Rauber 1995, pp.31, 33.
18 Arnold 1992.
19 Roush 1995, p.3; Helvarg 1994a, pp.122-3; Brick 1995, p.19; Arnold and Gottlieb 1989, p.vii; Kriz 1995, p.30.
20 Arnold 1992.
21 Poole 1992, p.61.
22 Gottlieb 1989, p.xx.
23 Arnold and Gottlieb 1993, p.vii.
24 Arnold and Gottlieb 1993, pp.7, 38.
25 Perry Pendley, Mountain States Legal Foundation, quoted in Satchell 1991, p.76.
26 Satchell 1991, p.75.
27 Arnold and Gottlieb 1993, pp.10, 33.
28 Ridgeway and St.Clair 1995, p.16; Brick 1995, p.36.
29 Lois Gibbs, quoted in O'Callaghan 1992, p.84.
30 Quoted in Helvarg 1994a, p.137.
31 Satchell 1991, p.76; O'Callaghan 1992, p.83; Goldberg 1994; Roush 1995, p.3.
32 Rowell 1996, p.21.
33 Quoted in Lapp 1993, p.24.
34 Quoted in Helvarg 1994a, p.140 and also Lapp 1993, p.24.
35 Maughan and Nilson 1994
36 O'Callaghan 1992, p.86;

Chapter 3 continued

Arnold 1992; CDFE 1996.
37 CDFE 1996.
38 CDFE 1996.
39 Arnold 1992.
40 Stapleton 1992, p.35
41 Brick 1995, p.19.
42 Quoted in Helvarg 1994b
43 Quoted in Helvarg 1994b
44 Knox 1993.
45 Watkins 1995, p.51.
46 Satchell 1991, p.75;
   Ridgeway and St. Clair
   1995, p.15; Helvarg 1994a,
   p.9.
47 Cordtz 1994.
48 Stapleton 1992, p.35.
49 Burke 1994, p.6.
50 Stapleton 1992; Ridgeway
   and St. Clair 1995, p.15;
   O'Callaghan 1992, p.86.
51 O'Callaghan 1992, p.86;
   Burke 1994, p.4; Grumbine
   1994, p.241.
52 Bielski 1995, pp.33-35;
   Ridgeway and St. Clair
   1995, pp.15-16.
53 Stapleton 1992, p.37;
   Burke 1994, p.5;
   O'Callaghan 1992, p.87;
   Greenpeace 1994; Baum
   1991, p.92.
54 Burke 1994, p.6;
   O'Callaghan 1992, p.88.
55 Kriz 1995, p.29; People
   for the West!, Home Page,
   World Wide Web, 1996.
56 Baca 1995; Baca 1995,
   p.53; Stapleton 1992,
   pp.36-37; Carl Deal 1993,
   p.78; Megalli and Friedman
   1991, p.15; O'Callaghan
   1992, p.85; Watkins 1995,
   p.51; Satchell 1991, p.76.
57 Stapleton 1992, p.36;
   Poole 1992, p.88; Deal
   1993 p.77; Megalli and
   Friedman 1991, p.159;
   Helvarg 1994b.
58 O'Callaghan 1992, p.88;
   Megalli and Friedman
   1991, p.159; Satchell 1991,
   p.76; Kriz 1995, p.29; Baca
   1995, p.54; Deal 1993
   p.77.
59 Stapleton 1992, p.36;
   Baca 1995, p.54; Helvarg

1994b
60 Baca 1995, p.54.
61 Deal 1993 p.78.
62 Stapleton 1993, p.34.
63 Stapleton 1993, pp.32-4.
64 Satchell 1991, p.74.
65 Helvarg 1994a, p.11;
   Poole 1992, p.92;
   Carothers 1994.
66 Arnold and Gottlieb 1993,
   pp.19, 23; CDFE 1996.
67 Ness 1995, p.21.
68 Helvarg 1994a, p.11.
69 Arnold and Gottlieb 1993,
   p.20.
70 Echeverria 1995, p.145.
71 Burke 1994, pp.7-8.
72 Toor 1993; Lavelle 1995,
   p.36.
73 Mazza and Beneville 1994.
74 Toor 1993.
75 Quoted in Echeverria
   1995, pp.147-8.
76 Lavelle 1995, p.39; Mazza
   and Beneville 1994; Toor
   1993.
77 Carothers 1994.
78 Lavelle 1995, p.40; Ness
   1995, p.21.
79 Satchell 1991, p.75; Poole
   1992, p.88; Grumbine
   1994, p.241.

Chapter 4

1 Lippin 1991, p.15.
2 Pring and Canan 1993,
   p.380.
3 Hoare 1993, p.10;
   Goldberg 1992/3, pp.1-3.
4 Jamieson and Plibersek
   1991
5 Kriz 1995, p.33; Gottlieb
   1989, p.15.
6 Pring, Canan, and Thomas-
   McGuirk 1994, p.3.
7 Schemo 1992.
8 Bishop 1991.
9 Pring & Canon 1993,
   pp.381-5.
10 Goldberg 1992/3, p.2;
   Nye 1994, p.15.
11 Costantini and Nash
   1991, p.420.
12 Davis and White 1994.
13 Quoted in Pring & Canon
   1993, p.382.

14 Quoted in Pring & Canon
   1993, p.381.
15 Dold 1992, p.36.
16 Schemo 1992.
17 Lippin 1991, p.15.
18 Dold 1992, p.36.
19 Quoted in Pring & Canon
   1993, p.382.
20 Pring & Canon 1993,
   p.387.
21 Goldberg 1992/3, p.2.
22 Canan and Pring 1988,
   p.515; Pring & Canon
   1993, p.381.
23 Tollefson 1994, p.207.
24 Dold 1992, p.36.
25 Nye 1994, p.15.
26 Anon. 1995j, p.15.
27 Dold 1992, p.36.
28 Wilson 1993.
29 Wilson 1993.
30 Anon. 1996j.
31 Anon. 1994e; Background
   Briefing, Radio 2RN,
   Australian Broadcasting
   Corporation, 30/4/95.
32 Anon. 1994e; Background
   Briefing, Radio 2RN,
   Australian Broadcasting
   Corporation, 30/4/95.
33 Starmer 1997.
34 Starmer 1997.
35 Lyall 1996; Midgley 1996;
   Zoll 1997.
36 Tollefson 1994, pp.201,
   205.
37 Mirabelle 1993.
38 Fairlie 1993, p.165.
39 Rowell 1996, pp.344,
   347-8.
40 Anon. 1993j.
41 Anon. 1993k.
42 CJ Gleeson, Judgement,
   Council of the Shire of
   Ballina v Ringland, The
   Supreme Court of NSW
   Court of Appeal, 25 May
   1994, p.19.
43 Supreme Court, Ensile Pty
   Ltd and Lady Carrington
   Estates Pty Ltd vs James
   Edward Donohoe, Jennifer
   Donohoe and Timothy
   Tapsell, Amended
   Statement of Claim, filed
   10th May 1994.
44 Keim 1994, p.45.
45 Marr 1996.

Chapter 4 continued

46 Lewis & Cornwall 1993; Prest 1994, p.22..
47 Personal communication, Alistair Harris, former Trade Union Liaison Officer, Greenpeace Australia, April 1995.
48 Jamieson & Plibersek 1991, p.4; Personal communication, Lara Crew, former Greenpeace campaigner, April 1995.
49 Jamieson & Plibersek 1991, p.4; Personal communication, Lara Crew, former Greenpeace campaigner, April 1995.
50 Jamieson & Plibersek 1994, p.4.
51 Alistair Harris, Trade Union Liaison Officer, Wilderness Society, evidence to the Senate Committee on Employment, Education and Training, 20 August, 1993.
52 Nelson 1996, p.21.
53 Bishop 1991.
54 Schemo 1992; Pring, Canon & McGuirk 1993, p.7.
55 Anon. 1995k.
56 Goldberg 1992/3, p.2.
57 Keim 1994, p.44.
58 Costantini & Nash 1991, p.425.
59 See for example Martin et. al. 1986; Beder 1993, pp.36-41.

Chapter 5

1 O'Sullivan 1993), p.4.
2 Gregg Easterbrook quoted in Desai 1994, p.32.
3 Blackburn 1995, p.18.
4 Gellner 1995, p.505; Ricci 1993, p.162.
5 Regan and Dunham 1995, pp.48-9.
6 Smith 1991, p.20.
7 Carey 1995, p.90.
8 Katz 1992, p.53.
9 Ricci 1993, p.157.

10 Ricci 1993, p.169; Blackburn 1995, p.18; Hood 1995.
11 James 1993, p.494; Smith 1991, pp.xv-xvi.
12 Ricci 1993, p.180; Smith 1991, p.206.
13 Abelson 1995, p.100.
14 Gellner 1995, p.502; Ricci 1993, p.171; Georges 1995; Smith 1991, p.201.
15 Quoted in Hood 1995.
16 Smith 1991, p.287; Ruben 1995; Weaver 1989, p.572.
17 Bencivenga cited in Weaver 1989, pp.161-2; Georges 1995; Abelson 1995, p.106; Katz 1992, p.53.
18 Anon. 1992a; Shanahan 1993.
19 Smith 1991, p.286; Ricci 1993, pp.2, 161; Swomley 1996; Saloma 1984, p.29.
20 Gellner 1995, p.503; Georges 1995; Blackburn 1995, p.18; Deal 1993, p.59; Smith 1991, p.286; Swomley 1996, p.49.
21 Smith 1991, p.201.
22 Kinsley 1993, p.6.
23 Hood 1995; Weaver 1989, p.572.
24 Smith 1991, p.221.
25 Anon. 1992a.
26 Weaver 1989, p.573; Deal 1993, p.40.
27 Crane 1995; Hood 1995; Karey 1995; Connolly 1995; Fan 1995.
28 Smith 1991, p.229; O'Sullivan 1995, p.4; Feulner 1995; James 1991, p.492.
29 Desai 1994, p.29.
30 Desai 1994, p.29; Anon. 1989a, p.53.
31 Robinson 1996.
32 Cockett 1994, p.140; Desai 1994, p.29.
33 Desai 1994, p.29; Cockett 1994, pp.183-4, 188-9.
34 James 1991, p.495; Cockett 1994, pp.132, 182-3, 237; Desai 1994, p.30.
35 Desai 1994, p.31.
36 Desai 1994, p.31.

37 Butler 1995.
38 James 1991, p.497; Desai 1994, p.28.
39 Quoted in Cockett 1994, p.173.
40 Carey 1995, p.227; Lindsay 1995.
41 Lindsay 1995.
42 Carey 1995, p.123; CIS 1995.
43 IPA Report, Institute of Public Affairs Ltd, 1991, p.1.
44 Burton 1995, p.27; Pusey 1991, p.227; IPA Report, Institute of Public Affairs Ltd, 1991, pp.1-3.
45 CIS 1995.
46 Rowell 1996, p.243; Carey 1995, pp.100-101, 122.
47 Carey 1995, pp.101-2.
48 Pusey 1991, p.27.
49 Swomley 1996, p.92; Saloma 1984, p.24.
50 Greider 1992, p.52.
51 Gellner 1995, p.505.
52 Weaver 1989, p.570.
53 Ricci 1993, pp.41-49.
54 Gellner 1995, p.499; Anon. 1991; Smith 1991, p.xv; Abelson 1995, p.108; Weaver 1989, pp.570-1.
55 Abelson 1995, pp.108-9; Smith 1991, pp.206-7; Weaver 1989, pp.569, 571.
56 Anon. 1991.
57 Smith 1991, p.207; Gellner 1995, p.500; Stoesz 1987.
58 Smith 1991, p.206.
59 Anon. 1989a, p.53.
60 Pusey 1991, p.297.
61 Pusey 1991, p.8.
62 Pusey 1991, pp.4, 133.
63 M.C and L.C.S. 1990, p.26; Smith 1991, p.200; Deal 1993, p.58.
64 Niskanen 1995; Anon., The Good Think-Tank Guide.
65 Cited in Ricci 1993, p.2.
66 Anon. 1992a.
67 James 1991, p.492.
68 James 1991, pp.322, 497, 501; Desai 1994, pp.32, 34; Anon. 1989a, p.53.
69 Georges 1995; Anon. 1994d; Cato Institiute,

Chapter 5 continued

1995.
70 Georges 1995; Anon.
 1994d; Feulner 1995.
71 Anon. 1994d; Ruben
 1995.
72 Anon. 1994d; Georges
 1995.
73 Ruben 1995.
74 Warder 1994, p.436.
75 Carey 1995, p.92.
76 Anon. 1989a, p.54.
77 Cockett 1994, p.323;
 Trend 1988, p.10; Desai
 1994, p.36; Anon. 1994,
 p.85.
78 Cockett 1994, p.322.
79 Desai 1994, p.60.
80 Malcom 1991, p.6.
81 Warder 1994, p.435;
 Kinsley 1993, p.57; James
 1991, p.492; M.C and
 L.C.S. 1990, p.27.
82 Pusey 1991, p.228.
83 Davidson 1992, p.58.
84 Smith 1991, p.222.

Chapter 6

1 Kriz 1995, p.28; Jacobson
 1995, pp.1769-70; CEI
 1996c; Rowell 1996, p.93.
2 CEI 1996c; Jacobson 1995,
 pp.1770-1; CEI 1996b.
3 Lesly 1992, p.331.
4 CEI 1996a.
5 Shanahan 1992.
6 Shanahan 1992; CEI
 1996a.
7 Bailey 1995, front cover
 and p.472; Balling 1995,
 p.84.
8 CEI 1996a.
9 Shanahan 1992.
10 Rowell 1996, p.328.
11 Tucker 1995, p.35.
12 Rowell 1996, p.141.
13 Lieberman 1996.
14 Bailey 1993, p.120.
15 Bailey 1993, p.121.
16 Ridley 1996.
17 Miller 1996, p.320.
18 Deal 1993, pp.89-90;
 Helvarg 1994a, p.21.
19 Deal 1993, p.89; Helvarg
 1994a, p.21.

20 Rowell 1996, p.143.
21 Montague 1995
22 Miller 1996, pp.319-20;
 Taubes 1993, pp.1581-2.
23 Roberts 1994, p.22;
 Roberts 1995, p.26.
24 Quoted in Taubes, 1993.
25 Lee and Solomon 1990,
 pp.66-7.
26 Roberts 1994.
27 Kiernan 1995, p.8.
28 Kiernan 1995, p.8.
29 Hecht 1996, p.49.
30 Bailey 1995, pp.4-6; Sedjo
 1995, p.178; Moore 1995,
 p.110.
31 Cato Institute 1995.
32 Ettore 1992.
33 Ettore 1992; CEI 1996d.
34 Anon. 1991f, pp.5, 8.
35 Quoted in Deal 1993,
 p.58; Cato Institute 1995.
36 Hyde 1991, p.3.
37 Brunton 1991, p.1.
38 Brunton 1991, p.1.
39 Shanahan and Wilson
 1995.
40 Cox 1995.
41 Kazman 1995.
42 CEI 1995a; CEI 1996e.
43 Shanahan 1992.
44 Cato Institute 1995.
45 Anderson and Leal 1991,
 p.171.
46 Savage and Hart 1993,
 p.3.
47 Hood 1995a.
48 Commonwealth
 Government of Australia
 1990, p.14.
49 Savage and Hart 1993,
 p.3.
50 Schelling 1993, p.19.
51 Kellman 1983, p.297.
52 CEI 1995b.
53 Ruben 1995; Rosner
 1992; Eckersley 1995,
 pp.xi-xii.
54 Moran, Chisholm, and
 Porter 1991, back cover.
55 CIS 1995.
56 Kellman 1983, p.302.
57 Quoted in Rosner 1992
58 Stavins and Whitehead
 1992, p.29.
59 Schmidheiny and BCSD
 1992, chapter 2.
60 Beder 1996a.

61 Jacobs 1993, p.7.
62 Stavins and Whitehead
 1992, p.8.
63 Bernstam 1996.
64 Quoted in Helvarg 1994a,
 p.19.
65 Shanahan 1993.
66 Hood 1995a.
67 Beder 1996a; Goodin
 1992.
68 Anderson and Leal 1991,
 p.23.
69 Adler 1996.
70 CEI 1996f.
71 Sas-Rolfes 1996.
72 White 1992, p.150.

Chapter 7

1 Carlisle 1993, p.22.
2 Carey 1995, p.81; Blyskal
 and Blyskal 1985, p.68.
3 Chomsky 1989, p.16;
 Carey 1995, p.22.
4 Carey 1995, pp.21, 28.
5 Quoted in Carey 1995,
 p.82.
6 Carlisle 1993, p.22; Seitel
 1995, pp.2, 40; Montague
 1993; Sherrill 1990, p.389;
 Brody 1992, p.351.
7 Josephs and Josephs 1994;
 Aylmer 1996.
8 Bleifuss 1995a, pp.4-5.
9 Bleifuss 1995a, pp.4,9;
 Stauber and Rampton
 1995a, p.173; Ridgeway
 1995, p.15.
10 Anon. 1993b.
11 Harrison 1991, p.32.
12 Morris Wolfe quoted in
 Nelson 1989, p.17.
13 Blyskal and Blyskal, PR,
 pp.76, 143.
14 Smith 1995.
15 Hallahan 1994.
16 Hill and Knowlton, home
 page, World Wide Web,
 1996; Pratt 1994, p.280.
17 Nelson 1993a, p.27;
 Stauber and Rampton
 1995c, p.207.
18 Carlisle 1993, p.20; Hill
 and Knowlton, home page.
19 Nelson 1993a, pp.26-7;
 Dillon 1993, p.34; Rauber
 1994, p.49; Carothers

Chapter 7 continued

1993, p.14.
20 Tokar 1995, p.151;
   Goldberg 1993; Landler
   and Melcher 1991;
   Roschwalb 1994, p.270.
21 Carlisle 1993, p.22;
   Landler and Melcher 1994,
   p.270; Trento 1992, pp.vii-
   viii, 62.
22 Nelson 1993a, pp.26-7;
   Dillon 1993, p.34; Rauber
   1994, p.49; Carothers
   1993, p.14.
23 Hill and Knowlton, home
   page.
24 Patton 1995.
25 Carothers 1993, p.14;
   Nelson 1993a, p.28.
26 Nelson 1993a, p.29.
27 Beder 1996b, pp.xxii-xxiv;
   Carothers 1993.
28 Nelson 1993a, p.30.
29 Nelson 1993a, pp.30-2.
30 Quoted in Nelson 1993a,
   p.31.
31 Nelson 1993b, p.8.
32 Walters and Walters 1992,
   pp.31-32; Nelson 1989,
   p.43.
33 Nelson 1989, pp.44, 50,
   53.
34 Walters and Walters 1992,
   p.33.
35 Lee and Solomon 1990,
   p.66.
36 Walters and Walters 1992,
   pp.33, 43; Carlisle 1993,
   p.22; Lee and Solomon
   1990, p.66; Blyskal and
   Blyskal 1985, p.28.
37 Blyskal and Blyskal 1985,
   pp.28, 68; Nelson 1989,
   p.18.
38 Weaver and Elliot quoted
   in Walters and Walters
   1992, p.32.
39 Adams 1992.
40 Nelson 1989, pp.43-4, 46.
41 Walters and Walters 1992,
   p.34.
42 Blyskal and Blyskal 1985,
   p.69.
43 Blyskal and Blyskal 1985,
   pp.88-9.
44 Blyskal and Blyskal 1985,
   pp.170-1.

45 Blyskal and Blyskal 1985,
   pp.171-2.
46 Blyskal and Blyskal 1985,
   p.172.
47 Blyskal and Blyskal 1985,
   pp.172-173.
48 Munday, Rowse, and
   Arana 1992.
49 Munday, Rowse, and
   Arana 1992.
50 Shell 1992; Greenberg
   1994.
51 Auerbach 1985, p.19;
   Blyskal and Blyskal 1985,
   p.87.
52 Shell 1992; Blyskal and
   Blyskal 1985, p.87; Warren
   1995; Jacobson and Mazur
   1995, p.57; Peters et al.
   1993, p.16; Marlow 1994.
53 Shell 1992; Greenberg
   1994.
54 Lee and Solomon 1990,
   p.65.
55 Stauber and Rampton
   1995/96 , p.25; Jacobson
   and Mazur 1995, p.57;
   Shell 1992.
56 Shell 1991; Greenberg
   1994.
57 Warren 1995.
58 Warren 1995.
59 Williams 1995, pp.16-17.
60 Williams 1995, p.17.
61 Williams 1995, p.16.
62 Shell 1992.
63 Carey 1995, pp.88-90.
64 Stauber 1994b.
65 Mellow 1989, p.38;
   Trento 1992, p.63.
66 Trento 1992; Mellow
   1989, p.37; Munday et. al.,
   1992.
67 Montague 1993, p.16; Sir
   Bernard Ingham, Lobby
   Fodder, Hill and Knowlton,
   home page; Mellow 1989,
   p.36.
68 Carlisle 1993, p.19;
69 Carlisle 1993, p.19;
   Stauber 1994b.
70 Glover 1993, p.40.
71 Auerbach 1985, p.19;
   Nelson 1993b, p.9.
72 Blyskal and Blyskal 1985,
   p.153.
73 Blyskal and Blyskal 1985,
   p.79.

74 Stauber and Rampton
   1995c, pp.80-81.
75 Munday et. al. 1992.
76 Munday et. al. 1992.
77 Lewis and Ebrahim 1993.
78 Gergen 1996, p.84.
79 Nixon 1996.
80 Carey 1995, p.12.
81 Tymson and Sherman
   1990, p.5.
82 Tymson and Sherman
   1990, p.13.
83 Carey 1995, p.20; Seitel
   1995, pp.4, 12.
84 Quoted in Delwiche
   1995b.
85 Lee and Lee 1995;
   Fleming 1995; Delwiche
   1995
86 Gismondi et al. 1996
87 Gismondi et al. 1996
88 Anon. 1996a
89 Delwiche 1995a

Chapter 8

1 Lindheim 1989, p.492.
2 Lindheim 1989, p.492.
3 Lindheim 1989, p.493.
4 Lindheim 1989, p.492.
5 Lindheim 1989, p.493.
6 Brody 1992, p.352.
7 Katz 1993.
8 Beder and Shortland 1992,
   pp.139-40.
9 Epley 1992, p.111.
10 Price 1994, p.33.
11 Hunter 1991; Beder
   1996b, pp.235-8.
12 Mellow 1989, p.39.
13 Dowie 1994, p.32.
14 Dowie 1994, p.33.
15 Quoted in Tymson and
   Sherman 1990, p.223.
16 Quoted in Roschwalb
   1994, p.270.
17 Makower 1996.
18 Arnstein 1994, p.29.
19 Arnstein 1994, p.29.
20 Quoted in Beers and
   Capellaro 1991.
21 Jenkins 1990, p.19.
22 Dadd and Carothers 1990,
   p.10.
23 Anon. 1994b; Lanouette
   1991; Nelson 1989, p.138.
24 Shell 1990, p.9.

Chapter 8 continued

25 Shell 1990, p.16.
26 Whitehead 1995.
27 Nelson 1989, p.131.
28 Kwittken 1994, p.27.
29 Anon. 1992c, p.3.
30 Editor's note in Ludford 1991.
31 Ludford 1991.
32 Asher 1991.
33 Asher 1991.
34 Rauber 1994.
35 Bleifuss 1995a, p.3.
36 Jenkins 1990, p.19.
37 Rauber 1994, p.48.
38 Bleifuss 1995a, p.3.
39 Greenberg 1993a; Greenberg 1993b
40 Flynn 1993.
41 Harris 1992, p.24.
42 Harrison 1993, p.190.
43 Quoted in Bleifuss 1995a, p.4.
44 Rauber 1994, p.48; Anon. 1993c.
45 Lesly 1992, p.329.
46 Lesly 1992, p.330.
47 Stauber and Rampton 1995/96, p.20.
48 Macken 1996.
49 Stauber and Rampton 1995/96, p.21; Kaplan 1994, p.4.
50 Kaplan 1994, p.5.
51 Quoted in Kaplan 1994, p.5.
52 Stauber and Rampton 1995/96, p.21.
53 Bleifuss 1995a, p.3.
54 Bleifuss 1995a, pp.2, 4.
55 Lesly 1992, p.328.
56 Lesly 1992, p.329.
57 Quoted in Montague 1993.
58 Montague 1993.
59 Quoted in Montague 1993.
60 Montague 1993.
61 Rauber 1994, p.49; Cox 1994, p.34.
62 Cass 1993.
63 Cass 1993.
64 Helvarg 1994a, p.4.
65 Lesly 1992, p.332.
66 Montague 1993; Stauber 1993a, p.2; MBD internal document quoted in

Stauber 1993a, p.4.
67 MBD internal document quoted in Stauber 1993a, p.5.
68 Montague 1993; Dillon 1993, pp.34-36; Stauber and Rampton 1995/96, pp.18-19.
69 Stauber 1993a, p.2; Stauber 1993b.
70 Stauber 1993b, p.7.
71 Stauber 1994a, pp.2-3.
72 Bleifuss 1995b, p.8.
73 Ridgeway 1995, p.16.
74 Hutchings 1990.
75 Bleifuss 1995b, p.9; Ridgeway 1995, p.16.
76 Blyskal and Blyskal 1985, pp.90-91.
77 Blyskal and Blyskal 1985, p.92.
78 Carlisle 1993, pp.20-21; Roschwalb 1994), p.268; Trento 1992, p.viii; Munday, Rowse, and Arana 1992.
79 Connor 1994.
80 Connor 1994.
81 Beder 1990.
82 Joint Taskforce on Intractable Waste 1989, pp.2/13.
83 Nelkin and Pollak 1977, p.334.
84 Joint Taskforce on Intractable Waste 1989, pp.2/19.
85 Waste 1989, pp.2/17-19.
86 Joint Taskforce on Intractable Waste 1989, p.2/13.
87 Joint Taskforce on Intractable Waste 1989, pp.2/20.
88 Joint Taskforce on Intractable Waste 1989, pp.2/15.
89 Beder and Shortland 1992.

Chapter 9

1 Roberts 1991a, p.624; Hay 1989.
2 Johnson 1995, p.25 A.
3 Gibbs and Waste 1995, p.1.
4 Casten 1992, p.13.

5 Weinberg 1995, part 5.
6 Weinberg 1995.
7 Weinberg 1995.
8 Nelson-Horchler 1990.
9 Megalli and Friedman 1991; Weinberg 1995, part 5.
10 Houk 1992, p.13.
11 Fumento 1993, pp.100-101.
12 Gibbs and Waste 1995, pp.8-9.
13 Montague 1996a; Roberts 1991a, p.626.
14 Quoted in Lapp 1991, p.121; Montague 1996a.
15 Coppolino 1994, p.24; Montague 1996b.
16 Gibbs and CCHW 1995, p.5.
17 Gibbs and CCHW 1995, p.6; Montague 1990a.
18 Gibbs and CCHW 1995, p.14.
19 Gibbs and CCHW 1995, pp.16.
20 Gibbs and CCHW 1995, p.17; Lapp 1991, p.10.
21 Gibbs and CCHW 1995, p.18.
22 EPA scientists quoted in Fumento 1993, p.53.
23 Roberts 1991a, p.624.
24 Harrison and Hoberg 1991, p.13; Gibbs and CCHW 1995, p.13.
25 Quoted in Gibbs and CCHW 1995.
26 Bailey 1992, p.A4; Thorner 1987, p.22; Harrison and Hoberg 1991, p.13.
27 Thorner 1987, pp.22, 26.
28 Gibbs and CCHW 1995, p.6.
29 Commoner 1988, p.30.
30 Commoner 1988, pp.30-1.
31 Johnson 1995, p.24A; Roberts 1991a; Gibbs and CCHW 1995, p.7.
32 Quoted in Gibbs and CCHW 1995, p.7.
33 Gibbs and CCHW 1995, p.7; Montague 1996b.
34 Montague 1991a.
35 Montague 1991b; Casten 1992, p.12; Cullton 1991.

Chapter 9 continued

36 Houk 1992, p.15.
37 Quoted in Monks 1993; Lapp 1991, p.9.
38 Bailey 1992.
39 Lapp 1991, p.10; Roberts 1991b, pp.866-7.
40 Clapp et al. 1995, p.30A; Roberts 1991a, pp.624-5.
41 Roberts 1991b, pp.866-7.
42 Quoted in Montague 1991a; Bailey 1992, p.A4.
43 Roberts 1991a, p.625.
44 Bailar 1991, p.260.
45 Bailey 1992, p.1; Quoted in Lapp 1991, p.9.
46 Quoted in Montague 1992a.
47 Montague 1992a; Lapp 1991, p.8.
48 Quoted in Bailey 1992, p.A4.
49 Quoted in Montague 1991b.
50 Gibbons 1993; Reichhardt 1994; Schmidt 1992, pp.25, 27.
51 Preuss and Farland 1993, p.24.
52 Quoted in Montague 1994b
53 Quoted in Johnson 1995, p.25A.
54 Johnson 1995, p.25A; Stone 1994; Reichhardt 1994.
55 US EPA 1995, p.26A.
56 US EPA 1995, p.26A; Johnson 1995, p.25A.
57 Weinberg 1995, part 4.3; Gibbs and CCHW 1995, p.278.
58 Howlett 1995; Sullum 1991; ARCC News, May 1996, WWW; Chlorophiles 1996a.
59 British Plastics Federation, home page, World Wide Web, 19/6/96.
60 Arnold and Gottlieb 1993, p.13.
61 Chlorine Chemistry Council, Chemical Manufacturers Association, quoted in Weinberg 1995, part 1.
62 Weinberg 1995, part 1.

63 Weinberg 1995, part 1.
64 AP Financial wire posted in charlie.cray@green2.green-peace.org, CEI Report called "Twisted Science" by ex-EPA official, dioxin-l discussion list, 23 April 1995; Malkin and Fumento 1995
65 Malkin and Fumento 1995.
66 ARCC News, May 1996, WWW.
67 Montague 1996d.
68 Montague 1996c.
69 Rowell 1996, p.321.
70 Malkin and Fumento 1995
71 CCC 1995; CCC 1996a.
72 CCC 1996a; ARCC News, May 1996, WWW.
73 King 1996.
74 CCC 1996a; Quoted in Montague 1994a.
75 Quoted in Montague, 1996d.
76 Gribble 1996.
77 Chlorophiles 1996a.
78 Arnold and Gottlieb 1993, p.13.
79 Howlett 1995.
80 Howlett 1995.
81 Howlett 1995.
82 Tolman 1995.
83 Priestly 1995.
84 British Plastics Federation, home page, World Wide Web, 19/6/96; Chlorophiles 1996b; Chlorophiles 1996c.
85 Mongoven 1994, p.9.
86 Montague 1996c.
87 Mongoven 1994, pp.7-8.
88 CCC 1996b.
89 CUES 1995, p.47.
90 CCC 1996c; CCC 1996d.
91 Englebeen 1996.
92 Englebeen 1996.
93 Weinberg 1995, part 4.3.
94 Smock 1994.
95 King 1996.
96 slester@essential.org, dioxin politics with the Texas PTA, dioxin-l discussion list, 19 October 1995.
97 King 1996.
98 Copy enclosed in

slester@essential.org, dioxin politics with the Texas PTA, dioxin-l discussion list, 19 October 1995.
99 King 1996.
100 MBD 1994, p.7.
101 Gibbs and CCHW 1995, p.280; Baker 1994, p.738; MBD 1994, p.7; Environ Dioxin Risk Characterization Expert Panel 1995.
102 Weinberg 1995, part 4.4.
103 SAB 1995, Executive Summary.
104 SAB 1995, Executive Summary.
105 Cited in Montague 1995c.
106 Gibbs and CCHW 1995, p.278.
107 Montague 1995b.
108 Citizen's Clearinghouse for Hazardous Waste 1995b.
109 Citizen's Clearinghouse for Hazardous Waste 1995a, Citizen's Clearinghouse for Hazardous Waste 1995b.
110 Maggrett 1995.

Chapter 10

1 Quoted in Durning 1992, pp.21-22.
2 Bagdikian 1983, p.188; Durning 1992, p.120.
3 Quoted in Jacobson and Mazur 1995, p.193.
4 Jacobson and Mazur 1995, p.16.
5 Mazur 1996.
6 Durning 1992, p.119.
7 Parenti 1986, pp.63, 65; Jacobson and Mazur 1995, p.13.
8 Kellner 1990, p.126; Lapp 1994, p.14; Kozol 1993, p.14; Aidman 1995; Wagner 1995, p.63; Karpatkin and Holmes 1995.
9 Teachers Federation quoted in Sunderland 1994, p.25.
10 Bednall 1996, p.51; Sunderland 1994, p.25;

Chapter 10 continued

Isles 1989, p.10.
11 Cole-Adams 1993, p.54; Bednall 1996.
12 Coulter 1995, p.14; Connell 1994.
13 Coulter 1995, p.14; Connell 1994; Tarrant 1996, p.62; Cole-Adams 1993, p.54; Gleick 1996, p.68; Ontario Secondary School Teachers' Federation 1995, p.3.
14 Quoted in Jacobson and Mazur 1995, p.21.
15 Rotenier 1995.
16 Quoted in Ontario Secondary School Teachers' Federation 1995, p.4.
17 Aidman 1995; Wagner 1995, p.63; France 1996; Karpatkin and Holmes 1995.
18 Anon. 1996k.
19 Lamont 1996; Sunderland 1994, p.25; Powell and Zuel 1993.
20 CUES 1995, p.1; Bagdikian 1983, p.187; Durning 1992, p.121.
21 Raphael 1993, p.38.
22 Quoted in Jacobson and Mazur 1995, pp.21, 24.
23 Frith 1996, p.13.
24 Karpatkin and Holmes 1995.
25 Mizerski 1995.
26 Frith 1996, pp.13-14; Mizerski 1995; Karpatkin and Holmes 1995; Jacobson and Mazur 1995, p.26.
27 Whittle quoted in France 1996; Manilov 1994, p.17; Kozol 1993, p.8; Brand and Greenberg 1994; Aidman 1995; Fox 1995.
28 Kozol 1993, p.8; Fox 1995; Manilov 1994, pp.17-18; Jacobson and Mazur 1995, p.29.
29 Brand 1996, p.32.
30 Brand 1996, p.30.
31 Cole-Adams 1993, p.52.
32 Aidman 1995; Manilov 1994, p.18; Greenberg 1994; Brand 1996, p.30.

33 Brand and Greenberg 1994; Brand 1996, pp.36-9; Mizerski 1995.
34 Fox 1995; Jacobson and Mazur 1995, p.30.
35 Brand 1996, p.29; Editors 1994, p.18; Murray 1991.
36 Murray 1991; Crispin quoted in Editors 1994, p.18.
37 Anon. 1996f.
38 Quoted in Anon. 1996f
39 Reproduced in Ontario Secondary School Teachers' Federation 1995, p.19.
40 Anon. 1996f; Fitzgerald 1996.
41 Ely-Lawrence 1994; Vandervoot 1991, p.18; Anon. 1995c.
42 Shenk 1995b; Karpatkin and Holmes 1995; Jacobson and Mazur 1995, p.31.
43 Quoted in Shenk 1995a
44 Quoted in Jacobson and Mazur 1995, p.31.
45 Quoted in Shenk 1995b and Wagner 1995, p.63.
46 Jacobson and Mazur 1995, p.31.
47 Shenk 1995a.
48 Quoted in Gleick 1996, p.68.
49 France 1996; Knaus 1992, p.16; Lapp 1994, p.17; Shenk 1995a.
50 Anon. 1996l.
51 Fried 1994.
52 Knaus 1992, p.15; Anon. 1996l.
53 Lapp 1994, p.14.
54 Anon. 1995c.
55 Molnar 1995.
56 Fried 1994; Anon. 1996k.
57 Anon. 1996k.
58 Anon. 1996k.
59 Quoted in Fried 1994.
60 Project Learning Tree, World Wide Web, 1996.
61 Ewen 1976, p.55.
62 Bovet 1994a, pp.24-5.
63 Quoted in Lapp 1994, p.16 and in Shenk 1995a.
64 Anon. 1993d; Anon. 1993e.
65 Anon. 1993d; CUES 1995, p.16.

66 Quoted in Anon. 1993d.
67 Anon. 1993d.
68 Quoted in Shenk 1995a.
69 Lapp 1994, p.16; Anon. 1995b.
70 Fattah and Hunter 1996.
71 Coulter 1995, p.10; Isles 1989, p.12; Anon. 1995b, p.18; Powell 1993.
72 Isles 1989, p.8.
73 Nelson 1989, pp.133, 138.
74 CUES 1995, pp.12-14, 45-46.
75 CUES 1995, pp.1, 13.
76 CUES 1995, p.2.
77 Satchell 1996; Ruben 1994a, p.20.
78 Ruben 1994a.
79 Richardson 1995.
80 Quoted in Satchell 1996.
81 Satchell 1996; Richardson 1995, p.19; Ruben 1994a, p.20.
82 Ruben 1994a, p.21; Richardson 1995.
83 Satchell 1996, School board guidelines quoted in Ruben 1994a, p.20.
84 Satchell 1996.
85 Knaus 1992, p.14.
86 Kozol 1993, p.8.
87 Lewis 1994; Powell 1993; Anon. 1995b, p.20.
88 Coulter 1995, p.15.
89 Coulter 1995, p.17.
90 Knaus 1992, p.16.
91 Manilov 1994.
92 Kozol 1993, p.10.
93 Jacobson and Mazur 1995, p.37.
94 Molnar 1995.
95 Durning 1992, p.34.

Chapter 11

1 Quoted in Jacobson and Mazur 1995, p.15.
2 Packard 1960, pp.22-23.
3 Packard 1960, p.27.
4 Packard 1960, pp.33-4.
5 Durning 1992, p.105; Packard 1960, p.28.
6 Anon. 1992d.
7 Vandervoot 1991, p.14.
8 Harris 1992, p.24.
9 Nelson 1990, p.12.

Chapter 11 continued

10 Nelson 1990, pp.12-13.
11 White 1990, p.49.
12 Irvine 1989, p.88.
13 Garcia 1990, p.16.
14 Hawken 1992.
15 Andre Carothers,
   Greenpeace quoted in
   Nelson 1990, p.12.
16 Packard 1960, p.23.
17 Packard 1960, p.24;
   Kellner, J 1990.
18 Varney 1994.
19 Winward 1991, p.113.
20 Quoted in Macken 1990,
   p.42.
21 LaCovey 1991.
22 Gutin 1992.
23 Gutin 1992.
24 Kellner, J. 1990.
25 Advertisement in Good
   Weekend, 12 June 1993,
   p.29.
26 Anon. 1991e.
27 Anon. 1991e; Anon.
   1993f.
28 Durning 1992, p.125.
29 Ellwood 1990.
30 Hynes 1991.
31 Plant and Plant 1991, p.7.
32 Lee and Solomon 1990,
   pp.59-60; Bagdikian 1983,
   p.188; Parenti 1986, p.62.
33 Jacobson and Mazur 1995,
   p.41.
34 Bagdikian 1983, pp.178,
   198, 201.
35 Twitchell 1996.
36 Franklin 1994, p.43;
   Carothers 1993, p.16;
   Mazur 1996; Jacobson and
   Mazur 1995, p.207.
37 Mazur 1996.
38 Day 1994, p.7.
39 Quoted in Warren 1996a.
40 Lee and Solomon 1990,
   pp.7, 64.
41 Anon. 1991d.
42 Lee and Solomon 1990,
   p.85; Jacobson and Mazur
   1995, p.54; Chomsky
   1989, p.8.
43 Quoted in Anon. 1993g,
   p.5.
44 Jacobson and Mazur 1995,
   p.51; Warren 1996b;
   Wright 1996.

45 Quoted in Chomsky
   1989, p.8.
46 Baum 1991, p.73;
   Jacobson and Mazur 1995,
   p.53.
47 Lee and Solomon 1990,
   pp.60-61.
48 Franklin 1994, p.44.
49 Jacobson and Mazur 1995,
   pp.43-44.
50 Bagdikian 1983, p.179;
   Lee and Solomon 1990,
   pp.61-2; Kellner, D. 1990,
   p.76; Ricci 1993, pp.89-90.
51 Twitchell 1996.
52 Quoted in Jacobson and
   Mazur 1995, p.42.
53 Jacobson and Mazur 1995,
   pp.42, 57.
54 Jacobson and Mazur 1995,
   pp.12, 57.
55 Quoted in Miller 1995,
   p.9.
56 Jacobson and Mazur 1995,
   pp.23-4.
57 Durning 1992, p.125.
58 Kellner, D. 1990, p.81.
59 Kellner, D. 1990, pp.87-8.
60 Quoted in Durning 1992,
   p.126.
61 Alan 1994; West and
   Francis 1996.
62 Himmelstein 1990, p.144.
63 Sethi 1977, p.4.
64 Sethi 1977, p.57; Fram,
   Sethi, and Namiki 1993.
65 Neill 1991, pp.336-7.
66 Neill 1991, p.338.
67 Sethi 1977, p.4.
68 Sethi 1977, p.17.
69 Lee and Solomon 1990,
   pp.67-8.
70 Mobil ad quoted in
   Parenti 1986, p.67.
71 Ricci 1993, p.168; Sethi
   1977, pp.16, 148-157.
72 Nelson 1989, pp.58-9.
73 Nelson 1989, pp.58-9.
74 Sethi 1977, p.65-7.
75 Sethi 1977, p.65-6.
76 Mobil 1996c.
77 Mobil 1996b.
78 Mobil 1996a.
79 Heller 1991.
80 Middleton 1991.
81 West and Francis 1996.
82 Bischoff 1996; Sethi 1977,
   p.292.

83 Sethi 1977, pp.292-3.
84 Stoesz 1987, p.8.
85 Elliott 1996; Anon.
   1995g, p.56; 'Latin
   America-Management
   Opportunities-Procter &
   Gamble', Online Career
   Centre, WWW, 1995; Hay
   1996; 'Awards/Honors/
   Recognitions', P&G Home
   Page, WWW, 1996;
   Vandervoot 1991, p.16.
86 Hay 1996; Landry 1996.
87 Swasy 1993.
88 Swasy 1993; Jacobson and
   Mazur 1995, p.43; Sloan
   1995; Anon. 1995f;
   Advertising Age, 1st April
   1996, p.41; Williamson
   1995, pp.1, 8.
89 Lapp 1994, p.15; Fried
   1994; Karpatkin and
   Holmes 1995.
90 Quoted in Lapp 1994,
   p.15.
91 Fried 1994; Karpatkin and
   Holmes 1995; CUES 1995,
   p.13; 'P&G History: 1945-
   1980', WWW, 1996;
   Kalish 1994.
92 Quoted in Lapp 1994,
   p.15.
93 Federation 1995, p.3;
   Energy Education
   Resources Guide, World
   Wide Web, 1995; CUES
   1995, p.46.
94 CUES 1995, p.48; text
   quoted in Jacobson and
   Mazur 1995, p.34.
95 Stisser 1994, p.28; Smith
   1991; Artzt quoted in
   Muller 1992.
96 Kiley 1991.
97 Rowell 1996, p.122; P&
   G quoted in Coeyman
   1994.
98 Koeppel 1989.
99 Latham 1992.
100 Hawken 1992.
101 Robert Shimp, head of
   environmental safety, P&G,
   quoted in Bell 1994.
102 Colford 1994, pp.1, 8.
103 'Awards/Honors/
   Recognitions', P&G Home
   Page, WWW, 1996;
   Vandervoot 1991, p.16;

Chapter 11 continued

Anon. 1995e.
104 Swasy 1993, p.215.
105 Swasy 1993, pp.207-209, 211-212, 217.
106 Leamy 1995.
107 Swasy 1993, pp.131, 150.
108 Swasy 1993, p.148.
109 Lee and Solomon 1990, p.61; Gamson et al. 1992, p.378.
110 Anon. 1995d; Leo 1995; Mandese 1995, p.1; Leo 1995.
111 Mandese 1995, p.8.
112 Wehling 1995.
113 Anon. 1995d.
114 Durning 1993a.
115 Quoted in Durning 1993b; Durning 1992, p.38.
116 Durning 1992, p.23; Jacobson and Mazur 1995, p.193; Motavelli 1996.
117 Twitchell 1996.
118 Durning 1993a.
119 Twitchell 1996.

Chapter 12

1 Parry 1995, p.6.
2 Saloma 1984, pp.104-7.
3 Schulman 1995, pp.11-12.
4 Saloma 1984, pp.111-2.
5 Jost 1994, pp.367-8.
6 Kurtz 1996, p.292.
7 Kurtz 1996, pp.298-300.
8 Kurtz 1996, p.301.
9 Quoted in Alterman 1996.
10 Parry 1995, p.6.
11 Kurtz 1996, p.291.
12 Dolny 1996, p.21; Solomon 1996a, p.10.
13 Dolny 1996, p.21.
14 Solomon 1996b, pp.26-7.
15 Anon. 1994h; Baker 1994; Anon. 1994f, p.19.
16 Lee and Solomon 1990, pp.26-7.
17 Gamson et al. 1992, p.382.
18 Croteau, Hoynes, and Carragee 1993, p.13.
19 Anon. 1995h, p.18.
20 Croteau, Hoynes, and Carragee 1993, pp.9-14; Entman 1989, p.32.
21 Spencer 1992, p.13.
22 Ruben 1994.
23 Entman 1989, p.18; Spencer 1992, pp.16-17; McNair 1994, p.48.
24 Ryan 1991, p.34.
25 Ricci 1993, p.99.
26 Walter Karp quoted in Lee and Solomon 1990, p.18; Kellner 1990, p.106.
27 Lee and Solomon 1990, p.18.
28 Himmelstein 1990, p.150; Parenti 1986, p.41; Kurtz 1996, p.204.
29 Kurtz 1993, p.137.
30 Chomsky 1989, p.8.
31 Kurtz 1996, p.203.
32 Fallows 1996a, p.103.
33 Fallows 1996a, p.103.
34 Fallows 1996a, p.106.
35 Ward 1995; Carmody 1995.
36 Anon. 1989b.
37 Cohen and Solomon 1995, p.10.
38 Franklin 1994, p.13.
39 Kurtz 1993, p.139.
40 Stone 1993; Kurtz 1996, p.310.
41 Parenti 1986, p.52; Kurtz 1993, p.137.
42 Glover 1993, p.40; Kohler 1997
43 Sherrill 1990, p.401.
44 Quoted in Anon. 1996g.
45 Harwood 1995, p.29; Fallows 1996a, p.78; Kurtz 1996, p.206; Sherrill 1990, pp.390, 400; Parenti 1986, p.39.
46 Fallows 1996a, p.77.
47 Parenti 1986, p.40.
48 Martínez and Head 1992, p.29.
49 Nelkin 1987, pp.103-4.
50 Entman 1989, p.30; Nelkin 1987, p.91.
51 McNair 1994, p.47.
52 McNair 1994, p.47.
53 Entman 1989, p.32; Nelkin 1987, p.94.
54 Lee and Solomon 1990, p.16.
55 Nelkin 1987, p.96.
56 Spencer 1992, p.13.
57 Parenti 1986, p.52; Bagdikian 1983, p.182.
58 Grossman 1992.
59 Spencer 1992, p.17; Parenti 1986, p.218.
60 Spencer 1992, p.18.
61 Entman 1989, pp.37-8; Jim Naureckas, editor of Extra! quoted in Ruben 1994.
62 Shabecoff 1994.
63 Rauber 1996.
64 Bagdikian 1983, p.182; Ryan 1991, p.176.
65 Bagdikian 1983, p.181.
66 Ryan 1991, pp.10, 176.
67 Kellner 1990, pp.113-4.
68 Quoted in Lyman 1994, p.39.
69 Sharon Begley, Newsweek, quoted in Lyman 1994, p.39.
70 Kurtz 1993, p.148.
71 Ryan 1991, p.68.
72 Cohen 1989.
73 Parenti 1986), p.35.
74 Nelson 1989, p.133; Parenti 1986, pp.35, 50.
75 Spencer 1992, p.15.
76 Lazare 1991.
77 Ralph Miliband quoted in McNair 1994, p.45.
78 Gitlin 1980, p.3.
79 Gitlin 1980.
80 Parenti 1986, p.91.
81 McNair 1994, p.32.
82 Parenti 1986, p.99.
83 Kellner 1990, p.122.
84 Bagdikian 1983, pp.180-1, 201-2.
85 Ryan 1991, p.31.
86 Windschuttle 1988, p.274.
87 Glover 1993, p.40.
88 Gold 1994 ; Ricci 1993, p.94; Levy 1992, p.70.
89 Levy 1992, p.70.
90 Ricci 1993, pp.94-5.
91 Quoted in Ryan 1991, p.34.
92 Windschuttle 1988, p.268.
93 Quoted in Ryan 1991, p.31.
94 McNair 1994, p.46; Spencer 1992, p.13.
95 Entman 1989, p.19.
96 Ricci 1993, p.95.

Chapter 12 continued

97 Gersh 1992.
98 Kaufman quoted in Russell 1990, p.5.
99 Ryan 1991, p.44.
100 Ricci 1993, p.95.
101 Entman 1989, p.21; Kurtz 1996, p.25.
102 Fallows 1996a, p.21; Waldman 1996; Kurtz 1996, p.25.
103 Barnett 1994, p.39.
104 Glover 1993, p.40.
105 Fallows 1996b.
106 Hoggart 1995.
107 Gamson et al. 1992, p.387; Spencer 1992, p.16; Lee and Solomon 1990, pp.202, 222.
108 Kellner 1990, pp.107-8.
109 Parenti 1986, pp.110-11.
110 Spencer 1992, p.13.
111 Dumanoski 1994.
112 Entman 1989, p.32; Parenti 1986, p.43.
113 Ryan 1991, p.119.
114 Lee and Solomon 1990, p.98.
115 Quoted in Williams 1995.
116 Selcraig 1995.
117 Gamson, Croteau et al. 1992, p.376; Lichter and Noyes 1995, pp.4-5.
118 Quoted in Rosen 1996.
119 Ryan 1991, p.121.
120 Lichter and Noyes 1995, p.5.
121 Edward Herman quoted in Ryan 1991, p.117.

Chapter 13

1 Carmody 1995; Letto 1995, p.22; Spencer 1992, p.14.
2 Quoted in Letto 1995, p.22.
3 Letto 1995, p.22.
4 Atlanta Constitution quoted in Spencer 1991, p.6.
5 Spencer 1991, pp.6-7.
6 Spencer 1992, p.15.
7 Spencer 1992, p.20.
8 Boff 1992, p.25.

9 Boff 1992, p.23.
10 Anon. 1995i.
11 Smith 1992, p.39.
12 Tokar 1995, p.153.
13 Carmody 1995.
14 Carmody 1995.
15 Quoted in Rauber 1993, p.40.
16 Quoted in Monks 1993.
17 Spencer 1993, p.8.
18 Spencer 1993, p.8.
19 Quoted in Spencer 1993, p.21; Rowell 1996, p.29.
20 Spencer 1992, p.16; Rauber 1993.
21 Nixon 1995, p.25.
22 Rowell 1996, pp.320-1.
23 Ruben 1994 ; Carmody 1995.
24 Peter Montague quoted in Ruben 1994.
25 Rauber 1996.
26 Ryan 1992.
27 Savage 1992.
28 Shabecoff 1994.
29 Earth First! 1996.
30 Goldin and Motavalli 1995.
31 Epstein 1995, p.11.
32 McLamb quoted in Epstein 1995, p.11.
33 Quoted in Epstein 1995, p.11 and Goldin and Motavalli 1995.
34 Quoted in Epstein 1995, p.11 and Goldin and Motavalli 1995.
35 Lapp 1991, p.9.
36 Monks 1993.
37 Quoted in Monks 1993.
38 Ray and Guzzo 1994, p.143.
39 Montague 1991b.
40 Lapp 1991, p.12.
41 Monks 1993.
42 Ryan 1993.
43 Ryan 1993.
44 Ryan 1993.
45 Johnson 1995, p.24A.
46 Nash 1994, p.70.
47 Quoted in Nash 1994, p.70.
48 Quoted in Montague 1996e.
49 Quoted in Montague 1996f.
50 Monks 1993; Lapp 1991, p.10; Montague 1990a.

51 Monks 1993.
52 Sherrill 1990, pp.398-99; Kellner 1990, p.82.
53 Sherrill 1990, p.394; Bagdikian 1983, p.xv; Kellner 1990, pp.82-87.
54 Herman & Chomsky quoted in Gamson et al. 1992, pp.379-80.
55 Chomsky 1989, pp.7-8.
56 Chomsky 1989, p.8.
57 Windschuttle 1988, p.264.
58 Bagdikian 1983, p.32.
59 Windschuttle 1988, pp.264-5; Brewster 1996; Abramsky 1995, p.16; Gomery 1996, p.52; Franklin 1994, p.34.
60 Abramsky 1995, p.16.
61 Williams 1995.
62 McNair 1994, pp.40-42.
63 Osler 1996, p.11; Bogart 1996; Gamson et al. 1992, p.378.
64 Bagdikian 1983, p.xv; Cohen and Solomon 1995, p.2.
65 Ryan 1991, p.119.
66 Miller 1995, p.9; Gunther 1995.
67 Parenti 1986, p.107; Littwin 1995, p.14.
68 McNair 1994, p.42.
69 Lichter and Noyes 1995 , p 24.
70 Lichter and Noyes 1995, p.4.
71 Chomsky 1989, pp.11-12.
72 'NBC and Microsoft Announce Joint Venture', World Wide Web, 1996.
73 Lee and Solomon 1990; GE Fact Sheet, WWW, 1997; General Electric Co, General BusinessFile ASAP, Infotrack SearchBank, 1995; Greider 1992, pp.335, 340, 341; Carley 1996; Kellner 1990, p.82.
74 Lee and Solomon 1990, pp.77-81; Naureckas 1995
75 Putnam 1991.
76 Gunther 1995, p.40.
77 FAIR 1991.
78 Anon. 1992f.
79 Lee and Solomon 1990, p.78.

Chapter 13 continued

80 Grossman 1993, p.6.
81 Grossman 1993, p.6.
82 Lee and Solomon 1990, p.210.
83 Tenenbaum 1990.
84 Stapleton 1992, p.34; O'Callaghan 1992, p.86.
85 Quoted in Knoll 1993; Jacobson and Mazur 1995, pp.51, 53.
86 Greider 1992, pp.337, 340.
87 Greider 1992, pp.336-7; Lee and Solomon 1990, p.77; Kellner 1990, p.172.
88 Greider 1992, p.341.
89 Greider 1992, pp.341-2.
90 Lee and Solomon 1990, pp.76-7.
91 Kellner 1990, p.172.
92 Greider 1992, p.339; Megalli and Friedman 1991, p.186; Rowell 1996, p.85.
93 Kellner 1990, p.83.
94 Greider 1992, p.339.
95 Lee and Solomon 1990, p.84.
96 Lee and Solomon 1990, pp.82-3; Anon. 1992f, p.6.
97 Lee and Solomon 1990, pp.76, 80, 82-3; Anon. 1992f, p.6; Greider 1992, pp.337, 350; Husseini 1994, p.14; Byrnes 1994.
98 Greider 1992, p.350.
99 Lee and Solomon 1990, p.80.
100 Quoted in Husseini 1994, pp.13-14.
101 Husseini 1994, p.13.
102 Ozone Action 1995; Otis 1995.
103 Greider 1992, pp.351-5; Kellner 1990, p.82; Lee and Solomon 1990, p.80.
104 Coppolino and Rauber 1994.
105 Rice 1993.
106 Rice 1993.
107 Anon. 1993h.
108 Greider 1992, p.334.
109 Greider 1992, pp.42-43.
110 Greider 1992, p.44.
111 Greider 1992, p.44.
112 Greider 1992, pp.44-45.

113 Anon. 1991c.
114 Megalli and Friedman 1992, p.16.
115 Quoted in Anon. 1991c.
116 Sibbison 1990, p.4.
117 Stauber and Rampton 1995/96 , p.24.
118 Quoted in Lee and Solomon 1990, p.75.
119 Kellner 1990, p.94-5.

Chapter 14

1 Dunlap, Jr, and Gallup 1993.
2 Pettinico 1995, pp.28, 30; Rockland and Fletcher 1994.
3 Anon. 1995i.
4 Levathes 1995, p.16.
5 Beale 1994a; Southam 1994, p.28.
6 Beale 1994b, p.7A.
7 Southam 1994, p.28.
8 Gilchrist 1995.
9 Parenti 1986, p.93.
10 Seitel 1995, p.32.
11 Carey 1995, p.18.
12 Chomsky 1989, p.48.
13 Wanna 1992, p.105.
14 Bell 1992, p.51.
15 Carothers 1993, p.15.
16 Anderson and Mann 1994.
17 Wanna 1992, p.71.
18 Ricci 1993, p.8, 152-3; Gellner 1995, p.501; Greider 1992, p.47.
19 Ricci 1993, p.41.
20 Greider 1992, p.47.
21 Johnson 1993, pp.98-99; Williamson 1989, pp.2, 54-7.
22 Greider 1992, p.50.
23 Carey 1995, p.105.
24 Greider 1993, pp.8-9; Greider 1992.
25 Greider 1992, pp.35-36.
26 Greider 1992, pp.108-9.
27 Roschwalb 1994, p.270.
28 Carlisle 1993, p.25.
29 Quoted in Montague 1993.
30 Domhoff 1985, p.21.
31 Sherrill 1990, p.363.
32 See for example the Australian, October 16

1996, p.1.
33 Rowell 1996, p.78.
34 Rowell 1996, p.78.
35 Rowell 1996, p.80.
36 Anderson and Mann 1994.
37 The Ecologist, Campaigns & Updates, Nov/Dev 1995, p.2.
38 New Scientist, 15 March 1997, p.11.
39 Greider 1992, p.107.
40 Bell 1992, p.47.
41 Williamson 1989, p.57.
42 Bell 1992, p.56.
43 Ball and Millard 1986, p.24.
44 Chomsky 1989, p.22.
45 Dowie 1995, p.2.
46 Stauber and Rampton 1995, p.14.
47 Tom Gitlin quoted in Ryan 1991, p.18.
48 Kellner 1990, p.94.
49 Stauber quoted in Montague 1993.
50 Chomsky 1989, p.48.
51 Sherrill 1990, p.351.
52 Stauber and Rampton 1995, p.78; Tokar 1995, p.155; Sherrill 1990, pp.359-60.
53 Quoted in Smith 1996.
54 Bennett 1992, p.402.
55 Bennett 1992, p.404.
56 Fallows quoted in Rosen 1996.
57 Kellner 1990, p.105; Ricci 1993, p.88.
58 Saltzman 1989, p.87.
59 Gamson et al. 1992, p.373.
60 Franklin 1994, p.11.
61 Franklin 1994, p.11.
62 Jacobson and Mazur 1995, pp.47-8.
63 Ryan 1991, pp.7, 130.
64 Noam Chomsky quoted in Szykowny 1991, p.28.
65 Noam Chomsky quoted in Szykowny 1991, p.30.
66 Kellner 1990, p.119.
67 Stauber and Rampton 1995, p.206.
68 Hightower 1995, p.32.

Bibliography

Abelson, Donald E. 1995. 'From Policy Research to Political Advocacy: The Changing Role of Think Tanks in American Politics', *Canadian Review of American Studies* 25 (1):93-126.
Abramsky, Sasha. 1995. 'Citizen Murdoch: The shape of things to come?', *Extra!*, Nov/Dec, 16-17.
Adams, William C. 1992. 'The role of media relations in risk communication', *Public Relations Quarterly* 37 (4):28-32.
Adler, Jonathan. 1996. Environmental Studies Program, Competitive Enterprise Institute, World Wide Web, (www.cei.org/esp.html).
Aidman, Amy. 1995. *Advertising in Schools,* University of Illinois, Illinois: ERIC Clearinghouse on Elementary and Early Childhood Education.
Alan, Richard. 1994. 'Issues communication and advocacy: contemporary and ethical challenges', *Public Relations Review* 20 (3):225-231.
Alterman, Eric. 1994. 'Fighting Smart', *Mother Jones* 19 (4):59-61.
Alterman, Eric. 1996. 'The GOP's Strike Force', *Rolling Stone,* 8 February, 30-31+.
Anderson, Paul and Mann, Nyta. 1994. 'A Cure of Sleaze?', *New Statesman & Society* 7(327):14-16.
Anderson, T., and D. Leal. 1991. *Free Market Environmentalism,* Pacific Research Institute for Public Policy, San Francisco.
Anon. 1987a. 'Misguided Health Priorities Could Affect Economy', *International Insurance Monitor* 41 (6):16-17.
Anon. 1987b. 'Dr blasts US health care priorities', *Cash Flow* 91 (47):28-29.
Anon. 1989a. 'Of Policy and Pedigree', *The Economist,* 6 May, 52-54.
Anon. 1989b. 'Cronkite for Hire' in *Extra!,* Oct/Nov.
Anon. 1991a. 'Think-tanks: The carousels of power', *The Economist* 319 (7708):23-26.
Anon. 1991b. 'H&K leads PR charge in behalf of Kuwaiti cause' in *O'Dwyer's PR Services* 5 (1):1,8.
Anon. 1991c. 'Toxic Times', *Extra!,* Nov/Dec, 15.
Anon. 1991d. 'Capitalist Tool, PR Executive's Dream', *Extra!,* Jan/Feb, 16.
Anon. 1991e. 'The World Cosmetics Industry: Facing Up', *The Economist* 320 (July 13):71-2.
Anon. 1991f. 'How much recycling should we do?', *Institute of Public Affairs Facts* 39 (4):2.
Anon. 1992a. 'The Good Think-Tank Guide', *The Economist* 321 (7738):49-53.
Anon. 1992b. 'ESD—Winding Up or Grinding Down?', *Choice,* May, 27.
Anon. 1992c. 'Research Group says some Green Marketers are only Pretending', *Marketing News* 26 (2):3.
Anon. 1992d. Beyond the Consumer Society. Unesco Courier 3 (March):32-33.
Anon. 1992e. 'Any Ideas?' *The Economist,* 7 November, 64.
Anon. 1992f. 'General Electric: You have the right to remain silent', *Extra!,* June, 6-7.
Anon. 1993a. 'Business groups endorses Clinton's climate policy', *Chemical Marketing Reporter* 244 (22):22.
Anon. 1993b. 'Environmental issues, corporate image top business concerns for '94', *Public Relations Journal,* October, 28.
Anon. 1993c. 'Wilson's open version of PR', *Marketing,* 20 May, 23.
Anon. 1993d. 'Learning to be "caretakers all"', *Agri Marketing* 31 (5):92-3.
Anon. 1993e. 'Beef industry aims lobbying effort at elementary students', *Marketing News* 27 (3):5.
Anon. 1993f. 'Cosmetics through the looking glass', *Drug & Cosmetic Industry* 152 (6):28-39.
Anon. 1993g. 'Corporate Messages', *Extra!,* Sept/Oct, 5.
Anon. 1993h. 'America's worst toxic polluters; eight companies with poor environmental records', *Business and Society Review* 84 (Winter):21-23.
Anon. 1993i. 'Going Global', *New Internationalist,* August, 18-19.
Anon. 1993j. 'Sewage will still flow into sea, group says', *The Northern Star,* 2 April 1993.
Anon. 1993k. 'No sewage in ocean: Apology', *The Northern Star,* 10 April 1993.

Anon. 1994a. 'Coalition urges resistance to greenhouse gas demands', *Chemical Marketing Reporter* 246 (8):5.
Anon. 1994b. 'Flack Attack, Part II', *Environmental Action*, Summer, 9.
Anon. 1994c. 'Greenwash Inc.', *Environmental Action*, Summer, 8-9.
Anon. 1994d. 'The new boys (2): Tanked up', *The Economist* 333 (7893):26-27.
Anon. 1994e. 'McLibel', *Chain Reaction* 72:9.
Anon. 1994f. 'NAFTA's Knee-Jerk Press', *Extra!*, Jan/Feb, 19.
Anon. 1994g. 'Political Intellectual: The Old New Right', *The Economist*, 2 July, 85.
Anon. 1994h. 'Debunking the "Liberal Bias" in Network News', *Extra!*, Jan/Feb, 26.
Anon. 1994i. 'Public Interest Pretenders', *Consumer Reports* 59 (5):316-320.
Anon. 1995a. '"Environment in Schools" through Commercialism', *Environment Writer*, June.
Anon. 1995b. 'Australia's petroleum industry goes back to school', *Petroleum Gazette* 30 (1):18-23.
Anon. 1995c. 'Commercial pressures on kids at schools', *Education Digest* 61 (1):4-8.
Anon. 1995d. 'TV Briefs: Procter & Gamble washes hands of 4 sleazy daytime shows', *The Detroit News*, 16 November.
Anon. 1995e. 'Labour Party backs Green P&G range', *Marketing Week* 17 (March 10):8.
Anon. 1995f. 'P&G and Paramount venture sign on NBC as a new broadcaster', *The Wall Street Journal*, 15 November, 14.
Anon. 1995g. 'Profiling America's biggest ad spenders', *Advertising Age* 66 (27 September):40-62.
Anon. 1995h. 'All the right moves: How the Republicans get their way at PBS', *Extra!*, March/April, 18-19.
Anon. 1995i. 'Environmental Policy: Could Try Harder', *The Economist*, 21 October, 32-33.
Anon. 1995j. '"Food Slander" is now a crime', *Earth Island Journal* 10 (4):15.
Anon. 1995k. 'Court Gives New Protections to Critics of Development', *Los Angeles Times*, 24 March, 12.
Anon. 1996a. 'What you can learn from radical environmentalists', *EnviroScan* (137).
Anon. 1996b. 'Confidence Game: B-M's PR Plan for Silicone Breast Implants', *PR Watch* 3 (1):9-12.
Anon. 1996c. 'Science Under Pressure: Dow-Funded Studies Say "No Problem"', *PR Watch* 3 (1):13-15.
Anon. 1996d. 'Senate Approves Agent Orange Benefits', *Los Angeles Times* (September 6).
Anon. 1996e. 'Rating Environmental Education Programs', *The Kansas City Star*, 29 June.
Anon. 1996f. 'Web of Deception: Threats to Children from Online Marketing', World Wide Web: Center for Media Education.
Anon. 1996g. 'Sizzle Over Substance', *Newsweek*, 29 January, 62-65.
Anon. 1996h. 'Murdoch doubles donations to US election campaigns', *Sydney Morning Herald* (November 21).
Anon. 1996i. 'Astroturf Group Wants to "Save" Headwaters', *E-Link*, 23 July, newsdesk@envirolink.org.
Anon. 1996j. 'McDonald's Censorship Strategy', McSpotlight, World Wide Web.
Anon, 1996k. 'Commercialisation of Education', Media Awareness Network, World Wide Web (http://www.screen.com/mnet/eng/met/class/edissue/commed2.htm).
Anon. 1996l. 'What Business Does Big Business Have in our Schools?', Media Awareness Network, World Wide Web.
Arnold, Ron. 1992. Transcript of Closing Remarks. Paper read at Maine Conservation Rights Institute Second Annual Congress, 20th April.
Arnold, Ron, and Alan Gottlieb. 1993. *Trashing the Economy: How Runaway Environmentalism is Wrecking America*, Free Enterprise Press, Bellevue, Washington.
Arnstein, Caren. 1994. 'How companies can rebuild credibility and public trust', *Public Relations Journal*, April, 28-29.
Asher, Joseph. 1991. 'When a good cause is also good business', *Bank Marketing* 23 (6):30-32.
Auerbach, Stuart. 1985. 'PR gets entrenched as a Washington business', *The Washington Post*, 18 February, 1, 19.
Aylmer, Sean. 1996. 'Accountability remains key issue for PR firm', *Business Sydney*, 8 April, 1, 21.

Baca, Jim. 1995. 'People for the West! Challenges and Opportunities', in *Let the People Judge*, edited by J. D. Echeverria and R. B. Eby. Island Press, Washington, DC.
Bagdikian, Ben H. 1983. *The Media Monopoly*, Beacon Press, Boston.
Bailar, John C. 1991. 'How Dangerous is Dioxin', *The New England Journal of Medicine* 324

(January 24):260-262.

Bailey, Jeff. 1992. 'Dueling Studies: How Two Industries Created a Fresh Spin on the Dioxin Debate', *Wall Street Journal*, 20 February, 1, A4.

Bailey, Ronald. 1993. *Eco-Scam: The False Prophets of Ecological Apocalypse*, St. Martin's Press, New York.

Bailey, Ronald, ed. 1995. *The True State of the Planet*, The Free Press, New York.

Baker, Beth. 1994a. 'The Case Against Dioxin', *Environmental Action*, Fall, 22-23.

Baker, Beth. 1994b. 'The Dioxin Dilemma Remains Unresolved', *BioScience* 44 (11):738-9.

Baker, Beth. 1995. 'A Feather in Their Caps', *Environmental Action Magazine* 27 (3):29-33.

Baker, Dean. 1994. 'Trade Reporting's Information Deficit', *Extra!*, Nov/Dec, 8-9.

Ball, Alan R., and Frances Millard. 1986. *Pressure Groups and the Distribution of Power: A Comparative Introduction*, Macmillan, London.

Balling, Robert C. 1995. 'Global Warming: Messy models, decent data, and pointless policy' in *The True State of the Planet*, edited by R. Bailey, The Free Press, New York.

Baran, Josh. 1991. 'Every day is Earth Day', *Public Relations Journal*, April, 22-23.

Barnett, Steven. 1994. 'Packaging Politics: Political Communications in Britain's Media Democracy', *New Statesman & Society* 7 (May 27):39.

Baum, Dan. 1991. 'Wise Guise', *Sierra*, May/June, 71-73, 92-3.

Beale, Bob. 1994a. 'Most say environment more important than economy', *Sydney Morning Herald*, 12 April.

Beale, Bob. 1994b. 'We're All Going Green', *Sydney Morning Herald*, 11 June, 7A.

Beder, Sharon. 1989. *Toxic Fish and Sewer Surfing*, Allen & Unwin, Sydney.

Beder, Sharon. 1990. 'No Smoke Without Fire', *Australian Society*, July, 5-6.

Beder, Sharon. 1991. 'Hazardous Waste: An Intractable Problem', *The Bulletin* (30 July):92-96.

Beder, Sharon. 1993. 'Engineers, Ethics and Etiquette', *New Scientist*, 25 September, 36-41.

Beder, Sharon. 1996a. 'Charging the earth: The promotion of price-based measures for pollution control', *Ecological Economics* 16:51-63.

Beder, Sharon. 1996b. *The Nature of Sustainable Development*, 2nd ed., Scribe Publications, Newham, Australia.

Beder, Sharon, and Michael Shortland. 1992. 'Siting a hazardous waste facility: the tangled web of risk communication', *Public Understanding of Science* 1:139-160.

Bednall, John. 1996. 'The Coles/Apple Programme', in *Innocent Advertising? Corporate Sponsorship in Australian Schools*, edited by T. Newlands and S. Frith. New College Institute for Values Research, University of NSW, Sydney.

Beers, David, and Catherine Capellaro. 1991. 'Greenwash!', *Mother Jones*, March/April, 88.

Bell, Stephen. 1992. 'The Political Power of Business', in *Business-Government Relations in Australia*, edited by S. Bell and J. Wanna, Harcourt Brace Jovanovich, Sydney.

Bell, Stephen, and John Warhurst. 1992. 'Political Activism Among Large Firms', in *Business-Government Relations in Australia*, edited by S. Bell and J. Wanna, Harcourt Brace Jovanovich, Sydney.

Bell, Sally. 1994. 'Use of 'green' labels is labeled harmful', *Supermarket News* 44 (18):63-4.

Bennett, Jeff, and Walter Block, eds. 1991. *Reconciling Economics and the Environment*, Australian Institute for Public Policy, West Perth.

Bennett, W. Lance. 1992. 'White Noise: The Perils of Mass Mediated Democracy', *Communication Monographs* 59 (December):401-406.

Bernstam, Mikhail S. 1996. 'The Wealth of Nations and the Environment', World Wide Web: Institute of Economic Affairs.

Bielski, Vince. 1995. 'Armed and dangerous: the Wise Use movement meets the militias', *Sierra*, September/October, 33-35.

Bird, Hedda. 1994. 'Marketing is dead, long live consumer marketing', *Pulp & Paper International* 36 (2):57, 59.

Bischoff, Dan. 1996. 'Corporate money dominates issues advertising', *St. Louis Journalism Review* 26 (July-August):11-12.

Bishop, Katherine. 1991. 'New Tool of Developers and Others Quells Private Opposition to Projects', *New York Times* (26 April).

Blackburn, Thomas E. 1995. 'Right-thinking conservative think tanks', *National Catholic Reporter* 31 (41):18.

Bleifuss, Joel. 1995a. 'Covering the Earth with "Green PR"', *PR Watch* 2 (1):1-7.

Bleifuss, Joel. 1995b. 'Journalist, watch thyself: Keeping tabs on the messengers', *PR Watch* 2 (1):8-10.

Bleifuss, Joel. 1995c. 'Science in the Private Interest: Hiring Flacks to Attack the Facts', *PR Watch* 2 (1):11-12.
Blyskal, Jeff, and Marie Blyskal. 1985. *PR: How the Public Relations Industry Writes the News,* William Morrow and Co., New York.
Boff, Richard B. Du. 1992. 'Government Regulation: All Cost, No Benefit', *Lies of Our Times,* July-August, 23-25.
Bogart, Leo. 1994. 'Who pays for the media?', *Journal of Advertising Research* 34 (2):11-18.
Bogart, Leo. 1996. 'Media and democracy: hand in hand?', *Current* 8380 (February):3-7.
Bovet, Susan Fry. 1994a. 'Teaching Ecology: A new generation influences environmental policy', *Public Relations Journal,* April, 24-27.
Bovet, Susan Fry. 1994b. 'Leading companies turn to trade associations for lobbying', *Public Relations Journal* 50 (7):13-14.
Brand, Jeffrey E. 1996. 'Teaching students to want: TV advertising in American schools and lessons for Australia', in *Innocent Advertising? Corporate Sponsorship in Australian Schools,* edited by T. Newlands and S. Frith, New College Institute for Values Research, University of NSW, Sydney.
Brand, Jeffrey E., and Bradley S. Greenberg. 1994. 'Commercials in the classroom: the impact of Channel One advertising', *Journal of Advertising Research* 34 (1):18-27.
Brante, Thomas. 1993. 'Reasons for Studying Scientific and Science-Based Controversies', in *Controversial Science: From Content to Contention,* edited by T. Brante, S. Fuller and W. Lynch, State University of New York Press, Albany, NY .
Brewster, Deborah. 1996. 'News calls for media ownership deregulation', *The Australian,* 13 November, 6.
Brick, Phil. 1995. 'Determined Opposition: The Wise Use Movement Challenges Environmentalism', *Environment* 37 (8):17-20, 36-42.
Brody, E. W. 1992. 'The Domain of Public Relations', *Public Relations Review* 18 (4):349-364.
Brunton, Ron. 1991. *Environmentalism and Sorcery,* paper read at Reconciling Economics and the Environment, 3 September, at Sydney.
Budd, John F. 1994-5. 'How to Manage Corporate Reputations', *Public Relations Quarterly* 39 (4):11-15.
Burbury, Rochell. 1993. 'Planet takes environmental initiative', *Sydney Morning Herald* (30th March).
Burke, William Kevin. 1994. 'The Wise Use Movement: Right-wing anti-environmentalism', *Propaganda Review* (11):4-10.
Burton, Bob. 1994. 'Nice names - pity about the policies - industry front groups', *Chain Reaction* (70):16-19.
Burton, Bob. 1995. 'Right wing think tanks go environmental', *Chain Reaction,* no. 73-74.
Burton, Bob. 1996. 'Mothers Opposing Pollution (MOP)-all washed up', *Chain Reaction* (76):28-31.
Burton, Douglas. 1995. 'To win the battle of ideas, send in the think tanks', *Insight on the News* 11 (10):15-17.
Butler, Daniel. 1995. 'Radicals without reins', *Accountancy* 116 (1224):36-38.
Byrnes, Nanette. 1994. 'The Smoke at General Electric', *Financial World,* 16 August, 32-34.

Callahan, Michael. 1989. 'Dioxin Pathways: Judging Risk to People', *EPA Journal,* May/June, 29-30.
Canan, Penelope, and George W. Pring. 1988. 'Strategic Lawsuits Against Public Participation', *Social Problems* 35 (5):506-519.
Carey, Alex. 1995. *Taking the Risk Out of Democracy,* edited by A. Lohrey, UNSW Press, Sydney.
Carley, William M. 1996. 'General Electric posts record profit for quarter, year', *The Wall Street Journal,* 19 January, 4.
Carlisle, Johan. 1993. 'Public Relationships: Hill and Knowlton, Robert Gray, and the CIA', *CovertAction* (44):19-25.
Carmody, Kevin. 1995. 'It's a jungle out there', *Columbia Journalism Review* 34 (1):40-45.
Carney, Eliza Newlin. 1992. 'Industry plays the grassroots card', *National Journal* 24 (5):281-3.
Carney, Eliza Newlin. 1993. 'From the K Street Corridor', *National Journal* 25 (8):466.
Carothers, Andre. 1993. 'The Green Machine', *New Internationalist,* August, 14-16.
Carothers, Andre. 1994. 'Anatomy of a Retreat', *GreenDisk* 3 (3).
Cass, Penny. 1993. 'The Effects of Schema Priming in the Labeling of Environmentalists', casspa@cs.orst.edu.

Casten, Liane Clorfene. 1992. 'Dioxin Charade Poisons the Press', *Extra!*, January/February, 12-13.

Cato Institute. 1995. 'Media Comments', World Wide Web (http://www.cato.org), November.

CCC (Chlorine Chemistry Council) 1995. 'Chlorine protects public health', EnviroScan - World Wide Web, April.

CCC. 1996a. Products, World Wide Web.

CCC. 1996b. Curriculum Resources, World Wide Web.

CCC. 1996c. 'Chlorine in Our Lives', World Wide Web.

CCC. 1996d. RISK, World Wide Web.

CDFE. 1996. 'The Center's Issues and Positions', World Wide Web: Center for the Defense of Free Enterprise.

CEI. 1995a. 'Clean Water Act Reform, Environmental Briefing Book for Congressional Candidates', Competitive Enterprise Institute, World Wide Web, (http://www.cei.org/ebb4.html).

CEI. 1995b. 'Energy Taxes, Environmental Briefing Book for Congressional Candidates', Competitive Enterprise Institute, World Wide Web, (http://www.cei.org/ebb9.html).

CEI. 1996a. 'Global Climate Change, Environmental Briefing Book for Congressional Candidates', Competitive Enterprise Institute, World Wide Web, (http://www.cei.org/ebb12.html).

CEI. 1996b. 'Automobile Fuel Economy Standards, Environmental Briefing Book for Congressional Candidates', Competitive Enterprise Institute, World Wide Web, (http://www.cei.org/ebb2.html).

CEI. 1996c. 'What is CEI?', Competitive Enterprise Institute home page, World Wide Web, (http://www.cei.org/about.html).

CEI. 1996d. 'Mandatory Recycling, Environmental Briefing Book for Congressional Candidates', Competitive Enterprise Institute, World Wide Web, (http://www.cei.org/ebb14.html).

CEI. 1996e. 'Risk Assessment, Environmental Briefing Book for Congressional Candidates', Competitive Enterprise Institute, World Wide Web.

CEI. 1996f. 'Free Market Environmental Vision', Competitive Enterprise Institute, World Wide Web, (http://www.cei.org/fme.html).

Chlorophiles. 1996a. 'Who are the Chlorophiles?', World Wide Web, 8 September.

Chlorophiles. 1996b. 'Chlorine and Cancer', World Wide Web, 17 August.

Chlorophiles. 1996c. 'Chlorine and Hormonal Changes', World Wide Web, 1 September.

Chomsky, Noam. 1989. *Necessary Illusions: Thought Control in Democratic Societies*, Pluto Press, London.

Chomsky, Noam. 1995. Letter from Noam Chomsky. CAQ 52 (Fall).

CIS (Centre for Independent Studies, The). 1995. Publications. World Wide Web (http://www.cis.org.au/bklist.html).

Citizen's Clearinghouse for Hazardous Waste. 1995a. *Congressional Dioxin Hearings*, Citizen's Clearinghouse for Hazardous Waste.

Citizen's Clearinghouse for Hazardous Waste. 1995b. *PAC Money*, Citizen's Clearinghouse for Hazardous Waste.

Clapp, Richard, Peter deFur, Ellen Silbergeld and Peter Washburn. 1995. 'EPA on Right Track', *Environmental Science and Technology* 29 (1):29A-30A.

CLEAR. 1996. 'Clearing the Air with Burson-Marsteller', *Earth First!*, August/September, 18.

Cockett, Richard. 1994. *Thinking the Unthinkable: Think-Tanks and the Economic Counter-Revolution 1931-1983*, Harper Collins.

Coeyman, Marjorie. 1994. 'P&G reformulates away from STPP', *Chemical Week* 154 (2):12.

Cohen, Jeff. 1989. 'Propaganda from the Middle of the Road: The Centrist Ideology of the News Media', *Extra!*, October/November.

Cohen, Jeff, and Norman Solomon. 1995. *Through the Media Looking Glass: Decoding Bias and Blather in the News*, Common Courage Press, Monroe, Maine.

Cole-Adams, Kate. 1993. 'Soft Sell Goes to School', *Time Australia* 8 (46):52-55.

Colford, Steven W. 1994. 'Fade-out for green?', *Advertising Age*, 5 December, 1, 8.

Collins, Clark. 1995. 'Off Highway Vehicle Enthusiast Input Needed on Endangered Species Act (ESA) Re-authorization', BlueRibbon Coalition - World Wide Web.

Commoner, Barry. 1988. 'Acceptable Risks: Who Decides?', *Harpers Magazine* 276 (1656):28-32.

Commonwealth Government of Australia. 1990. *Ecologically Sustainable Development: A Commonwealth Discussion Paper*, Australian Government Printing Service, Canberra.

Connell, Jennifer. 1994. 'Parents and Teachers Slice Schools' Pizza Cash Scheme', *Sydney Morning*

Herald, 16 November, 7.
Connolly, Paul. 1995. 'Think tanks chide AGA for petitioning against DOE's demise', *The Oil Daily* 45 (63):4.
Connor, Desmond M. 1994. *Preventing and Resolving Public Controversy*, Connor Development Services, Victoria, BC, Canada.
Cooper, Mario H. 1993-4. 'Winning in Washington: From Grasstops to Grassroots', *Public Relations Quarterly* 38 (4):13-15.
Coppolino, Eric F. 1994. 'Dioxin Critic Sued', *Lies Of Our Times*, May, 23-24.
Coppolino, Eric F., and Paul Rauber. 1994. 'Pandora's Poison', *Sierra* 79 (5):40-45+.
Cordtz, Dan. 1994. 'Green Hell: foes of environmental rules are starting to fight back, and they're winning a few skirmishes', *Financial World* 163 (2):38-42.
Costantini, Edmond, and Mary Paul Nash. 1991. 'SLAPP/SLAPPback: The Misuse of Libel Law for Political Purposes and a Countersuit Response', *Journal of Law and Politics* VII:417-478.
Coulter, Jane. 1995. *Who profits from public education? An internal audit of private provision of services to public education*, Public Sector Research Centre, University of NS, Sydney.
Council, Chlorine Chemistry *see* CCC.
Cox, Hank. 1995. 'Powerful agencies join endangered species list', *Insight on the News* 11 (29):15-17.
Cox, Rory. 1994. 'Ketchum if you can-Cloroz versus Greenpeace', *Propaganda Review* (11):34.
Crane, Edward H. 1995. The Cato Institute, home page on the World Wide Web, (http://www.cato.org/people/crane.html).
Croteau, David, William Hoynes, and Kevin Carragee. 1993. 'Public Television & the Missing Public', *Extra!*, Sept/Oct, 6-14.
Crowley, Chris. 1992. 'With Environmental Opposition to Projects, Fight Fire with Fire', *Oil & Gas Journal* 90 (31):30-31.
CUES. 1995. *Captive Kids: Commercial Pressures on Kids at School*, Consumers Union Education Services, New York.
Cullton, Barbara J. 1991. 'US government orders new look at dioxin', *Nature* 352 (29 August):753.

Dadd, Debra Lynn, and Andre Carothers. 1990. 'A bill of goods?', *Greenpeace* 15 (3):8-12.
Davidson, Kenneth. 1992. 'Defrocking the Priests', in *The Trouble with Economic Rationalism*, edited by D. Horne, Scribe Publications, Newham, Victoria.
Davis, Cameron, and David White. 1994. 'The Unslapped: A Primer for Protecting You and Your Affiliate Against SLAPP Suits', elaw.public.interest, January 26.
Day, Charles R. 1994. 'Stop talkin' (and showin') trash', *Industry Week* 243 (3):7.
Deal, Carl. 1993. *The Greenpeace Guide to Anti-Environmental Organisations*, Odonian Press, Berkeley, California.
deButts, C. Read. 1995. 'In defense of grassroots lobbying', *Campaigns & Elections* 16 (11):67, 75.
Delwiche, Aaron. 1995a. 'Why Think About Propaganda', Institute for Propaganda Analysis, World Wide Web, (http://carmen.artsci.washington.edu/propaganda/home.htm).
Delwiche, Aaron. 1995b. 'Propaganda Techniques', Institute for Propaganda Analysis, World Wide Web (http://carmen.artsci.washington.edu/propaganda/home.htm).
Delwiche, Aaron. 1995c. 'Examples: How Newt Gingrich Uses These Techniques', Institute for Propaganda Analysis, World Wide Web (http://carmen.artsci.washington.edu/propaganda/home.htm).
Desai, R. 1994. 'Second-Hand Dealers in Ideas: Think-Tanks and Thatcherite Hegemony', *New Left Review* 203 (Jan-Feb):27-64.
Diamond, Sara. 1991. 'Free Market Environmentalism', *Z Magazine* (December):54.
Dillon, John. 1993. 'PR giant Burson-Marsteller thinks global, acts local: Poisoning the Grassroots', *CovertAction* (44):34-38.
Dixon, Catherine. 1993. 'Tree Power Grows On', *Public Power* 51 (5):50-51.
Doern, G.Bruce, and Thomas Conway. 1994. *The Greening of Canada: Federal Institutions and Decisions*, University of Toronto Press, Toronto.
Dold, Catherine. 1992. 'SLAPP Back!', *Buzzworm: The Environmental Journal* IV (4):34-36.
Dolny, Michael. 1996. 'The think tank spectrum: for the media, some thinkers are more equal than others', *Extra!*, May/June, 21.
Domhoff, G. William. 1985. 'The Power Elite and Government' in *Taking Sides: Clashing Views on Controversial Political Issues*, edited by G. McKenna and S. Feingold, Dushkin Publishing

Group, Guildford, Connecticut.

Dowie, Mark. 1994. 'Saving Face: Could Public Relations have Rescued Exxon's Image', *Propaganda Review* (11):32-34.

Dowie, Mark. 1995. 'Introduction: Torches of Liberty', in *Toxic Sludge is Good For You! Lies, Damn Lies and the Public Relations Industry*, edited by J. Stauber and S. Rampton, Common Courage Press, Monroe, Maine.

Drew, Elizabeth. 1983. *Politics and Money: The New Road to Corruption*, MacMillan Publishing Company, New York.

Dumanoski, Dianne. 1994. 'Mudslinging on the Earth-beat', *The Amicus Journal* 15 (4):40-41.

Dunlap, Riley E., George H. Gallup Jr, and Alec M. Gallup. 1993. 'Of Global Concern: Results of the Health of the Planet Survey', *Environment* 35 (9):6-15, 33-39.

Durning, Alan Thein. 1992. *How Much is Enough: The Consumer Society and the Future of the Earth*, edited by L. Starke, Worldwatch Environmental Alert Series, Earthscan, London.

Durning, Alan Thein. 1993a. 'Can't live without it', *World Watch* 6 (3):10-18.

Durning, Alan Thein. 1993b. 'Long on things, short on time', *Sierra* 78 (1):60-67.

Earth First! 1996. 'ABC is spreading lies', *E-Link*, 10 April.

Echeverria, John. 1995. 'The Takings Issue', in *Let the People Judge*, edited by J. D. Echeverria and R. B. Eby, Island Press, Washington DC.

Echeverria, John D., and Raymond Booth Eby, eds. 1995. *Let the People Judge: Wise Use and the Private Property Rights Movement*, Island Press, Washington DC.

Eckersley, Robyn, ed. 1995. *Markets, the State and the Environment: Towards Integration*, MacMillan Education, South Melbourne.

Editors. 1994. 'What are kids learning?', *Environmental Action*, Spring, 18.

Elliott, Stuart. 1996. 'Advertising: Consistency is not a hobgoblin', *The New York Times*, 6 February, 21.

Ellwood, Wayne. 1990. 'Scandal!', *New Internationalist*, January, 19.

Ely-Lawrence, Deborah. 1994. 'Writing classroom materials that make the grade', *Public Relations Journal*, April, 26.

Englebeen, Ferdinand. 1996. 'Chlorophile Activities', Chlorophiles, World Wide Web, 29 August.

Entman, Robert M. 1989. *Democracy Without Citizens: Media and the Decay of American Politics*, Oxford University Press, New York.

Environ Dioxin Risk Characterization Expert Panel. 1995. 'EPA Assessment Not Justified', *Environmental Science & Technology* 29 (1):31A-32A.

Epley, Joe S. 1992. 'Public relations in the global village: an American perspective', *Public Relations Review* 18 (2):109-116.

Epstein, Robin. 1995. 'Flaks in Green Clothing: "Ecology Channel" Tied to Polluters' PR Firm', *Extra!*, January/February, 10-11.

Ettore, Barbara. 1992. 'Are we headed for a recycling backlash?', *Management Review* 81 (6):14-17.

Ewen, Stuart. 1976. *Captains of Consciousness: Advertising and the Social Roots of the Consumer Culture*, McGraw-Hill, New York.

FAIR. 1991. 'GE Irrelevancies', *Extra!*, January/February, 4.

Fairlie, Simon. 1993. 'SLAPPs Come to Britain', *The Ecologist* 23 (5):165.

Fallows, James. 1996a. 'Why You Hate Us', *Newsweek* 127 (Jan 29):62-65.

Fallows, James. 1996b. *Breaking the News: How the Media Undermine American Democracy*, Pantheon Books, New York.

Fan, Aliza. 1995. 'Energy Department makes as much sense as 'sporting goods agency,' speaker says', *The Oil Daily* 45 (10):7.

Fattah, Hassan, and David Hunter. 1996. 'Responsible Care goes to school, emphasising educational outreach', *Chemical Week* 158 (July 3):71-2.

Faucheux, Ron. 1995. 'The Grassroots Explosion', *Campaigns & Elections* 16 (1):20-30, 53-58.

Feulner, Edwin J. 1995. 'Global Warming', *National Review* 47 (23):87-90.

Fitzgerald, Nora. 1996. 'Watching the Kids: the Internet opens a new front in the battle over children's ads', *ADWEEK* Eastern Edition 37 (May 6):26-7.

Fleming, Charles A. 1995. 'Understanding Propaganda from a General Semantics Perspective', *Etc.* 52 (1):2-12.

Flynn, John M. 1993. 'European site inspection opens dialogue among wary stakeholders', *Public Relations Journal* 49 (5):26-28.

Fox, Roy F. 1995. 'Manipulated kids: teens tell how ads influence them', *Educational Leadership* 53 (1):77-79.
Fram, Eugene H., S. Prakash Sethi and Nobuaki Namiki. 1993. 'Newspaper advocacy advertising', *USA Today* 122 (July):90-92.
France, David. 1996. 'This lesson is brought to you by...' *Good Housekeeping*, February, 80-83.
Franklin, Bob. 1994. *Packaging Politics: Political Communications in Britain's Media Democracy,* Edward Arnold. London.
Fried, John J. 1994. 'Ongoing Corporate Polluters Flood Schools with Environmental Lesson Aids', *Knight-Ridder/Tribune Business News*, 28 March.
Friedman, S. M., and C. Rogers, eds. 1986. *Scientists and Journalists,* Free Press, New York.
Frith, Stephen. 1996. 'What's the Problem?', in *Innocent Advertising? Corporate Sponsorship in Australian Schools,* edited by T. Newlands and S. Frith, New College Institute for Values Research, University of NSW, Sydney.
Feulner, Edwin Jr. 1995. home page, World Wide Web, (http://www.heritage.org/heritage/staff/feulner.html).
Fumento, Michael. 1993 *Science Under Siege: Balancing Technology and the Environment,* William Morrow and Co., New York.

Gamson, William A., David Croteau, William Hoynes and Theodore Sasson. 1992. 'Media Images and the Social Construction of Reality', *Annual Review of Sociology* 18:373-93.
Garcia, Shelly. 1990. 'When it comes to green media, ad rules are gray', *ADWEEK Western Advertising News* 40 (39):16.
Gardner, James N. 1991. 'Loybbing, European-Style', *Europe*, November, 29-30.
Gellner, Winand. 1995. 'The Politics of Policy "Political Think Tanks" and their Markets in the U.S.-Institutional Environment', *Presidential Studies Quarterly* 25 (3):497-510.
Georges, Christopher. 1995. 'Conservative Heritage Foundation finds recipe for influence: ideas plus marketing equal clout', *Wall Street Journal,* August 10, 10.
Gergen, David R. 1996. 'And now, the fifth estate?', *U.S. News & World Report* 120 (17):84.
Gersh, Debra. 1992. 'Covering solid waste issues', *Editor & Publisher* 125 (August 29):15-16.
Gibbons, Ann. 1993. 'Dioxin Tied to Endometriosis', *Science* 262 (26 November):1373.
Gibbs, Lois Marie, and The Citizens Clearinghouse for Hazardous Waste. 1995. *Dying from Dioxin*, South End Press, Boston, MA.
Gilchrist, Gavin. 1995. 'Secret Strategy Undermines Greenhouse Fight', *Sydney Morning Herald,* 7 August, 1.
Gismondi, Michael, Joan Sherman, Joan Richardson and Mary Richardson. 1996. 'Goldfish, Horse Logging, Jock Talk, and Star Wars: Debunking Industry's Green PR', *Alternatives Journal,* Fall.
Gitlin, Todd. 1980. *The Whole World is Watching: Mass Media in the Making and Unmaking of the New Left,* University of California Press, Berkeley.
Gleick, Elizabeth. 1996. 'Blackboards as billboards', *Time* 147 (24):68.
Glover, Richard. 1993. 'Blink and You'll Miss it', *Sydney Morning Herald,* 7 August, 40.
Gold, Philip. 1994. 'Just say no to infotainment', *Insight on the News* 10 (28):37-8.
Goldberg, Kim. 1992/3. 'SLAPPs Surge North: Canadian Activists Under Attack', *The New Catalyst,* Winter, 1-3.
Goldberg, Kim. 1993. 'Axed', *This Magazine* XXVII (August).
Goldberg, Kim. 1994. 'More wise use abuse', *Canadian Dimension* 28 (3):27.
Goldin, Greg, and Jim Motavalli. 1995. 'Is TV Going Green?', *E: The Environmental Magazine* 6 (1):36-41.
Gomery, Douglas. 1996. 'A Very High-Impact Player', *American Journalism Review,* July/August, 52.
Goodell, Rae. 1987. 'The role of the mass media in scientific controversy', in *Scientific Controversies: Case Studies in the Resolution and Closure of Disputes in Science and Technology,* edited by H. T. Engelhardt and A. L. Caplan, Cambridge University Press, Cambridge.
Goodin, Robert. 1992. 'The ethics of selling environmental indulgences', paper read at Australasian Philosophical Association Annual Conference, July, at University of Queensland.
Gopsill, Tim. 1995. 'Even Stephen says it's all up for grabs', *Journalist* (June/July):14-15.
Gorman, Christine. 1991. 'The Double Take on Dioxin', *Time*, 26 August, 52.
Gottlieb, Alan, ed. 1989. *The Wise Use Agenda: The Citizen's Policy Guide to Environmental Resource Issues,* The Free Enterprise Press, Bellevue.
Greenberg, Keith Elliot. 1993a. 'Practitioners pick top environmental trends of 90s', *Public*

Relations Journal 49 (4):7.

Greenberg, Keith Elliot. 1993b. 'The Impact of a "Greener" White House', *Public Relations Journal* 49 (4):6, 10.

Greenberg, Keith Elliot. 1994a. 'Clinton's "green" agenda still taking shape', *Public Relations Journal*, April, 6.

Greenberg, Keith Elliot. 1994b. 'Video releases with a twist make news', *Public Relations Journal* 50 (7):22-24.

Greenpeace. 1994. *The Things you need to know about Ron Arnold and the "Wise Use" Movement*, Greenpeace Fact Sheet, GreenDisk 3 (3).

Grefe, Edward A., and Marty Linsky. 1995. *The New Corporate Activism: Harnessing the Power of Grassroots Tactics for Your Organization*, McGraw-Hill, New York.

Greider, William. 1992. *Who Will Tell the People: The Betrayal of American Democracy*, Simon & Schuster, New York.

Greider, William. 1993. 'Grassroots organizing, PR-style: Democracy for Hire', *PR Watch* 1 (1):8-9.

Gribble, Gordon. 1996. *The Future of Chlorine*, Heartland Institute.

Grossman, Karl. 1992. 'Survey Says: Newspapers Boost Nukes', *Extra!*, March, 14.

Grossman, Karl. 1993. 'Three Mile Island: "They Say Nothing Happened"', *Extra!*, July/August, 6-7.

Grumbine, R. Edward. 1994. 'Wildness, Wise Use, and Sustainable Development', *Environmental Ethics*, Fall, 227-249.

Gunther, Marc. 1995. 'All in the Family', *American Journalism Review*, October, 37-41.

Gutin, JoAnn. 1992. 'Plastics-A-Go-Go', *Mother Jones* 17 (2):56-59.

Hallahan, Kirk. 1994. 'Public relations and the circumvention of the press', *Public Relations Quarterly* 39 (2):17-19.

Harding, Thomas. 1993. 'Mocking the Turtle', *New Statesman & Society* 6 (271):45-48.

Harris, James. 1992. 'Working with environmental groups', *Public Relations Journal*, May, 24-25.

Harrison, Bruce. 1991. 'Plowing new ground in environmental affairs', *Public Relations Journal*, April, 32-33.

Harrison, E. Bruce. 1993. *Going Green: How to Communicate Your Company's Environmental Commitment*, Business One Irwin, Homewood, IL.

Harrison, Kathryn, and George Hoberg. 1991. 'Setting the Environmental Agenda in Canada and the United States: The Cases of Dioxin and Radon', *Canadian Journal of Political Science* XXIV (1):3-27.

Harwood, Richard. 1995. 'Are Journalists Elitist?', *American Journalism Review*, June, 27-29.

Hawken, Paul. 1992. 'The Ecology of Commerce', *Inc* 14 (4):93-100.

Hay, Alistair. 1989. 'Dioxins in the dock', *Nature* 340 (3 August):353.

Hay, H. 1996. *Procter & Gamble - Company Report*, Prudential Securities Inc., Ohio.

Hecht, Jeff. 1996. 'Triumph of dogma over reason', *New Scientist*, 27 January, 49.

Heller, Karen. 1991. 'Reaching the public', *Chemical Week* 149 (December 11):26-7.

Helvarg, David. 1994a. *The War Against the Greens: The "Wise-Use" Movement, the New Right, and Anti-Environmental Violence*, Sierra Club Books, San Francisco.

Helvarg, David. 1994b. 'Anti-Enviros are Getting Uglier', *The Nation*, November 28, 646-651.

Helvarg, David. 1994c. 'Grassroots for sale: the inside scoop on (un)Wise Use', *Amicus* 16 (3):24-29.

Helvarg, David. 1995. 'Red Herrings of the Wise Use Movement', *The Progressive*, November, 18-20.

Hightower, Jim. 1995. 'Get the hogs out of the creek!', *Earth Island Journal* 11 (1):32.

Hileman, Bette. 1993. 'Plan to prevent climate change pleases industry', *Chemical & Engineering News* 71 (11):6.

Himmelstein, Jerome L. 1990. *To the Right: The Transformation of American Conservatism*, University of California Press, Berkeley.

Hoare, Brent. 1993. *SLAPP Suits: Silencing the Opponents of Destruction*, World Rainforest Report 25:10-11.

Hoggart, Simon. 1995. 'Filleted Fish', *New Statesman & Society*, 24 March, 20-21.

Holzinger, Albert G. 1994. 'Thriving on Challenges', *Nations Business* 82 (4):51-52.

Hood, John. 1995a. 'How green was my balance sheet: The environmental benefits of capitalism', *Policy Review*, Fall.

Hood, John. 1995b. 'Send in the Tanks', *National Review* 47 (23):80-81.

Houk, Vernon N. 1992. 'Dioxin', *Consumers' Research*, February, 13-15.
Howlett, C. T. 1995. 'Chlorine: Basic Benefits, Universal Uses', paper read at United Nations Economic Commission for Europe Working Party on the Chemical Industry, September 27, at Geneva.
Howlett, C. T. 1995. 'Chlorine: The Issue, the Reality and the Solution', paper read at American Chemical Society, August 22, at Chicago, Illinois.
Hunter, David. 1991. 'Turning the touchstone to gold', *Chemical Week* 149 (20):4.
Husseini, Sam. 1994. 'Felons on the Air: Does GE's Ownership of NBC Violate the Law?', *Extra!*, November/December, 12.
Hutchings, Vicky. 1990. 'Being Prepared', *New Statesman & Society*, 24 August, 12-13.
Hyde, John. 1991. 'Politicising the Environment', paper read at Reconciling Economics and the Environment, 3 September, at Sydney.
Hynes, Patricia H. 1991. 'The race to save the planet: will women lose?', *Women's Studies International Forum* 14 (5):473-8.

Irvine, Sandy. 1989. 'Consuming fashions? The limits of green consumerism', *The Ecologist* 19 (3):88-93.
Irvine, Ross. 1993. 'How to use communications technology to compete with radical environmentalists', paper read at 1993 Wise Use Conference, July 25, at Reno, Nevada.
Isles, Jacqueline. 1989. 'Corporations in the Classroom', *Consuming Interest* 42 (October):7-14.

Jacobs, Michael. 1993. 'Economic instruments: objectives or tools?', paper read at 1993 Environmental Economics Conference, November, at Canberra.
Jacobson, Louis. 1995. 'Tanks on the Roll', *National Journal*, July 8, 1767-1771.
Jacobson, Michael F., and Laurie Ann Mazur. 1995. *Marketing Madness*, Westview Press, Boulder, Colorado.
James, Simon. 1993. 'The Idea Brokers: The Impact of Think Tanks on British Government', *Public Administration* 71 (Winter):491-506.
Jamieson, Robert, and Ray Plibersek. 1991. 'Legal Rights of Industry Against Conservationists', paper read at Third Annual Pollution Law Conference, at Sydney 28-29 October and Melbourne 30-31 October 1991.
Jenkins, Jolyon. 1990. 'Who's the Greenest?', *New Statesman & Society*, 17 August, 18-20.
Johnson, David. 1993. 'The Canadian Regulatory System and Corporatism: Empirical Findings and Analytical Implications', *Canadian Journal of Law and Society* 8 (1):95-120.
Johnson, Jeff. 1995. 'Dioxin Risk: Are We Sure Yet?', *Environmental Science & Technology* 29 (1):24A-25A.
Johnson, Tamara. 1993. 'The workers' environmental story', *American Metal Market* 101 (228):14.
Joint Taskforce on Intractable Waste. 1989. *Phase 2 Report*, Joint Taskforce on Intractable Waste.
Josephs, Ray, and Juanita W. Josephs. 1994. 'Public Relations, the U.K. Way', *Public Relations Journal* 50 (4):14-18.
Jost, Kenneth. 1994. 'Talk show democracy: are call-in programs good for the political system', *CQ Researcher* 4 (16):363-380.

Kalish, David E. 1994. 'P&G's lessons on environment provoke criticism', *Marketing News* 28 (6):7.
Kaplan, Sheila. 1994. 'Lobby-PR giant makes hay from client 'cross-pollination': Porter/Novelli plays all sides', *PR Watch* 1 (2):4-7.
Karey, Gerald. 1995. 'Regulation and the Environment', *Platt's Oilgram News* 73 (237):3.
Karpatkin, Rhoda H., and Anita Holmes. 1995. 'Making schools ad-free zones', *Educational Leadership* 53 (1):72-76.
Katz, Jeffrey L. 1992. 'The Conservative Idea Machine', *Governing*, February, 51-55.
Katz, David M. 1993. 'Press role eyed for pollution consultants', *Cash Flow* 97 (20):1, 49.
Kazman, Sam. 1995. 'Public Interest Group Calls for Congress to Recognize the Risky Nature of Government Risk Regulation', CEI Press Release, 13 March.
Keim, Gerald D. 1996. 'Strategic grassroots: Developing influence', *Electric Perspectives* 21 (2):16-23+.
Keim, Stephen. 1994. 'Dealing with SLAPP Suits', *Australian Environmental Law News* 2 (June):42-48.
Kellman, S. 1983. 'Economic incentives and environmental policy: Politics, ideology, and

philosophy', in *Incentives for Environmental Protection*, edited by T. Schelling, MIT Press, Cambridge, Mass.

Kellner, Douglas. 1990. *Television and the Crisis of Democracy*, Westview Press, Boulder, Colorado.

Kellner, Juliet. 1990. 'Beware the green con', *New Internationalist*, Jan, 18-20.

Kiernan, Vincent. 1995. 'Leave ozone hole to nature, say Republicans', *New Scientist*, 30 September, 8.

Kiley, David. 1991. 'EPA charged with gutting report; P&G and Scott lend a helping hand for a government manual', *Adweek's Marketing Week* 32 (July 8):6.

King, Michael. 1996. 'The Chemical Industry and the TNRCC Lay Siege to Texas Moms', *The Texas Observer*, 26 January.

Kinsley, Michael. 1993. 'The Envelope, Please', *The New Republic* 209 (12-13):6, 57.

Knaus, Holley. 1992. 'The Commercialized Classroom', *Multinational Monitor*, March, 14-16.

Knoll, Erwin. 1993. 'Conflict of Interest', *The Progressive* 57 (3):4.

Knox, Margaret. 1993. 'The World According to Cushman', *Wilderness*, Spring, 28-31, 36.

Koeppel, Dan. 1989. 'P&G's "environmental lobby" hits the halls of Congress', *Adweek's Marketing Week* 30 (November 27):53.

Kohler, Alan. 1997. 'It's a hairy ride on the superhighway', *Sydney Morning Herald*, 18 January.

Kozol, Jonothan. 1993. 'The sharks move in', *New Internationalist*, October, 8-10.

Kriz, Margaret. 1995. 'Land Mine', in *Let the People Judge*, edited by J. D. Echeverria and R. B. Eby, Island Press, Washington DC.

Kuipers, Dean. 1994. 'The Gambler's Summit: At a Wise Use conference in Reno, Nevada', *Propaganda Review* (11):16-21, 63.

Kurtz, Howard. 1993. *Media Circus: The Trouble with America's Newspapers*, Times Books, New York.

Kurtz, Howard. 1996. *Hot Air: All Talk, All the Time*, Random House, New York.

Kwittken, Aaron Renner. 1994. 'Planning proactive corporate environmental communications', *Public Relations Journal*, April, 27.

LaCovey, A. Joseph. 1991. 'Business Changes Its Ways', *Public Relations Journal*, April, 23.

Lamont, Leonie. 1996. 'Challenge to children's advertising', *Sydney Morning Herald*, 28 May, 2.

Landler, Mark, and Richard A. Melcher. 1991. 'The PR Problem at Hill & Knowlton', *Business Week* 3229 (2 September):50.

Landry, B. L. 1996. *Procter & Gamble - Company Report*, Morgan Stanley & Co. Inc., Ohio, Switzerland.

Lanouette, William. 1991. 'Painting themselves green', *The Bulletin of the Atomic Scientists*. 4.

Lapp, David. 1991. 'Defenders of Dioxin: The Corporate Campaign to Rehabilitate Dioxin', *Multinational Monitor*, October, 8-12.

Lapp, David. 1993. 'Wise Use's Labor Ruse', *Environmental Action*, Fall, 23-26.

Lapp, David. 1994. 'Private Gain, Public Loss', *Environmental Action*, Spring, 14-17.

Latham, Valerie. 1991. 'Green group tears into P&G's paper nappy claims', *Marketing*, 25 July, 6.

Latham, Valerie. 1992. 'ASA chides P&G over green nappy claims', *Marketing* (March 19):7.

Lavelle, Marianne. 1995. 'The "Property Rights" Revolt: Environmentalists Fret as States Pass Reagan-Style Takings Laws', in *Let the People Judge*, edited by J. D. Echeverria and R. B. Eby, Island Press, Washington, DC.

Lazare, Daniel. 1991. 'Press Ignores the Obvious in U.S. Energy Policy', *Extra!*, May/June, 4.

Leamy, Ben. 1995. 'Boycott Procter & Gamble', Uncaged, World Wide Web.

Lee, Alfred McClung, and Elizabeth Briant Lee. 1995. 'The iconography of propaganda analysis', *Etc.* 52 (1):13-17.

Lee, Martin A., and Norman Solomon. 1990. *Unreliable Sources: A Guide to Detecting Bias in News Media*, Carol Publishing Group, New York.

Leo, John. 1995. 'A lovely day for haranguing', *US News & World Report*, November 13, 33.

Lesly, Philip. 1992. 'Coping with Opposition Groups', *Public Relations Review* 18 (4):325-334.

Letto, Jay. 1995. 'TV Lets Corporations Pull Green Wool Over Viewers' Eyes', *Extra!*, July/August, 21-24.

Levathes, Louise. 1995. 'Easy Money: How Congressional Candidates are Cleaning up with the Dirty Water PACs', *Audubon*, Nov/Dec, 16-22.

Levy, Mark R. 1992. 'Learning from Television News', in *The Future of News: Television-Newspapers-Wire Services-Newsmagazines*, edited by P. S. Cook, D. Gomery and L. W. Lichty, The Woodrow Wilson Center Press, Washington, D.C.

Lewis, Charles, and Margaret Ebrahim. 1993. 'Can Mexico and Big Business USA Buy Nafta?',

The Nation 256 (January 4/11):826-839.
Lewis, Daniel and Deborah Cornwall. 1993. 'Trial of Greens "Risk to Rights"', oz.green, 12 July 1993.
Lewis, Julie. 1994. 'Profit Seen in Poor Schools', *Sydney Morning Herald*, 1 November, 10.
Lichter, S. Robert, and Richard E. Noyes. 1995. *Good Intentions Make Bad News: Why Americans Hate Campaign Journalism*, Rowman & Littlefield, Lanham, Maryland.
Lieberman, Ben. 1996. 'The High Cost of Cool: The Economic Impact of CFC Phaseout', Competitive Enterprise Institute, World Wide Web, (http://www.cei.org/cfcsum.html).
Lindheim, James. 1989. 'Restoring the Image of the Chemical Industry', *Chemistry and Industry* 15 (7 August):491-494.
Lindsay, Greg. 1995. The Centre for Independent Studies, home page, World Wide Web, (http://www.cis.org.au/oldindex.html).
Lippin, Tobi. 1991. 'Uncivil Suits', *Technology Review* 94 (3):14-15.
Littwin, Angela. 1995. 'The Interconnected World of the Cable Oligopoly', *Extra!*, Nov/Dec, 14-15.
Lord, Michael D. 1995. 'An agency theory assessment of the influence of grassroots political activism', *Academy of Management Journal*, Best papers Proceedings, 396-400.
Ludford, Lowell F. 1991. '3P program pays off in costs savings of $500 million for 3M', *Public Relations Journal* 47 (4):20-21.
Lyall, Sarah. 1996. 'Britain's Big 'McLibel Trial' (It's McEndless, Too)', *New York Times*, 28 November.
Lyman, Francesca. 1994. 'Mudslinging on the Earth-beat', *The Amicus Journal* 15 (4):39.

M.C, and L.C.S. 1990. 'TV's Favorite Think Tanks. Expertise: Self-Promotion', *Mother Jones*, Feb/March, 26-27.
Macken, Deirdre. 1990. 'It's not easy being green', *Sydney Morning Herald*, 14 September, 37-42.
Macken, Deirdre. 1996. 'Full Circle: The Conversion of Paul Gilding', *Sydney Morning Herald*, 8 June, 51-52.
Maggrett, Dick. 1995. 'Anti-dioxin activists fight effort to slow ban on use', *The Stars and Stripes*.
Makower, Joel. 1996. 'Just the facts', *E: the Environmental Magazine* 7 (2):48, 50.
Malcom, Noel. 1991. 'The clever Tories who are far too clever to have any new ideas', *The Spectator*, 21 September, 6.
Malkin, Michelle, and Michael Fumento. 1995. 'Rachel's Folly: The End of Chlorine', CEI Environmental Studies Program.
Mandese, Joe. 1995. 'Talk show stalwart P&G pans "trash"', *Advertising Age*, November 20, 1, 8.
Manilov, Marianne. 1994. 'Whittling Away Students' Education', *Environmental Action*, Spring, 17-19.
Marlow, Eugene M. 1994. 'Sophisticated "news" videos gain wide acceptance', *Public Relations Journal* 50 (7):15-21.
Marr, David. 1996. 'It's legal, but is it moral?', *Sydney Morning Herald*, 21 December.
Martin, Brian et al, eds. 1986. *Intellectual Suppression: Australian Case Histories, Analysis and Responses*, Angus and Robertson, North Ryde.
Martínez, Elizabeth, and Louis Head. 1992. 'Media White-Out of Environmental Racism', *Extra!*, July/August, 29-31.
Maughan, Ralph, and Douglas Nilson. 1994. *What's Old and What's New About the Wise Use Movement*, GreenDisk 3 (3).
Mazur, Laurie Ann. 1996. 'Marketing Madness', *E Magazine* 7 (May-June):36-41.
Mazza, David, and Craig Beneville. 1994. 'Takings: The latest arrow in the Wise Use quiver', *Earth First!*, Yule, 27.
MBD. 1994. 'MBD Update and Analysis', *PR Watch* 3 (2):5-7.
McIntosh, Philip. 1990. 'Most prepared to put environment ahead of growth', *Sydney Morning Herald*, 15 June.
McNair, Brian. 1994. *News and Journalism in the UK*, Routledge, London and New York.
Megalli, Mark, and Andy Friedman. 1991. *Masks of Deception: Corporate Front Groups in America*, Essential Information.
Mellow, Craig. 1989. 'Remaking PR's Image', *Across the Board* 26 (7):33-39.
Middleton, Kent R. 1991. 'Advocacy advertising, the First Amendment, and competitive advantage: a comment on Cutler & Muehling', *Journal of Advertising* 20 (2):77-81.
Midgley, Carol. 1996. 'Trial That's Made A Meal of It', *The Times*, 13 December.
Miller, Mark Crispin. 1995. 'Demonopolize Them! A Call for a Broad-Based Movement Against

the Media Trust', *Extra!*, Nov/Dec, 9-11.

Miller, G. Tyler. 1996. *Living in the Environment*, 9th ed. Wadsworth, Boulder.

Mirabelle. 1993. 'Multinationals Get SLAPP-Happy: Strategic Lawsuits Against Public Participation', *Earth First!*, Lughnasadh.

Mizerski, Richard. 1995. 'The relationship between cartoon trade character recognition and attitude toward product category in young children', *Journal of Marketing* 59 (4):58-70.

Mobil. 1996a. 'Energy and Earth Day: an oxymoron no more', *New York Times*, 25 April.

Mobil. 1996b. 'Car Crazy: A Hard Habit to Break', Mobil Home Page, World Wide Web, 25 January, http://www.mobil.com.

Mobil. 1996c. 'Climate Change: We're all in this together', Mobil Home Page, World Wide Web, 5 August, http://www.mobil.com.

Molnar, Alex. 1995. 'Schooled for Profit', *Educational Leadership* 53 (1):70-71.

Mongoven, Jack. 1994. 'Memorandum', PR Watch 3 (2):8-9.

Monks, Vicki. 1993. 'See no evil', *American Journalism Review* 15 (5):18-25.

Montague, Peter. 1990a. 'Dioxins and Cancer: Fraudulent Studies', *Rachel's Hazardous Waste News* (171).

Montague, Peter. 1990b. 'Report Links Herbicide Exposure to Illness Among Vietnam Vets', *Rachel's Hazardous Waste News* (212).

Montague, Peter. 1991a. 'A Tale of Science and Industry', *Rachel's Hazardous Waste News* (248).

Montague, Peter. 1991b. 'Dioxin Dangers - What's Going On?', *Rachel's Hazardous Waste News* (249).

Montague, Peter. 1992a. 'EPA's Dioxin Reassessment - Part 1', *Rachel's Hazardous Waste News* (269).

Montague, Peter. 1992b. 'Young Male Rats are 'Demasculinized' and 'Feminized' by Low Doses of Dioxin', *Rachel's Hazardous Waste News* (290).

Montague, Peter. 1993. 'PR firms for hire to undermine democracy', *Rachel's Hazardous Waste News* (361).

Montague, Peter. 1994a. Turning Point for the Chemical Industry. Rachel's Hazardous Waste News (405).

Montague, Peter. 1994b. 'Dioxin Reassessed - Part 1', *Rachel's Hazardous Waste News* (390).

Montague, Peter. 1995a. 'Ignorance is Strength', *Rachel's Environment & Health Weekly* (467).

Montague, Peter. 1995b. 'Dioxin Inquisition', *Rachel's Hazardous Waste News* (457).

Montague, Peter. 1995c. 'Dioxin and Health', *Rachel's Hazardous Waste News* (463).

Montague, Peter. 1996a. 'How They Lie, Part 1', *Rachel's Hazardous Waste News* (503).

Montague, Peter. 1996b. 'Bill Gaffey's Work', *Rachel's Hazardous Waste News* (494).

Montague, Peter. 1996c. 'Chemical Industry Strategies, Part 1', *Rachel's Hazardous Waste News* (495).

Montague, Peter. 1996d. 'Chemical Industry Strategies, Part 2', *Rachel's Hazardous Waste News* (496).

Montague, Peter. 1996e. 'Dangers of Chemical Combinations', *Rachel's Hazardous Waste News* (498).

Montague, Peter. 1996f. 'Our Stolen Future - Part 1', *Rachel's Hazardous Waste News* (486).

Moore, Stephen. 1995. 'The Coming Age of Abundance', in *The True State of the Planet*, edited by R. Bailey, The Free Press, New York.

Moran, Alan, Andrew Chisholm and Michael Porter, eds. 1991. *Markets, Resources and the Environment*, Allen & Unwin and the Tasman Institute, North Sydney.

Motavelli, Jim. 1996. 'Enough!', *E: the Environmental Magazine* 7 (2):28-35.

Muller, E. J. 1992. 'The quest for a quality environment', *Chilton's Distribution* 91 (1):32-34.

Munday, Alicia, Arthur E. Rowse and Ana Arana. 1992. 'Is the Press any Match for Powerhouse PR?', *Columbia Journalism Review* 31 (3):27-34.

Murray, John. 1991. 'TV in the Classroom: News or Nikes?', *Extra!*, Sept/Oct.

Nash, J. Madeleine. 1994. 'Keeping Cool About Risk', *Time* 144 (12):70.

Naureckas, Jim. 1995. 'Corporate Ownership Matters: The Case of NBC', *Extra!*, Nov/Dec, 13.

Neill, Roger. 1991. 'The Vital Role of Advertising in Successful Economies: Getting the Message Across', *Vital Speeches of the Day*. 336-340.

Nelkin, Dorothy. 1987. *Selling Science: How the Press Covers Science and Technology*, W.H.Freeman & Co., New York.

Nelkin, Dorothy, and Michael Pollak. 1977. 'The Politics of Participation and the Nuclear Debate in Sweden, the Netherlands, and Austria', *Public Policy* 25 (3):333-357.

Nelson, Joyce. 1989. *Sultans of Sleaze: Public Relations and the Media*, Between the Lines, Toronto.

Nelson, Joyce. 1990. 'Deconstructing Ecobabble: Notes on an attempted corporate takeover', *This Magazine* 24 (3):12-18.

Nelson, Joyce. 1993a. 'Great Global Greenwash: Burson-Marsteller, Pax Trilateral, and the Brundtland Gang vs. the Environment', *CovertAction* (44):26-33, 57-8.

Nelson, Joyce. 1993b. 'Burson-Marsteller, Pax Trilateral, and the Brundtland Gang vs. the Environment', *The New Catalyst* (26):1-3, 8-9.

Nelson, Joyce. 1996. 'Japanese Timber Giant SLAPPs Canadian Natives', *Earth Island Journal*, 4 January, 21.

Nelson-Horchler, Joani. 1990. '"We were wrong"; acts of contrition brighten a company's tarnished image', *Industry Week* 239 (8):20-25.

Ness, Erik. 1995. 'Taking it All Away: The Private-Property Movement Carves up America', *The Progressive*, November, 21-23.

Niskanen, William A. 1995. Home page on the World Wide Web, (http://www.cato.org/people/niskanen.html).

Nixon, Ron. 1995. 'Limbaughesque Science: "Eco-Realism" vs. Eco-Reality', *Extra!*, July/August, 25-26.

Nixon, Ron. 1996. 'Divide and confuse: Selling Nigeria to American Blacks', *Nation* 262 (20):19-22.

Nye, Peter. 1994. 'Surge of SLAPP Suits Chills Public Debate', *Public Citizen*, Summer, 14-19.

O'Callaghan, Kate. 1992. 'Whose Agenda For America?', *Audubon*, September/October, 80-91.

O'Keefe, Micheal, and Kevin Daley. 1993. 'Checking the right', *Buzzworm* 5 (3):38-44.

O'Sullivan, John. 1993. 'Send in the Tanks', *National Review*, May 10, 4.

Ontario Secondary School Teachers' Federation. 1995. *Commercialization in Ontario Schools: A Research Report*, Ontario Secondary School Teachers' Federation.

Orchard, Deborah. 1991. 'The Green Plan: A National Challenge for Canada', *Journal of Air Waste Management Association* 41 (3).

Osler, Dave. 1996. 'Broadcasting Bill Starts Media Merger Merry-Go-Round', *Journalist*, April/May, 10-11.

Otis, L.H. 1995. 'Reinsurers Sue Mass. over GE captive', *National Underwriter* 99 (December 18/25):50.

Ozone Action. 1995. 'Ozone Action and Environmental Law Foundation File Suit', Press Release, 19 October.

Packard, Vance. 1960. *The Waste Makers*, Penguin, Harmondsworth, Middlesex.

Parenti, Michael. 1986. *Inventing Reality: The Politics of the Mass Media*, St Martin's Press, New York.

Parry, Robert. 1995. 'The Rise of the Right-Wing Media Machine', *Extra!*, March/April, 6-10.

Patterson, Sally J. 1996. 'Your grassroots resources', *Electric Perspectives* 21 (2):24.

Patton, Baz. 1995. 'Bad public relations', *Green Left*, 6 December.

Perkins, Peter. 1990. 'Developing a Program to Satisfy the Community's Concerns', paper read at NSW Agriculture & Fisheries DAs Conference.

Peters, Nick, Patrick Pharris, Bob Kimmel and Dan Johnson. 1993. 'A beginner's guide to VNRs', *Public Relations Journal* 49 (12):16.

Pettinico, George. 1995. 'The Public Opinion Paradox', *Sierra*, Nov/Dec, 28-31.

Plant, Christopher, and Judith Plant. 1991. *Green Business: Hope or Hoax?*, New Society Publishers, Gabriola Island, BC and Green Books, Devon.

Poole, William. 1992. 'Neither wise nor well', *Sierra*, Nov/Dec, 59-61, 88-93.

Pope, Carl. 1995. 'Going to extremes: Anti-environmental groups hide their extremism', *Sierra* 80 (5):14-15.

Powell, Sian. 1993. 'School's Amway deal attracts criticism', *Sydney Morning Herald*, 24 November.

Powell, Sian, and Bernard Zuel. 1993. 'Marketers' influence over young challenged', *Sydney Morning Herald*, 3 September.

Pratt, Cornelius B. 1994. 'Hill & Knowlton's Two Ethical Dilemmas', *Public Relations Review* 20 (3):277-294.

Prest, James. 1994. 'The Muzzling of the Dingo Forest Mob', *Chain Reaction* (70).

Preuss, Peter W., and William H. Farland. 1993. 'A Flagship Risk Assessment', *EPA Journal*,

Jan/Feb/Mar, 24-26.

Price, Charles M. 1992. 'Signing for fun and profit: the business of gathering petition signatures', *California Journal* 23 (11):545-548.

Price, Stuart V. 1994. 'Learning to Remove Fear from Radioactive Waste', *Public Relations Quarterly* 39 (3):32-34.

Priestly, B. G. 1995. 'Environmental Oestrogens - A danger to men and women - or to neither?', paper read at Environmental Health Short Course, December 1.

Pring, George W., and Penelope Canan. 1993. '"SLAPPs"—"Strategic Lawsuits Against Public Participation" in Government — Diagnosis and Treatment of the Newest Civil Rights Abuse', in *Civil Rights Litigation and Attourney Fees Annual Handbook*, Clark Boardman.

Pring, George W., Penelope Canan and Vicky Thomas-McGuirk. 1994. 'SLAPPS: A New Crisis and Opportunity for the Government Attorney, Part 1', *National Environmental Enforcement Journal* (April):3-9.

Pusey, Michael. 1991. *Economic Rationalism in Canberra*, Cambridge University Press, Cambridge.

Putnam, Todd. 1991. 'The GE Boycott: A Story NBC Wouldn't Buy', *Extra!*, Jan/Feb, 4-5.

Raghavan, Chakravarthi. 1995. 'TNCs control two-thirds of the world economy', *Third World Resurgence* (65/66):31-32.

Rampton, Sheldon, and John Stauber. 1995a. 'Spin Doctors amputate health reform', *PR Watch* 2 (2):1-4.

Rampton, Sheldon, and John Stauber. 1995b. 'Yes, in your back yard: Flacking at the grassroots level', *PR Watch* 2 (2):5-8.

Raphael, Murray. 1993. 'Are you kidding?', *Direct Marketing* 56 (3):38-9.

Rauber, Paul. 1993. 'Cost/benefit journalism', *Sierra* 78 (5):40-43.

Rauber, Paul. 1994. 'Beyond Greenwash: An insider's guide to duping the public', *Sierra* 79 (4):47-50.

Rauber, Paul. 1995. 'Wit and Wisdom of the Wise Users', *Sierra* 80 (6):31,33.

Rauber, Paul. 1996. 'The uncertainty principle', *Sierra* 81 (Sept-Oct):20-22.

Ray, Dixy Lee, and Lou Guzzo. 1994. *Environmental Overkill: Whatever Happened to Common Sense?*, HarperCollins, New York.

Regan, Mary Beth, and Richard S. Dunham. 1995. 'A think tank with one idea: the newt world order', *Business Week* (July 3):48-49.

Reichhardt, Tony. 1994. 'EPA rebuffs challenge to its assessment of dioxin data', *Nature* 371 (22 September):272.

Ricci, David. 1993. *The Transformation of American Politics: The New Washington and the Rise of Think Tanks*, Yale University Press, New Haven.

Rice, Faye. 1993. 'Who scores best on the environment', *Fortune*, 26 July, 114-122.

Richardson, Valarie. 1995. 'Environmental curriculum may pollute kids' minds', *Insight on the News* 22 (6):12-13.

Ridgeway, James, and Jeffrey St.Clair. 1995. 'Where the buffalo roam: The Wise Use Movement Plays on Every Western Fear', *Village Voice*, July 11, 14-16.

Ridgeway, James. 1995. 'Greenwashing Earth Day', *Village Voice*, 25 April, 15-16.

Ridley, Matt. 1996. 'Down to Earth: A Contrarian View of Environmental Problems', Institute of Economic Affairs, World Wide Web, (http://www.iea.org.uk/pubs/se/se_03.html).

Roberts, Leslie. 1991a. 'Dioxin Risks Revisited', *Science*, 8 February, 624-6.

Roberts, Leslie. 1991b. 'Flap Erupts Over Dioxin Meeting', *Science*, 22 February, 866-7.

Roberts, Leslie. 1991c. 'EPA Moves to Reassess the Risk of Dioxin', *Science*, 17 May, 911.

Roberts, Paul Craig. 1994. 'What's Flying out the Ozone Hole? Billions of dollars', *Business Week*, 13 June, 22.

Roberts, Paul Craig. 1995. 'Quietly, now, let's rethink the ozone apocalypse', *Business Week*, 19 June, 26.

Robinson, Colin 1996. 'Energy Policy: Errors, Illusions and Market Realities', Institute of Economic Affairs, World Wide Web, (http://www.iea.org.uk/pubs/op/op_90.html).

Rockland, David B., and Gwyn L. Fletcher. 1994. 'The economy, the environment, and public opinion', *EPA Journal* 20 (3-4):39-40.

Roschwalb, Susanne A. 1994. 'The Hill & Knowlton Cases: A brief on the controversy', *Public Relations Review* 20 (3):267-276.

Rose, Merrill. 1991. 'Activism in the 90s: changing roles for public relations', *Public Relations Quarterly* 36 (3):28-32.

Rosen, Jay. 1996. 'Breaking the News: How the media undermine American democracy', *The Nation*, 5 February, 25-28.

Rosenberger, Jack. 1996. 'A wolf in sheep's clothing?', *E Magazine* 7 (2):19-23.

Rosner, Jeremy D. 1992. 'Market-based environmentalism', *Los Angeles Business Journal* 14 (40):2A(2).

Rotenier, Nancy. 1995. 'She's kidding', *Forbes* 156 (September 11):266.

Roush, Jon. 1995. 'Freedom and Responsibility: What we can learn from the Wise Use Movement', in *Let the People Judge*, edited by J. D. Echeverria and R. B. Eby, Island Press, Washington, DC.

Rowell, Andrew. 1996. *Green Backlash: Global Subversion of the Environment Movement*, Routledge, London and New York.

Ruben, Barbara. 1992. 'Root Rot', *Environmental Action*, Spring, 25-30.

Ruben, Barbara. 1994a. 'Reading and Writing, But not Recycling', *Environmental Action*, Spring, 19-22.

Ruben, Barbara. 1994b. 'Back talk', *Environmental Action* 25 (4):11-16.

Ruben, Barbara. 1995. 'Getting the wrong ideas', *Environmental Action* 27 (1):21-26.

Ruiz-Marrero, Carmelo. 1994. 'The International PR Machine: Environmentalism à la Burson-Marsteller', *Earth First!* (Brigid):9.

Russell, Dick. 1990. 'EPA Official Accuses Nightline of Distortions', *Lies of Our Times*, June, 5.

Ryan, Charlotte. 1991. *Prime Time Activism: Media Strategies for Grassroots Organizing*, South End Press, Boston, MA.

Ryan, Charlotte. 1993. 'An NPR Report on Dioxin: How 'Neutral' Experts Can Slant a Story', *Extra!*, April/May.

Ryan, William A. 1992. 'Media Warms to Earth Summit Coverage', *Lies of Our Times*, July-August, 12-13.

SAB, Science Advisory Board. 1995. *Dioxin Reassessment Review*, US EPA, Washington.

Sale, Kirkpatrick. 1993. *The Green Revolution: The American Environmental Movement, 1962-1992*. Hill and Wang, New York.

Saloma, John S. 1984. *Ominous Politics: The New Conservative Labyrinth*, Hill and Wang, New York.

Saltzman, Joe. 1989. 'Style vs. Substance', *USA Today*, January, 87.

Sas-Rolfes, Michael. 1996. 'Rhinos: Conservation, Economics and Trade-Offs', Institute of Economic Affairs, World Wide Web, (http://www.iea.org.uk/pubs/se/se_04.html).

Satchell, Michael. 1991. 'Any color but green', *US News & World Report*, October 21, 74-76.

Satchell, Michael. 1996. 'Dangerous Waters? Why environmental education is under attack in the nation's schools', *US News & World Report* 120 (23):63-4.

Savage, J. A. 1992. 'Environment Got Lost in Earth Summit Coverage', *Extra!*, September, 6.

Savage, E., and A. Hart. 1993. 'Environmental economics: Balancing equity and efficiency', paper read at 1993 Environmental Economics Conference, November, at Canberra.

Schelling, T., ed. 1993. *Incentives for Environmental Protection*, MIT Press, Cambridge, MA.

Schemo, Diana Jean. 1992. 'Silencing the Opposition Gets Harder', *New York Times*, 2 July.

Schmidheiny, S, and The Business Council for Sustainable Development. 1992. *Changing Course: A Global Business Perspective on Development and the Environment*, MIT Press, Cambridge, Mass.

Schmidt, Karen. 1992. 'Dioxin's Other Face: Portrait of an "environmental hormone"', *Science News* 141 (January 11):24-27.

Schulman, Beth. 1995. 'Foundations for a Movement: How the Right Wing Subsidizes its Press', *Extra!*, March/April, 11-12.

Sedjo, Roger A. 1995. 'Forests: Conflicting Signals' in *The True State of the Planet*, edited by R. Bailey, The Free Press, New York.

Seitel, Fraser P. 1995. *The Practice of Public Relations*, 6th ed., Prentice Hall, Englewood Cliffs, New Jersey.

Selcraig, Bruce. 1995. 'Print no evil', *Sierra* 80 (1):36-7.

Sethi, S. Prakash. 1977. *Advocacy Advertising and Large Corporations*, Lexington Books, Lexington, MA.

Shabecoff, Phil. 1994. 'Mudslinging on the Earth-beat', *The Amicus Journal* 15 (4):42-3.

Shanahan, John. 1992. *A Guide to the Global Warming Theory*, Heritage Foundation Backgrounder (896).

Shanahan, John. 1993. 'How to help the environment without destroying jobs', Memo to

President-elect Clinton #14, The Heritage Foundation.

Shanahan, John, and Mark Wilson. 1995. *Using Appropriations Riders to Curb Regulatory Excess*, The Heritage Foundation.

Shell, Adam. 1990. 'Earth Day spawns corporate "feeding frenzy"', *Public Relations Journal*, Jan/Feb, 9, 16-17.

Shell, Adam. 1991. 'Will Europe be the next frontier for VNRs?', *Public Relations Journal* 47 (12):10-13.

Shell, Adam. 1992. 'VNRs: in the news', *Public Relations Journal* 48 (12):20-23.

Shenk, David. 1995a. Ethics, Inc. World Wide Web: Ethics Institute Home Page.

Shenk, David. 1995b. 'The pedagogy of pasta sauce; pretending to help teachers, Campbell's teaches consumerism', *Harper's Magazine* 291 (September):52-3.

Sherrill, Robert. 1990. *Why They Call it Politics: A Guide to America's Government*, 5th ed., Harcourt Brace Jovanovich, San Diego.

Sibbison, Jim. 1990. 'The EPA Speaks', *Lies of Our Times*, June, 4.

Silas, C. J. 1990. 'The Environment: Playing to Win', *Public Relations Journal*, January, 10, 34.

Sloan, Pat. 1995. 'P&G/Paramount deal to be mimicked', *Advertising Age* 66 (March 6):2.

Smith, Doug. 1992. 'Rio and all the R-words', *Canadian Dimension* 26 (5):39.

Smith, Gar. 1995. 'The Media Militia: Behind the PR Curtain', *Earth Island Journal.*

Smith, James A. 1991. *The Idea Brokers: Think Tanks and the Rise of the New Policy Elite*, Free Press, New York.

Smith, S. L. 1991. 'The greening of American business', *Occupational Hazards* 53 (9):112-118.

Smith, Trevor. 1996. 'Citizenship, community and constitutionalism', *Parliamentary Affairs* 49(2):262-272.

Smock, Doug. 1994. 'How will the toxics' debate affect plastics?', *Plastics World* 52 (22):27-31.

Solomon, Norman. 1996a. 'The Media's Favorite Think Tank', *Extra!*, July/August, 9-12.

Solomon, Norman. 1996b. 'Right-wing populists and limousine liberals galore', *Extra!*, Jan/Feb, 26-27.

Southam, Kate. 1994. 'Why Green Australia got such a black mark', *Sydney Morning Herald*, 12 February, 28.

Spencer, Miranda. 1991. 'Cold War Environmentalism: Reporting on Eastern European Pollution', *Extra!*, January/February, 6-7.

Spencer, Miranda. 1992. 'US Environmental Reporting: The Big Fizzle', *Extra!*, April/May, 12-22.

Spencer, Miranda. 1993. 'The New York Times and Environmental Cleanup: Green is the Color of Money', *Extra!*, July/August, 7-8, 21.

Stapleton, Richard. 1992. 'Green vs. green', *National Parks*, Nov/Dec, 32-37.

Stapleton, Richard. 1993. 'On the Western Front: Dispatches from the war with the Wise Use Movement', *National Parks*, January/February, 32-36.

Starmer, Keir. 1997. 'Kier Starmer on the trial, the judge and Dave and Helen's legal career', McSpotlight, World Wide Web.

Stauber, John. 1993a. 'Spies for hire—Mongoven, Biscoe & Duchin, Inc.', *PR Watch* 1 (1):1-5.

Stauber, John. 1993b. 'Spy operation costs Kaufman million dollar-a-year account', *PR Watch* 1 (1):7.

Stauber, John. 1994a. 'Strange Bedfellows at PR Conference on Activism', *PR Watch* 1 (2):1-3.

Stauber, John. 1994b. 'Sound Bites Back', *PR Watch* 1 (2):11.

Stauber, John C, and Sheldon Rampton. 1995a. '"Democracy" For Hire: Public Relations and Environmental Movements', *The Ecologist* 25 (5):173-180.

Stauber, John, and Sheldon Rampton. 1995b. 'How the American Tobacco Industry Employs PR scum to continue its murderous assault on human lives', *Tuscon Weekly* (Nov 22-Nov 29).

Stauber, John, and Sheldon Rampton. 1995c. *Toxic Sludge is Good For You! Lies, Damn Lies and the Public Relations Industry*, Common Courage Press, Monroe, Maine.

Stauber, John, and Sheldon Rampton. 1995/96. 'Deforming Consent: The public relations industry's secret war on activists', *CovertAction Quarterly* (55):18-25, 57.

Stavins, R., and B. Whitehead. 1992. 'Dealing with pollution: Market-based incentives for environmental protection', *Environment* 34 (7):7-11, 29-42.

Stisser, Peter. 1994. 'A Deeper Shade of Green', *American Demographics*, March, 24-29.

Stoesz, David. 1987. 'Policy Gambit: Conservative Think Tanks Take on the Welfare State', *Journal of Sociology & Social Welfare* 14 (4):3-20.

Stone, Peter H. 1993. 'Wearing too many hats?', *National Journal* 25 (36):2161.

Stone, Peter H. 1996. 'Fortress Tobacco Strengthens its Walls', *National Journal*, April 20.

Stone, Richard. 1994. 'Dioxin Report Faces Scientific Gauntlet', *Science* 265 (16

September):1650.

Sullum, Jacob. 1991. 'Dioxin Doubts', *Reason*, Dec, 12.

Sunderland, Kerry. 1994. 'Corporate Sponsorship in the Classroom', *Youth Studies Australia*, Autumn, 24-28.

Swasy, Alecia. 1993. *Soap Opera: The Inside Story of Procter & Gamble*, Random House.

Swomley, John M. 1996. 'Funding for the culture war', *The Humanist* 56 (3):34-5.

Szykowny, Rick. 1991. 'Manipulating People: The Role of the Media is Serving Power', *Third World Resurgence* 12 (August):27-30.

Tarrant, Judith. 1996. 'Sponsorship and the Early Years', in *Innocent Advertising? Corporate Sponsorship in Australian Schools*, edited by T. Newlands and S. Frith, New College Institute for Values Research, Univ. of NSW, Sydney.

Taubes, Gary. 1993. 'The Ozone Backlash', *Science* 260 (11 June):1580-1583.

Tenenbaum, Brian. 1990. 'G.E. Farben?', *Lies of Our Times*, August, 17.

Thompson, Jennifer. 1996. 'Greens sound alarm on secondary boycotts', *Green Left*, 13 November.

Thorner, John. 1987. 'The "That's Old News" Strategy', *Harper's magazine*, February, 22, 26.

Tokar, Brian. 1995. 'The "Wise Use" Backlash: Responding to Militant Anti-Environmentalism', *The Ecologist* 25 (4):150-156.

Tollefson, Chris. 1994. 'Strategic Lawsuits Against Public Participation: Developing a Canadian Response', *The Canadian Bar Review* 73:200-233.

Tolman, Jonathan. 1995. *Nature's Hormone Factory: Endocrine Disrupters in the Natural Environment*, CEI Environmental Studies Program.

Toor, Will. 1993. 'The Wise Use Movement, Property Rights, and the Environment', *New Liberation News Service*, January.

Trend, Michael. 1988. 'Mrs Thatcher's Kindergarten', *The Spectator*, 23 April, 9-10.

Trento, Susan B. 1992. *The Power House: Robert Keith Gray and the Selling of Access and Influence in Washington*, St Martin's Press, New York.

Trudel, Mary R. 1992. 'PR professionals and TV producers: the new alliance for good television', *Public Relations Quarterly* 37 (1):22-3.

Tucker, Brian. 1995. 'The Greenhouse Panic', *Engineering World*, Aug, 35-38.

Twitchell, James B. 1996. 'But first, a word from our sponsor', *The Wilson Quarterly* 20 (3):68-77.

Tymson, Candy, and Bill Sherman. 1990. *The Australian Public Relations Manual*, revised ed., Millenium Books, Sydney.

US EPA. 1995. 'EPA's Dioxin Reassessment', *Environmental Science & Technology* 29 (1):26A-28A.

Vandervoot, Susan Schaefer. 1991. 'Big "Green Brother" is Watching: New directions in Environmental Public Affairs Challenge Business"', *Public Relations Journal*, April, 14-19, 26.

Varney, Wendy. 1994. '"Environmental" Toys: Selling Consumerism Dressed in Green', University of NSW, Wollongong, NSW.

Vidal, John. 1997. 'Welcome to McHell', *The Big Issue*, 24 February.

Vogel, David. 1989. *Fluctuating Fortunes: The Political Power of Business in America*, Basic Books, New York.

Wagner, Betsy. 1995. 'Our class is brought to you today by... Advertisers target a captive market: school kids', *US News & World Report* 118 (16):63.

Waldman, Amy. 1996. 'Breaking the News: How the Media Undermine American Democracy', *Washington Monthly* 28 (Jan-Feb):43-45.

Walters, Lynne Masel, and Timothy N Walters. 1992. 'Environment of Confidence: Daily Newspaper Use of Press Releases', *Public Relations Review* 18 (1):31-46.

Wanna, John. 1992. 'Furthering Business Interests: Business Associations and Political Representation', in *Business-Government Relations in Australia*, edited by S. Bell and J. Wanna, Harcourt Brace Jovanovich, Sydney.

Ward, Bud. 1995. 'Crossing the line?', *American Journalism Review* 17 (1):12-13.

Warder, Michael. 1994. 'The Role of Think-Tanks in Shaping Public Policy: Our Society is Well Served by Thinkers', *Vital Speeches of the Day*: 434-437.

Warren, Agnes. 1995. 'Video News Releases', Radio National, *ABC Radio*, 21 December.

Warren, Agnes. 1996a. 'Advertorials', Radio National, *ABC Radio*, 14 March.

Warren, Agnes. 1996b. 'Whistleblowing, Sponsorship and "Your ABC"', Radio National, *ABC Radio*, 1st August.

Watkins, T. H. 1995. 'Wise Use: Discouragements and Clarifications', in *Let the People Judge*, edited by J. D. Echeverria and R. B. Eby, Island Press, Washington, DC .

Weaver, R. Kent. 1989. 'The Changing World of Think Tanks', *PS: Political Science and Politics* 22 (Sept.):563-78.

Wehling, R.L. 1995. 'A positive impact on TV show content', *Advertising Age*, November 20, 8.

Weinberg, Jack. 1995. 'Dow Brand Dioxin: Dow Makes You Poison Great Things', Greenpeace, peg.haz.forum.

West, Darrel M., and Richard Francis. 1996. 'Electronic advocacy: interest groups and public policy making', *PS: Political Science and Politics* 29 (1):25-29.

White, Rob. 1992. 'Towards a green political economy: The market', paper presented at the Ecopolitics V Proceedings, University of NSW, Sydney.

White, Sally. 1990. *Green is Good*, Clemenger/BBDO.

Whitehead, Wendy R. 1995. '25th Earth Day will be a local affair', *Environment Today* 6 (2):3, 11.

Williams, Granville. 1995a. 'New Times', *New Statesman & Society*, 24 March, S7-S11.

Williams, Granville. 1995b. 'Whose News?', *Journalist*, October/November, 16-17.

Williamson, Debra Aho. 1995. 'P&G goes Hollywood for interactive ally', *Advertising Age* 66 (August 31):1, 8.

Williamson, Peter. 1989. *Corporatism in Perspective: An Introductory Guide to Corporatist Theory*, edited by P. S. Cawson, Sage Studies in Neo-Corporatism, Sage Publications, London.

Wilson, Kelpie. 1993. 'Sapphire Six Sacrificed by Oregon Supreme Court'. *Earth First!*, Mabon, 30.

Windschuttle, Keith. 1988. *The Media: A new analysis of the press, television, radio and advertising in Australia*, 2nd ed., Penguin, Ringwood, Victoria.

Winward, John. 1991. 'Consumer Preferences and the Environment', in *Green Futures for Economic Growth: Britain in 2010*, edited by T. Barker, Cambridge Econometrics, Cambridge.

Wright, Tony. 1996. 'QC attacks whistleblower sacking', *Sydney Morning Herald*, July 20, 4.

Zoll, Daniel. 1997. 'Big Mac Attack: A British trial puts McDonald's on the grill', *San Francisco Guardian*, 29 January.

Index